Hospital and Healthcare Security
Fourth Edition

Hospital and Healthcare Security

Russell L. Colling

Butterworth–Heinemann

Boston   Oxford   Auckland   Johannesburg   Melbourne   New Delhi

Copyright © 2001 by Butterworth–Heinemann
A member of the Reed Elsevier group
All rights reserved.

No part of this publication may be reproduced, stored in a retrieval system, or transmitted in any form or by any means, electronic, mechanical, photocopying, recording, or otherwise, without the prior written permission of the publisher.

Recognizing the importance of preserving what has been written, Butterworth–Heinemann prints its books on acid-free paper whenever possible.

∞ Butterworth–Heinemann supports the efforts of American Forests and the Global ReLeaf program in its campaign for the betterment of trees, forests, and our environment.

Library of Congress Cataloging-in-Publication Data

Colling, Russell L.
 Hospital and healthcare security / by Russell L. Colling.—4th ed.
   p. cm.
 Previously published under the title: Hospital security.
 Includes bibliographical references and index.
 ISBN 0-7506-9892-6 (alk. paper)
  1. Hospital–Security measures. I. Colling, Russell L. Hospital Security. II. Title.
RA969.95 .C64 2001
362.1'1'0684—dc2   00-062089

British Library Cataloguing-in-Publication Data

A catalogue record for this book is available from the British Library.

The publisher offers special discounts on bulk orders of this book.
For information, please contact:
Manager of Special Sales
Butterworth–Heinemann
225 Wildwood Avenue
Woburn, MA 01801-2041
Tel: 781-904-2500
Fax: 781-904-2620

For information on all Butterworth–Heinemann publications available, contact our World Wide Web home page at: http://www.bh.com

10 9 8 7 6 5 4 3 2 1

Printed in the United States of America

CONTENTS

1	**Hospitals and the Healthcare Security Services Environment**	**1**
	Categories of Healthcare	4
	Types of Hospitals	5
	Staffing the Medical Care Facility	6
	Physician Role Impacted	7
	The Healthcare Security Administrator	7
	The Joint Commission on Accreditation of Healthcare Organizations (JCAHO)	8
	References	11
2	**The Foundation of Health Care Security: Risks and Vulnerabilities**	**13**
	Basic Healthcare Security Risk/Vulnerabilities	14
	Primary Security Vulnerabilities	14
	Security-Related Vulnerabilities	34
	Safety-Related Vulnerabilities	35
	Facility Security Survey	36
	Terms	43
	References	43
3	**Protecting Healthcare Organizations**	**45**
	Defining Healthcare Security	46
	Unique Aspects of Hospitals	47
	Rationale for Healthcare Security	48
	Evolution of Healthcare Security	50
	Progression of Hospital Security in the United States	50
	Healthcare Security Personnel	53

Expansion of Healthcare Security	57
Security and Risk Management	57
Safety Programming	59
Developing the Security System	63
Security Safeguards Relating to the Individual Decision-Making Process	67
Design and Development of the Organizational Protection Program	72
One Program Approach to Security	74
References	75

4 Managing Security and Basic Program Services **77**

Maintaining an Orderly Facility	80
Preventive Patrol (Inspection Services)	80
Incident Reporting and Investigation	83
Response to Requests for Service	84
Accident Reporting and Investigation	84
Security Education and Training	85
Applicant Background Investigation	85
Parking and Traffic Control	85
Reaction to Internal and External Emergencies	86
Enforcement of Rules and Regulations	86
Access Control	87
Liaison with Public Safety and Other Government Agencies	88
Internal Audits	89
External Audits (Inspections)	90
Locks and Keys	90
Supportive General Services	90
Public/Employee/Community Relations	96
References	97

5 Security Management Planning **99**

Security Mission Statement	100
Program Authority	100
Position Descriptions/Activities	102
Security Program Overview (Duties and Activities)	104

	Security Management Cycle	112
	Security Strategic Plan	113
	Utilization of Physical Security Safeguards	118
	Employee/Staff Involvement in the Protection Program	119
	Building Configuration and Design	120
	Unique Strategic Plans	120
6	**Security Department Organization and Staffing**	**121**
	Security Department Reporting Level and Support	121
	The Functional Organization Chart	123
	Types of Security Staff	126
	How Large a Staff Is Needed?	139
	Incremental Facility Security Staffing	142
	References	144
7	**Security Force Administration**	**145**
	Management	145
	Supervision	149
	Communication	155
	Motivation	156
	Morale and Negative Attitudes	156
	Handling Subordinate Complaints	157
	Handling Problem Employees	157
	Determining How Many Security Supervisors Are Needed	158
	The Security Officer	159
	Selecting Security Personnel	163
	Retention	169
	Full-Time Versus Part-Time Security Officers	169
	Wage Compensation	171
	Security Force Discipline	172
	Rules and Regulations	174
	Punishable Offenses	175
	Equipping Security Personnel	178
	Managing the Firearms Program	184
	Terms	193

	Resource Information	194
	References	194
8	**Training the Security Force**	**197**
	Training Concepts	199
	IAHSS Basic Security Officer Training	201
	IAHSS Advanced Security Officer Training	202
	IAHSS Supervisory Training	204
	IAHSS Safety Training	204
	Specialized or Supplemental Training	205
	Elective Training	207
	On-the-Job Training	207
	Training Resources and Records Requirements	209
	Terms	211
	References	212
9	**Deployment of the Security Staff**	**215**
	Deployment Objectives	216
	Scheduling the Security Staff	218
	Deployment Patterns and Concepts	219
	Post Assignments	220
	Basic Patrol Deployment Plans	222
	Patient Care Units/Areas	226
	Entrances and Exits	227
	Basic Patrol Concepts	227
	Security Officer Response	242
	Patrol Problems	244
	Terms	245
	References	245
10	**Records and Reports**	**247**
	Purposes of Records	247
	Documentation Policy	250
	Report Formats	250
	Basic Records	252
	Keeping Departmental Records Current	271
	Records Retention	273

	Terms	273
	References	274
11	**The Interrelationship of Security with Patients and Visitors**	**275**
	Patients	276
	Visitors	303
	References	310
12	**Security and Public Safety Agencies**	**311**
	Requests for Law Enforcement Service	311
	Police Interaction with Patients and Employees	313
	Emergency Room Activity	314
	Detaining Patients	316
	Prisoners and Police Holds	316
	Requests for Information	317
	Security and Law Enforcement Liaison	323
	Security and Non-Police Liaison	324
	References	325
13	**Human Resources and Staff Contributions to a Secure Environment**	**327**
	Considerations in Hiring and Managing Employees	327
	Employee Identification	331
	Security-Oriented Personnel Policies	334
	Employee Assistance Programs	344
	Loss of Employee Property	344
	Employee Security Attitudes	345
	Employee Security Education and Motivation	347
	Hospital Watch	350
	References	350
14	**Investigative Activity in the Healthcare Setting**	**351**
	Types of Investigations	353
	Investigators and Their Tools	361
	References	364

15	**Physical Security**	**365**
	Electronic Security Systems	365
	The Central Security Station	366
	Alarms	369
	Closed-Circuit Television	373
	Non-Electronic Physical Security Safeguards	380
	Locks and Keys	384
	Windows and Glass Areas	392
	Fastening Down Equipment	393
	Marking Property	393
	Safes	394
16	**Managing Workplace Violence**	**397**
	The Who (Perpetrators/Visitors)	399
	The What and the Why	402
	The When and the Where	403
	The Management of Healthcare Violence	404
	Preventing Violence in the Workplace	407
	References	408
17	**Security Sensitive Areas and Security-Related Sentinel Events**	**411**
	Security Sensitive Areas	411
	Infant Abductions from U.S. Healthcare Facilities	413
	Emergency Department Security	427
	The Hospital Pharmacy	436
	The Security-Related Sentinel Event	439
	References	441
18	**Special Security Concerns, Offsite Facilities, and Community Healthcare Provider Services**	**443**
	Narcotics and Dangerous Drugs	443
	Internal Hospital Drug Controls	449
	Medical Records	451
	Computer Operations (Information Services)	452
	Materials Management	453

	Laundry and Linen Control	457
	The Research Laboratory (Animal)	460
	Daycare Centers	463
	Off-Site Facilities	464
	Home Healthcare (Community Provider Services)	465
	References	470
19	**Parking Control and Security**	**471**
	Types of Parking Areas	473
	Closed-Circuit Television Monitoring (CCTV)	477
	Signage	478
	Shuttle Service and Valet Parking	478
	Types of Parkers	479
	Automated Controls	481
	Traffic Flow and Space Allocation	481
	Pay Parking	482
	Parking System Violators	482
	Computers and Parking Control	485
	References	485
20	**Emergency Planning and Operations**	**487**
	Common Emergency Codes	489
	Mutual Aid	489
	Fire Prevention and Control	490
	Natural Disasters	498
	Bombs and Bomb Threats	503
	Strikes and Picketing	508
	Terrorism	515
	Mob and Gang Activities	516
	Civil Disturbances	518
	References	524
Index		**525**

CHAPTER 1

Hospitals and the Healthcare Security Services Environment

The rapidly changing dynamics of our healthcare delivery system are creating new and unique challenges for the healthcare security administrator. Today's hospital is vastly different from what it was just a few years ago. In many instances, the single-unit hospital has been transformed into a medical center with many freestanding buildings. It is not uncommon for medical centers and hospitals alike to find themselves as parts of a large healthcare system. These healthcare systems may have dozens of facilities serving communities near the main facility, or they may be part of a system with facilities many states removed. Our healthcare delivery system has moved from a simple process, in which both consumers and providers had choices, to a complex system, in which there is little choice for either consumers or providers. Cost and reimbursements have largely driven this change. The complex challenge for healthcare professionals today is something known as "managed care," which is further complicated by increasing government control.

This challenge translates into drastic changes in the methods and philosophies regarding protection of our healthcare organizations. The protection of the healthcare organization cannot be completely dependent on the security department. Many aspects of protecting healthcare organizations reach far beyond the control of the commonly accepted elements of a healthcare security department. Today, in order to achieve a high level of security, managers, top executives, and boards of directors must be more involved, through appropriate funding levels, with managing and supporting security issues. These leaders must accept a greater responsibility and ownership for security in their day-to-day management obligations.

The recent breach of security at the University of Minnesota illustrates this point. There, a researcher died from a cocaine overdose while conducting a study on pain that involved cocaine and other controlled substances. The researcher had ordered 140 grams of cocaine hydrochloride in 28 different shipments over a period of several years. He held a federal license from the Drug Enforcement Administration to research the drug under a grant from the National Institutes of Health.[1] The supervision of this researcher in ordering, storing, and accounting for this 140 grams was not the direct responsibility of security. It was the responsibility of the researcher's supervisor, as well as others in the organization's chain of command.

The United States leads the world in per capita spending on healthcare, from aspirin to heart transplants. This spending is currently estimated to be between 14 and 15 percent of the U.S. gross domestic product (GDP). This expenditure compares to that of Switzerland, the second-highest buyer of healthcare services, which spends approximately 10 percent of their GDP on healthcare. U.S. healthcare spending can be viewed in a number of ways. In terms of per capita spending, each American accounts for approximately $4,000 per year. This spending results in an annual cost of approximately $1.1 trillion. Private funding provides 54 percent of this dollar amount, while public programs pick up the remaining 46 percent.[2]

Despite private, free-standing ambulatory care centers, declining inpatient days, long-term care facilities, wellness programs, and advances in outpatient and home care, the hospital remains the primary source of healthcare in terms of dollars expended. Currently, hospitals consume approximately 40 percent of the U.S. healthcare dollar. It is expected, however, that this percentage will drop at least 10 percent before the year 2010.[3]

U.S. residents make about 400 million visits to general practice physicians and osteopaths each year. In over 75 percent of those visits, drug therapy is prescribed. As the aging of our population continues, this level of drug therapy will increase, as will the use of assisted care, long-term care, home care, and hospice-type services. While persons 65 years and older make up 13 percent of the U.S. population today, this group is expected to reach 20 percent of the population by the year 2020.

Nursing homes are also experiencing drastic changes in their delivery of service, driven primarily by payment methods. The change to Medicare's prospective payment system will further impact the ability to deliver quality medical services. Under the prospective payment system, the facilities will be paid a flat rate. The rate will then be adjusted according to the patient's projected use of services. This change in payment structure will force many smaller nursing homes to close, merge, or consolidate with other similar provider organizations.

The future for home healthcare agencies is also rather dreary. According to the American Federation of Home Health Agencies, over half of the nation's 9,700 home healthcare agencies will be forced to close unless reimbursement systems are changed.[4] This situation is rather paradoxical, given that home healthcare is viewed as the most economical and productive way to deliver a step-down approach to medical care. While the issue of reduced funding for home healthcare is being discussed, the U.S. Department of Health and Human Services has awarded a $400,000 grant to the University of California San Francisco to develop a Masters of Science program in advanced-practice home care nursing.[5]

The focus of managed care is to produce short-term financial gains. This focus severely threatens the future of clinical research and the survival of academic medical centers conducting research. While expansion of managed care was a key factor in moderating increases in healthcare costs during the early and middle 1990s, it is doubtful that it will continue to be in the next century. A case in point is the much-respected health maintenance organization Kaiser Permanente, which posted a large loss in the late 1990s.[6]

It is clear that health maintenance organizations must continue to raise premiums that cannot be absorbed entirely by employers. The increased cost to employees will most likely lead to more workers declining coverage. These workers will add substantially to the some 43 million Americans who are currently uninsured, and who receive emergency care through charity and government programs.

The continuing development of new healthcare information systems will have a significant impact on how our healthcare delivery systems will operate in the future. These information systems will provide more information to patients and managed care organizations. In the case of the provider, there will be more standard procedures and protocols, often referred to as "clinical pathways," which are "cookbook recipes" for patient treatment and projected outcomes. The pathway becomes the record of care and reduce or eliminate the need for a good deal of paperwork.

The emerging model for efficient and quality healthcare is the Integrated Health Delivery Network (IHDN). The IHDN is a group of hospitals, physicians, other providers, insurers, and/or community agencies working together to coordinate and deliver a broad spectrum of services to a community. A well-designed and well-managed integrated delivery system will require a program that provides for a broad continuum of care services that are linked together for a smooth patient transition to all components of the system. This concept is often referred to as "vertical integration."

Another term used in talking about an IHDN is "horizontal integration." This term simply means expanding the delivery of services to a greater geographic area. This expansion would be designed to improve accessibility and reduce duplication of costly equipment, staff, and facilities through the optimizing of resource utilization. This change in the way healthcare services are delivered means the healthcare administrator will be involved in developing, implementing, and managing a broader security program. There will be many opportunities to provide better protection services at a lower cost if the IHDN meets the planned objectives.

CATEGORIES OF HEALTHCARE

Direct clinical care of patients is being delivered in all kinds of organizations and in all types of facilities. This diversity of care is generally the result of a particular entity wanting greater patient market share, and is creating environments with low overhead to maintain cost control. A basic concept is to bring the delivery of care geographically closer to the patient. Lower unit costs are also intended to provide greater patient accessibility to quality care. This geographical spread of organizational facilities is based on the great amount of outpatient procedures once done only in the hospital. Healthcare can be viewed on a continuum from assisted living (low acuity) to acute care (high acuity). This progression follows these basic steps:

- **Assisted Living.** Assisted living provides help with day-to-day living activities, often including transportation services to healthcare delivery sites, some limited medical care presence in the living facility, and general staff watchfulness.

- **Home Care.** In home care, healthcare staff generally visit with a coordinated plan of treatment and services.

- **Outpatient Services.** Outpatient services include surgery, clinic visits, physical therapy, psychological counseling, speech therapy, and dental care.

- **Intermediate Care.** Intermediate care provides 24-hour oversight, and is often tied closely to geriatric care.

- **Skilled Care.** Skilled care requires intervention skills by caregivers as opposed to caretakers.

- **Short-Term Acute Care.** Short-term acute care is generally medically complex and includes post-surgical intensive rehabilitation, respirator care, and intensive oversight.

- **Acute Care.** Acute care occurs when a patient is medically unstable and includes extensive use of invasive procedures, high level of staff skills, close monitoring, and complex care plans.

A current trend in senior care is to build facilities on a campus that provides independent living, assisted living, long-term care, and even a hospice facility. This arrangement is especially convenient for spouses who may have different medical needs. This arrangement is also helpful to families who visit or oversee parents or other close relatives.

TYPES OF HOSPITALS

Hospitals can be viewed according to their type of ownership and specialty regarding medical care. In terms of ownership, four different types of facilities exist:

- Not-for-profit hospitals

- Investor-owned hospitals

- Federal government facilities

- State or local government facilities

The not-for-profit and investor-owned facilities have undergone dramatic changes within the last 10 years. The closing of facilities, the buying and selling of facilities by large publicly owned companies, as well as affiliations and mergers have completely reshaped the management and often the mission of medical care delivery. One aspect of this change is a reduction in the number of hospitals both in the private and federal government arenas. The American Hospital Association decided in 1995 to discontinue its annual hospital closing report, which revealed that over 675 hospitals closed between 1980 and 1993.[7]

The merger of hospitals does reduce the space requirements needed on a per-bed basis. This reduction in space is most noticeable in facility support services and patient/visitor intake and processing space. This reduced need for inpatient space is often lost, however, on the expanding need for outpatient facilities. The cost to convert inpatient bed space is often too costly to convert to outpatient services, and thus this space is often left vacant depending on the age and condition of the structure.

In addition to the ownership of hospitals, the type of medical specialty is another way to differentiate facilities. Basic medical specialties include pediatric, medical/surgical, rehabilitative, long-term care, and psychiatric facilities. The teaching hospital generally has elements of these specialties in addition to research, education, and clinic activities. Each of these specialty care facilities presents unique security and safety challenges, which will be explored throughout this text.

STAFFING THE MEDICAL CARE FACILITY

The delivery of medical care is very labor-intensive, and utilizes a wide range of professional and service staff. The staff-to-patient ratio is extremely high in the pediatric facility and is quite low in the nursing home facility. The diversity of technical positions continues to increase as new equipment and care procedures develop, yet nurses continue to be the backbone of the direct clinical care of the patient. The number of nursing specialties, along with certification programs, also continues to increase. This specialization is expected to create a nurse shortage beginning in the year 2001.

A multitude of models has been developed to care for patients in a more economical and quality way. The terms "total patient care," "primary care," "team nursing," "patient-focused care," and the like have all, at some point, been promoted as the wave of the future. Most of these models of care have come and gone, yielding to one major theme: to provide routine bedside care with less skilled, less expensive personnel. It is estimated that 97 percent of all hospitals today utilize some type of unlicensed assistant personnel (UAP) for direct clinical care or unit support. One criticism of the UAP approach is that no standard educational curriculum exists for this type of worker, and thus individual institutions must often develop, implement, and evaluate their own customized approach.[8]

PHYSICIAN ROLE IMPACTED

The physician has been severely impacted by managed care and other changes in the healthcare delivery system. The physician specialty has seen less demand and less pay for services. In addition, a tremendous increase has taken place in the number of family practice physicians, often referred to as primary care physicians and gatekeepers for payer groups. The physician solo or partner practices have given way to various group practices, which have banded together to negotiate reimbursements, purchasing power, physician-hospital partnerships, and direct employment by provider organizations. All of these changes have generally resulted in less physician income and control over patient care decisions. In fact, the primary care physician is often monetarily rewarded for limiting the delivery of care.

THE HEALTHCARE SECURITY ADMINISTRATOR

Changes in the delivery of healthcare services, a focused attention on workplace violence, more defined Joint Commission on Accreditation of Healthcare Organizations (JCAHO) accreditation standards, a demand by organization management for greater security program justification (that is, performance measurements and return on investment), and generally reduced operating budgets have changed the healthcare security business. The strong, business-approach-minded security administrator has thrived in this new environment, while the weak, traditional-approach-minded administrator has often fallen by the wayside.

THE JOINT COMMISSION ON ACCREDITATION OF HEALTHCARE ORGANIZATIONS (JCAHO)

The JCAHO, through its standards and intents, has had the most significant impact of any single element in the improvement of safety and security in our nations healthcare facilities in the past five years.

In the area of security, this impact is, however, beginning to erode as commission surveyors tend to "broad brush" security or to ignore it altogether. It appears the "surveyor" may not have "his arms" entirely around security, preferring to address the more defined area of Life Safety.

The Commission was founded in 1951 as the Joint Commission on Accreditation of Hospitals (JCAH), until 1987, when it adopted the current name. Its mission is to improve the quality of health care provided to the public through the provision of health care accreditation and related services that support performance improvement in health care organizations. The Commission evaluates and accredits more than 5,000 hospitals and nearly 10,000 other health care organizations that provide home care, long term care, behavioral health care, laboratory, and ambulatory care services. More recently the Joint Commission has begun to accredit networks and health plans and develop international standards. An independent, not-for-profit organization, the Joint Commission is the nation's oldest and largest standards-setting and accrediting body in health care.

There are currently JCAHO manuals that include standards for:

- Ambulatory Care

- Behavioral Health Care

- Health Care Networks

- Home Care

- Hospital

- Long Term Care

- Long Term Care Pharmacies
- Managed Behavioral Health Care
- Pathology and Clinical Laboratory Services
- Preferred Provider Organizations

The security standards and intents of concern in this text are found in the *Comprehensive Accreditation Manual for Hospitals*, which is a subscription series with quarterly updates. The subject of security is specifically addressed in the chapter entitled Management of the Environment of Care (EC). In addition, there are other standards that have a direct bearing on security in terms of action and compliance requirements. These standards are considered whole house, applicable to all hospital staff, and are principally found in the chapters on Human Resources (HR), Leadership (LD), Improving Organization Performance Standards (PI), and Management of Information (IM). The healthcare security administrator must coordinate with other departments and functions to determine specific action items and compliance oversight regarding security standards.

Design and Implementation

The format of the standards is broken into two categories, referred to as Design and Implementation. The first category is concerned with the organization plan for compliance. The plan is developed through the assessment process and the application of organization (or outsourced) resources. The second category is putting the plan into action to achieve the compliance goal. Immediately upon implementation, the plan and performance objectives are measured as an ongoing activity in a cycle to constantly improve (or maintain) performance. This cycle can be referred to as the EC management process that includes:

- Design
- Teach

- Implement
- Measure and assess
- Improve (redesign)

Organization Surveys

An organization seeking accreditation is generally surveyed on a three-year cycle. Random surveys, surveys for cause, and sentinel events can result in a limited review survey within the three-year cycle. No accreditation, conditional accreditation, or accreditation with Type II or I recommendations status can result in various remedial and follow-up actions by the Commission.

An unannounced random survey of 5 percent of accredited organizations will occur between 9 and 30 months after an organization's full accreditation survey. The selection of the organization to receive the random survey is not based on how well the organization did on their last regular survey.

Scoring of Standards

The survey team will assign scores to each of the grid elements contained on a Hospital Accreditation Services-Accreditation Decision Grid. Scoring is on the following basis:

Score 1—Substantial compliance
Score 2—Significant compliance
Score 3—Partial compliance
Score 4—Minimal compliance
Score 5—Noncompliance

The lowest score possible is the survey objective for the organization. A score of 3, 4, or 5 will generate a Type I or supplemental recommendation, and can affect the accreditation status of the organization.

The JCAHO Healthcare Safety Committee

The Healthcare Safety Committee addresses all seven elements of the Environment of Care. It advises Commission staff and reviews changes to the EC standards and intents. New standards, or clarification of standards, are discussed in this committee and may be forwarded on to other committees such as a Professional Technical Advisory Committee for discussion and feedback. The Commission staff coordinates these communications and makes recommendations to the JCAHO Board concerning substantive changes, deletions, or new standards.

REFERENCES

1. "School to Repay Grant Money for Cocaine after Overdose Death," *Denver Post*, June 4, 1999, p. 56A.

2. *Health Affairs*, Vol. 17, #6, November/December 1998, p. 99.

3. "Here's What Ails You," *Hospital and Health Networks*, November 5, 1996, p. 18.

4. "1999 Day of Reckoning for Nation's Nursing Homes," *Modern Healthcare*, January 4, 1999, p. 32.

5. "Home is Where the Nurse Is," *Hospitals and Health Networks*, November 5, 1996, p. 12.

6. "The Uncertain Future of Managed Care," *The New England Journal of Medicine*, Vol. 340, #2, January 14, 1999, p. 144.

7. "AHA to Drop Controversial Closure Report," *Modern Healthcare*, June 5, 1995, p. 2.

8. Pamela L. Blyth, "Patient-Focused Care: Can Multi-Skilled Workers Work for You," *Health Facilities Management*, February, 1997, p. 40.

CHAPTER 2

The Foundation of Healthcare Security: Risks and Vulnerabilities

The protection of any organization requires the identification and risk assessment of security vulnerabilities. The terms "risk" and "vulnerability" have often been used interchangeably. They are, in fact, different terms. In this text, the term "vulnerability" will be used to describe the *type* of security threat, while the term "risk" will be used to describe a *degree of risk* relative to each type of threat. As an example, all organizations face the *vulnerability* of fire; however, the *risk* of fire will be somewhat different for different organizations.

Risk does not only refer to the probability of occurrence, but also to the consequences (or damages) that can result from such an occurrence. In the healthcare organization, basic security vulnerabilities fall into several areas, including assaults on employees, patients, and visitors; disturbances; pilferage and theft of supplies and equipment; loss of patient and employee property; malicious destruction of property; civil disobedience; strikes; and terrorism. Additional vulnerabilities may be more properly categorized as safety concerns. These include fire, accidents, and other internal and external emergencies that could disrupt the operation of the healthcare organization.

Many facilities operate with the assumption that security and safety problems generally occur someplace else, and they consider their risks to be minimal. Others, however, do conduct a comprehensive vulnerability and risk analysis, taking their responsibility seriously.

Basically, all organizations apply some measure of management effort to security. Someone in the organization is responsible for managing missing property, fire control, accident reports, safety regulations, the approval of new locks, and other functions commonly associated with security. In extremely small organizations, these functions are often fragmented: the maintenance department takes care of the locks, keys, and fire equipment; the administrator or business manager reviews all claims and reports of missing property; and the human resources person is responsible for general safety. This system can work well in a small facility because of the daily interaction of the relatively small group of personnel.

In larger organizations, where communication and coordination are more difficult, serious questions concerning the proper management of these responsibilities arise. As an organization grows, it will find that the workload is sufficient to warrant coordinating these responsibilities under one person or department. It is through the process of assessment and evaluation that the protection system evolves and becomes formalized. A standard of the International Association for Healthcare Security and Safety (IAHSS) states that "each healthcare institution, regardless of size, should have a person at an administrative level responsible for the security function."[1] The Joint Commission on Accreditation of Healthcare Organizations (JCAHO) has a similar requirement outlined in its environment of care standards.

BASIC HEALTHCARE SECURITY RISK/VULNERABILITIES

All healthcare facilities, regardless of size, are subject to basic security vulnerabilities. These vulnerabilities have been grouped into several major categories for the purposes of this text. The magnitude of the vulnerability, which varies to a considerable degree, determines the risk to the organization. The vulnerabilities, shown in Table 2-1, must be individually assessed by each facility.

PRIMARY SECURITY VULNERABILITIES

The following sections detail the primary security vulnerabilities of healthcare services.

Assaults

All facilities face the multifaceted and extremely acute problem of assaults to patients, staff, and visitors. The vulnerability of assault for the

Table 2-1 Healthcare Services Basic Security Vulnerabilities

Assault/Grounds* • Simple • Aggravated	Homicides and Suicides
Assaults/Interior* • Simple • Aggravated	Hostage-Taking
Bomb Threats/Bombing	Imposters
Burglary (Breaking & Entering) • Facilities • Vehicles	Kidnappings • Stranger • Domestic
Civil Disturbances	Labor Disputes
Destruction of Property (Vandalism)	Loss of Information
Disturbances • Internal • External	Patient Elopement
Drug Abuse/Loss	Robbery • Armed • Unarmed
Fire/Explosion	Stalking
Fraud/Kickbacks	Terrorism
Gambling	Theft • Patient • Staff • Organization

* Includes sexual assault

purposes of this text can be viewed in terms of simple assault or aggravated assault. *Simple assault* refers to the threatening of injury to another, while *aggravated assault* refers to the actual striking or touching of another with the intent to inflict serious injury or harm. Assaults can take place inside facilities and on the grounds, and incidents range from simple threats to rape. Serious assaults, which require immediate attention by administration, account for the majority of lawsuits against healthcare facilities where a security issue is involved.

Patients are particularly at risk to attack due to their physical and mental condition as well as to their accessibility. A person would never check in to a hotel and go to sleep at night with the corridor door open; yet in a hospital, patients do just that, with the added problem that they are sick or injured, and thus less able to protect themselves. The patient is at risk of assault by other patients, visitors, or even legitimate caregivers charged with rendering patient care. In fact, caregivers are responsible for the majority of assaults against patients, particularly sexual assaults. These incidents run the gamut of fondling patients in dentist chairs to reported rapes of patients in recovery rooms by recovery room nurses. Nursing home patients are also at risk for rough handling (assaults) and sexual assaults. In 1995, a nurse aid in New York was arrested on charges of raping a patient in a chronic vegetative condition. The patient became pregnant and delivered a baby. The attacker had been fired numerous times from previous jobs as a caregiver for such conduct as propositioning an invalid's wife, peeking under stall doors of women's restrooms, making lewd remarks to a mentally ill patient, and sending sexually explicit letters to a nurse who had spurned him.[2]

It is not always the patient who is the victim of assault, however. Employees and visitors are also at risk. Examples include a nurse who was pulled from a stairwell into a construction area and raped, and a visitor who was sexually assaulted in a parking structure. Although sexual assaults command the most attention, other assaults also occur. These include assaults between patients and staff, between staff and visitors, and among family members.

Hospital emergency departments and psychiatric treatment areas are frequently the scenes of assaults to staff. Within the hospital, nurses and ancillary staff often work in remote areas alone at night. In a Florida hospital, a hospice patient appeared at the nursing station and beat the two nurses on duty so severely that both required lengthy inpatient medical treatment. In addition, some nursing units may have only two staff members on duty; when one staff member is absent, the other may be at greater risk.

Facility grounds, parking facilities, and streets surrounding the facility also offer opportunities for assaults to occur. Healthcare organizations often experience difficulty in recruiting staff for evening and night shifts because of this security risk. It is not uncommon for organizations to provide patrols on nearby streets, and many offer escort services to bus stops and nearby residential areas for employees and visitors. In addition, escorts walk people to their destination, or a vehicle shuttle service may exist.

Bomb Threats/Bombings

Bomb threats involving healthcare facilities are not as prevalent today as they were in the late 1960s and 1970s. The vulnerability is very real, however, and requires constant readiness. The motives for such threats range from extortion to revenge to the excitement of causing trouble. Despite the number of bomb threat calls, each call must be treated as though it were genuine. Action must be based on planning and on the nature of the information received.

Burglary (Breaking and Entering)

Loss of assets does not always occur through theft and robbery. Burglary, too, is common in healthcare facilities. Although one might suspect that the hospital pharmacy would be a primary target, the advent of 24-hour pharmacies and the alarming of closed pharmacies have reduced the number of burglaries to a very few. There are numerous other targets for burglary in a hospital, however. The operating room narcotics supply tops the list, as it is generally isolated and closed at night. The physician's office and dental offices are also frequent burglary targets. Since very few drugs are kept in these areas, the burglar is usually after money and computer equipment. In some cases, expensive medical equipment is also taken. Optical shops are at high risk for the theft of eyeglass frames. As with robbery, anywhere cash is stored—whether in large or small amounts—is vulnerable to burglary. This includes storerooms, work areas, and offices.

Civil Disturbances

Healthcare facilities learned during the numerous civil disturbances of the late 1960s and the more recent Los Angeles riots that they are not immune from incurring damage to facilities and injury to staff. Up until then, most disaster planning had focused on one basic need: how to handle mass casualties due to a disaster. The types of casualties expected in an explosion, fire, or plane or train accident are considerably different from those sustained during a riot. Not only are the injuries different, so are the victims. Experience has shown that the victims of civil disturbances are generally a mix of rioters, prisoners, bystanders, and law enforcement officers.

Medical care facilities themselves may be the target of civil disturbances or demonstrations. Anti-abortion and animal rights protesters have created media and public relations problems for many facilities across the country, as well as inflicting major property damage and injuries. Protesters carrying signs and chanting slogans have become frequent images on our television screens, as they parade in and around lobbies, clinics, parking lots, and medical facilities. Security tactics in this situation include:

- A large amount of pre-protest planning by the public relations department, which generally has a liaison with members of the media

- Interacting only when required to keep property secure and the public and staff safe; this usually involves keeping demonstrators out of buildings and on public property

The list of security concerns to be managed during a civil disturbance varies, depending to a large extent on whether the hospital is located within the disturbance area or outside it. Problems common to both situations include:

- The separation of injured rioters and riot control personnel while they are being treated

- Strict visitor control, as injured rioters often are accompanied to the facility by friends or relatives who wish to continue their confrontations

- An area-wide curfew, which can affect the reporting and releasing from duty of employees

- The housing of personnel who cannot return home and of people from the community who may seek refuge within the facility

In addition to these common factors, a facility that is the target of civil disturbance or that is located within the area of the disturbance must deal with the following:

- Employees seeking access to a controlled area when attempting to report for work

- Safety of arriving and discharged patients

- Safety of personnel traveling within the controlled area

- Sniper fire at or around the facility

- Fires set within the facility

- Fire bombs thrown into the facility or onto low roofs

- Sabotage of the physical plant

- The acquisition of additional supplies and equipment, and the general need for increased housing

Planning for civil disturbance activities can generally be viewed as an extension of, or an annex to, the management of the normal security vulnerabilities of the facility's mass casualty disaster plan.

Destruction of Property (Vandalism)

The malicious destruction of property is a constant threat for all healthcare facilities. In general, facilities are relatively open, and it is extremely difficult to guard against destructive acts, which can take place at any time, quickly and unexpectedly. Reported incidents of malicious destruction range from writing on walls to the complete shutdown of a computer operation. Disgruntled employees and employees who leave under less-than-favorable conditions are prime causes of malicious acts.

Gang activity and so-called "taggers" can cause thousands of dollars in damage in a relatively short period of time. The courts' generally *laissez-faire* attitude towards dealing with persons who deface property is a significant factor in the high volume of such activity.

Disturbances

Continuing security vulnerabilities also include disturbances or disorderly conduct incidents. These incidents can occur virtually anywhere within or outside the facility, including in parking lots, employee locker rooms, lobbies, work areas, and even patient rooms. Disturbances can involve patients, visitors, or staff. Many incidents of disturbance simply involve verbal arguments of varying degree; however, these verbal arguments frequently lead to assault and the destruction of property. The number of disturbances taking place can often be correlated directly to the size, location, and type of facility. The type of patient, which relates to the type of visitor to some degree, must also be factored into the risk of disturbances.

A common area for disturbances is the emergency/outpatient department. Large urban hospitals with busy emergency rooms can experience incidents on almost a daily basis. Many such facilities have found it necessary to station at least one security officer in the emergency area on a 24-hour basis. Patients who become combative in an emergency room are usually intoxicated, drug-impaired, mentally impaired, or police-involved patients.

The patient is not the only source of disturbances. People accompanying the patients are often involved. Many such incidents are precipitated by long waits for medical treatment, lack of information, or alleged improper treatment. Many incidents that have ended with physical confrontation and property destruction could have been avoided had the medical personnel informed the patient and accompanying people of the reason for delayed treatment or the type of treatment to be rendered.

A particularly dangerous source of trouble is the person who comes to the facility with the intention of engaging in a domestic confrontation with a spouse. These incidents often lead to serious injuries, and the security officer can easily become injured in attempting to control these confrontations.

Another fairly common occurrence involves a visitor who is intoxicated or under the influence of drugs and demands to visit a patient after visiting hours. These people can usually be escorted from the property before causing a disturbance. This type of incident often requires a show of force and must be handled very quickly.

Drug Abuse/Loss

A security vulnerability that seems to be more prevalent in recent years is that of drug abuse among healthcare employees. Although drug abuse is not unique to employees in the healthcare field, it is of great concern because patients may be placed in danger. In one case, an anesthesiologist in Pennsylvania admitted he stole patient anesthetics, thus subjecting patients to agonizing pain on the operating table. These thefts fed his own drug addiction. He pled guilty to felony charges of acquiring drugs under false pretenses, to theft of drugs and burglary, and to 16 counts of assault for his role in operations on 12 patients.[3]

It is well known among healthcare security administrators that a great number of employees in healthcare facilities have purposely selected the facility with the intent of diverting drugs. Narcotics addiction among doctors and nurses is a much more serious problem than is generally recognized. The ease with which these people can obtain narcotics contributes significantly to the problem. In fact, today's healthcare facilities are a major source of the nation's drug traffic involving legally manufactured drugs. This is especially a problem in the area of barbiturates and amphetamines.

Fire/Explosion

Arson is a security vulnerability that can have grave consequences not only with regards to property damage, but to human suffering as well. Incidents involving arson are quite frequent in healthcare facilities. Disgruntled employees, or ex-employees, are often responsible for these acts. Labor disputes sometimes spawn this type of act, thus organizations should be especially aware during these times. Areas that require close attention include storerooms, employee locker rooms, lounge areas, machine rooms, linen storage areas, loading docks, and employee and public washrooms.

Fraud/Kickbacks

Many forms of kickback, fraud, and embezzlement occur in medical care organizations. One of the problems in dealing with kickbacks is the definition of the term. Most organizations do not regard a free lunch or dinner as a kickback, but just where is the line drawn?

Healthcare fraud and abuse has been estimated at $80 billion to $90 billion per year.[4] The vast majority of this fraud involves false claims of government reimbursement for patient care services and supplies. Still, a large number of fraud and kickback schemes are perpetuated by employees, costing healthcare organizations large sums of money. In fact, a report by the head of the National Healthcare Anti-Fraud Association (a group of insurers and law enforcement agencies) cites that healthcare fraud costs Americans up to $150 billion annually.[5]

One example of insurance fraud took place in a Colorado hospital that provided self-funded insurance to its employees. One employee turned in a claim for himself and his child for treatment supposedly received while on vacation in another country. All documentation appeared to be in order, and the claim was paid. Several months later, another claim was made on behalf of the employee's spouse. Investigation revealed that the services were not provided to either spouse or to the child. The employees must have believed that because the scheme worked once, it would work again—a premise that often portends the undoing of many schemes.

Hundreds of such schemes are used to defraud organizations. One of the most common methods is to sign for, and cause the organization to be subsequently invoiced for, more goods than are actually received. Another common method is to accept a lower quality product than shown on the invoice. At a Detroit, Michigan, hospital, the manager of purchasing and three outside suppliers were arrested for conspiring to defraud the hospital of more than $400,000 over a period of five years.

A relatively common scam involves sending phony invoices for goods that were never sent, often by bogus companies. In a recent case, postal inspectors intercepted over 650 bogus bills sent to hospitals by a nonexistent firm. The invoices from General Diagnostics Industries, Inc., were found to have originated from a phony mailbox at a vacant apartment.

Embezzlement does not always occur at the main cashier's station or in complicated bookkeeping manipulations. Parking lot cash collection requires close security and control.

Gambling

Gambling is a problem generally associated with larger organizations. Organized rings often prey on workers in the support areas, such as laundry, housekeeping, and food service employees. Although organized gambling has been a problem in some medical care facilities, it has not been of the magnitude found in many other organizations.

Homicides and Suicides

This vulnerability occurs with more frequency than most people realize. Each year, numerous homicides and suicides occur within healthcare organizations. Perhaps the most tragic case of a hospital-related homicide took place in Cincinnati, Ohio in 1987. There, Donald Harvey killed 24 patients over the span of one year while he worked as a nurse's aide at Daniel Drake Hospital. Harvey, currently serving three concurrent life sentences, may have killed more than 70 patients over a period of several years.

The Richard Speck murder case, which occurred in 1966 in Chicago, Illinois, also involved multiple homicides. Speck killed eight student nurses in the townhouse living quarters provided by South Chicago Community Hospital. A jury deliberated just 49 minutes before convicting him of these murders. Speck died in 1991 at age 49 in prison.

Disgruntled employees, former employees, patients, and visitors have been responsible for shootings and homicides in numerous healthcare facilities. In 1992, a 68-year-old patient gunned down his doctor in an examining room at a University of Michigan hospital. The doctor, John Kemink, had just been listed in a magazine as being among the top 10 pediatric specialists in the nation. According to a report of the incident, Dr. Kemink was the eighth physician to die in a work-related incident since 1985.[6]

Hostage-Taking

Healthcare organizations have experienced a relatively high number of incidents in which hostages have been taken. These incidents have been most prevalent in the emergency department setting; however, physician offices, administrative offices, clinics, and pharmacies have not been immune to such incidents.

Impostors

Impostors represent another security vulnerability that occurs with a high degree of frequency. Certified nurse assistants (CNAs) or licensed practical nurses (LPNs) with fraudulent identification indicating they are registered nurses (RNs) appear in all segments of the healthcare industry. There have also been numerous accounts of people who claimed to be physicians, visited patients, gave care, and interacted in their assumed role for considerable lengths of time before their false identity was discovered. In Ohio, a man impersonated a physician for over four years until his true identity was discovered by a "patient" he had treated. The patient was a police officer who, after knowing the imposter for a number of years, became suspicious. Subsequent investigation resulted in the arrest of the physician imposter, but not before he had treated individuals, utilizing space, supplies, and equipment from several Cincinnati hospitals. In addition, hundreds of patients had the confidentiality of their medical records compromised as the imposter regularly made rounds posing as a medical student, intern, and resident.

At Belleview Hospital in New York City, a vagrant wandered the halls wearing a doctor's smock and stethoscope. He was charged with raping and murdering a pregnant pathologist who worked at the hospital.[7] In another case, an imposter, who was vice president and general counsel of a large corporation, was charged with impersonating staff physicians by telephone. He ordered enemas for female patients and then called the patients and asked them to describe the procedure.

Another case of physician impersonation occurred in Texas where as many as 17 fake surgeons may have contributed to 10 deaths.[8] In these cases, phony doctors took part in hundreds of operations as diverse as brain surgery and hip replacements.

Kidnappings

The threat of abduction is a security problem that must be seriously considered in analyzing an organization's vulnerabilities. This risk is generally associated with newborn and pediatric patients; however, there have been incidents of abductions of adult patients and employees. In a strange case at a large Detroit, Michigan, hospital, a 76-year-old man fell victim to a kidnapping of sorts. He was waiting in a car while his daughter sought a wheelchair. The woman saw a stranger jump in the car and drive off with her father. The victim was later released, and a police car took him back to the hospital.

The subject of infant abductions from hospitals has received more media attention and subsequent implementation of hospital security safeguards than perhaps any other hospital security vulnerability. The vast majority of these infant abductions result in recovery of the newborn. An infant abduction from an Illinois hospital in 2000, however, resulted in the death of the infant. In this case the abductor saw the police at her door and placed the abducted infant in a clothes hamper. The police took the abductor to the police station where a confession was obtained. When the police returned to the home of the abductor, the infant was found in the hamper. The infant died as the result of apparent suffocation.[9]

Labor Disputes

In 1974, healthcare employees came under the jurisdiction of the National Labor Relations Act. The Act gives employees the right to collective bargaining representation. In order to preclude interference with patient care during the process of unionization, the National Labor Relations Board defines what groups are eligible for bargaining representation. It should be noted that the law provides that an employer is not obligated to recognize a union for security personnel at a specific healthcare facility if the proposed union represents any other employee group.

Labor disputes can create a myriad of protection problems, including threats, harassment, destruction and damage to property, intimidation, sabotage, and injury to both the innocent person and the person who is either represented by a union, seeks representation, or is simply sympathetic to the organized labor cause.

Protection problems encountered during a strike are somewhat similar to those encountered during a civil disturbance. These problems include:

- The disruption of services from within

- The disruption of external services, such as deliveries and trash removal

- Malicious destruction of facility-owned property and the personal property of employees, such as parked vehicles

- Intimidation and assault of pro-management employees

- Harassment in general, such as illegal secondary boycotts

- Altercations between pro-union and anti-union persons

Loss of Information

The theft of confidential or privileged information is a security vulnerability that is often overlooked in medical clinics and hospitals. Of primary importance are the medical records of the patients. These records often contain valuable information concerning lawsuits and other legal action. The methods of stealing information have changed radically over the years with the advent of fax machines and computers. Thus, a whole new industry regarding the protection of information has evolved. Loss of information can occur as the result of a theft of computer hardware and diskettes, unauthorized access, unsecured networks, and inadequate security for database files. The growing use of telehealth/telemedicine systems by healthcare providers opens up a whole new area for the compromise of information, including misuse and theft. Other types of proprietary data that must be properly safeguarded include unusual incident reports, bid specifications, certain financial records, and personnel records.

Patient Elopement

Healthcare providers assume a high degree of responsibility for the safety and welfare of patients, whether they are inpatients or outpatients. Maintaining an accountability of their whereabouts during treatment varies to a degree depending on the type of patient. There is, of course, a high expectation in terms of this accountability regarding the mental health patient and the pediatric patient. A patient leaving during the treatment process, without notifying the caregiver, is generally referred to as an "elopement." In simple terms, the patient has left the facility, either by rational decision or due to impaired mental capacity. In the latter case, the patient may be subject to great injury or death for various reasons, including weather conditions, potential accidents, and the failure to take life-saving medication and/or treatment.

Robbery

Armed robbery within and on the grounds of healthcare facilities is a continuing security problem. Although the number of robberies is low, a main threat to a medical center involves the pharmacy, which routinely stocks large quantities of narcotics and other dangerous drugs. While neighborhood pharmacies face the threat of an armed robbery, it is generally the result of seeking cash as opposed to drugs. Although most armed robberies in the medical center involve the pharmacy, there have also been reports of robberies occurring in the emergency room and at nursing stations.

Another goal of armed robbery is cash. The main cashier is a likely target, but robberies of cafeterias, gift shops, outpatient cashiers, and other areas where cash is handled or stored have occurred. The robber's timing, however, is not always right. In one case, two armed people held up a cafeteria cashier at 3:30 P.M. and escaped with less than $20. Just minutes before, the breakfast and lunch cashier had cashed out her full register drawer.

Robbery is also of major concern on medical center grounds. Victims are often visitors, which leads to negative public relations. The patient becomes upset, especially if the victim is a spouse. Other patients quickly learn of the incident, and word spreads to relatives and friends. Thus the healthcare organization becomes a secondary victim.

Stalking

The healthcare environment provides many opportunities for the stalker to operate. A stalker is someone who tracks his victim and generally attempts to make unwanted personal contact. While the contacts are usually in person, the stalker will sometimes pursue his victim through telephone calls, faxes, letters, or even electronic mail. Stalking can be a precursor to escalating threats and physical confrontation. Researchers report an estimated 1,006,970 women are stalked each year, compared to 370,992 males.[10] The high number of female staff and the openness of medical center campuses result in a high number of stalking incidents. Most stalking problems are based on a previous relationship of the two persons; however, stranger-to-stranger cases also exist. In the case of the latter, the victim is often a well-known personality in the community. As with bomb threats, each reported incident must be taken seriously and proactive preventive steps must be taken. A common proactive step is the obtainment of a restraining order. However, a recent survey reported that 80 percent of these decrees were violated.

Terrorism

The terrorist act is actually a combination of other vulnerabilities, including fire, bomb threats, destruction of property, and kidnapping (hostage-taking). It is, however, considered a separate vulnerability due to the distinct motive that precipitates the act. As in strikes and civil disturbances, the primary safeguards to be applied are the expansion of the everyday protection elements in place; that is, increased security personnel, greater facility restricted access, and increased staff awareness and attention to good security practices.

Theft

The pilferage or theft of supplies, equipment, and personal property is a reality for all healthcare organizations. There are as many estimates of the extent of theft in hospitals as there are estimators. A generally accepted estimate of loss for U.S. hospitals by industry experts is between $4,000 and $4,500 per bed per year. In terms of losses for all healthcare organizations, a conservative estimate projects an annual cost exceeding $20 billion.

It is virtually impossible to calculate the specific losses of any single facility. Like an iceberg, only a small part of the problem actually surfaces, and it is often difficult to properly attribute the loss to theft, waste, or loss of accountability. In the opinion of knowledgeable administrators, however, loss is a substantial item in the cost of operating any medical care facility, regardless of size or location.

What Is Being Taken?

Because more than 3,000 items purchased by hospitals are usable in the home, the list of items being taken from hospitals is quite lengthy. Items that top the list are drugs, linens, food supplies, and maintenance parts and materials. But, it is not always the obvious items that are being stolen from hospitals. In Cologne, West Germany, physicians, nurses, and administrators were implicated in a scheme in which they removed pacemakers from the dead, according to the public prosecutor's office. In another case, a pathologist and three other people were charged with the illegal sale of human organs, tissues, and fluids, which were in the custody of a Veterans Administration hospital in California. These body parts, removed during autopsies, were sold to biomedical companies, which use human organs and fluids to conduct research and develop diagnostic tests.

Meanwhile, a recent series of equipment thefts from Florida hospitals indicates how large amounts of expensive medical equipment can be stolen in a short time. The Florida Hospital Association reports that from October 1997 to mid-October 1998, medical equipment thefts from 48 different hospitals were reported, while some hospitals reported more than one incident. These known thefts totaled nearly $2.5 million. Primary items being stolen were cardiac monitors, pulse oximeters, life pack defibrillators, endoscopes, anesthesia machines, and even c-arm fluoroscopic units.[11] In a Texas incident, two men were able to remove a c-arm fluoroscopic unit from a hospital building in less than 15 minutes.[12]

Employee Theft

Security practitioners agree that the majority of hospital losses from theft can be attributed to employees. The employee thief works every day, creating a constant drain on resources, as opposed to people from outside the organization who generally do not have recurring opportunities to steal. Numerous ingenious employee theft schemes have been

Table 2-2 Most Common Thefts by Percentage

Took tools or equipment	8 percent
Received excess expense reimbursement	2 percent
Paid for more time than worked	9 percent
Took or used medication	10 percent

revealed. Indeed, theft by only one employee can lead to rather substantial losses. However, the biggest loss comes from the magnitude of employees who dip into supplies with only a slight chance of being caught.

Although the data was collected almost 20 years ago, the most in-depth research into employee theft in hospitals was conducted by the Sociology Department at the University of Minnesota under a Law Enforcement Assistance Administration grant.[13] The study surveyed nine retail operations, 10 electronic manufacturing firms, and 16 hospitals in the general Minneapolis area. This research was also conducted in Dallas and Cleveland for comparison. Thirty-seven percent of hospital employees who responded to the survey indicated that they had been involved in taking hospital supplies. Eleven percent of those employees admitted engaging in the theft of supplies on a monthly or more frequent basis. In addition to the theft of general supplies, the study revealed several other areas of interest to the hospital security administrator, which are depicted in Table 2-2.

Study findings were based on questionnaires sent to a cross-section of employees. Although the number of employees revealing misdeeds was high, the percentage of actual malefactors was probably higher. Some respondents most likely were unsure whether the questionnaire could be traced back to them, even though the study process was completely anonymous, and were thus less likely to turn it in. In addition, most people tend to deny any wrongdoing as a matter of course. These two factors alone would certainly account for some understating of the magnitude of the problem.

Factors in Employee Theft

An objective of the Minnesota study was to determine the circumstances under which employee theft was most likely to occur. Although the study did not focus on counterproductive behavior, its incidence appears to have a direct correlation to theft. The employees who reported above-average theft levels were also quite prone to above-average counterproductive behavior, such as taking extra long lunch and coffee breaks, working slowly or poorly, using drugs or alcohol at work, and abusing sick leave. The study concluded that younger and never-married employees have a high level of theft involvement. An explanation for this is that they are less vulnerable to management sanctions, including dismissal, because they have no dependents and generally a low seniority status.

Job dissatisfaction also leads to higher theft involvement, especially in the younger workforce. The most consistent source of employee dissatisfaction was found to be in the employee-supervisor relationship. The study also concluded that employees who frequently got together with co-workers after hours were in a higher theft level category.

The most consistent predictor of theft involvement found by the study was the employee's perceived chance of being caught with the potential of being fired or arrested. When there was opposition to theft on the part of management and co-workers, the amount of theft decreased. It is of interest that the inferred sanctions imposed by co-workers appear to have had a much stronger influence in shaping behavior than did the more formal action of management.

Effects of Controls on Employee Theft

Another important goal of the Minnesota study was to determine how effective certain actions or controls imposed by the organization were on reducing the amount of employee theft. The controls reviewed were the security department, management policy, inventory, financial procedures, and pre-employment screening. The study indicated that the level of sophistication of a security department has little effect on theft reduction. This is not surprising as the major thrust of most security operations reviewed addressed external theft control, grounds safety, employee safety, and other non-employee theft-related activities.

As one would expect, clearly defined theft policies, inventory programs geared to detecting losses, and the effective pre-employment screening of job applicants all tend to lower the level of theft in an organization. Joe Mele, of the National Crime Prevention Institute, points out several management activities in addition to written, published, and enforced anti-theft policies that can lower theft rates. He recommends that managers:

- "Roam the ship"; chatting with employees and asking routine questions fosters communication and increases management visibility

- Be involved in the inventory process

- Insist on tidy work areas and do not allow items to accumulate and become a hiding place for stolen goods; clear work areas also make shortages more visible to everyone

- Prohibit employees from parking their vehicles near exits

Reporting Healthcare Facility Property Losses

It is extremely difficult to develop a program of theft control unless the extent of the problem can be measured. One method of measurement is a good reporting system that requires all employees to report missing property. It is in this area, however, that hospitals have failed miserably. It is estimated that security departments receive reports of hospital property losses in only 1 to 2 percent of cases. The chief reason for poor reporting is that the supply lines are so open that stocks are quickly replenished. In addition, employees do not want to get involved, especially when the hospital does not seem to care. Property losses can also be viewed as supervisory failures, and thus employees tend to ignore the problem when possible.

Patient Property Losses

Loss of patient property is a continual concern for all healthcare provider organizations. Although the value of most lost patient property is minimal when compared to the loss of facility property, most organizations place more emphasis and more effort on protecting patient property and investigating patient losses than they do on protecting their own assets. Missing patient property can seriously affect public relations, and the patient can interpret this problem as an indication that the medical care may also be inferior. In some instances, patients become so upset over a theft of their property that their medical condition is adversely affected.

The healthcare employee is not always responsible for patient property losses. In one case, a patient in a nursing home could not locate his false teeth. Investigators solved the case when the teeth were discovered in the mouth of another patient.

One of the serious questions facing an organization when a loss is reported is whether the matter is one of accountability or actual loss. Many patient belongings are reported stolen when in actuality the property has been misplaced, accidentally discarded, or taken home by a family member or friend. In such cases where property has unknowingly been taken home, the claim of theft is usually made in good faith, and most patients advise the hospital when the item is found. Some patients, however, rationalize that since the hospital thinks something was stolen, it might reimburse them for the loss. It is not uncommon for these patients to feel that they deserve anything the hospital pays them because they are paying extremely high hospital charges. Other patients may be embarrassed that they caused trouble over nothing and thus hesitate to inform the hospital that the lost item has been located.

The question of responsibility or liability is usually raised in the investigation of a loss that is not successfully recovered. Laws vary, of course, but the hospital generally cannot be held responsible for all property brought into the facility by a patient or visitor. The hospital must take every reasonable precaution to see that the patient's property is safeguarded so that losses do not occur, but it is generally accepted that any loss is the responsibility of the patient and that the hospital should not automatically reimburse patients for losses. An exception exists when the hospital has a valuables-protection system. In such a system, where the patient has actually been given a receipt for the property and the property is subsequently controlled by the hospital, the organization would, of course, be liable for any loss.

A complicating factor concerning patient property is that the property in the custody of the patient is not constant. Patients rarely go home with the same property they had when they checked into the hospital. Visitors often bring gifts, and the patient often requests that additional items be brought to the hospital by relatives and friends. Thus the property belonging to the patient is in a constant state of flux. Control of patient property is discussed further in Chapter 11.

Employee Property Losses

The loss of employee property is another problem that confronts virtually all hospitals, clinics, and long-term care facilities. This vulnerability can generally be correlated to the size of the organization. In a large facility, the anonymity factor and the erosion of interpersonal relationships combine to create an environment that increases the theft of employee property. This does not imply that larger organizations necessarily have more theft. The application of safeguards can effectively manage this vulnerability, resulting in a good record of theft prevention.

The most common loss among employees is the purse left on an open shelf at a nursing station or under an office desk. Other commonly stolen items include shoes and articles of clothing. Although theft can occur at any time, experience shows that it can sometimes be predictable. A prime example is the theft of winter coats and vehicle batteries in places that have fairly severe winters. There is generally a rash of these thefts at the onset of the winter season, but they taper off as the thieves get what they need to see them through the winter. The holiday seasons also provide more opportunities for theft.

As with patient property, the dollar value of employee property losses is quite low compared to organizational losses. Regardless of dollar amounts, however, employee property loss is often a key factor in employee relations. No one wants to work in a facility in which losses, distrust, and suspicion are ongoing problems. In contrast to the extremely low reporting level of hospital property losses, it is estimated that security receives reports on up to 95 percent of all employee property losses.

SECURITY-RELATED VULNERABILITIES

Certain vulnerabilities facing healthcare organizations often receive attention as security issues, but are not directly related to the security program. These security-related issues are actually more clinically related and should be managed and controlled within the operating department. Although the security function may play a supporting role, the ownership of the vulnerability does not belong to security. Two good examples of such security-related vulnerabilities are the misuse of medical record information and the infrequent but serious problem of infant switching.

Healthcare providers have a responsibility to protect patient medical information from loss, misuse, and the compromising of confidentiality. This responsibility rests with the functional department in possession of the information as well as with the information systems department. The use of electronic patient information systems mandates that the whole area of computer access be addressed. Nursing units must protect their point of contact information and the medical records department must guard against theft and improper release of such information.

The baby-switching problem is one of providing proper clinical management within the specific medical care unit. The protocols of infant identification, staff and mother education, and compliance with established policy and procedure rests squarely with the operating unit. These mix-ups can go undetected for many years, as was the case at a medical center in Virginia. In 1998, it was discovered that an infant switch had taken place over three years earlier. In 1999, a Southern California hospital discovered a baby mix-up within several hours of the occurrence. While one infant had been discharged with the wrong parents, the second baby was still at the hospital, and the error was corrected quickly through blood antibody testing.

SAFETY-RELATED VULNERABILITIES

Among the safety-related risks that affect the protection level of the organization and relate directly to the security program are accidents, fires, and disasters.

Accidents

All facilities must be concerned with employee, visitor, and patient safety. Safety in this regard refers principally to preventing injury caused by unsafe physical conditions or by an inadvertent act.

It is somewhat paradoxical that the safety record of some healthcare facilities is inferior to those of the major industries that send accident victims to them for care. Because they treat a wide variety of accident cases, hospitals should have a special awareness of the need to maintain an adequate safety program. However, many accidents involving healthcare employees are similar in nature to those occurring in other industries.

The courts have consistently ruled that all medical care facilities are required to maintain safe premises. The costs of medical care, loss of services, malpractice and public insurance liability, loss of materials and equipment, human suffering, and loss of public goodwill are just some of the reasons why medical care facilities must constantly guard against accidents.

Fires (Accidental)

Fires in medical care facilities can contribute to a high loss of life and property. The incidence of accidental fires and explosions in healthcare facilities has decreased over the past years. This reduction in the number of fires, and certainly in the severity, has been due, in large part, to the JCAHO standards, NFPA guidelines, and local fire department fire prevention efforts. The issue of accidental fires and explosions clearly falls within the safety function, with a good deal of support from security. Fires can start anywhere; however, the most common location in hospitals and nursing homes is patient rooms.

Internal and External Emergencies (Disasters)

Security concerns during an external disaster center around controlling visitors, safekeeping patient valuables, controlling external traffic of pedestrians and vehicles, providing extra security support to the treatment areas, and designating an area for the dissemination of information concerning the injured. As disasters strike, new and often unanticipated factors present themselves to challenge even the most comprehensive and well-developed disaster plans.

FACILITY SECURITY SURVEY

The identification of specific vulnerabilities, with their associated risk, generally begins with a security survey. Although the initial survey is the basic step in developing a protection system, the importance of an ongoing program to identify changing risks and a periodic audit/survey cannot be overemphasized.

Who Should Conduct the Survey?

A basic question that must be answered is, Who should conduct the survey? As one might expect, there are several approaches. The first approach is to delegate this task to the person who is responsible for the day-to-day security program. An advantage of this approach is that the individual already possesses a general knowledge of the environment, including past problems, community assessment in terms of criminal activity, organizational philosophy, and the organizational structure. This person most likely has good access to department heads and supervisors, all of whom may be more candid in their discussion of operational procedures and problems than they would be with an outsider.

A second approach is to use an outside consultant. The major advantage of this approach is that an outsider can often be more objective. The consultant can generally perform the survey task in much less time than the insider, and can bring a broad range of operational experience. In other words, the consultant does not need to find solutions from scratch and does not have personality conflicts with facility staff or preconceived opinions regarding the organization.

The third survey method involves using someone from the organization *and* an outside consultant. This method combines the advantages of the other two approaches. The consultant selected to co-conduct the survey must be familiar with the healthcare delivery process and with security issues surrounding the healthcare environment.

Regardless of who does the survey, employees often view it as an investigation rather than part of a security needs assessment. The healthcare administrator must use every avenue available to communicate the objective of the review process, which is to assist departments in the performance of their specific objectives.

How Detailed Should the Survey Be?

A great variety of security surveys exists, and they are designed for a number of purposes. The tendency to group all security surveys into a single category should be avoided. Not all surveys—in fact, only a very few—are intended to examine every facet of the entire healthcare facility. It is important to keep in mind that the security survey discussed here is a formal review project to identify general security risk levels. Security evaluation, review, and recommended actions are a continual, everyday process of a less formal nature.

A security survey must be viewed in terms of the depth of the review process. A security survey is most often a general review process. An in-depth review may more properly be referred to as a *security audit*, as opposed to a *security survey*.

What Should the Survey Include?

A general security survey of a healthcare facility need not be overly structured. There are no ready-made checklists that fit every organization. Keep in mind that every facility is unique. Checklists and guidelines are only resources that may assist in the review process. Just as there are no set guidelines on what should be reviewed, there is no exact starting point. The survey should review the physical facilities and the major functions of the organization.

A good place to begin is with the physical facilities on the extreme perimeters of the property. Security can be referred to as *a system of perimeters*. In this concept, the application of security safeguards becomes more strict (or stringent) as one advances to the interior. A simplified example of this concept is the protection of a hospital's main narcotic supply. The grounds may be fenced; there may be limited traffic control, well-trimmed shrubs, and night lighting. Next is the building in which the pharmacy is located. This perimeter will be protected by walls, doors and locks, window protection, and limited-access control. Next is the pharmacy area, which will again be protected by walls, doors and locks, window protection if required, as well as good access control including an alarm system. The final perimeter may be the safe or vault within the pharmacy.

Assessing Risk

Each of the vulnerabilities identified must be assessed in terms of the degree of threat (real, perceived, and potential) to the organization. In rendering this assessment, basic sources of information should be utilized. These information sources are shown in Table 2-3.

Table 2-3 Basic Sources of Risk Assessment Information/Data

- Location of facility in terms of crime and social/economic profile
- Past security incidents
- Type of facility and patient/visitor characteristics
- Customer feedback
- Site/facility inspection
- Current information relative to the scope and practice of healthcare security
- Case law

Analyzing risk in terms of real or perceived threats is more easily addressed than in terms of potential threats. Environmental criminology is the study of the spatial patterns of wrongdoing, perceptions and space awareness of the criminal, criminal mobility patterns, target selection, and the decision to commit a crime. Although these factors pertain more directly to crime outside the organization, they do relate to varying degrees of internal crime and other negative acts.[14]

In addition to the foregoing, the legal implications of *foreseeability* must be taken into consideration. The courts consistently take the position of "totality of circumstances," as opposed to the strict view of whether a similar incident previously occurred that would put the organization on notice. Such notice can go far beyond the organization's property to include situations or incidents occurring down the street or across the nation. The best example of being on national notice is the vulnerability of infant kidnapping from hospitals. It would be very difficult for any hospital to defend itself on the premise that it was not knowledgeable that this type of event could occur.

The assessment of each risk can be expressed in a number of ways, such as low, medium, or high on a scale of 1 to 10. The higher the risk, the greater the effort required to introduce safeguards that will provide an adequate level of protection. Figure 2-1 is an example of a matrix used to list vulnerabilities and to assess the degree of risk.

Risk levels should be expressed in terms of addressing the threat by considering current safeguards that are in place, not the prevalence of the vulnerability. For example, the vulnerability of fire is well known; however, a well-trained staff, fire control construction, fire-safe practices, and physical fire detection and control equipment may produce a very low risk.

Area/ Function	Vulnerabilities						
	Assault	Theft		Robbery	Drug Abuse	Fire	(continue adding vulnerabilities)
		Personal	Facility				
Pharmacies							
Main	2	1	4	2			
ED	6	2	3	7			
Nurseries							
Well Baby	1	0	1	0			
Neonatal	1	0	1	0			
Materials Management							
Main Stores	1	1	6	1			
Dock	3	1	7	1			
Medical Records							
Main	4	4	6	2			
Dead Files	6	0	3	0			
Admitting	4	3	2	1			
Cashier							
Gift Shop							
Parking Lot							
Lot 1							
Lot 2							
Lot 3							
Structure							
(continue with area/functions)							

SECURITY RISK ASSESSMENT WORKSHEET

Instructions: Each organization should add vulnerabilities and area/functions as appropriate. Place a number between zero (0) and ten (10) in each block to indicate the current degree of security risk. A zero indicates no risk and a ten indicates a risk of the highest degree. An assigned risk of five or higher requires additional security safeguards to reduce the risk to an acceptable level to a four or below.

Figure 2-1 An Example of a Security Risk Assessment Worksheet

Matching Safeguards to Risk

After the assessment is completed and the degree of risk is calculated, each vulnerability is viewed in relation to additional safeguards that are needed to maintain an acceptable risk level. In some cases, the safeguards are the direct responsibility of the security function, and in others, a specific operating department may be responsible. The application of all safeguards is seldom the responsibility of one particular department; rather, responsibility is usually a combination of security and the operating department. Further, a given safeguard applied to a specific vulnerability will, in many cases, also bear on many other vulnerabilities. For example, the security guard force is a safeguard utilized to help manage a high percentage of all the known vulnerabilities.

In assessing risk and applying safeguards, the security professional is concerned not only with existing vulnerabilities evidenced by incidents, but also with potential vulnerabilities, as prevention is a key concept. In practical terms, it is difficult to obtain resources and gain organizational support for preventive safeguards. Unfortunately, many safeguards currently in place are due to past incidents.

In this section of the text, the main focus is on identifying vulnerabilities and assessing risk rather than on reviewing the specific safeguards and applications available. The following example, however, will help you understand the conceptual model of matching safeguards to multi-department responsibilities in managing a specific vulnerability. In this example, the problem is protecting people in various parking lots.

Vulnerability: Personal safety in parking areas

Safeguards

1. Security Force:

    - Patrol parking areas

    - Fix post assignments during specific shift changes

    - Escort people on request

    - Provide various departmental in-service education programs

- Follow up and investigate incidents

2. Install emergency communication devices in highly visible locations that are connected directly to the security dispatch center

3. Monitor designated parking areas by closed-circuit television (CCTV)

4. Operating Departments:

    - Standardize work shifts with other departments when possible
    - Advise employees of security escort service

5. Provide adequate night lighting

6. Check trees and shrubs for proper placement and keep well pruned

7. Personnel Department:

    - Give parking lot safety and services information to new employees
    - Address parking lot safety and services in the employee handbook

8. Nursing/Admissions:

    - Inform visitors and patients of security escort services and means of requesting this service

As you can see, the above safeguards and defined responsibilities are somewhat similar to those that would be considered in addressing the risk of break-ins and damage to vehicles in the parking areas.

A Continuous Process

Once the process of risk assessment has been completed, an abatement plan has been devised, and safeguards have been blended into a security program, this process begins again. The identification of security vulnerabilities and risks is an ongoing one. Risks previously identified may no longer exist, and new risks may appear as the dynamics of a healthcare environment continually change.

TERMS

Aggravated assault: Unlawful intentional causing of serious bodily injury with or without a deadly weapon, or unlawful intentional attempting or threatening of serious bodily injury or death with a deadly weapon.

Elopement: In the healthcare context, this term refers to a patient who has "run away" without conveying this intent to a caregiver or going through a discharge process.

Fraud: Deceit of intentional misrepresentation with the purpose of illegally depriving a person or organization of property or legal rights.

Kickback: Money or something of value given to an employee by a vendor or contractor in exchange for consideration.

Simple assault: Unlawful intentional inflicting, or attempted or threatened inflicting, of injury upon another.

Stalking: A course of conduct directed at a specific person that involves repeated physical or visual proximity, non-consensual communication, or verbal, written, or implied threats.

REFERENCES

1. International Association for Healthcare Security and Safety, *IAHAA Standards*, P.O. Box 637, Lombard, IL, 60148.

2. "Nurse's Aid to be Tried in Sex Attack on Patient," *Rocky Mountain News*, February 10, 1997, p. 31A.

3. "Doc Stole Drugs from Patients Going Under Knife," *Rocky Mountain News*, February 5, 1997, p. 34A.

4. "Fraud Costs Billions," *Rocky Mountain News*, July 15, 1990.

5. *Special Issues in Environmental Management*, 8.9 Corporate Compliance, ECRI, Plymouth, PA, Volume 1, August 1997, p. 1.

6. "Man Charged in Killing of His Doctor," *Lansing State Journal*, June 27, 1992.

7. "Fake Doctor Held in Killing," *Detroit News*, January 10, 1989.

8. "Fake Doctors 'Aided' Hundreds of Operations, Lawsuit Says" *Rocky Mountain News*, September 3, 1996, p. 15B.

9. 7. "Incident is First to End in Death," *Daily Southtown*, Chicago, IL, May 8, 2000.

10. "Survey: 1 in 12 Women Stalked at Least Once," *Rocky Mountain News*, November 14, 1997, p. 44A.

11. Wade Edwards, *Medical Equipment Theft Memo*, Florida Hospital Association, January 18, 1999, p. 1.

12. Paulette Standefer, *Another Report of Hospital Equipment Theft-C-Arm Fluoroscopic Unit*, Dallas, Fort Worth Hospital Council, December 10, 1998.

13. J. P. Clark and R. C. Hollinger, "Theft by Employees," *Security Management*, September, 1980.

14. Daniel B. Kennedy, "Case Your Space," *Security Management*, April, 1989, p. 47.

CHAPTER 3

Protecting Healthcare Organizations

In the past, healthcare organizations were slow to recognize the importance of providing protection services for those who utilize and staff the various components of our healthcare delivery systems. However, in just the last few years, those same organizations have taken security and safety much more seriously. This change has been brought about by ever-increasing security-related litigation, financial control mandates, the creation of larger organizations, requirements of regulatory agencies, and accreditation processes. The whole issue of workplace violence has put many of our healthcare organizations in news headlines.

In addition to facing an increasing crime rate, healthcare facilities are becoming larger and have new characteristics. Medical centers are building physician office buildings and are constructing satellite care facilities many miles away from their main facilities. New and enlarged outpatient treatment facilities are commonplace, as are large parking decks and daycare centers. The protection system must be modified to manage this new environment so that it not only creates unique protection applications, but also brings an increasing number of people to our patient care facilities. As the number of people in a given area increases, so does the number of probable interactions.

The products used in healthcare facilities are also changing. The high use of disposable products has left more items vulnerable to theft, and the problem of disposing of these products is a new area for risk management. Even equipment design provides more opportunity for loss. The lightweight, collapsible wheelchair has become a major loss item for most organizations. The downsizing of computers and electronic items such as VCRs has added to the problem.

Continued changes in the U.S. criminal justice system have also had a significant impact on the protection needs of all organizations, including those in the healthcare field. The emphasis on individual rights has resulted in less protection for society as a whole. Those who are inclined toward criminal acts have found these changes to be particularly lucrative. Shrinking law enforcement resources place increasing emphasis on organizational security self-reliance.

DEFINING HEALTHCARE SECURITY

The term *security* might seem vague and elusive. It is in fact a relatively ill-defined concept that has taken on different connotations in different settings. In the context of protecting healthcare facilities, it continues to be defined as a system of safeguards designed to protect the physical property of the facility and to achieve relative safety for all people interacting within the organization and its environment. This definition, however, does not solve the problem of defining *relative safety*. What is safe today, may not be safe tomorrow. It is difficult to evaluate the environment of a particular facility to determine whether relative safety has in fact been achieved. Protection, or security, is supposed to reduce the probability of detrimental incidents, not to eliminate all risks. Security, then, is not static and can be viewed as a state or condition that fluctuates. As environmental and human conditions change, so does the status of protection. It is this phenomenon that requires the constant reevaluation of any system of protection.

Many people in the field attempt to view security too strictly or too definitively. The organization being served is the entity that provides the ultimate definition of the security system; after all, the organization provides the funding. This is not to say that the protection program and the philosophy and objectives of the principal security administrator do not have a strong influence on molding the organizational definition.

A common error for healthcare organizations is to view security as being closely aligned with the law enforcement function. Although some common ground may exist between security and law enforcement, at least 90 percent of their respective activities are different. Security must be viewed as internal protection, while law enforcement must be viewed as external protection that attempts to uphold the law for all of society. See Table 3-1 for a comparison of security and law enforcement characteristics.

The military, as an exception to this general rule, does blend law enforcement and security. Provost Marshal Don Devaney of Tripler Army Medical Center, Honolulu, runs a crime prevention program that

Table 3-1 Comparison of Security and Law Enforcement Characteristics

Security	Law Enforcement
Prevention	Apprehension
General Services	Prosecution
Proactive	Reactive
Organization Defined	Statute Defined
Protect an Organization	Protect a Society
Private Funding	Tax Supported

combines security and law enforcement approaches. The three primary elements of this program are:

1. **Prevention:** Elimination of the will to commit a crime by taking away the opportunity.

2. **Enforcement:** Timely detection, investigation, apprehension, and prosecution of offenders.

3. **Correction:** Removal of offenders from the community, rehabilitation, and return to duty, or removal from the army of those unwilling to respond to rehabilitation.

UNIQUE ASPECTS OF HOSPITALS

Healthcare organizations—from hospitals, to freestanding outpatient facilities, to dental/physician offices, to clinics—must operate 24 hours a day. Service—or, in the language of the industrial complex, production—cannot be shut down at night and on the weekends; the facility must remain open to admit the sick and injured at any hour, to permit the patient to see visitors, and to carry on normal business. With people entering and exiting through numerous entrances at all hours, it is extremely difficult to determine who belongs and who doesn't belong, who is legitimate and who may be a threat to the organization.

Hospital patients and visitors present unique problems not found in most other social settings. Patients are involuntary consumers, because they generally have no desire to be in the hospital or to undergo major treatment. With the proliferation of HMOs and the concept of managed care, an increasing number of patients are being told which physician and which hospital they must use. Patients directly or indirectly pay the bills, and their wants must be considered within the organizational framework of the institution. This is no simple matter because patients are presumed to be somewhat impaired due to illness or injury. Many patients are helpless. The newborn child, for example, is certainly in a helpless state. Pediatric patients can also be classed as helpless in many situations, either because they are non-ambulatory or because they are unable to define a clear course of action in a situation that affects their welfare and safety.

Similar considerations can be applied to hospital visitors. When a member of the family or a close friend is ill, the visitor's actions and reactions to management practices may not always be completely rational. Thus tolerance for abnormal behavior, within limits, resulting from stress must be a major consideration in any hospital protection program.

RATIONALE FOR HEALTHCARE SECURITY

The first of several basic reasons for providing a protection system is moral responsibility. Every organization, especially if it serves the public, has an obligation to manage its environment in such a way that it minimizes the possibility of injury or death to all people on the premises. It is also the organization's moral responsibility to take reasonable steps to preclude the destruction, misuse, or theft of property so that the physical facility remains intact to carry on its business.

A second justification for providing protection services is legal responsibility. The healthcare organization has a duty to exercise care and skill in the day-to-day management of corporate affairs. A specific example of this general obligation is the duty to preserve property by preventing fire and safety hazards and to protect people from the actions of others. The healthcare organization's obligation to its patients is contractual in that the organization assumes certain responsibilities toward them. The duty of protection becomes even greater when patients are unable to take care of themselves, as is the case for the critically ill, the elderly, infants, children, and the mentally impaired.

The issue of liability in the management of patient care facilities has become more acute in recent years. An organization may be held liable for corporate negligence or for the negligence of an individual employee under the doctrine of "respondent superior." Corporate negligence occurs when the organization maintains its buildings and grounds in a negligent fashion, furnishes defective supplies or equipment, hires incompetent employees, or in some other way fails to meet accepted standards and such failure results in harm or injury to a person to whom the organization owes a duty. In terms of employee negligence, two general factors are requisite for imposing liability on the corporation: an employer-employee relationship must exist and the employee's act or failure to act must occur within the scope of his or her employment.

One aspect of the legal rationale is of the growing element of punitive damages. Jury awards that punish organizations for not taking appropriate security measures are increasing in frequency and size. An added concern is that in many jurisdictions, punitive damage awards cannot be covered by insurance and must be paid from the organization's funds. Another important reason for maintaining a safe and secure environment is the responsibility of complying with accreditation standards imposed by the Joint Commission on Accreditation of Healthcare Organizations (JCAHO). The Occupational Safety and Health Act and other federal, state, and local regulatory agencies also play an important part in a safe facility.

Another rationale for providing a protection system is to maintain a sound economic foundation for the organization. In this regard, healthcare has faced mounting criticism, especially due to the rapidly escalating costs of delivering quality medical care. Authorities estimate that between 3 and 20 percent of hospital expenditures could be saved if proper security controls were implemented. Yet in most cases, the protection budget for healthcare facilities is generally less than 3 percent of the total operating budget. It would seem that the economic stimulus of increased profits would be especially important to investor-owned hospitals and freestanding healthcare facilities. Yet as a group, they appear to go no further than other healthcare providers in providing adequate loss prevention and protection systems.

Lastly, a safe and secure environment is required to maintain good public and employee relations. Although this reason does not appear to be as important as the others, it has probably been responsible for providing more funds for the security budget than the other justifications combined. Healthcare administrators who face bad media coverage relative to a security problem, or restless employees threatening to walk out over a security incident somehow find the funds to make necessary adjustments in the protection plan.

EVOLUTION OF HEALTHCARE SECURITY

The evolution of healthcare security is based on hospital security. Although this book often focuses on hospital security as it pertains to U.S. hospitals, much of the heritage of hospital security can be found in the history of Great Britain. And during the past 25 years, an increased dialogue and exchange of information has occurred between hospital security personnel in the U.S. and colleagues across the oceans.

History reveals that one of the first traces of an organized hospital in the United Kingdom was the St. Bartholomew Hospital at Smithfield in London, founded in 1123. The hospital was granted a Royal Charter by King Henry VIII in 1546. In 1552, the House of Governors authorized the implementation of "the Order of the Hospital"—what are now known as job descriptions. The Office of the Porter, for example, was responsible for the beadles (or the stationed guards). This marked the beginning of healthcare security.

Until 1948, hospitals in the United Kingdom operated under boards of governors. In 1948, the Department of Health and Social Security was created, and the Social Services Act went into effect. At this time, some hospitals in major cities employed a security officer known as a "house detective." In the late 1950s and early 1960s, the position title was changed to "security advisor." During the early 1970s, hospitals made a concerted effort to create a more efficient protection system and now have very good protection programs in place. Today, the most senior position in hospital security is that of district security officer. A person with this title is generally responsible for 10 to 20 hospitals in a geographic district.[1]

PROGRESSION OF HOSPITAL SECURITY IN THE UNITED STATES

To better understand the current status of healthcare security, a review of the way in which hospital security has evolved over the last 100 years in the U.S. is in order. For purposes of this discussion, this history has been divided into five periods, each of which reflects a somewhat different philosophy or approach to the concept of hospital security.

1900–1950

From 1900–1950, little mention was made of the term "security" in relation to protecting the hospital. Initially, the basic protection activities were performed entirely by maintenance workers as they completed their physical plant duties. As facilities grew in size, some hospitals hired a guard to make the rounds to relieve the maintenance person of the security task. The primary emphasis of the guard's rounds was the fire watch. Maintaining the physical plant, including the fire watch, was the primary responsibility of the engineering/maintenance function.

1950–1960

After 1950, protection was expanded to include aspects of law enforcement. The fire watch continued to be an important protection function; however, the fire watch and law enforcement operated independently of each other. It was during this time that an abundance of police officers could be found in many of the larger police departments, and criminal activities were beginning to be noticed in and around hospitals. It become fairly common for larger police departments to station a police officer at the hospital or at least to use the hospital as the hub of the neighborhood beat. The police presence at hospitals came at taxpayer's expense, but at this time the nation's hospitals were viewed as public and community institutions. As the need for more protection become apparent, hospitals naturally hired off-duty policemen to provide additional security. The shift from the beat officer to vehicle patrols basically eliminated city-funded coverage for most hospitals.

1960–1975

Beginning around 1960, hospitals became aware that protection of the organization was not limited to fire hazards and illegal activities. The need was perceived as a specialized management service touching all departments and functions of the healthcare organization. The idea of security as a management service created the need to review the reporting procedure of the protection function. The result was the creation of a security department that reported to an administrative-level position, often to the Director of Maintenance and Engineering. The use of off-duty police officers declined during this period and security departments began to be staffed by in-house personnel.

1975–1990

The management services concept continued to prevail during this period, but the definition and day-to-day functions of security expanded. The most noticeable activity in this regard was in the area of safety. Many security departments became so involved in safety that they were renamed "Security and Safety." In addition, the department director became more involved as a member of the top management team. During this period, the mission of the security department changed from being primarily a reactive function to being a proactive (prevention) type of program.

1990 into the Next Century

In the early 1990s, rapid change began to take place. The concept of risk management, introduced in the 1980s, was now maturing and bringing a new appreciation for the protection effort. Security departments were expanding their service roles while at the same time facing budget constraints. They were being asked to do more with less in many programs. There also developed a great diversity of security programs with a general trend to break safety away from security, resulting in two complementary but separate departments. On one hand, some security departments were downsizing in terms of manpower, function, and budget, while other programs were growing. The growing programs simply had a broader view of security and the interrelations of other hospital functions to the protection program. In these programs the security department often took up the slack in other functions due to the downsizing of other hospital support programs. A good example of this change is the merging of security and hospital telecommunications into a single department. Another area of consolidation is the merging of transportation services and security into a new department.

Currently, out-sourced services continue to replace proprietary security departments as well as other hospital support departments such as food services, environmental services, bio medical engineering, and laundry services. Along with security, support services are reorganized as healthcare organizations continue to merge or form other types of affiliations.

HEALTHCARE SECURITY PERSONNEL

According to *Hallcrest Report II*, more than 1 million people were working in the security field in 1990.[2] Approximately 528,000 people worked in proprietary security forces, and 520,000 worked in contract security. Contract security now employs approximately 800,000 people, and proprietary security employs approximately 400,000. The exact number of security personnel in the healthcare field is difficult to determine. Using past data and projections of current survey data, it is estimated that more than 50,000 people are now engaged in healthcare protection services.

Professional Growth

The number of healthcare security personnel continues to grow at a very slow pace and is expected to stay somewhat flat through the year 2010. Growth has been limited due to a variety of factors, not the least of which has been the closing of facilities, consolidation of services, and greater use of physical security safeguards. However, numbers do not relate to quality. Growth must also be reviewed in terms of professional advancement.

The term "professional security officer" is frequently used to denote superior effort rather than to define a true professional. Although definitions of the word professional vary considerably, the generally accepted criteria suggest that the hospital security officer, as with all security officers, has considerable distance to cover before reaching this status. These criteria involve (1) a basis of systematic defined theory; (2) an authority recognized by those being served; (3) broad community sanction and approval of this authority; (4) a code of ethics; and (5) a professional culture sustained by formal professional associations.

Various writers suggest that attaining professional status is a process and as such implies a sequence of events. The first step may well be the establishment of a professional association with definite membership requirements. Next would be the development and promulgation of a code of ethics and the explicit utilization of systematically accumulated general knowledge in the solution of problems.

The International Association for Healthcare Security and Safety (IAHSS), formed in 1968, has over 1,700 members, and, at present, functions as the major professional organization for healthcare security. Although many splinter groups provide for local needs, it is the larger group that has had an impact on truly advancing the field. The American Society for Industrial Security has a Healthcare Committee, which also provides professional leadership for the field.

An important step toward professionalism was undertaken by the IAHSS at their 1981 annual meeting, when the organization adopted a formal code of ethics, which is shown in Figure 3-1.

In 1990, the association sponsored the first annual Healthcare Security Officer/Security Officer Week to recognize the efforts of all security and safety personnel who contribute to the security and well-being of healthcare facilities. Hospital Shared Services of Denver developed and produced the first poster for this event, which was distributed to all IAHSS members and is pictured in Figure 3-2.

It is generally agreed that today's professional is distinguished by performance rather than academic degrees, and there is increasing pressure to eliminate from the field those who no longer function as professional. Performance is linked to a recognized body of knowledge, which must be developed. This knowledge must then be transmitted to those individuals seeking professional status.

Professional growth is further stimulated by the numerous four- and five-year college-level programs now in existence, and the growth of two-year college programs that lead to degrees in security. These programs require courses in business, science, psychology, and sociology, as well as courses directed to the technical and administrative aspects of protection services.

Code of Ethics

PREAMBLE

"Recognizing that the overall quality of healthcare delivery is directly related to the professional services rendered by the International Association for Healthcare Security & Safety, the following Code of Ethics is hereby mandated as a consideration of membership."

As a healthcare security professional, I pledge to dedicate myself to providing a safe and secure environment to the people and institution(s) I serve by:

Supporting patient care and awareness within my health care facility;

Recognizing that my principal responsibilities are security and/or safety services to the healthcare community that I serve;

> to protect life and property and reduce crime through the implementation of recognized crime prevention and investigative techniques, and

> to provide a safe environment of care in support of the mission of the healthcare facility

Respecting the moral and constitutional rights of all persons while performing my duties without prejudice,

Ensuring that confidential and privileged information is protected at all times,

Maintaining open communication with other professionals with whom I conduct business,

Striving to further my education, both academically and technically, while encouraging professional development and/or advancement of other security/safety personnel,

Promoting and exemplifying the highest standards of integrity to those whom I serve while dedicating myself to my chosen profession.

Figure 3-1 Formal Code of Ethics, International Association for Healthcare Security and Safety

Figure 3–2 International Association for Healthcare Security and Safety Code of Ethics (Courtesy of Healthcare Security Services, Denver, Colorado)

EXPANSION OF HEALTHCARE SECURITY

Although this book focuses on hospital security to a large degree, other areas of healthcare security either are growing or have recently emerged.

The extended-care facility, the largest segment of which comprises nursing homes, is constantly upgrading its protection efforts and faces the same general problems confronting the hospital industry. The overall magnitude of the problem is decreased, however, because the extended care facility's size and scope of activity are considerably less than those of the general hospital.

There is also significant growth in the concept of one campus serving a wide variety of persons with varying degrees of medical care needs. Typical of these organizations is the provision of independent residential units, assisted living units, a nursing home, and a hospice facility. This concept provides for a person's changing needs with minimal disruption and is especially convenient when a spouse or significant other may each need different accommodations or care.

In the 1980s, freestanding neighborhood clinics, emergency centers, surgery centers, physical rehabilitation offices, and wellness centers emerged. Some are owned and operated by hospitals, with the intent of transferring patients to or from the main hospitals.

In the past few years, home health care has experienced a phenomenal growth rate and this growth is expected to continue, subject to adequate funding mechanisms. The delivery of healthcare services in the home has created a whole host of security issues for both the patient and the caregiver.

SECURITY AND RISK MANAGEMENT

The term "risk management" is relatively new compared with the term "security," at least in the healthcare environment. Healthcare risk managers are a relatively new group of staff support personnel for healthcare provider organizations. Their role developed less than 20 years ago as medical malpractice claims became a major concern.

The goal of risk management in the healthcare setting is to prevent patient injury and prevent or limit financial loss to the healthcare organization. Risk managers often spend a great deal of time dealing with

Typical Components of Risk Management

1. Security
2. Employee Health
3. Patient Safety
4. Employee Safety
5. Patient Representative
6. Infection Control
7. Disaster Program
8. Bio-Medical Instrumentation Testing
9. Insurance/Claims Management
10. Incident Reporting/Review/Action
11. Environmental Safety (Including Fire)
12. Product Evaluation
13. Medical Audits
14. Contracts Evaluation

Figure 3-3 Typical Components of Risk Management

contracts, equipment technology, insurance administration, and problems involving potential or actual liability. It is thus not surprising to find that many risk managers have a background in law and/or clinical experience.

Components of Risk Management

Although it varies from institution to institution, a written statement of function, authority, and responsibility is absolutely essential to the effective functioning of a risk management program. The security effort is considered an element of total organization risk management however security rarely reports to risk management. As shown in Figure 3-3, numerous elements can be integrated into a coordinated program.

Centralization of Information

A basic foundation of the risk management program is the maintenance of a central record system. All incidents and accident reports, committee minutes, follow-up investigative reports, support documents, and correspondence are thus readily available.

The incident report is the basic document of the risk management program. It forms the basis of the investigation, review, and evaluation of the incident. The form must be comprehensive enough to ensure completeness yet simple enough to enable a wide variety of personnel to complete it accurately. The security department must have a formal understanding regarding which types of security-generated incident reports will be forwarded to risk management.

SAFETY PROGRAMMING

Despite apparent recognition of the need for active hospital safety programs by the public, employees, patients, insurance companies, JCAHO, and a whole host of governmental agencies, hospitals generally remain only partially committed to this need. The equipment, processes, and procedures used to cure illnesses and mend injuries combine to create an environment requiring a high level of safety programming.

There is an inter-relationship between security and safety in that the goal of each is to prevent human suffering and avoid costs to the organization. Safety deals primarily with acts and conditions where there is generally no conscious rationale to do harm. Security deals with acts where there is a conscious decision or rationale to do harm. An example is fire. Safety is basically concerned with accidental fire, while security would be directly concerned with arson. Both security and safety play an important role in the prevention of fire regardless of the cause.

OSHA and NIOSH

The purpose of the Occupational Safety and Health Act of 1970 (U.S. public law 91-596 and as amended by P.L. 101-552, Section 3101, 1990) is to ensure safe and healthful working conditions for employees and to preserve human resources. The law authorized the National Institute for Occupational Safety and Health (NIOSH). The Institute's mission is to develop and establish recommended occupational safety and health standards, conduct research, and develop experimental programs to further new and improved practices and standards for worker safety.

In 1996, OSHA introduced a document entitled *Guidelines for Preventing Workplace Violence for Health Care and Social Service's Workers* (OSHA-3148). These guidelines are not a new standard or regulation. They are advisory in nature and only address the violence inflicted by patients or clients against staff. The general spirit of these guidelines can, however, be enforced under the OSH Act referred to as the "General Duty Clause." A violation of the General Duty Clause can occur when there is a recognized hazard of workplace violence within the organization and the organization has not taken reasonable steps to prevent or abate the hazard. These guidelines are very compatible with the JCAHO security standards and work well for those developing healthcare security programs.

Foundation of the Safety Program

Safety is not the organization's primary concern; its basic mission must come first. A safety program is neither more nor less important than supply, personnel, budget, or other administrative functions that are vital to the total operation of the healthcare facility. It should, however, become a part of the facility's every operation in order to contain costs and enhance the quality of every facet of the organization.

Safety activity in its broadest sense revolves around

- Management and personnel involvement

- Accident investigation and reduction of the probability of recurrence

- Facility inspections

- Policy and standards

Obviously, each of these activities has many subcategories that are necessary elements of a successful safety effort.

Accident Reporting

The prevention of accidents is, of course, the primary objective of the safety effort, but accidents cannot be reduced unless problems are first identified. Identification of the problems through inspection must be supplemented by good accident and hazard reporting. Reporting accidents is the responsibility of every employee, and the stimulation and motivation of this responsibility are continuing functions of the total protection program.

Timeliness of reporting is important. In organizations of any size, reports are often delayed because several people must sign or evaluate the document. At least one copy should be forwarded to the designated administrative office by the end of the shift during which the incident occurred. Even though this copy may not be complete, it serves as a timely notification of the incident.

Patient Accidents

Reporting patient accidents is generally the responsibility of nursing service because it clearly falls into the realm of patient care. Only in rare circumstances would a security officer be called on to conduct an investigation or to file a report. The most common of these "rare circumstances" include a suicide or an attempted suicide, the disappearance of a patient, a fire, an assault, and a patient accident in a public area of the facility.

Employee Accidents

The responsibility for reporting employee accidents is usually assigned to the head of the department or unit where the employee works. Thus, responsibility is fixed through chain of command. Where the accident occurred is not germane to the responsibility of reporting it.

The accident report should include the medical care that was rendered. Also, initial reports should not be overly complicated or time consuming; this will result in the delay or failure to report accidents on a timely basis.

Accident reports prepared by departmental heads are often incomplete. Supervisors intent on completing their regular departmental duties tend to complete the accident report as quickly as possible and often leave out important causative facts regarding the cause of the accident.

Another major problem is that supervisors often view the report as a fault-finding rather than a fact-finding tool. Supervisors, either consciously or subconsciously, try to protect the employee and the department from being "blamed" for the occurrence.

In some organizations, all employee accidents are reported via telephone to the security department. A security officer then responds to the scene of the accident and is responsible for the investigation and the reporting process. More complete recording generally results from this system. It is much more efficient to train security staff in the proper completion of an accident report than to train the many department supervisors of an organization. This approach is highly recommended for all organizations that have an organized security department.

Visitor Accidents

The reporting and investigation of visitor accidents is frequently neglected, despite the fact that the visitors are the source of many litigation proceedings against healthcare facilities. The basic problem appears to be that the responsibility for reporting visitor incidents is not fixed on a specific individual or department. Because it is everyone's responsibility, it is sometimes not accomplished. The investigation of all visitor accidents should be a security function responsibility.

Hazard Reporting

Accident prevention also requires the reporting and correction of hazards. In their own areas, all employees should become the eyes and ears of the safety effort. Two types of hazards exist: major hazards and minor hazards. Although major hazards are generally reported immediately, often no one bothers to report minor hazards, such as a broken piece of floor tile or a loose piece of molding. As for accident reporting, the system for reporting safety hazards must be simple. For organizations that maintain a 24-hour security staff, a simple telephone call is the obvious method for reporting hazards.

Safety Inspections

Employees cannot realistically report all hazards. Periodic structured safety inspections are thus a necessary element of the safety program. The inspection of certain areas may require technical, operational, and procedural expertise. Regardless of the inspection area, the prime goal is to locate unsafe conditions and to observe unsafe acts. Where the latter are noted, the inspector should not correct the employee unless it is a matter of extreme urgency. Corrective behavior is the responsibility of the department supervisor, who must be made aware of the unsafe practice. The unsafe act may be an individual situation, or it may indicate the need for retraining an entire group of employees.

Safety inspections help to promote employee awareness. A safety inspector's presence in various hospital work areas, interacting with employees, forces employees to think about safety, however briefly. The activity of the safety inspector is tangible, not just a concept in the employee's mind.

Need for Safety Professional

There is hardly an authority in existence who does not believe that a good safety program will not only pay for itself but also save money and prevent human suffering. Why, then, is it so difficult to obtain funding for a safety professional from a hospital administrator?

One reason may be that the work of the safety person seems abstract. Furthermore, results of the safety program are not always evident, at least not in financial terms, for several years. In addition, the intangibility of safety in the mind of the administrator often means that the safety effort is assigned a low priority. Many administrators simply do not fully understand the relationship between safety and quality patient care. Regardless of the size of facility, the JCAHO requires that responsibility for safety be fixed in a specific organizational job description.

Two or more healthcare facilities can develop a joint safety program and thus share the cost of the safety professional. Safety professionals spend much of their time reviewing material, attending meetings and seminars, researching problems, advising on purchasing, and performing other activities that are redundant from program to program.

DEVELOPING THE SECURITY SYSTEM

A healthcare security system is developed by applying security safeguards to manage the vulnerability and risks identified by the orga-

Table 3-2 Common Physical and Psychological Security Safeguards

PHYSICAL	PSYCHOLOGICAL
Security Officers	Signage
Alarms	Visitor Badges
Closed Circuit Television	Visitor Sign-in Logs
Glazing	Marking/Labeling
Barriers	Policy/Procedure Enforcement
Lighting	Investigative Activity
Safe/Containers	
Locks	
Identification Badges	

nization. A safeguard is simply an element of the protection system. Safeguards can be viewed in two basic categories: physical safeguards and psychological safeguards.

Although one can differentiate between psychological and physical security control, most physical controls carry an element of psychological protection. A good example is night lighting. Just because a parking lot is well lit does not mean that it is more difficult to commit a crime there than in a poorly lit lot. The lighting itself is a physical control, but it also functions as a psychological deterrent. The television camera or monitor cannot reach out to stop an incident or to catch a malefactor. It serves as a psychological deterrent, however, because the would-be criminal probably does not know the extent of the system; that is, who is watching, what resources may be deployed, and whether a video recorder is translating the picture into evidence.

Psychological Deterrents

Realizing that physical controls cannot protect all things in all places, professionals also use psychological deterrents, which are directed at the decision-making process of the individual. For the purposes of security planning a *psychological deterrent* is defined as an individual's interpretation of a situation in which the potential positive or negative aspects of behavior serve to prevent or preclude the expression of that behavior.

Factors in Motivation

When people act in any way, good or bad, it is because they are motivated to act. Behavior is observed as a contemporary event—a dynamic relationship between the organism and its environment. Motives, on the other hand, are not directly observable in the sense that actions and even emotions, learning, memory, and intelligence are observable; rather, motives are inferred or hypothesized from behavior.

Age

In a study conducted by researcher Alice Peckett Franklin, 12 percent of the workforce at a retail outlet was between the ages of 18 and 22. This group was associated with 69 percent of the reported thefts. One explanation for this phenomenon, offered by Richard C. Hollinger and John P. Clark in *Employee Theft*, is that younger workers do not feel as committed to an employer as senior workers do. Older workers risk losing their vacation, sick time, retirement benefits, and longevity pay, which younger workers have not yet achieved.[3]

Society and Motives

Motives that involve other people, either directly or indirectly, are called *social motives*. They are distinguishable from psychological drives because their form is usually determined by the individual's culture through rules, regulation, and taboos. Human behavior must fit into the pattern of activity that society dictates, or the individual risks rejection.

Most people resist some of their tendencies toward antisocial behavior, not because of moral qualms, but because of their fear of the consequences. The inhibition of antisocial tendencies is acquired in the course of individual development, and depends on the moral code and convention of the given culture.

Differences in motivation often account for the fact that different people may react differently when confronted by the same set of circumstances, and one person may behave differently when confronted by a particular set of circumstances on different occasions. This variability presents a challenge to the healthcare security practitioner.

Conscious versus Unconscious Motivation

Only a very small part of an individual's knowledge can be in his or her consciousness at any given moment. The belief that humans are rational animals who make their plans with foresight is appealing, but it is an incomplete statement of human nature. Analytical experience of psychologists demonstrates that the conscious self-restraint of instincts plays only a modest role compared with such emotional factors as the desire for love or the fear of punishment. Actions are determined more by unconscious than by conscious motivation.

There is, however, a constant interplay between the conscious and unconscious mind. The unconscious mind contains knowledge accumulated in various ways throughout life. The vast storehouse contains past experiences of finding gratification for needs, the consequences of these past efforts, and the feelings they aroused. As the environment changes and new possibilities are offered for gratification, the memories of past experiences that are most similar and pertinent to the current external conditions are recalled.

The unconscious mind, the reservoir of total memory and intuitive judgment, is the part most influenced by suggestion and imagination. A suggestion that seems to strengthen ideas already present usually produces action. In this regard, a strong and viable protection system will strengthen the individual's inclination to maintain acceptable social behavior.

Security preventive programming is concerned primarily with one area of motivation: directing behavior through the fear of being caught and the possibility of being punished. It has long been recognized that fear strongly motivates human behavior, and the threat of punishment has a retarding effect on the individual's impulses. Parents use fear to direct the conduct of their children. School, church, and state institutions also use fear to produce a desired form of behavior, when necessary.

This is not to imply that fear is the only reason people do no exhibit negative behavior. Other motives, including perceived needs; conscience; conditions like fatigue, illness, or anxiety; past experiences; and personal goals, play an important part in determining this behavior.

External Motivation

In *The Organization Man*, William Whyte describes how significantly humans have changed over the years. Several decades ago they were "inner-directed," but today they have become "outer-directed." By this Whyte means that individuals get their "motivation orders" from outside.[4]

It is because humans today are most susceptible to outside influence that they can be influenced consciously as never before. Their attitudes and beliefs can be shaped without their being aware of it. They are willing and waiting to be motivated because they want to know what is expected of them.

SECURITY SAFEGUARDS RELATING TO THE INDIVIDUAL DECISION-MAKING PROCESS

The healthcare employee will be exposed to a variety of organization elements that will psychologically impact their "decision-making" relative to security activities and practices. The goal is to influence these decisions to produce positive outcomes.

Conditions of Employment

In many organizations, an applicant must sign a form entitled "Security Conditions of Employment." These conditions are generally aspects of security policy that are highlighted to establish an understanding between the applicant and the organization. Examples of these conditions include the organization's policies on employee identification badges, parking, locker inspections, package inspections, and the use of personnel entrances.

In the same programs, these security rules and regulations are included in the employee handbook with other general personnel policies.

Regardless of the method used to inform employees of organization policy, all employees should be required to complete a form that states that they have read and understand what is expected of them during their employment. This form becomes a permanent part of the employee's personnel record.

New Employee Orientation

The security portion of orientation for new employees serves several purposes, one of which is to psychologically create an image of protection. New employees, who begin their jobs with the understanding that the organization takes its protection responsibility seriously, will be less inclined to become involved in undesirable activities.

The security orientation should be presented in a positive fashion, stressing that the security system is provided for the welfare of the organization and the employees. It is also recommended that the presentation indicate the organization's strong position when people become involved in security situations. This position should include the organization's policy on criminal prosecution and strict enforcement of the disciplinary system. This presentation sets the stage for further security education, which must be carried out on a continuing basis.

Badges and Visitor Log Books

The direct value of employee badges and visitor access control in preventing incidents may be open to challenge in regard to a cost/benefit relationship. The indirect value is an important preventative measure, however. As Tom Kramer, a nationally known healthcare security consultant notes, "There is a psychology in giving a visitor a pass." A person who goes through the procedure of obtaining a visitor pass often assumes that there is more control than may actually be the case. An access control system that includes employee badges and visitor checks tells the staff that the hospital cares about who comes and goes. This is all part of the psychological deterrent and image of protection, and is JCAHO mandated.

Security Uniforms

Most healthcare security officers wear uniforms. The uniform provides identity and visibility for the security program. It serves as a deterrent to would-be wrongdoers and identifies the security officer to the public. The security uniform denotes help to most individuals. Security programs in which officers wear blazers or other street clothes lose much of the positive effect of this visibility and subsequent benefit.

Security vehicles are generally marked for the same reasons that security officers are generally uniformed. One Midwestern hospital has reported a reduction in parking lot assaults during the night shift since the security vehicle began patrolling with the top light revolving. One might argue that the light makes it easier for a wrongdoer to determine the security officer's location. On the other hand, people who want to be protected can see the officer's location and enter the lot at the most advantageous time.

Security Patrols

One of the primary purposes of security officer patrol is to prevent security incidents both by physically preventing the act and by creating the image that the organization is properly protected. No part of a complex is too remote or too unimportant to receive unannounced inspectional patrols by security. Employers who are performing their assigned job as well as legitimate visitors view the patrolling officer as a support service and derive a feeling of added safety. Dishonest employees and illegitimate visitors will view the officer as an important reason to refrain from negative behavior. It is well recognized that as patrol increases, the number of incidents decreases.

Signs

Signs and notices have significant value as psychological deterrents. Almost everyone has seen and reacted to such signs as "Beware of Dog" and "Radar Patrolled." Many security companies use a sign or decal to advertise their presence with the intent of deterring criminal activity.

EMERGENCY
711

Figure 3-4 Security Telephone Sticker (Courtesy of Mission Hospital Regional Medical Center, Mission Viejo, CA)

Employee lockers receive all the security deterrent effort available. Employee lockers are sometimes receptacles for such items as stolen property, gambling equipment and data, drug abuse paraphernalia, and contraband such as liquor or weapons. A conspicuous sign that indicates locker inspections or one that offers a reward for information leading to the arrest and conviction of people responsible for theft or malicious destruction of property is good advertising. This type of sign reinforces the protection image and can result in receiving good information from concerned staff.

Another method of reinforcing the protection image through signs is the telephone sticker used in many programs. The sticker generally gives the security telephone number and sometimes numbers for fire or other emergencies. The main purpose of the sticker is to provide personnel with easy access to the correct numbers. People consciously read these emergency numbers while using the telephone for normal calling, at least the first couple of times. After a few times the caller no longer consciously reads the sticker but subconsciously makes note of the numbers, this reinforcing the protection image. Figure 3-4 illustrates an actual security telephone sticker. One method of attracting conscious attention to the emergency numbers is to change the color of the telephone stickers periodically.

False Security Expectations

In applying psychological security deterrents there is a difference between inhibiting negative behavior and creating a false sense of security. In the former, the target is the potential perpetrator; in the latter, the focus is on the victims. Creating a false sense of security has legal ramifications. A false sense of security can be created in several different ways, but generally involves physical security, signage, or written material that either is false or exaggerates the level of protection provided. Examples of false security are dummy CCTV cameras and signs that claim there is a security patrol or electronic surveillance when there is not. A false sense of security can occur when compensating security safeguards are not implemented during a malfunction or temporary absence of a normal safeguard. An example of the latter is a parking lot that is normally protected by a chain link fence. If a section has been removed for construction, an additional safeguard must be implemented to equate the protection normally in place.

Investigations

Incident investigation is a very real, tangible security activity that also has certain psychological deterrent ramifications. In some programs, the investigation responsibility is taken lightly, with little or no follow-up, especially in the area of property losses. In some facilities, a nurse or department supervisor prepares the loss report, which is forwarded to the administration with no further action. If the loss is due to an employee, the perpetrator sees no activity resulting from the crime. The organization conveys the message that it does not care, which makes it easier for the criminal to repeat the crime without inhibition and with little fear of consequences. Also, in this ineffective system, the nurse or supervisor may find it relatively easy to neglect to file a report of the incident because of the perception that nothing will be done.

All protection programs must provide an immediate field response to security incidents. In larger programs a security officer responds to the incident location; in smaller programs an administrative aide, maintenance worker, or nursing supervisor may respond. That someone in authority is concerned and is asking questions about the problem is important. A follow-up inquiry is also important in many cases to bring the incident to a successful conclusion.

The objective of any incident investigation is to record the facts properly and to resolve the problem. One should not infer that making a show or going through the motions is the objective. Rather, the demonstration of security is a by-product of proper investigation, and it has positive effects on preventing incidents.

Each Malefactor Is Different

There is no question that each malefactor is different. The system of physical security and psychological deterrence in the healthcare setting is intended to prevent as many negative acts as possible. The security fence cannot be built high enough to exclude or deter all those who wish to prey on healthcare organizations. How high to build the "fence" in a particular organization is a management decision based largely on the value or importance that the organization places on security.

DESIGN AND DEVELOPMENT OF THE ORGANIZATIONAL PROTECTION PROGRAM

At this point in the text, the security vulnerabilities and risks have been identified, and the rationale for healthcare security has been explored. In addition, the two primary security safeguards of physical and psychological elements have been developed. It is now time to determine the specific safeguards that will provide the protection aspect of the program. The total program will also include the additional component of services to be provided, which will be discussed in the following chapter.

An important step in security program design is to determine the degree of risk the organization is willing to accept, the image that the program intends to project, the conformance with generally accepted healthcare security standard practice, and conformance to regulatory and accreditation standards. Each organization must decide on an overall philosophical level, from a simple watchman approach to an aggressive police approach.

The approach to security is determined, to a large extent, by location, size, and security risks. Figure 3-5 portrays a continuum from a passive to an aggressive program approach. Most healthcare organizations will fall into a window between 4 and 7 on this continuum. A small rural facility may fit at a 2 while a large, urban facility in high-crime area many warrant a program that is a 9 or 10. Aside from the overall program philosophy, there will be certain aspects of the program that may be a 6, but the protection level of the emergency department may warrant a level of 8 or 9.

THE SECURITY PHILOSOPHY/LEVEL

```
     Passive                              Aggressive
            1 – 2 – 3 – 4 – 5- 6 – 7 – 8 – 9 – 10
     Watchman                              Police
```

Figure 3-5 A Continuum of Protection Program Philosophy

Determining the Correct Application of Safeguards

Once the safeguards that can be properly applied to manage a given vulnerability are established, another important step is required. This is to determine the degree or quantity of the safeguard to be used. It is the degree and manner in which the safeguard is applied that form the real test of an administrator's ability. Because all safeguards will undoubtedly cost money, and because most safeguards cause some inconvenience to the organization, the proper application must be well calculated. The truly correct application is one in which the problem is resolved within a cost-effective framework that facilitates good personal relationships with a minimum of change or disruption to normal work procedures.

In terms of desired results, the healthcare organization must provide some input to this goal. The questions is, What degree of risk is the organization willing to assume? As safeguards are applied, it is a matter of rationalization to decide how much is enough. In viewing the security officer coverage of the parking lots to prevent physical assault, the manpower commitment could range from a 24-hour guard to a few random patrols. This commitment must, of course, be viewed within the application of other interrelating safeguards. The process involves designing a protection system using varying degrees of different safeguards much the same as an architect would design a building.

Blending Safeguards into a System

The security administrator must take several factors into consideration when selecting safeguards and deciding to what degree each safeguard will be used to achieve the proper blend. Although it is difficult to separate these factors into categories of importance because of their interdependent relationship, cost considerations often prevail.

A second consideration involves the organization's acceptance of and compliance with the safeguards being applied. It may be a good security concept to restrict all employees to a single entry and exit; however, if parking accommodations are greatly fragmented, it may be impractical to achieve this goal.

Image is also a factor for consideration. Security visibility and procedure should not be so great that employees, patients, and visitors view the environment as unsafe. A security system must help create an environment of relative safety, good will, service, and human concern. It must be an ingredient that contributes to the overall mission of the healthcare organization.

ONE PROGRAM APPROACH TO SECURITY

There are many approaches to developing a sound and effective healthcare security program. It is the outcome that is the ultimate test of program design. Donald E. Futrell, Director Facilities Operations, University of Chicago Hospitals, has developed a concept, which he calls "layering," to address the design of a well-rounded security program.[5] This concept has six interlocking elements or layers:

- Effective screening (visitation and identification policy and procedures)

- Effective use of security technology

- Appropriate security staffing (numbers, training, skill mix, and deployment)

- An informed and involved hospital staff

- Continuous quality improvement

- Effective communication with staff

There are of course many subsets within these six basic layers. Each organization will have subsets that are somewhat unique to the specific individual healthcare facility.

REFERENCES

1. The author gratefully acknowledges John E. Nichols, District Security Officer of the British Health Service and author of *Guide to Hospital Security* (Gower Publishing Co. Ltd., Aldeshot, Hampshire, England, 1983), for this information.

2. William C. Cunningham, John J. Strauchs, Clifford W. Van Meter, "Private Security Trends 1970 to 2000," the *Hallcrest Report II*, Butterworth-Heineman Publishing, 1990, p. 196–197.

3. J. P. Clark and R. C. Hollinger, "Theft by Employees," *Security Management*, September, 1980.

4. William Hollingsworth Whyte, *The Organizational Man*, Simon and Shuster, 1956.

5. John R. Lion, M.D., William R. Dubin M.D., and Donald E., Futrell, *Creating a Secure Workplace*, American Hospital Publishing, Inc., 1996, p. 46–47.

CHAPTER 4

Managing Security and Basic Program Services

The function of a security program goes far beyond simply addressing security vulnerabilities. The program must provide a whole host of services. In this chapter we will review the various functions of a healthcare security program that work together to reduce security risks and provide tangible services in support of the organizational mission. Each organization must determine how the functional security program elements will be implemented and managed. They may be assigned to different individuals and departments, or they may be brought together under a specific department or division. In this respect not all elements of a protection system are performed by one department. An example of this concept is the background investigation of applicants seeking employment. The background investigation is an element of the protection system but is generally performed by the human resources department rather than by security.

Security programs must be structured to protect the organization within the restrictive factors of budget, organization philosophy, layout, employee and community relations, and the operational requirements of the organization. The security function should not be applied in such a manner that it is unduly restrictive in terms of the operational efficiency of providing quality patient care. The healthcare security function must be viewed as an element of management that supports professional patient care. This support will involve numerous systems and subsystems of protective services.

The security function in all organizations is not static; rather, it undergoes continuous change. It must remain flexible to cope with the constant changes in security vulnerabilities that occur in a changing patient-care environment. It must also be evaluated as an ongoing process to ensure that the function is fulfilling the organization's objectives.

The security function has a different focus, however slight the difference, in each and every facility. Despite this, security practitioners agree on one point: the security function must always be viewed from a service-oriented management perspective and not solely from a law enforcement orientation. The law enforcement function is designed to provide protective services from an external or environmental standpoint, and it cannot provide the internal safeguards that comprise up to 80 percent of an organization's security system. In support of this concept, Donald Bing, former Director of Safety/Security/Communications, Baton Rouge General Medical Center, feels that safety and security are about 90 to 95 percent prevention, education, and public relations. The remaining 5 to 10 percent involves investigative and punitive activity.

Security programs tend to develop along the lines that reflect the strengths and weaknesses of the person responsible for the program rather than organizational needs. For example, if the responsible person has a background as a firefighter, the protection program will often be structured toward a strong fire prevention and control system. A person with a strong background in investigation will use investigation as the backbone of the program, and the other elements support this emphasis.

It cannot be stated strongly enough that the organization—not the individual responsible for security—defines the security function. This does not mean that the security administrator cannot draw up the security plan or provide directional input. However, in the final analysis the organization must give approval designating the responsibility, authority, and funds necessary to implement the system.

Smaller healthcare organizations often assign various protection safeguards to various departments and to specific employees. The assignment of responsibility is often unwritten and vague; however, in small organizations it does not necessarily have to be as formalized as in larger organizations. In the case of medical clinics and nursing homes, the entire responsibility often rests with the business manager. One of the inherent problems in small organizations is that an individual often wears many hats, and no one can be completely knowledgeable in all fields. When one individual must perform many varied tasks, the protection system is often given low priority.

A security operation cannot be superimposed, like an umbrella, on a healthcare organization with any degree of effectiveness. Rather it must be integrated into the routine operations of the organization. To produce the maximum return for the investment, security must be a serviceoriented entity.

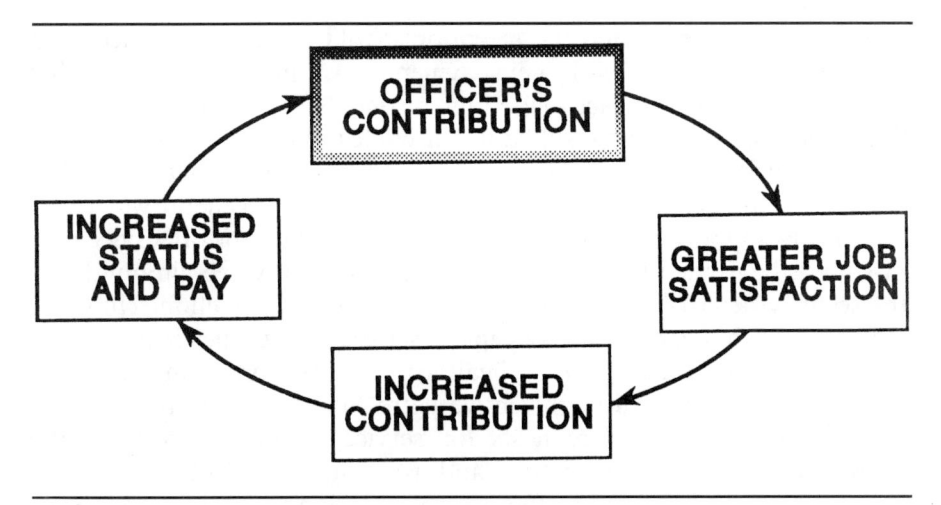

Figure 4-1 Relationship of Security Officers' Effort to Job Status

When security officers perform general services, they become a viable part of the system, and the officers themselves have a better understanding of the environment. As officers begin to contribute to an organization, three very important things can occur. First, they find greater job satisfaction. Second, the officer's status is generally elevated in the eyes of the entire organization. Third, as a person or function becomes more valuable to a system, the payment for services is generally increased. All organizations review their programs in terms of worth, or return on investment. The complementary interrelationship of these factors is illustrated in Figure 4-1.

In general, although security officers perform management services, they also provide a deterrent patrol image and are available for emergencies if needed. Moreover, in the course of providing services, the officer's interaction with other employees is often instrumental in collecting information concerning the protection of the organization that would never have been reported or would not be available elsewhere. In other words, conversations and observations that occur in the course of providing services often yield valuable security information.

A case in point concerned the theft of a considerable amount of money from a medical clinic. As the security officer escorted a receptionist to her vehicle, he remembered that she had previously told him she was afraid her car might be repossessed because she was behind in her payments. Several weeks later, the receptionist told the security officer that she was now current with her payments. An inquiry revealed that the receptionist had in fact made four payments the day after the theft. Subsequent investigation resulted in her confession.

Security administrators do not need much imagination to find ways to be of service to the organization, either in a general way or by specifically supporting a single department. The concept of service can, or course, be carried too far, and one must constantly keep in mind that the security department's primary responsibility is protection. However, the program that carries the concept of service to extremes is rare.

The basic functions of a healthcare security program are: maintaining an orderly facility, preventive patrol, incident reporting and investigation, response to requests for service, accident reporting and investigation, security education and training, applicant background investigation, parking and traffic control, reaction to internal and external emergencies, enforcement of rules and regulations, access control, liaison with law enforcement and other government agencies, internal and external audits, locks and keys, and a host of supportive services. Table 4-1 is a listing of the variety of services provided by the Police and Security Department of a Massachusetts General Hospital.

MAINTAINING AN ORDERLY FACILITY

Wherever there are crowds of people, there will be manifestations of disorderly conduct, including destructive and disruptive acts, that must be controlled. There is often a fine line between settling a minor incident by handling it internally and having to call for police assistance. The function of maintaining orderly premises relates directly to the other roles of providing patrol and supportive services. The main objective is to prevent incidents entirely or to handle problems effectively when they occur, with a minimum of disruption, harm to persons, or adverse publicity.

PREVENTIVE PATROL (INSPECTION SERVICES)

A fundamental security role is the patrol or surveillance of an area to determine that conditions are normal and to serve as a deterrent to negative conduct. This element of protection is usually performed by a

Managing Security and Basic Program Services 81

Table 4-1 Listing of Functions, Activities, and Services of a Large Security Program. (Courtesy of Massachusetts General Hospital, Boston, Massachusetts)

- Access control maintenance
- Administrative escorts
- Adverse weather condition information provided
- Alarm monitoring
- Ambassadorial services
- Animal rights intelligence
- Arrests and court adjudication
- Bomb threat investigation
- Brain tissue delivery and storage
- Call for taxi service
- Child abuse protection
- Code call responses
- Communications monitored with shuttle buses
- Community education
- Community patrol
- Confidential information handling
- Crime prevention information/literature
- Currency escorts
- Daycare security
- Departmental information dissemination
- Directions provided
- Domestic violence issues investigated
- Disaster committee participation
- Door openings
- Educational seminars conducted
- Elevator entrapment assists
- Fairs and special events organization
- Fingerprinting services
- Fire-drill responses
- Gunshot wound evidence
- Handgun retention
- Handwriting analysis
- Hate crime information dissemination
- Hazardous material spills protection
- Helipad responders
- Homeless person assistance
- Information provided of street closings
- Intelligence gathering/dissemination
- Internal affairs investigations conducted as needed
- Investigations (diverse)
- Key control
- Liaison with law enforcement agents

Table 4-1 *Continued*

- Lost and found system
- Media assists
- Medical assists
- Missing person searches
- Monitor parking coupons for volunteers/chaplains
- Motor vehicle assists: jump-starts, lock out, flat tires, locating lost vehicles, assist "block ins," record motor vehicle accident incidents
- Notary public service
- Operation identification
- Package delivery
- Panic alarm responses
- Pathology escorts, medical examiners, funeral directors, organ donation representatives, family members
- Patient restraints
- Patient searches
- Patient standbys
- Patient valuables assist
- Patrol 50 MGH buildings
- Personnel escorts
- Phone referrals
- Photographing of patients
- Photo identification processing
- Policy and procedures creation
- Property retrieval and dissemination
- Radio system monitoring
- Record keeping
- Reported incidents documentation
- Security surveys/risk assessment
- Solicitors removed
- Store luggage for visitors
- Surveillance
- Threat analysis
- Timely postings maintenance
- Tow illegally parked motor vehicles
- Traffic control

variety of different people from within and outside the organization. Medical clinics, for example, may rely on police or security patrols to randomly check the exterior of the premises during the night. Hospitals may perform this function by assigning the task to employees: for example, maintenance personnel in the normal course of their duties, nursing supervisors conducting their rounds, and the security officer on patrol. Preventive patrol is a 24-hour requirement. However, when a facility is closed or shut down, surveillance takes on additional meaning and increased responsibility, especially at nighttime.

INCIDENT REPORTING AND INVESTIGATION

No security program can be effective without proper reporting of security incidents and investigative follow-up of these incidents. An important factor in reporting incidents is to maintain a simple and easy-to-access procedure. One telephone call should be all that is required of an employee, visitor, or patient to report a security incident.

A major element of protection is investigation, required regardless of the size of the healthcare organization. In this frame of reference, the term "investigation" takes on a rather broad meaning and is not limited to the initial response or follow-up of a criminal incident. It refers to the collection and preservation of data or materials and the proper analysis of collected materials to manage criminal or civil actions, business situations, and as a basis for protective services programming.

Investigation is necessary for such general purposes as the following:

- To discover the facts and to determine the cause of an incident that may have resulted in loss or possible injury to staff, visitors, or patients

- To determine adequate procedures and safeguards to manage the various organizational protection vulnerabilities (for example, to analyze the system of handling patient valuables to ensure safekeeping or to determine whether such handling is designed to minimize the risk of various malefactions)

- To successfully resolve a crime

- To determine if in fact a crime has been committed

- To determine the facts and causes of employee work accidents

- To obtain additional information for law enforcement agencies in cases in which the organization may have an interest

- To determine the truthfulness of an improper conduct allegation against an employee

RESPONSE TO REQUESTS FOR SERVICE

The response to requests for assistance is a major facet of a healthcare security system. Some security professionals disagree about the type of requests that are appropriate for security interaction. In most programs, security responds to almost any situation when called on, even though at times it is necessary to refer action to another department or outside agency. Successful security departments have learned that requests for service must be encouraged and handled with efficiency regardless of the inappropriateness of some requests. It is much better to receive some requests that are inappropriate than to receive no requests at all. The success of a security effort can, in large part, be determined by the number of people who access the services being offered. In other words, when the telephone stops ringing, the program is not only in jeopardy, it is dead.

ACCIDENT REPORTING AND INVESTIGATION

Properly recording the facts concerning injury to employees, visitors, and vendors is an essential security function. Many organizations assign the responsibility for employee accident reporting to the employee's supervisor. A more comprehensive investigation will be conducted when a security representative accomplishes this task. This does not mean that a departmental supervisor should not be involved in the reporting procedure or in any follow-up action that may be required.

The security officer should also be responsible for investigating and recording visitor or vendor accidents. Many unnecessary claims have been paid because an accident report was not filled out or because of an incomplete investigative report. Organizations sometimes fail to assign this responsibility specifically. When it is everyone's responsibility, it often ends up being no one's. Without proper records it can be extremely difficult to defend a case in which the plaintiff has all the facts and the organization has no facts or incomplete facts.

SECURITY EDUCATION AND TRAINING

A major element of a successful security program is to stimulate, educate, and motivate employees to be conscious of protection needs and to practice good security. Personnel must be trained in the proper response to fire, bomb searches, evacuation procedures, work safety, and taking an ownership in their security responsibilities. In small medical clinics, this function is rather informal and spontaneous; in larger facilities, a more formalized approach, using many different communication media, is necessary.

Organizations are taking on the broader task of helping employees to be safe and secure outside the workplace. Classes on self-defense, home security, babysitting security, and other topics are offered as an employee benefit on the premise that security awareness must constantly be reinforced.

Promoting security awareness among patients and visitors is also an element of security. Visitors and patients often are victims of various crimes, many of which could be prevented through safer practices.

APPLICANT BACKGROUND INVESTIGATION

Investigating prospective employees is generally the responsibility of the personnel department or, in small organizations, the person who actually hires the employee. Other organizations often rely on security assistance when considering an applicant for a sensitive position, such as cashiers, storeroom clerks, pharmacists, and top-echelon supervisors. As our society becomes more mobile, incidents of false credentials, overstated education, overstated experience, and applicants "forgetting" about their criminal history are becoming altogether too commonplace. The number of lawsuits and the subsequent awards for negligent hiring are increasing each year.

PARKING AND TRAFFIC CONTROL

Parking and the control of traffic are basic services required by most healthcare organizations. The degree to which security is involved in parking depends on program development. In some cases the control of parking is delegated to a special unit of security or even to the maintenance and grounds department.

The volume of vehicle traffic entering and leaving the grounds each day produces a significant problem for most medical care facilities. The need to keep fire lanes open, assist in minor accidents, ensure orderly parking, and protect parked vehicles is a multifaceted task that requires many resources.

In systems where special parking areas are designated, the sticker is a popular means of control. The vehicle sticker, which provides ready identification of the owner or driver of the vehicle, is useful in notifying drivers of lights left on, flat tires, damage, or the need to move the vehicle.

REACTION TO INTERNAL AND EXTERNAL EMERGENCIES

One of the security system's primary responsibilities is to react to the unexpected to minimize the negative impact caused by non-criminal emergency situations. A main concern of healthcare facilities is, thus, fire prevention and control. Fire prevention is activity designed to prevent a fire, while fire control refers to the procedures to be followed in an actual fire. Fire safety is not only essential to the preservation of life and organizational assets, but is also required by law and by the Joint Commission on Accreditation of Healthcare Organizations (JCAHO).

Other types of internal or external emergencies that concern security are explosions; severe weather that causes property damage or injury; chemical spills and other hazardous situations; loss of power, water, or communications; and isolation from the rest of the community in a disaster situation.

ENFORCEMENT OF RULES AND REGULATIONS

The enforcement of organizational rules and regulations is generally considered a security function. This role, however, should not be isolated from the supervisory authority and responsibility throughout the organization. In organizations with an established security force, the supervisor's responsibility is often de-emphasized; as a result, security is looked to for enforcement. This is a mistake. It forces security personnel into a relationship with other employees and with visitors that takes on negative tones. A good example is the policy requiring that all employees wear their identification badge. Even though the security force acts to ensure compliance, the job should not be identified solely with security; it requires the support of and enforcement by every supervisor and administrator of the organization.

ACCESS CONTROL

Although access control to facilities varies widely, such control is a function of the security system and supported by operating units. The proper channeling of visitors and patients into and about the healthcare facility is good security, and a good business practice as well. In some larger cities and some larger hospitals, access control is tightly administered 24 hours per day, with various checkpoints for visitors, vendor logging and badging, and employee identification systems. In some facilities, restricted access is instituted only during the night hours by locking certain doors and access points. All facilities with inpatients and 24-hour emergency medical service should designate one or more entrances as night entrances. These entrances should be controlled by a staff person or physical access control hardware. This person may be a security officer, a switchboard operator, or clinical staff. Regardless of the degree of control, the security function must take on a greater responsibility for determining who belongs or does not belong during the evening, night, and weekend time periods.

Access to Locked Areas

All protection systems use locked doors to preserve the integrity of a given office or work area. Likewise, all efficient organizations must provide a system to grant access to these areas under special circumstances. The term "special circumstances" underscores the need to control special areas and to provide services to people who require legitimate access but do not have a key, an access card, code, or other lock-release device.

Because providing access to locked areas is generally considered to be a security function, certain controls must be established, or the security officer will quickly become an errand runner. People who need frequent access to a given area should be provided with a means for such access. Basically, the security officer is called on to grant special access to areas that require a high degree of control, such as storerooms, medical records areas, libraries, equipment rooms, and other places where a record of entry is required.

Access to locked areas can also be achieved by holding keys in a central area to which those who desire entry must report to check out the required key. This function works well when responsibility is assigned to the security department in organizations that maintain a 24-hour security desk. In smaller programs, the keys can still be maintained by security if the patrolling officer responds to calls for assistance.

Efficiently granting access to authorized individuals is a service that improves the overall efficiency of the organization. People mislay keys, lock themselves out, lose keys, and forget keys. The security department should provide quick response, so that the necessary work of the organization can progress without undue delay. If these requests appear to be too frequent, the problem should be handled administratively, not through a delay of service.

Access to Employee Lockers

A greatly appreciated security service is providing access to lockers when an employee does not have a key or cannot remember a combination. This service eliminates the need for employees to break into their lockers when they have misplaced or forgotten their locker key. In some programs, a key that will fit only the specific locker is loaned to the employee. In others, the security department uses a master key to open the lockers. Where the master key system is used, the key should not be checked out to the employee; instead, the security officer should provide the access.

LIAISON WITH PUBLIC SAFETY AND OTHER GOVERNMENT AGENCIES

All organizations, regardless of the sophistication of their security effort, eventually need to call on government public safety services. Even if this need seldom arises, the government agencies themselves frequently request assistance of the healthcare organization. There is so much duplication of effort, jurisdictional disputing, red tape, and disorganization among various agencies that a medical facility must set up a clearinghouse to be able to work effectively with these agencies. The clearinghouse approach can best be handled by the person or department created to handle the facility's day-to-day security effort.

As police agencies become increasingly overtaxed and underfunded, today's healthcare facilities must look more closely into providing a greater amount of self-protection against criminals. As healthcare security increases and develops, a partnership with law enforcement is emerging. Both partners must understand that the proper role of security is not to supplant the police, but rather to supplement and assist them.

INTERNAL AUDITS

Another important function of any protection effort, and one that is often neglected, is to test the procedures designed to protect the organization against such malefactions as internal theft or fraud. Many fraudulent schemes have been discovered by spot checks and internal audits. There are basically three kinds of internal audits. The first is an unannounced inspection of a procedure. An example would be to check the patient personal property envelopes that are being held for safekeeping to determine that all are accounted for in accordance with the system (that is, serial numbers properly listed, inventories as required, double signatures for deposits). The second type of control involves spot-checking incoming or outgoing goods to determine whether the records match the actual commodity. One example would be to randomly weigh meat as it is delivered. Another would be to measure the fuel oil delivery before it is transferred to facility storage tanks. The third type of check involves the use of an undercover operative to monitor a service to determine whether correct procedures are being followed. An example would be to determine whether cashiers ring up the proper amount, especially after a customer pays the exact amount due. Security operations are also subject to audit and should receive the same review and scrutiny as other areas of the organization.

EXTERNAL AUDITS (INSPECTIONS)

An external audit is a survey that is concerned mainly with the hardware of the protection system. At periodic intervals, locks should be inspected, external and stairwell lights checked, and alarm systems activated to ensure that they are operating correctly. Advances in electronic security systems are providing automatic checking, which insures systems are operating properly. There will continue, however, to be a need for visual inspection of security elements such as doors, windows, external lighting, fencing, and shrubbery control (maintaining sight lines).

LOCKS AND KEYS

This protective function is perhaps the most neglected security safeguard, even though it is one that most facilities rely on quite heavily. It has been observed that it is not uncommon for a new lock-and-key system to be out of control within days or weeks of the installation. The control of locks and keys must be assigned to a level of the hierarchy that can effectively compel strict adherence to the program. Although electronic access systems are now rapidly replacing many locked access points, organization will always have the need for keys.

SUPPORTIVE GENERAL SERVICES

In addition to specific responsibilities, security must also provide support to the various departments and sections of the healthcare organization. Chief among these supportive activities is giving directions and helping people, especially patients, utilizing the facility. Other examples include accepting and properly storing shipments when the receiving department is closed, monitoring blood bank refrigeration temperatures, and escorting cashiers. The list can be exhaustive; however, the important point is that security should provide as many supportive services as possible as long as they do not interfere with security's primary protection responsibility. Security is a service organization, and service is a prime consideration when calculating security cost-effectiveness.

Lost and Found

Lost and found activity is usually a component of the protection system. The lost and found service benefits the entire organization and is of specific value to the security program. Although lost and found is operated as a service, it can contribute directly to resolving reports of stolen property. An efficient system of handling found property can clear up many instances of property loss that are reported as theft. Whenever property is missing in a busy medical facility, there is always the question of whether the item was lost, accidentally discarded, inadvertently taken by another person, or taken with the intent to deprive the rightful owner. The public and employee relations fostered by an efficient lost and found system are of tremendous value to any organization.

Conservation

Helping to conserve resources is a security function that goes hand in hand with support services and preventive patrols. Utility costs have made saving energy everyone's job in the medical care facility. Security officers on patrol can shut off and turn on lights at specific times, close windows that were inadvertently left open, report water leaks, and report equipment that is not functioning properly.

Removal of Bodies

Security involvement in handling deceased patients and their property can be found in numerous programs. This involvement may include safekeeping property, assisting in transporting bodies to the facility morgue, granting undertakers access to the facility, and releasing bodies. Although such tasks are generally considered unpleasant for the security officer, one or all of these assignments are appropriate security program responsibilities. As would be expected, much of this activity occurs during the night and on weekends.

The loss of deceased patients' property is a problem familiar to most security administrators. The question often arises whether the disappearance of property occurred before or after death. In some cases, relatives or visitors have removed property from patients as they lay helpless. The blame for the missing property is easily shifted to the facility by the family. Of course one cannot always place the blame for missing property on the relatives or friends of the patient; many cases have been resolved by ascertaining that a hospital employee was responsible.

Although it is common practice, it cannot be stressed enough that a complete inventory of all of the deceased's personal property should be made by two persons as soon as possible after the death. In some programs, this inventory is completed by the security department, and the property is removed for appropriate storage until it can be properly released.

Emergency Messages

Relaying emergency messages is a necessary activity of any organization. For the most part, relaying of messages is handled within the normal operating framework of the system. There are, however, important messages that must be properly handled after normal business hours and outside the routine system. Examples include telegrams granting consent for certain medical procedures and telephone calls to locate employees or visitors to advise them of emergency situations. The security department can and should provide any assistance possible in helping to locate persons and to expedite this relay of important information.

Cash Registers

The handling of cash is a problem for most organizations. According to the accounting firm of Ernst and Young, of all cash fraud techniques, cash taken by the failure to record sales accounts for about 30 percent of all losses.[1] The security department can lend support to the accounting department in several ways. First, cash registers should be read and cleared by a person other than the person handling the transactions. This poses a problem for many accounting departments because a number of registers must be cleared at various night hours and on weekends. In many cases, the security department is already responsible for providing escorts when the money is transported to the main vault or cash-holding area. It is a simple matter to provide the additional service of clearing the register and forwarding the tapes directly to internal auditing or another predesignated department.

A word of caution concerning cash escorts: the security officer should be just that—an escort. The officer should not be the sole transporter unless proper tamper-proof controls have been instituted. The route from the cash collection point to the holding area should be varied just as patrol patterns should be varied.

Emergency Shipments

A valuable support service is the receiving, signing for, and proper disposition of equipment and supplies that arrive at the facility during off-hours. It is sometimes impossible for a critical shipment to arrive before the regular receiving area closes. In this case, the security department can provide a valuable helping hand to the materials management department.

Clear guidelines must be established concerning this support service. Otherwise, outside delivery personnel may not make the effort to deliver on time because they know that security will accept the late shipment. They will deliver first to organizations that do not have after-hours receiving. It is thus important to perform this service on a prearranged request from the materials management department. It should be recognized, however, that flexibility must prevail because it is important that a critical delivery not be refused due to a breakdown in the prearrangement procedure.

Specific handling instruction should be recorded in the system used to pass on information so that all security personnel will be aware of the proper handling of the goods received. At the time the delivery is actually accepted, an entry should be made in the daily activity record indicating the time the delivery was received and where the property was taken for storage.

Package Check

It may be desirable to maintain a checking service for employee property bought into the facility. Not only does this service discourage organization-owned property from being added to the employee's personal property, but it also provides better protection for employee property than storage in a department. In addition to the security aspects, the housekeeping function is enhanced when personal suitcases, packages, boxes, and so on that do not pertain to the departmental responsibilities are stored elsewhere.

This system is quite common in department stores, where packages held by security are released as the employee leaves the building. Already practiced in some healthcare facilities, this procedure requires a firm, consistent policy prohibiting the employee from taking certain personal property to his or her work area.

Distribution of Reports and Equipment

In one hospital, the daily census report prepared by the admissions office is distributed each night by a patrolling security officer. Previously, the admissions employee was responsible for this task, which required approximately 30 to 45 minutes. Because only one admissions clerk was on duty at this time, the admitting function was left uncovered. The security officer frequently found people wandering around who needed admissions services. The security administrator determined that it would serve the best interests of the facility from a security standpoint if the security officer distributed the report. While providing this distribution service, the officer also conducts a patrol of the area. Because the reports are not always ready for distribution at the same time each day, the patrol round occurs on a nonpatterned basis.

The problem of providing wheelchairs at the proper time and place where needed occurs in all facilities, regardless of size. Although this need is predictable to a certain degree, employees frequently need to search for a wheelchair. The continuing need for wheelchairs defies real control, and it is generally impossible to determine the location of all wheelchairs at any given time. An added complication is the fact that patients' private wheelchairs are often brought to the facility. Most security operations can cite examples of missing patient wheelchairs that took days to find after an employee inappropriately used the chair to transport another patient.

In one program, all unit location markings were removed from the chairs and a standard was prepared that specified the number of wheelchairs that should be in a given location. According to this standard, during the late-night shift, the security department was responsible for redistributing the wheelchairs.

Flag Etiquette

It is not uncommon to assign the task of raising and lowering flags to the security department. Security officers, especially those in uniform, add a certain dignity to this activity. Although this function is strictly a service, it is one to which even security administrators who oppose the service concept can seldom raise a suitable objection. In one hospital, the security department not only takes great pride in handling the flag etiquette, but also buys the American flag for the facility through donations from security personnel. It is, however, common to continuously fly the flag with night lighting.

Miscellaneous Services

The number of security services is almost endless. Services should be implemented only if they fit into the system without jeopardizing the basic protection function. Some miscellaneous services other than those previously listed may be found in specific programs. One of these is turning equipment on or off. This may be a routine service, such as turning on kitchen equipment before food service employees arrive, or the specific control of a researcher's experimental project. Another service is providing storage for firearms belonging to patients. Controlling car pool areas and interacting in facility transportation systems is also frequently a role for security departments. In one hospital, the security officer records the number of people using hospital-controlled buses to provide important operational planning data. Another service frequently requested of security officers is helping with patients.

Services are limited only by the needs of the organization and the imagination of those in charge. Security administrators who continually object to requests because "that isn't a security function" may only be reflecting their own narrow view. One must always remember that security is part of the healthcare team, and patient needs are paramount. Figure 4-2 presents a diagram of the various healthcare security service activities and their functional organization impact.

Security Service Impact

- Administration
- Risk Management
- Corporate Compliance
- Non Clinical
- Loss Control
- Human Resources
- Clinical
- Quality
- HCFA / JCAHO / OSHA — Regulatory / Accreditation / Legal

Security
- Security Management Plan
- Security Assessment
- Investigations
- Patrols
- Access Control
- Documentation
- Background Checks
- Identification
- Threat Assessment
- Liaison
- Education/Training
- Design/Construction/Renovation
- Resource
- Crisis Response

- Ambulatory Outpatient/Surgery Center
- Long Term Care
- Assisted Living
- Home Health
- Physician Practices

Copyright © 1998 by Safety And Security Solutions, L.L.C. All rights reserved.

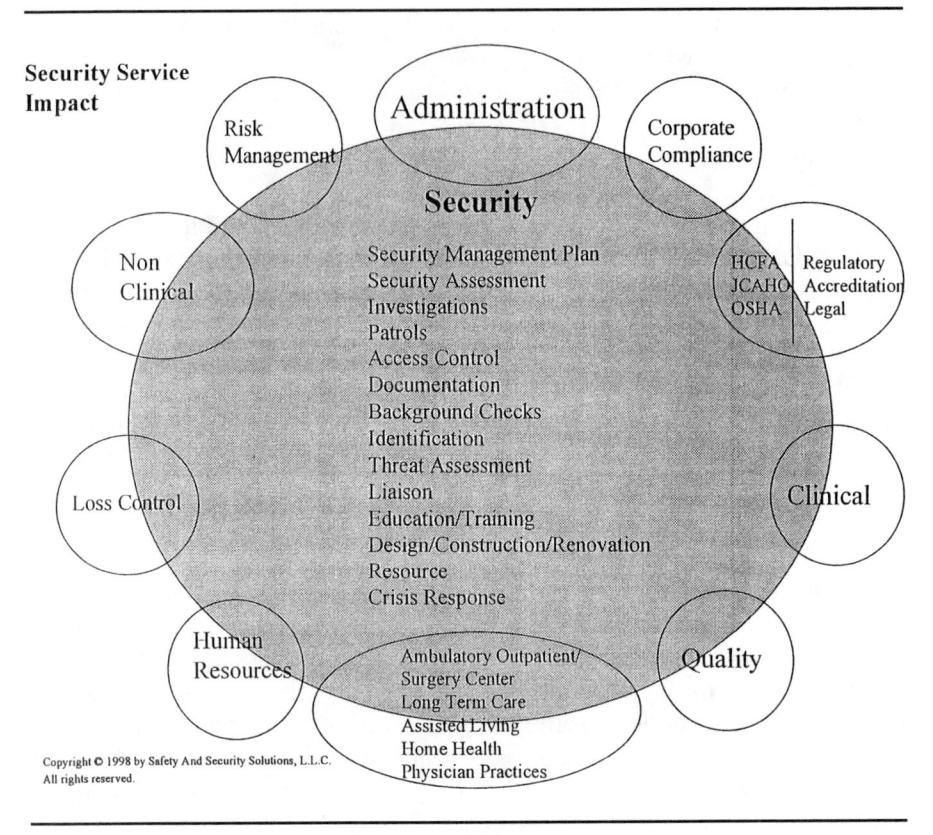

Figure 4-2 Basic Healthcare Security Service Activities and Functional Organization Impact (Courtesy of Safety and Security Solutions, L.L.C., Richmond, Virginia)

PUBLIC/EMPLOYEE/COMMUNITY RELATIONS

The security effort is created to serve the hospital. The organization is people—all sorts of people, including visitors, employees, patients, physicians, vendors, delivery people, repair technicians, researchers, and students. The overall security program must be accepted and understood by the organization it serves. Security personnel must exhibit a helpful and friendly attitude toward everyone they meet. In many instances, a security officer is the first person that a stranger to the hospital meets. The image projected by the officer can set the tone for that person's feelings toward the organization. Security cannot operate in a vacuum and must function as part of the team in providing quality patient care.

REFERENCE

1. Dale L. Gerboth, Jonathan B. Hoenecke, and Robert Briganti, "White Collar Crime: Loss Prevention Through Internal Control," Chubb Group of Insurance Companies, 1989, p. 8.

CHAPTER 5

Security Management Planning

Security management planning involves the formulation of two interrelated, but separate types of plans. The first is a security **management** plan that relates directly to the day-to-day protection program plan. This plan should be considered as a short-term plan that requires a formal review, evaluation, and modification on an annual basis. The second plan is the security **strategic** plan that relates more toward community involvement, long-term goals, objectives, philosophy, and program direction.

A security management plan is the design of the security program developed for an organization after evaluating the security vulnerabilities and risks of the organization. The term security management plan is a specific term utilized by the Joint Commission on Accreditation of Healthcare Organizations (JCAHO) in its Environment of Care Standards. A plan for security management should, however, be part of managing any healthcare organization.

No set format exists for a security management plan, and it can vary in length from a few pages to 25 pages or more. The plan should be just a plan and should not generally include policy and procedure in any great detail. The plan should address all the components of the program, and in a sense equates to a business plan without the financial aspects of one.

In general terms, the plan should include a security mission statement; the basis of authority and responsibility for the security program; a summary of the vulnerability and risk assessment evaluation; a security organization chart; a brief description of positions depicted in the department organization chart; a summary description of the general duties and responsibilities (activities) of the security program; a listing of physical security safeguards as elements of the program; a description of the security staff training program; a listing of the department operating policies and procedures including preparation and review protocols; elements of security awareness, prevention, and training provided to total organization staff and others if applicable (that is, patients, vendors, visitors, neighborhood); prepared and maintained records and reports; and performance standards, measurements, and improvement strategies.

SECURITY MISSION STATEMENT

The security mission statement is the foundation of a security program. It essentially states the reason or purpose of the program, and must relate to and support the overall mission of the organization. Figures 5-1 and 5-2 are examples of two healthcare security mission statements.

PROGRAM AUTHORITY

The authority and responsibility for the day-to-day operation of a security program must be assigned to a specific position within the organization. The day-to-day tasks of security may be delegated to others; however, the responsibility for getting the job done rests with the specific position designated by the organization. In most cases this position will be found in an organization chart. In other cases an organization chart may only portray a function rather than a position. In this case the security management plan should contain a memo from the chief executive officer, or the chief operating officer, granting a specific position the authority and responsibility for the security function.

When the organization chart is utilized in the security management plan it must include at least the next highest hierarchical position, or reporting level, of the security program. In most cases the organization chart will show reporting levels at least to the chief operating officer level. An organization chart may also show how the security department or program is organized. The department organization chart may be organized to show program functions, positions, or a combination of both position and function. A program organization chart can be quite helpful in showing the overall picture or concept of the security program. Figure 5-3 is an example of a security program organization chart showing a combination of positions and functions. (In Chapter 6 we will discuss standard security program organization charts that do not include a functional aspect of the position.)

WELLSTAR
Health System

SECURITY SERVICES DEPARTMENT

SECURITY MANAGEMENT PROGRAM MISSION STATEMENT

It shall be the mission of the WellStar Health System Security Services Department, through the administration of the security management program, to provide an orderly and peaceful atmosphere for the safety and security of the people who work at and use all system facilities. The Security Services Department staff will stand ready to react to internal and external emergencies, to respond proactively and/or reactively to crimes committed on system campuses, to enforce rules and regulations when necessary, to patrol all buildings and grounds for the safety and security of patients, visitors, employees, medical staff, and volunteers, to control parking on all lots, emergency traffic flow and/or traffic flow around the perimeters, and to protect system and personal property. In cooperation with the Safety Officer(s) and/or the Safety Committee(s) the Security Services Department will perform services as set forth in the safety management program to promote and insure a safe environment. The Security Services Department shall also perform services as required by other departments and/or government agencies during disasters and other emergency situations.
  The Security Services Department will have in place a reporting system to document any of these services as required. The Security Services Director, Operations Manager and Supervisors will evaluate the security management program annually and will establish goals for continued performance improvements of the program.

Thomas E. Hill
Chief Executive Officer
WellStar Health System

Stanley C. Bishop, CHPA
Director of Security Services
WellStar Health System

July 1, 1999
Date

Figure 5-1 An Example of a Healthcare Security Mission Statement (Courtesy of Wellstar Health System, Marietta, Georgia)

UNITED GENERAL HOSPITAL

SECURITY MISSION STATEMENT

The mission of security at United General Hospital (UGH) is to provide a reasonable and prudent level of protection from harm to all persons utilizing the campus of UGH and the protection of property. Security will also be responsible to provide a myriad of general services that will facilitate the efficient delivery of services and courtesies to visitors, staff, and patients.

The security department will be responsible to identify security risks, design protection safeguards to properly manage these risks, implement and manage security safeguards, evaluate effectiveness of safeguards, and improve systems of protection within a framework of cost effectiveness, efficiency, and consistent with the overall mission of the organization.

The security department will provide direct protection services, while assisting, educating, and coordinating the security efforts of all staff members and departments.

The security department will be responsible to coordinate the UGH protection effort with public safety agencies, regulatory agencies, and healthcare organization where the issue of security or law enforcement is involved. The specific goals, objectives, systems, and procedures of security operations will be delineated in the UGH Security Management Plan.

Figure 5-2 An Example of a Healthcare Security Mission Statement

POSITION DESCRIPTIONS/ACTIVITIES

The security program management plan should contain a brief description of the activities performed by each job position in the program. An option is to include the full position descriptions in an appendix to the plan and simply refer the reader to the appendix. With this option one may also want to use the appendix for other areas of the plan, such as defining skill and competency levels of various positions.

In the brief job descriptions, one may want to include the number of authorized full-time equivalent (FTE) staff for each position. Alternatively, each position could be expressed in terms of person-hours required for program implementation. Table 5-1 presents staff requirements according to FTE count and number of person-hours per week.

Security Management Planning 103

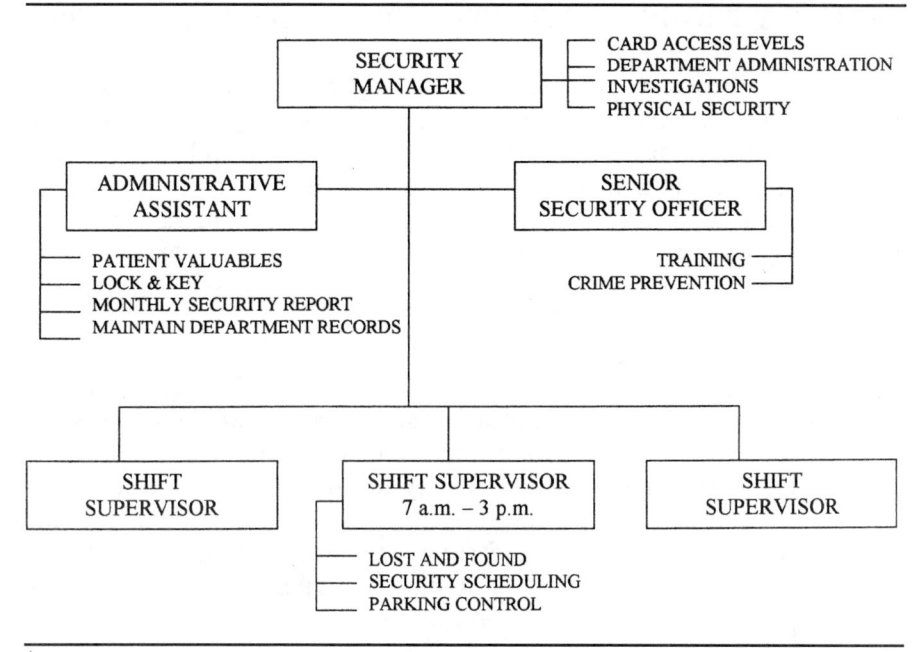

```
                    ┌─────────────┐  ── CARD ACCESS LEVELS
                    │  SECURITY   │  ── DEPARTMENT ADMINISTRATION
                    │   MANAGER   │  ── INVESTIGATIONS
                    └─────────────┘  ── PHYSICAL SECURITY
```

Figure 5-3 A Security Program Organization Chart Depicting Positions and Functions

Table 5-1 Authorized Security Program Staffing: Security Department Manpower Loading

Position	FTE	Hours/week
Security Manager	1	40
Shift Supervisor	4.2	168
Investigator	1.5	60
Training Officer	1	40
Security Officer I	11.4	456
Security Officer II	9.6	384
TOTALS	**28.7**	**1148**

SECURITY PROGRAM OVERVIEW (DUTIES AND ACTIVITIES)

This section of the security management plan is intended to provide the reader an understanding of what the program does (operations) on a day-to-day basis. This overview is intended to bridge the gap between mission statements, organization charts, and position descriptions to what activities are actually performed or accomplished by the program.

Security Physical Safeguards

All security programs utilize physical security safeguards to some degree. In this section of the plan, each safeguard should be listed with a general description and how the security department relates to the safeguard including objectives, responsibility for systems operation, and maintenance. Figures 5-4 and 5-5 show examples of how physical safeguards might appear in the security management plan description for lock and key programs and the utilization of security closed circuit television.

Security Staff Training

In this section of the plan there will be a review of the various elements of the training provided to security personnel. This training will vary considerably between organizations, but will always relate directly to the job description or other document that contains the skill levels required of each position. Since skill levels, training, and competency all tie together, this section would be a good place to describe competency procedures. Competency essentially means verifying skill levels and/or determining the training needs of each staff person.

Department Policies and Procedures

A simple listing of security policies and procedures is appropriate for this section. This information is often referred to as post orders, general orders, facility orders, or just security orders. A brief explanation on how these policies and procedures get prepared, approvals required,

PHYSICAL SECURITY

SYSTEM DESCRIPTION/PROTOCOL

TYPE: Mechanical Lock and Key Control
LOCATION: All Campus Facilities
OBJECTIVE: Determine proper locking devices and maintain integrity of the lock and key program (See Administrative Policy 107-2).

<u>GENERAL DESCRIPTION:</u> Administration of a centralized system to determine the need for any locking device, specify type of device, approve installation, approved distribution of keys, and maintain an accountability of all locks and keys in the organization excluding desks and filing cabinets.

<u>SYSTEM OPERATION:</u> The Director of Security or his designated representative has full authority and responsibility to control the organization's lock and key program.

All lock installation, or modification, will be approved through the issuance of a work order forwarded to the department of facilities for lock work or duplication of keys. All keys will be issued through the security department and be stamped with the proper location code. Keys will be issued to individuals upon approval of appropriate department managers.

The individual staff member or department manager will report any lost or stolen keys to security.

Staff terminating employment will surrender all organization keys, except desks and filing cabinets, to security and obtain a signature on their termination release statement. Staff members being terminated on the spot will surrender organization keys to the terminating supervisor and turned into security as soon as possible after the termination is effected.

Security will determine at what point a locking device has been compromised requiring a new or modified lock. All lock and key work will be charged to the department utilizing locking devices.

Figure 5-4 A Security Management Plan Description of an Organization's Lock and Key Program

PHYSICAL SECURITY

SYSTEM DESCRIPTION/PROTOCOL

TYPE: Closed Circuit Television (CCTV)
LOCATION: 4 North Newborn Nursery and Post Partum (Mother/Infant)
OBJECTIVE: General Surveillance/ Recorded Movement

GENERAL DESCRIPTION: This CCTV system utilizes four color cameras, a quad (4 screen) monitor, and a recording system. The recording system tapes images from all four cameras and a seven-day library of recorded images is maintained. The system monitor is located at the 4 North nursing station. It is intended that there will be live monitoring of the cameras only when staff randomly look at monitors or when there is a specific situation requiring attention.

CAMERA LOCATION/PURPOSE: Camera #1 is mounted in the ceiling of the main corridor entry to the mother/infant unit. The purpose of the camera is to record all persons entering the unit.

Camera #2 is mounted in the ceiling of the main corridor entry to the unit back-to-back of Camera #1. The purpose of this camera is to record all persons exiting the unit via this unit corridor.

Camera #3 is mounted in the ceiling of the unit's back corridor (W-E). This corridor cannot be visualized from the nursing station. There is a door at the end of this corridor, leading to a main facility corridor. This door is locked from the main corridor side. The camera is positioned to record all exiting persons and to provide staff at the nursing station a view of this unit's corridor when desired.

Camera #4 is mounted in stairwell #8 facing the stairwell exit door of the mother/infant unit. The purpose of this camera is to view any person exiting into the stairwell. The door is equipped with a 15 second delayed exit device and locked from the ingress side. An alarm is sounded at the nursing station immediately when pressure is exerted on the exit release bar on the door. Staff will immediately respond to the exit door when the alarm is activated.

SYSTEM OPERATION: The system requires security to change recorder tapes at 12 midnight each day at which time the stairwell exit alarm is also tested. The tape library is maintained at the central security office.

Figure 5-5 A Security Management Plan Description of an Organization's Utilization of Closed Circuit Television

COMMON HEALTHCARE SECURITY POLICIES AND PROCEDURES

Security Staffing and Deployment

Functional Relationship of Security Department Positions

General Security Officer Duties and Activities

Utilization of Security Equipment and Vehicles

Reporting for Duty

Security Assistance/Support
    Patients
    Staff
    Visitors
    Vehicle
    Departments/Programs

Critical Incident and Alarm Response

Outside Agency Interactions/Response

Legal Actions and Guidelines

Investigative Procedures

Report Preparation

Facility Access Control

Enforcing Organization Rules

Safety Services/ Response

Parking Control

Facility Property Control/Removal

Patient Property Control

Lost and Found

Security Officer Training
    Pre-Service
    In-Service

Figure 5-6   A List of Common Healthcare Security Policies and Procedures

and how they are maintained in a current status would help the reader in understanding the mechanics of this element of the security program. The listing referred to in this section does not include personnel policies covering staff conduct, disciplinary actions, pay, or benefits. Figure 5-6 shows an example of commonly utilized security policies and procedures.

Security Education (Security Awareness)

A comprehensive security program will include a program of education, training, and motivating persons to be security aware. Being security aware and adhering to good security practices prevents security incidents. While much of this educational effort is directed to staff, it should be clear in this section of the plan who is responsible to provide the various education activities. For example, new employee security training may be the responsibility of the security department or the human resources department. Another example is the JCAHO requirement for staff training relative to security in designated security-sensitive areas. Is this training the responsibility of the area supervisor or is it accomplished by the security department? Who develops training material? Where are training records maintained?

The typical security program will involve a variety of departments to accomplish employee security training. The security department should provide the coordination to blend all these efforts into the overall program.

Security Records and Reports

The security management plan should outline all security records and reports prepared and utilized in the security program. In this outline there should be a brief explanation of the objective of each document, who is responsible for preparation of the document, distribution protocols, and, very importantly, how and where each is document stored. Figure 5-7 shows a sample format that could be utilized for each document.

Performance Standards and Performance Improvement Measures

There must be program performance standards to determine whether program goals and objectives are being accomplished. A program

SECURITY DOCUMENTATION

SYSTEM DESCRIPTION/PROTOCOL

TYPE: Security Incident Report
LOCATION: All Campus Facilities
OBJECTIVE: The completion of an accurate and timely report of all security incidents occurring on facility property, or effecting the organization from a protection perspective. The report will clearly set forth facts and include all actions taken by personnel in relation to the incident.

GENERAL DESCRIPTION:

Security Incident Reports (SIR), form SD-104, will be completed by the assigned security officer responding to the incident or by off site personnel as directed by a member of the security department. The SIR will be completed as soon after the initial management of the incident has been accomplished. The completed report will be reviewed by the security shift supervisor and be placed in the investigators "in box" located in the central security control station.

REPORT UTILIZATION

The security shift supervisor, or the assigned investigator, will effect any emergency or routine notification of other appropriate parties relative to a security incident.

The assigned investigator will determine the need for any follow-up investigation of the incident and if so will coordinate this follow-up activity. The investigator will enter summary incident information into the computer log file after verifying the appropriate incident report classification. The computer log file will be utilized to generate the monthly, quarterly, and annual security incident report utilized by security administration and reporting to the facility safety committee.

REPORT STORAGE/RETENTION

The completed SIR, with attached supplemental reports if appropriate, will be filed chronologically as the master file. These reports will be maintained for a five year period except for a report where there is a perceived need for the report to be maintained in excess of five years. Retention of these reports will be determined on an individual basis by the Director of Security.

Figure 5-7 A Sample Format for Explaining the Security Incident Report in the Security Management Plan

must then measure actual activity to determine the level of service provided. A goal of all programs should be to develop a plan of improvement action for activities not meeting standards and to look for opportunities to set higher standards where possible. A key management responsibility is to ensure that standards are set at a realistic level. If standards are too low, the program stagnates with little incentive to improve. On the other hand, standards must be realistically achievable. Figure 5-8 shows an example of security performance standards.

JCAHO Security Management Plan

The security management plan required for JCAHO accreditation purposes is rather specific in terms of content. In seeking accreditation, the plan must include the specific element required but should not be limited to that element. Simply addressing that element alone will not provide a complete and comprehensive protection plan for an organization. It is also important to remember that not all JCAHO security management plan-required elements are contained in the Environment of Care Standards. Additional elements are found in Human Resources, Leadership, Improving Organization Performance, and Management of Information sections, which have whole-house as well as security implications. An example is found in the Management of Human Resources section regarding forensic staff and training to be provided. Since there is a direct relation between forensic staff and security operations, this aspect of operations should be addressed in the security management plan. Since the forensic staff-training requirement is in Human Resources, there would simply be a cross-reference to show that this standard is addressed in security.

The current security areas or elements that are required to be addressed as outlined only in the Management of the Environment of Care (CAMH, 2000) are summarized as follows:

- Designating personnel responsible for the security program (developing, implementing, and evaluating the security management plan and program)

- Identifying and addressing security issues involving patients, visitors, and staff, including property issues

HUNTINGTON MEMORIAL HOSPITAL

Safety Program 1999

SECURITY MANAGEMENT PLAN

STANDARDS FOR IMPROVING PERFORMANCE

STANDARD MEASURED	INDICATOR	HOW MEASURED	BASE TYPE	TARGET	HOW OFTEN	REPORTED TO
Huntington Hospital shall assure the manpower and processes necessary to provide a reasonable environment in which individuals are safe from harm.	During safety inspections, staff will be asked to verbalize the procedure to contact security in an emergency.	# Correct / # Asked	Rate	95%	Semi Annual	Safety Committee
Risks will be minimized as appropriate to incident.	Incident investigation utilized to determine/trend cause/area of visitor falls and theft.	Each occurrence	Event		Quarterly	Safety Committee

Should an indicator not meet established thresholds that are considered a significant issue. Issues should be identified in detail, actual or proposed corrective action noted and necessary follow-up indicated.
The status of event based monitors are to be reported as significant issues each time they are assessed. Findings, corrective actions (if any) and required follow-up (if any) are to be noted.

Figure 5-8 Examples of Healthcare Security Standards and Performance Measures (Courtesy of Huntington Memorial Hospital, Pasadena, California)

- Reporting and investigating all security incidents

- Providing an identification system for patients, visitors, and staff

- Controlling access in security-sensitive areas

- Providing vehicular access to urgent care areas

- Providing security orientation and education programs relative to minimizing risks for personnel in designated security-sensitive areas, as well as providing emergency procedures for security incidents and processes for reporting security incidents

- Monitoring performance of actual or potential risk of at least one of five areas listed by the commission

- Establishing emergency security procedures that address actions to be taken in the event of a security incident or failure including civil disturbances, VIP or media situations, and disasters

- Establishing a process for an annual evaluation of the security management plan, which addresses objectives, scope, performance, and effectiveness

Current JCAHO standards and intents should always be reviewed to determine any addition or deletions relative to the accreditation process and specific requirements.

SECURITY MANAGEMENT CYCLE

There really is no ending point in security management planning and operations. The protection program should be viewed as a cyclical and dynamic process geared to reacting to new issues and concerns as well as eliminating ineffective or obsolete practices. The starting point is, of course, identifying and quantifying security risks; however, this starting point is repeated daily as the management cycle continues to provide new information. Figure 5-9 displays such a security management process/cycle.

Security Management Planning 113

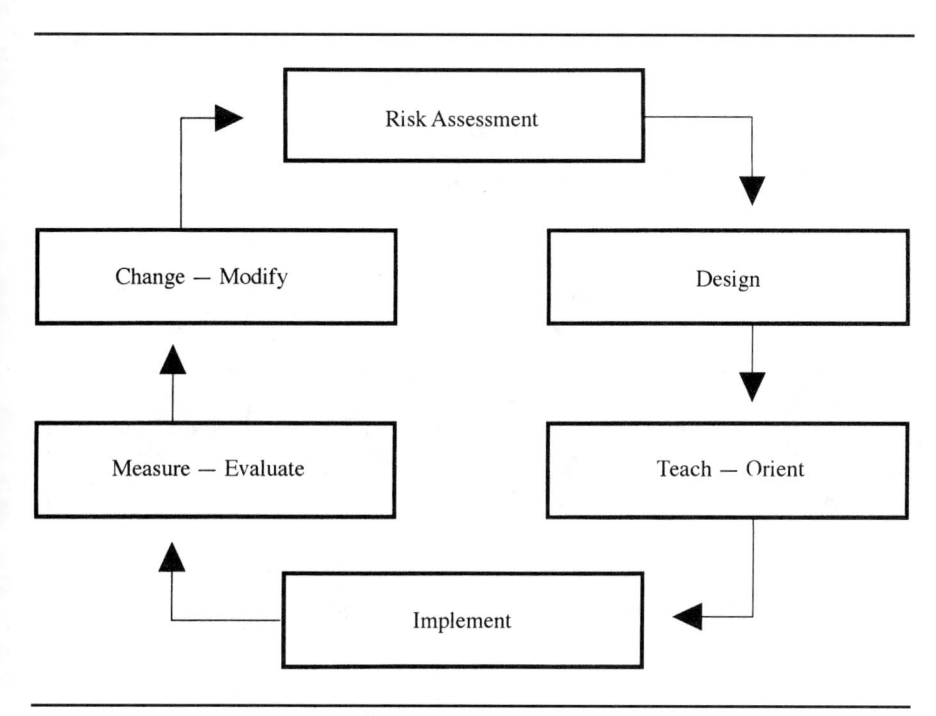

```
        ┌──────────────────────┐
        │   Risk Assessment    │
        └──────────────────────┘
          ▲                  │
          │                  ▼
┌──────────────────┐   ┌──────────────────┐
│ Change — Modify  │   │     Design       │
└──────────────────┘   └──────────────────┘
          ▲                  │
          │                  ▼
┌──────────────────┐   ┌──────────────────┐
│ Measure — Evaluate│   │  Teach — Orient  │
└──────────────────┘   └──────────────────┘
          ▲                  │
          │                  ▼
        ┌──────────────────────┐
        │      Implement       │
        └──────────────────────┘
```

Figure 5-9   The Security Management Process/Cycle

SECURITY STRATEGIC PLAN

The security strategic plan is the second major plan required of the healthcare organization. As opposed to the day-to-day security management plan, this plan sets the philosophy and direction of the protection program for the longer term and may include elements of financial planning. The major components of this plan are organization-wide security coordination and control, neighborhood stability and security/crime prevention involvement, public safety agency coordination, criminal justice system interface, a philosophy regarding the type and extent of physical security safeguards utilization, the degree of employee/staff involvement in the protection program (i.e., centralization versus decentralization), and building configuration and design considerations. Figure 5-10 lists the different components of the healthcare organization security strategic plan.

114 Hospital and Healthcare Security

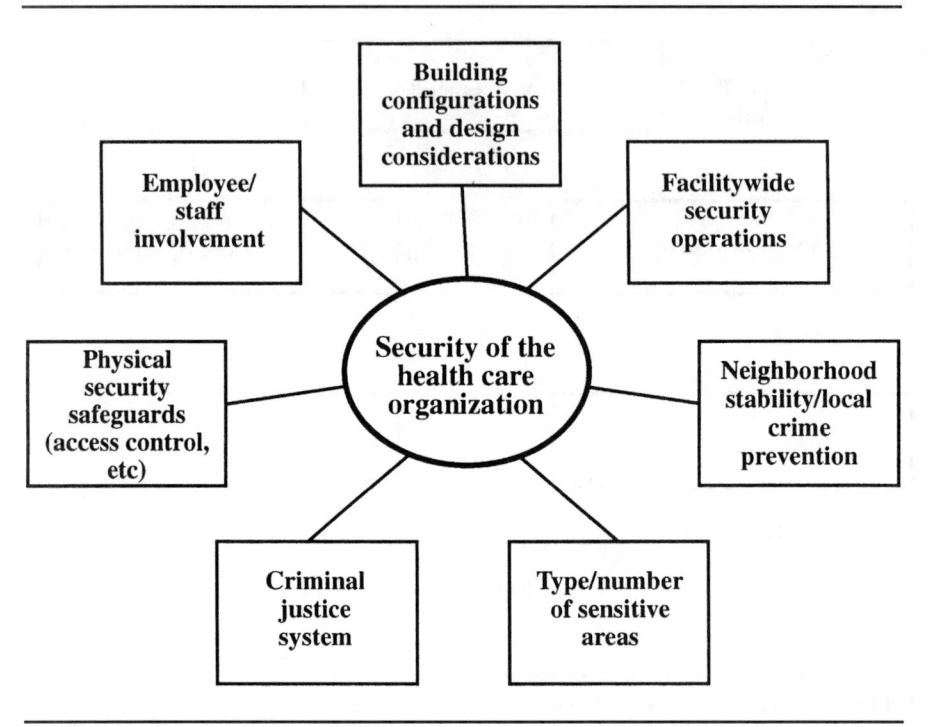

Figure 5-10 Components of the Healthcare Organization Security Strategic Plan

Organization-Wide Security Coordination

There must be basic organizational policy that creates a clear understanding of the authority and responsibility of the various layers of management in regard to the protection program. In this respect, the security department is seldom responsible for all the components of the protection, either partially or totally. Security personnel must ask themselves, What security responsibility and/or security decisions can be made within an operating department versus those reserved totally for the security department? This question involves the philosophy of security centralization versus decentralization. The same questions apply to an organization that may have two or three campus locations and a dozen or more freestanding patient facilities many miles removed from each other. Does security provide all the direct services as a mandate to the freestanding facility, or does management at the facility make independent decisions regarding reporting of incidents, key control, alarm systems, etc.? In a totally decentralized approach, the director of security on the main campus would serve only as a consultant upon the request of the autonomously operating facility.

Even within the main facility, various departments may be performing security-related functions almost totally removed from the security department. An example is background investigations of prospective employees. Background checks, including criminal histories, are a significant element of the protection program but may be almost exclusively the responsibility of the human resources department—not only in performing the activity, but in making the decision relative to the depth and methodology of such investigations.

The following are some of the questions that must be answered:

- Who has the authority and under what circumstances can the police be called to make an arrest?

- Who has the authority to make decisions in reference to locks and keys? Can any employee order a lock installed, removed, or changed? Who approves the issuance of keys?

- Can departments order and install a security alarm or camera in their department without security approval?

- What about physical security safeguard funding? What types of security equipment and supplies are purchased with security department funds versus operating department funds?

- Does the nurse decide if missing property will be reported? If reported, does the nurse or security prepare the missing property report? If the nurse completes the report, is it mandated to be sent to security, nursing administration, or risk management?

- Who decides restitution questions regarding property loss or damage relative to patients, staff, and visitors?

- When security is called to a patient treatment area due to inappropriate behavior of a patient or visitor, who is in charge relative to actions to be taken?

These and other questions require clear direction and shape the type of security program that evolves.

Neighborhood Stability and Security/Crime Prevention Activities

A healthcare security protection program goes beyond the physical property lines of the campus. Community involvement takes place to some extent in all protection programs. The environment surrounding the campus severely impacts the security risks to the organization and all persons coming to and from the facilities. It makes little difference to the public whether visitors and staff are assaulted on or off the hospital property in terms of their perception of feeling safe. In many cases an incident occurring a block or more from a facility will be reported as being "at the medical center." Some security departments work at community involvement and others tend to withdraw from this activity. Examples of security outreach are:

- **Security patrols of the neighborhood by organization security departments.** These patrols may be funded totally by the healthcare organization, or contracted by businesses, neighborhood associations or a cost-sharing arrangement.

- **Active involvement in neighborhood watch and community associations.** The healthcare organization may provide funding, meeting places, and sometimes allow use of equipment.

- **Home purchase assistance.** Home purchase assistance is a program to entice staff to relocate to the medical center neighborhood. It is an established fact that owner-occupied living units create an environment that tends to foster improved communities with lower crime rates. These programs basically provide cash and/or low cost loans to purchase a home. The employee must agree to personally live in the home for a certain number of years. In addition to organization financial support, there is pending federal legislation that provides tax credits or discount mortgage rates for renovation of living units in historic neighborhoods. Medical centers located in these neighborhoods may find a new source of funds to make owning in the area more attractive.

Security Management Planning 117

- **Block parties.** Block parties are popular events that blend the medical care campus into the surrounding neighborhood. These events provide tours, food, entertainment, and fun activities for old and young people alike. The concept is for the hospital to be a good corporate neighbor and an integral part of the community.

- **Alarm monitoring and response.** Alarm monitoring and response is another element of community involvement. Alarms generally pertain to businesses; however, a really involved outreach program could provide this service for private homes as well.

Public Safety Coordination

The primary public safety agencies that the security program must work with are law enforcement, fire, disaster, and possibly a governmental citywide ambulance service. The law enforcement coordination presents many additional issues and is generally covered in a separate section of the strategic plan. In these cases, the security strategic plan should include a reference to these important agencies, which refers the reader to the proper documents or department.

Criminal Justice Interface

This section of the plan requires specific policy to define appropriate staff interactions with law enforcement agencies at all levels—including prosecutors, probation, parole, and correctional personnel. A major issue is what will be reported to law enforcement and who will make these decisions as situations occur. On the surface, this appears to be quite simplistic, but as further questions develop it becomes more complex. Confidentiality issues and philosophical issues must be taken into account, especially between security and the human resources department, which often view the relationship of the organization to staff from different perspectives. Meanwhile, the police insist that all crime be immediately reported to them and then often don't want to be bothered with minor crimes. In some jurisdictions, the police will not even respond to the scene of certain crimes unless a suspect is being detained.

In this respect, does the organization report the loss of $1 from the bedside of a patient? What about $5, $20, $50, or $100? Or does the organization leave all reporting of missing personal property to the victim? Does the police agency permit, or foster, reporting certain crimes to a specialized investigative unit, or must all reporting be accomplished through a police dispatcher or mail-in report? An example is missing narcotics. In many jurisdictions, it is appropriate to report directly to the police narcotics unit; in others, this direct reporting is prohibited. It is often difficult to define some of these relationships, as law enforcement agencies often give out conflicting information and have frequently changing philosophies. These problems have been minimized in some jurisdictions where a specific municipal or county police liaison person has been assigned to the healthcare organization. There tends to be less liaison problems at state and federal levels as contacts are less frequent and issues are more situational with specific decision-makers readily available.

UTILIZATION OF PHYSICAL SECURITY SAFEGUARDS

Virtually all healthcare organizations utilize physical security (hardware) as a component of their protection system. This utilization ranges from lighting and fencing to state of the art electronics. Security manpower and physical security safeguards should complement each other in forming a balanced blend of manpower and equipment. Every component of physical security should fit into the overall protection plan. Unfortunately, however, many of our nation's healthcare organizations have ended up with a high-cost, uncoordinated conglomeration of ineffective equipment.

Physical security safeguards are usually purchased in relatively small amounts over a number of years due to budget considerations. It is thus important to keep a road map (plan) to insure that each purchase fits the technical aspects of being compatible with current equipment, product standardization from a cost maintenance and replacement viewpoint, and user buy-in and acceptance. The philosophy of the organization must also be factored into the direction of the program.

Closed-circuit television is utilized in many security programs and provides an example of how strategic planning can shape a system. The following series of questions regarding closed-circuit television will help shape the strategic safety plan.

- Will the system be centrally monitored, tape recorded, or departmentally monitored?

- What is the policy or plan regarding covert versus overt camera placement?

- Will the closed-circuit television system be integrated with other electronic physical security components and fire systems?

- Who will determine camera placement and utilization?

- Who will be authorized to purchase equipment?

- Will equipment be standardized as to manufacturer and/or technical specifications?

- Will equipment be maintained by in-house or vendor arrangement?

- What is the maintenance and equipment replacement schedule?

- What is the optimum size of the system in relation to the total security program?

Thus, there should be a business plan approach to the utilization of physical security safeguards. This plan should address the current year and project plans, objectives, and funding for a minimum of five years.

EMPLOYEE/STAFF INVOLVEMENT IN THE PROTECTION PROGRAM

It is universally agreed that staff must take ownership in helping protect the organization; however, there are issues beyond practicing good security. One of these issues is the authority for intervention. When security is called to a nursing unit because a patient is out of control, who is responsible for directing actions, security or nursing? The answer is that either one may be appropriate; however, this should be clear in the strategic plan and resultant policy. When there are drugs missing from the pharmacy, is this a pharmacy problem that security supports, or a pure security problem to be resolved only by security? When a laptop computer belonging to the organization is stolen, can the employee simply order another one, or does it require a report to security before purchasing will order a new one? These are the types of strategic questions that must be answered in the strategic plan to provide the proper operating fabric for the protection effort.

BUILDING CONFIGURATION AND DESIGN

The most cost-effective security is that which is designed and planned during renovation or new construction. Traffic patterns can be planned and new security hardware can be installed at far less cost than a retrofit situation. In addition, funding is sometimes more easily obtained when it is included in the total construction package. New construction will often present the opportunity to begin a phased approach for introducing a new system for the whole campus. The best example is that of introducing electronic card access. A system for a large campus could cost upwards of $800,000 or more at build-out. This large expenditure is typically spread out over several years. The first phase may be a physician office building with proper strategic planning that includes the basic hardware and software to accommodate the entire campus. The strategic plan should stipulate that no construction or installation of security hardware can be placed without the review and, if necessary, the approval of the director of security or the designated person responsible for total organization protection.

UNIQUE STRATEGIC PLANS

The security strategic plan will be unique to each specific organization as to form, format, and subject area. This plan, however, is necessary for all organizations to provide a clear program direction. Without the framework of strategic security policy and infrastructure, a program simply becomes one of nonproductive day-to-day reactions.

CHAPTER 6

Security Department Organization and Staffing

The security force is the basic component of the healthcare protection system. Although the security staff is the backbone of this effort, it is perhaps only 15 to 20 percent of a well-rounded security program. In fact, in some small facilities, there are successful security programs in which there are no full-time security personnel. However, in such cases there must be a designated security force response capability. It may be that the maintenance staff (or other hospital personnel) assume certain security responsibilities. Regardless of facility size, the security force must always be integrated into the other organizational resources that contribute to a cost-effective protection program. The achievement of this integration is the direct responsibility of the security program administrator.

SECURITY DEPARTMENT REPORTING LEVEL AND SUPPORT

The security function serves, supports, and is interrelated to all aspects of the healthcare organization. As such, security is considered an element of administration. A required component of the security management plan is to clearly specify the position that has the responsibility for security of the organization and the reporting level of that position. The level in the organization to which security reports reflects the importance that administration places on the security function.

It has been argued by some security practitioners that the security function must report only to the chief executive officer (CEO) or the chief operating officer (COO). This may sound good in theory, but it is generally neither practical nor a satisfactory situation. The basic problem is accessibility. Both the CEO and the COO are performing functions that, by necessity, do not generally involve day-to-day department operations.

On the other hand, the security function must not report at a level that negatively affects its productiveness. The security function, like many other functions in healthcare, has been a victim of organizational "flattening out." The various management levels in healthcare organizations that once existed are gone. As a result, security has been pushed lower in the organizational hierarchy and often "pushed around."

The important aspect of the reporting level is that it must provide the organizational authority necessary to properly carry out its mission. Security must, thus, report to an individual who has both the time and interest in the security function. In short, there must be proper administrative support for the program. This person must also have sufficient stature to carry the ball when a decision is outside his or her realm of direct authority or when information of a sensitive nature must be transferred to others at higher levels within the organization.

It is common that security reports to the vice president (or director) of facilities. Other highly successful programs report to the vice presidents of finance, human resources, and administration. Regardless of the reporting level, the professional security administrator must be cognizant of the organizational support level cycle. The concept of the cycle is that when necessary, security is a top priority of the organization. This results in a high level of support for security in terms of funding and philosophy relative to policy and procedures. At other times, such intensive support may not be necessary.

Dennis Dalton, in his book *The Art of Successful Security Management*, suggests that the support cycle consists of three phases: strong organization support, confusion, and a lack of support.[1] In Dalton's support cycle, the confusion phase is one that can slip up on the security administrator. This confusion phase can occur when the program is running smoothly and there is little or no perceived security threat. Management and staff feel safe and are thus totally focused on other management issues. Various signs and clues will alert the security administrator that the program is entering this confusion stage of the support cycle. Chief among these signs are:

- A general indifference toward the program by top management

- Inadvertent exclusions from meetings where issues clearly enter into the area of protection

- Planning of activities or events with security implications without security involvement

- Department heads and supervisors making assumptions about the security program without seeking clarifications or confirmation of program components

In the third stage of the support cycle, there is outright rejection of plans and programs, top management avoids security input or discussion, and staff show little support for the security function. This is a bad time for the security administrator, who must do everything possible to end this final stage of the cycle and return to the full support phase.

THE FUNCTIONAL ORGANIZATION CHART

In essence, the administrative plan for the entire organization is recapped in the functional organization chart, which defines the relationship of the components of the organization. This chart further establishes the chain of command. However, the chart specifies only formal authority relationships; it omits the many significant informal relationships. Further, it does not generally indicate the degree of authority that exists at any point in the structure.

The organization of a security department is limited only by the imagination and desires of the person responsible for the protection system. Organizational charts range from simple to complex. Each facility or organization has its own format, style, and procedure for preparing the department organization chart. The charts in Figures 6-1 and 6-2 are offered as examples of actual working charts in a single facility. They are not intended to be used as models, as each protection program is unique in scope, function, and reporting level.

The organizational chart and the delivery of security services of a healthcare system may look quite different than a single hospital facility. These healthcare systems, created by mergers, buyouts, and affiliations, develop their own specific management operating philosophies. These philosophies range from centralization, to quasi-centralization, to decentralization management styles, with variations of form in between.

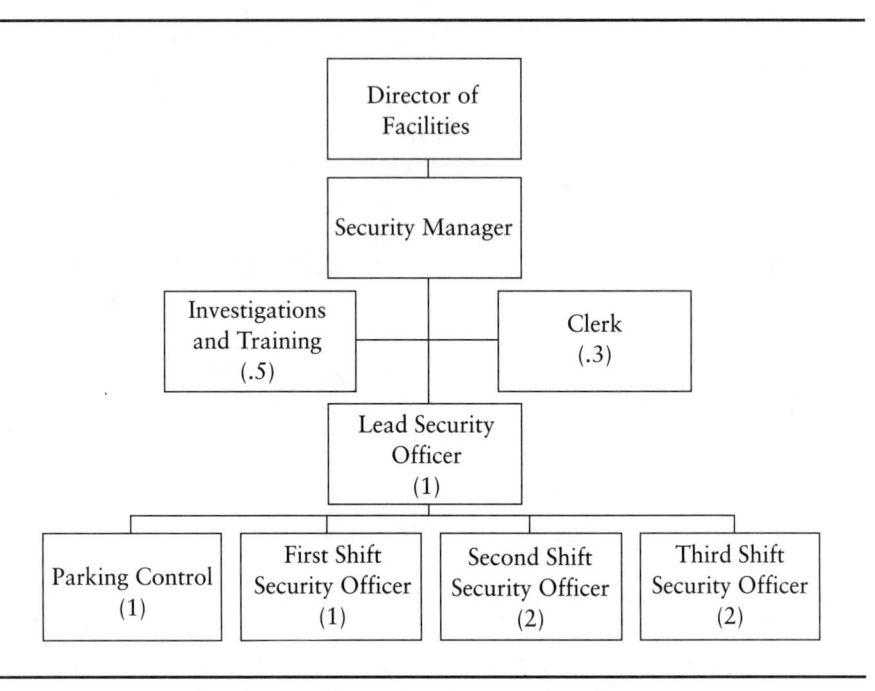

```
                    ┌─────────────────┐
                    │   Director of   │
                    │    Facilities   │
                    └─────────────────┘
                             │
                    ┌─────────────────┐
                    │ Security Manager│
                    └─────────────────┘
         ┌───────────────────┼───────────────────┐
┌─────────────────┐  ┌─────────────────┐  ┌─────────────────┐
│  Investigations │  │                 │  │     Clerk       │
│   and Training  │──┤                 ├──│     (.3)        │
│      (.5)       │  │                 │  │                 │
└─────────────────┘  └─────────────────┘  └─────────────────┘
                             │
                    ┌─────────────────┐
                    │  Lead Security  │
                    │     Officer     │
                    │       (1)       │
                    └─────────────────┘
```

| Parking Control (1) | First Shift Security Officer (1) | Second Shift Security Officer (2) | Third Shift Security Officer (2) |

Figure 6-1 Example of a Small Proprietary Security Department Organization Chart

In the complete centralized philosophy approach, there is one budget with full-line authority to operate a consolidated systems program. There may be some internal accounting expense allocations to different facilities being served, but from an operations standpoint, each facility receives security services as a one-campus approach.

The quasi-centralization philosophy, which is the most popular, operates with a central corporate budget and a facility-specific budget for security. In this approach, the central office provides support functions such as training, investigations, consultation, and documentation including Joint Commission on Accreditation of Healthcare Organizations (JCAHO) and strategic planning; equipment standardization including maintenance contracts; and a communications center. In some programs, the central office also provides for a common external grounds patrol or patrol/field supervision. The patrol field supervisor for the system has the authority of the individual facility supervisor during evenings, nights, and

Security Department Organization and Staffing 125

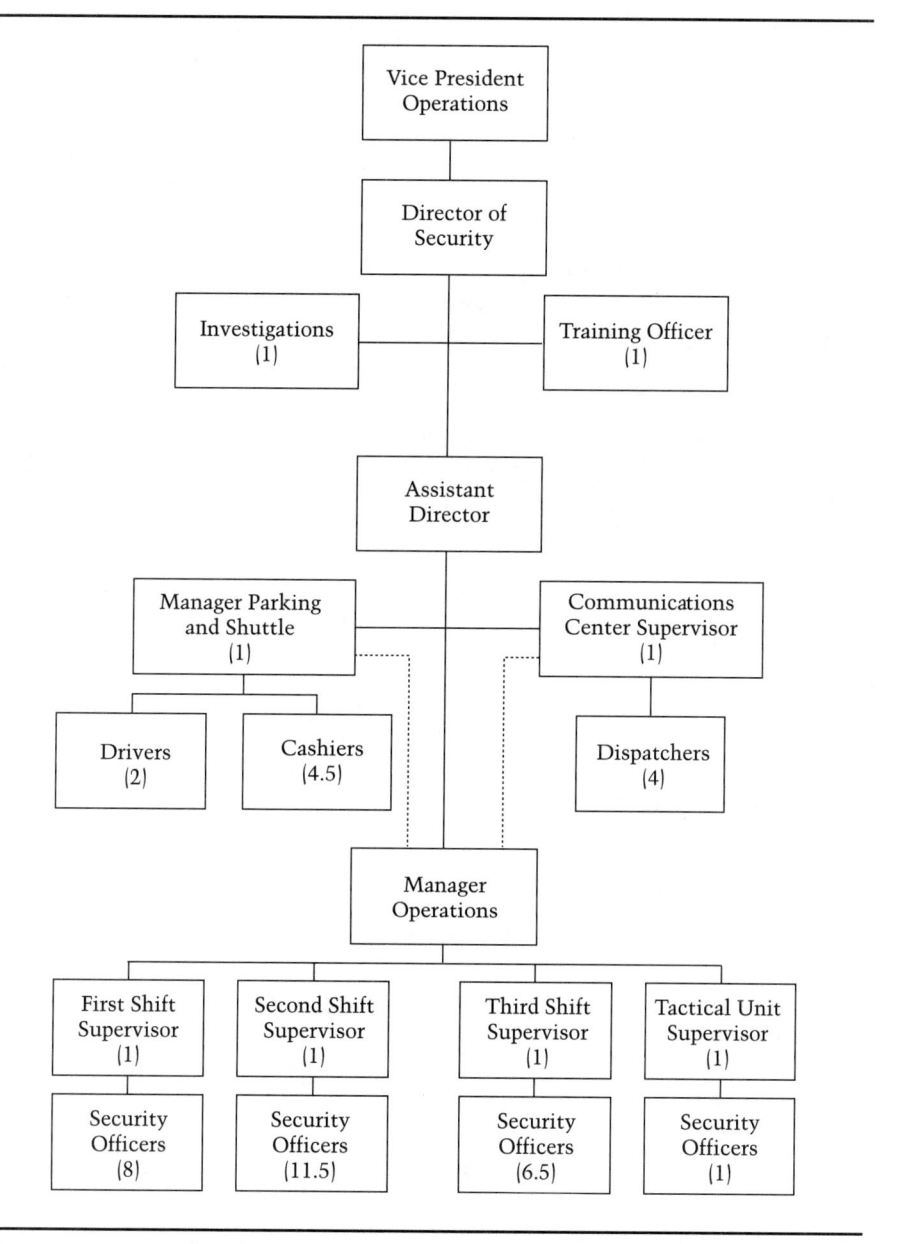

```
                    ┌──────────────────┐
                    │  Vice President  │
                    │    Operations    │
                    └────────┬─────────┘
                             │
                    ┌────────┴─────────┐
                    │   Director of    │
                    │     Security     │
                    └────────┬─────────┘
        ┌────────────────────┼────────────────────┐
┌───────┴────────┐            │           ┌───────┴────────┐
│ Investigations │            │           │ Training Officer│
│      (1)       │            │           │      (1)       │
└────────────────┘            │           └────────────────┘
                              │
                    ┌─────────┴────────┐
                    │    Assistant     │
                    │    Director      │
                    └─────────┬────────┘
      ┌───────────────────────┼───────────────────────┐
┌─────┴──────────┐            │           ┌───────────┴─────────┐
│ Manager Parking│            │           │   Communications    │
│  and Shuttle   │            │           │  Center Supervisor  │
│      (1)       │            │           │         (1)         │
└───┬────────┬───┘            │           └──────────┬──────────┘
    │        │                │                      │
┌───┴───┐ ┌──┴─────┐           │                 ┌────┴─────┐
│Drivers│ │Cashiers│           │                 │Dispatchers│
│  (2)  │ │ (4.5)  │           │                 │   (4)    │
└───────┘ └────────┘            │                 └──────────┘
                      ┌─────────┴────────┐
                      │     Manager      │
                      │    Operations    │
                      └─────────┬────────┘
    ┌──────────────┬────────────┼────────────┬──────────────┐
┌───┴──────┐ ┌─────┴─────┐ ┌────┴─────┐ ┌────┴──────┐
│First Shift│ │Second Shift│ │Third Shift│ │Tactical Unit│
│Supervisor │ │ Supervisor │ │Supervisor │ │ Supervisor │
│   (1)     │ │    (1)     │ │    (1)    │ │    (1)     │
├───────────┤ ├────────────┤ ├───────────┤ ├────────────┤
│ Security  │ │  Security  │ │ Security  │ │  Security  │
│ Officers  │ │  Officers  │ │ Officers  │ │  Officers  │
│    (8)    │ │   (11.5)   │ │   (6.5)   │ │    (1)     │
└───────────┘ └────────────┘ └───────────┘ └────────────┘
```

Figure 6-2 Example of a Large Proprietary Security Department Organization Chart

weekends. Also in this approach, the security staff members of individual facilities are hired by the individual facility supervisor and are generally paid as employees of that facility. The facility supervisor reports to the central (corporate) director and is paid through corporate funding. This creates a contract management concept for the facility. The facility security supervisor in turn works very closely with the facility administrative person responsible for facility security.

In the decentralized approach, each facility maintains complete control of their security effort with no line of authority outside of the specific facility. In this approach, a centralized security support function may exist; however, this function would only be advisory in nature.

The security organization chart shown in Figure 6-3 presents a systems structure that incorporates a centralization of security support services while maintaining a certain management autonomy and program function at the facility level.

TYPES OF SECURITY STAFF

Several options are available to healthcare administrators in selecting the type of security force for their facility. Each of the different models of staffing has its own advantages and disadvantages. The four basic types of security staffing are:

- A proprietary (in-house) staff

- An out-sourced staff (contract agency)

- A proprietary security manager or supervisory staff with outsourced security officers

- Off-duty law enforcement personnel

In addition, there are individual hybrid models utilizing various combinations of staff. An example of such a "combination" approach is the security force at Johns Hopkins Medical Institutions in Baltimore, Maryland. In this program, which utilizes some 335 security officers and

WELLSTAR HEALTH SYSTEM
SECURITY AND COMMUNICATIVE SERVICES

```
                          Stanley Bishop
                             Director
                              1 FTE
    ┌────────────────┬──────────────────┬──────────────────┬──────────────────┐
   Kirk Walsh       Penn Jones         Dan Berkner         Alex Jones
Operations Manager  Security Supervisor Security Supervisor Security Supervisor
    1 FTE            1 FTE              1 FTE              1 FTE
```

Kirk Walsh — Operations Manager (1 FTE)
- Lane VanPelt, Security Telecomm Asst. 1 FTE
- PBX Lead Operators 2 FTEs
- PBX Operators 22 FTEs
- Communication Officer WAB 1 FTE
- Investigative Services

Penn Jones — Security Supervisor (1 FTE)
- Sr. Security Officers 2 FTEs
- Security Officers Cobb Hospital 9.3 FTEs
- Security Officers Douglas Hospital 4.23 FTEs
- Security Officers Paulding Hospital 4.23 FTEs

Dan Berkner — Security Supervisor (1 FTE)
- Sr. Security Officers 2 FTEs
- Security Officers Kennettone Hospital 10.70 FTEs
- Parking Attendants Kennestone Hospital 2.5 FTEs
- Security Officers Atherton Place 4.23 FTEs
- Sr. Communications Officer Communications Ctr. 1 FTE
- Communications Officers Communications Ctr. 3.23 FTEs

Alex Jones — Security Supervisor (1 FTE)
- Security Officers PROMINA Support Center 5.2 FTEs
- Security Officers Windy Hill Hospital 3.3 FTEs

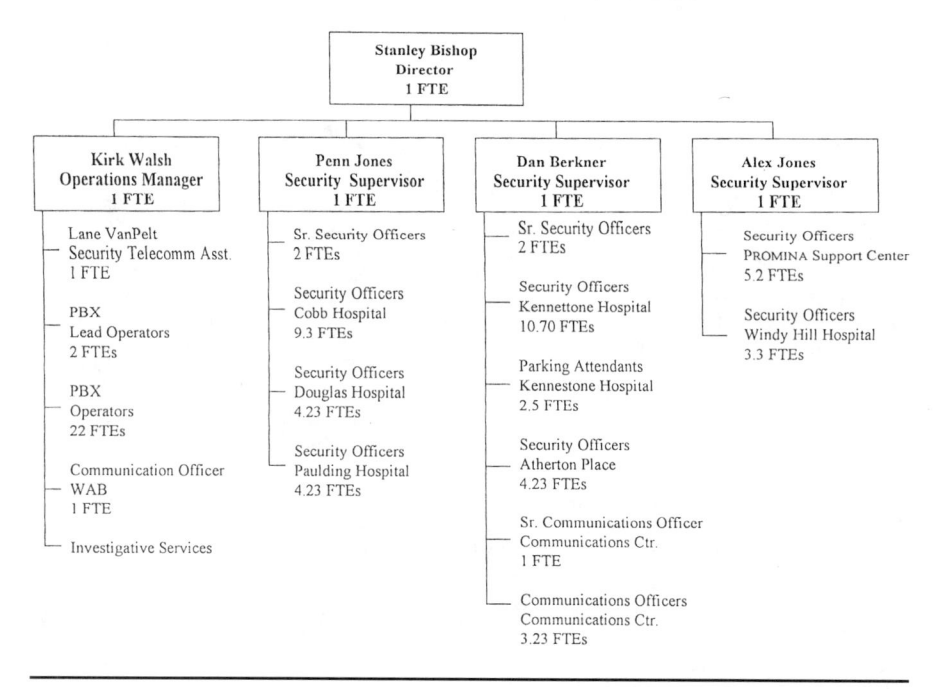

Figure 6-3 Example of a Healthcare System Proprietary Security Department Organization Chart (Courtesy of Wellstar Health System, Marietta, Georgia)

supervisors, there is a combination of proprietary and contracted officers plus off-duty Baltimore city police officers.[2] Figure 6-4 compares the various basic security staffing models.

There is a significant trend toward the use of outsourcing as a model for security staffing of healthcare security programs. Table 6-1 compares the security staffing models over a 10-year period. One reason that the proprietary model dropped so drastically with a corresponding rise in the combination model is that many healthcare organizations froze new hires but would allow vacancy replacements to be contract service employees.

128 Hospital and Healthcare Security

	Security Program Characteristics/Profile	Staffing Model			
		Proprietary	Outsource	Combination Out/Propr.	Off Duty
BUDGET	Cost	Fair/Poor	Very Good	Good	Very Poor
	Cost Control	Good/Fair	Very Good	Good	Poor
	Cost Effectiveness	Good	Very Good	Good	Poor
ORGANIZATION	Clear Chain of Command	Very Good	Good	Fair	Poor
	Organizational Control	Very good	Very Good	Very Good	Fair
	Effective Training	Very good	Good/Fair	Good	Poor
	Effective Supervision	Good	Good	Good/Fair	Very Poor
	Healthcare Expertise	Very Good	Fair	Good	Very Poor
	Effecting Program Change	Good	Good	Good	Poor
	Integration into Organization	Very good	Fair	Good/Fair	Poor
	Loyalty to Organization	Very Good	Fair	Good	Poor
	Lack of Tunover	Good	Fair/Poor	Fair	Fair
PROGRAM	Upward Mobility	Fair	Good	Fair	N/A
	Completing Good Documentation	Very Good	Fair	Good	Poor
	Quality of Investigation Activity	Very Good	Good	Very Good	Fair/Poor
	Crime Prevention Efforts	Very Good	Good/Fair	Good	Fair
	Officer Image	Very Good	Good	Good	Fair/Poor
RATING	Overall Effectiveness	Very Good	Good	Good	Poor

Figure 6-4 Comparing Basic Security Staffing Models

Proprietary Staff

The main advantage of the in-house staffing model is control. The organization can control the recruitment, selection, supervision, and training of security personnel. However, the degree of control will be adversely affected if security personnel belong to a union.

The in-house system is generally the most expensive in terms of labor costs, despite the fact that some of the expenses are absorbed by

Table 6-1 Comparing the Use of Healthcare Security Staffing Models Over a 10-Year Period

Staffing Model	1980	1990	2000
Outsourced/Contract	24%	30%	52%
In House/Proprietary	64%	60%	34%
Combination of Proprietary and Contract Staff	8%	7%	13%
Proprietary Management and Supervision with Contact Staff/Off-Duty Police	3%	2%	1%
Off-Duty Law Enforcement	1%	1%	0*

* Less than one percent.

other departments such as accounting, purchasing, employee health, and human resources. Fringe benefits for an in-house staff generally range between 25 to 35 percent of the base salary.

Some organizations ignore fringe benefits when computing program costs for periodic budget responsibility reports. The cost of fringe benefits can be controlled to some extent in larger forces by simply running a duty shift one or two employees short during holiday, vacation, or sick-leave absences. This cost-saving method is usually not available in other staffing models. However, if the protection system can operate without a given position, the question of overstaffing could certainly be an issue. The true hourly cost for proprietary staff runs 30 to 50 percent higher than for an outsourced staff. This fact is generally denounced by in-house budget staff, who ignore certain cost items in order to achieve lower cost projections.

A main disadvantage of the proprietary system, in addition to its high cost, is the tendency for a program and its security staff to become stagnant. The routine of security services can easily produce apathy among employees. It becomes increasingly difficult to stimulate and motivate officers in direct relation to their age and length of employment. The cliché "You can't see the forest for the trees" becomes a real problem as a security officer becomes one of the "well-settled" staff. This does not imply that all in-house programs deteriorate to an unacceptable level. The implementation of good management techniques can successfully counter this negative trend. As a general rule, however, proprietary security staff programs should not be considered for a staff of less than 20 to 24 full-time employees. An in-house staff of less than this number of employees may also be mandated in the absence of qualified outsourcing services.

Outsourcing (Contract Staff)

In addition to lower cost, organizations contract with an outside agency to be relieved of the burdensome administrative duties of operating an in-house security force. An additional incentive is that costs are fixed, and thus the organization can more accurately budget expenditures. According to *Security Magazine*, the use of contract security officers for all organizations grows by 12 percent annually.[3] About 10 percent of in-house programs in the U.S. convert to contract services each year. However, the net increase of contract services in healthcare security is closer to 2 percent. In addition, there are some cases in which a healthcare organization will convert to a proprietary staff from the contract-supplied model.

Many other advantages of contracting for security services are espoused in articles usually written by members of contract agencies. Many of these arguments could be valid; however, too few contract companies live up to their claims in actual field performance. When one security company bids against another for business, the lowest bid most probably excludes something. Usually, what is missing is quality. Many of the nations large contract agencies have formed special healthcare services units or have hired a healthcare security practitioner to proclaim their expertise in healthcare security. Such proclamations should be examined closely.

The advantages and disadvantages of contract services, and their countering or supporting comments, are as follows:

1. *A contract service usually means lower payroll costs.* Unfortunately, this is almost always achieved by paying contract personnel a low wage and using a substantial number of part-time employees. The contract agency's full-time officers must generally work more than 40 hours per week to earn a sufficient salary. In some cases, the wages are so low that overtime rates for contract security officers are lower than the straight-time wages of proprietary staffs. Excessively long working hours can be detrimental to the security effort, as coverage is not necessarily synonymous with good security. Having too many part-time employees and a high labor turnover

rate can reduce the continuity of effort essential to a high-quality program. These deficiencies can be controlled to a large extent by including in the contract agreement specifications regarding wages and benefits to be paid to the security staff.

2. *A contract service relieves the organization of administrative burdens.* This may be welcome relief for managers who do not want to concern themselves with management, but it can result in losing control of security. Management must be involved with these so-called burdens, together with the contract service, to maintain a good program.

3. *Contract services make available extra security officer coverage.* Employing extra officers on short notice or for a short duration of time may, however, require premium hourly payments. At best, additional security personnel who have never seen the facility may be of doubtful value. Further, when one client needs additional security officers due to a flood, civil disturbance, strike, etc., other clients may also need additional security coverage. All contract agencies have limits to the number of additional personnel they have available.

4. *Healthcare security personnel should be well versed in the specialized area of healthcare security.* The contract agency must obtain their business from many different types of organizations and settings. Thus, it becomes virtually impossible to serve solely hospitals, airports, hotels, department stores, etc. There simply must be movement of security personnel among the various types of accounts due to a variety of reasons, including promotions, disciplinary problems, personality conflicts, officers' geographical residence in relation to work site, and others.

5. *With contract officers, discipline can be handled by advising the contract agency that a particular officer is no longer acceptable for duty.* Contract agencies generally shift the officer to another client, who thus ends up with the first client's reject. And, of course, this system works in two ways. An exceptionally good officer can be reassigned by the contractor to another facility without notice. This mobility can create such a continuous shift of personnel that continuity of service is jeopardized.

6. *Fraternization is a problem in all security forces.* Contract security officers are less apt to develop friendships that result in their overlooking

problems that they should correct or report. They are often considered outsiders (this can be good or bad), and with their high turnover rate, they have little time to develop close ties. Consequently, contract security officers can be more objective in discharging their duties. On the other hand, they do not possess the same loyalty as regular employees and are not always as dependent on doing their best to ensure continued employment.

In competing for a contract security service, the lowest bidder usually provides only a warm body to fill a position. The lowest bidder is also probably the most expensive in terms of cost/benefit relationships. The cost of a security service should not be considered only in terms of labor cost, but in terms of the total annual expenses and what protection services are provided. In many cases, labor coverage can be reduced by using better-quality personnel, and annual costs can be maintained or even lowered despite a higher labor unit cost. A competent security consultant can be useful in analyzing vulnerabilities and objectively recommending the proper coverage.

A major deficiency in the contract security system can be traced to the client, not the contractor. This deficiency is a lack of involvement in the day-to-day protection needs of their facility. Management cannot eliminate its role in the security of the facility by simply delegating the responsibility of protection to a third party. A third party, no matter how competent, cannot by itself provide the protection required. The organization that expects the contractor to take care of all of its security is not properly managed. This practice, which can be viewed as the scapegoat syndrome, is characterized by organizational management that willfully or through ignorance is not concerned with security. If a large crime, fire, or disaster occurs, management can simply point the finger at the third party as the one who failed to perform the job properly. Incompetent management can thus "correct the situation" by replacing the contractor. Obviously, the real problem is only perpetuated.

Proprietary Management/Contract Security Officers

A staffing system of in-house supervision and contract security officers is used in a limited number of facilities. The basic premise of this approach is a partial answer to the control and supervision problems that can occur when all contract security personnel are utilized. Proponents of this combination system suggest that the in-house supervisor can develop a more in-depth program and make better use of security personnel. The in-house supervisor, an employee of the organization being served, presumably has direct lines of communication within the organizational structure. A very serious pitfall of this system results from an employee of one organization acting in a supervisory capacity over the employee of another organization. In-house supervisors tend to be overly critical of the quality of the contract personnel furnished, and they are less motivated to work with the security officer in dealing with deficiencies than if the supervisors had made the hiring decision themselves. The in-house manager tends to become less realistic in terms of personnel issues and loses some practicality in day-to-day operations.

Off-Duty Law Enforcement Personnel

The employment of off-duty police personnel is almost a thing of the past in most U.S. healthcare facilities. This system for securing a facility is the least desirable of all staffing systems. High costs, virtually no organized system, little or no security training, and lack of continuity are all basic reasons supporting this conclusion. Moreover, moonlighters of all types can be accused of just putting in their time because a second job provides supplementary income rather than the primary means of support.

Police authority often has appeal to organizations that are not well versed in their protection needs. The power to arrest is often cited as a primary advantage of the law enforcement officer. Most professional security administrators, however, view this authority as a disadvantage. Further, progressive police administrators prefer that their officers not work in part-time jobs requiring them to wear the police uniform. The potential for misconduct, which brings adverse publicity to the police agency and the possibility of litigation naming the police jurisdiction, should be avoided.

One recent case of police moonlighting gone bad occurred in Denver, Colorado, when two police officers were involved in a shooting incident that resulted in a death. The case was brought to civil court, and the city was accused of unreasonable force, depriving the victim of his constitutional rights against such force. Although no criminal charges were filed against the officers involved, the jury awarded the plaintiff $500,000.[4]

Another disadvantage of using law enforcement officers is availability. A facility may have no coverage at a time of critical need because of overtime required on the officer's regular police assignments (strikes, fires, civil disturbance, training, etc.), court time, and federal assistance programs that fund police operations through the payment of overtime work.

Commissioned Police Officers

There are a few limited programs, such as the Baylor Health Care System, which operate a security program as a full police agency. These programs are often referred to as Departments of Public Safety.

Another unique approach to providing security services via police officers is a law enforcement agency that has a security division. The security division is a contract agency available to private organizations. In this approach, the organization contracts for police officers, who are assigned to provide security/police services. The police officers thus perform their primary duties at the organization, as opposed to the off-duty approach. This type of program, however, is highly suspect in terms of value for the healthcare industry.

Shared Services Approach

During the last 10 years, the true shared service approach to providing security services has been supplanted somewhat by healthcare organization mergers, affiliations, and the growth of proprietary hospital organizations. These new "systems" simply combine facilities through an organizational structure as opposed to a shared service membership of separate, individually governed facilities. The advantages and disadvantages of the shared approach to security must now be applied to a systems approach.

The shared services security approach still exists and is operating successfully in a number of programs. The major roadblock to shared systems involving separate organizations continues to be politics, turf, and self interests. In addition, federal government requirements, through special interest group legislation and IRS rulings, have negatively impacted the efficient operation of a shared service approach.

There is another quasi-shared service approach operating to a limited degree. This approach is purchased services, or sold services, in which one healthcare organization markets a program to one or more other healthcare organizations. The organizational structure for this type of plan is relatively uncomplicated. An organization that has effective management and a specialized talent in security can generate additional revenue to offset costs while providing a quality, cost-effective service to other independent organizations. The marketing entity must maintain acceptable services within a price structure, and the consumer organization must accept some funding responsibility when extensive capital investments are required. In the case of capital investments, a long-term contract may be required to protect the provider organization. This approach is generally limited to and fostered when organizations are in a close proximity to each other.

Corporate (Systems) Approach

The systems approach, like the shared service approach, is an organizational structure as opposed to a staffing model. Security services provided to facilities through the systems approach can produce a high level of service within an extremely cost-effective framework. Protection service lends itself particularly to a system's concept because one of the major problems in healthcare security is one referred to as "islandism." Islandism simply means standing alone, attempting to protect oneself without the benefit of knowing what is happening in the other local or systems healthcare facilities.

Security problems that occur in one facility will very likely be transferred to other facilities in that geographical area. When thieves find out how easy it is to steal computer equipment in one medical care facility, they are quick to "case" other such facilities. Forged prescriptions, short-change operators, and "professional patients" provide other examples of problems that tend to travel the healthcare circuit. Healthcare workers who are terminated due to involvement in security-type problems invariably turn up in other healthcare facilities. Where else does a registered nurse find employment? Even housekeeping employees, food service workers, and maintenance people tend to seek employment in other healthcare facilities once they have been employed in the healthcare field.

In a health system centralized approach, cost containment is achieved through several factors. One is supervision. The combined effort can reduce the total number of supervisors from that required by individual programs. Another area of cost containment is the purchasing of supplies and equipment—otherwise known as economy of scale. Supplies such as forms and uniforms are less expensive when purchased in large quantities.

Although important, cost reduction is not the primary reason for a centralized systems approach to the security effort. The primary reason is to improve services. Improvement can occur in many areas, most notably in supervision, the training and quality of personnel, the investigative effort, and the efficient deployment of personnel, especially when the facilities are located within close proximity of each other.

Most facilities, except the very largest, may find it difficult to justify the high cost of hiring and retaining a top-quality security director. On the other hand, several facilities within a system can easily afford a competent security administrator and in turn receive a quality protection program.

The lack of direct supervision for line personnel is a deficiency of many hospital security programs. Generally, only the largest programs can efficiently and effectively provide 24-hour supervision. In many facilities there is only one security officer on duty, and it is not practical to provide one supervisor for one other officer. Some programs attempt to resolve this deficiency with a lead officer or senior officer when two are on duty at a time; however, this arrangement seldom provides quality supervision.

The systems supervisor concept is practical, efficient, and simple. When each facility is funding only a fraction of a wage, it is possible to pay a higher wage, thus attracting and retaining a better-qualified supervisor. The number of personnel and the size of the geographical area that a supervisor can effectively cover are determined by individual philosophy, workload, level of officer training, and other factors.

Virtually every review of security operations, in healthcare and other settings, cites a deficiency in officer training. There are probably few programs in which the training level is at an optimum; however, the systems approach provides a good opportunity to improve this effort. The large group of personnel, the different facility environments available, and the sharing of cost enable a systems program to improve officer training.

It is much more efficient to present a formal class to eight or more people than to pay one instructor for just a few officers. The large personnel base allows the placement of officers in different assignments depending on their aptitude and skill level, giving the training effort an added dimension for the trainee and the operations supervisor.

Training takes on many different forms. One important form provided by the systems approach is the rotation of assignments. An important aspect of training is to prevent officers from getting stuck in a routine. Rotating officers to other facilities within the system provides a unique training experience and fulfills the objective of having a pool of officers who have been trained in multiple facilities.

It could be argued that this advantage also exists for the contract agency, but there are some important differences. First, the contract agency must provide a more general security training since the officers may be working on airline, retail, factory, or other assignments. Furthermore, it is extremely difficult for the contract agency to assemble officers for training due to their coverage commitments.

A systems security program generally attracts a higher quality applicant than either contract agencies or single facility in-house programs. The main attraction for candidates is the career ladder that larger organizations can offer to individuals who strive to move up to supervisory positions. The training and challenge provided through experience in multiple facilities also contribute to attracting and retaining quality personnel.

Perhaps one of the most important and cost-effective benefits of the systems arrangement is in investigation. Just as police problems move from city to city, security problems move from facility to facility. The consolidation of records and reports enables system participants to resolve incidents and problems that they would be unable to solve individually. In addition, systems organizations have an opportunity to preclude problem staff members from moving from one facility to another in the system. This is preventive action of the highest level, and preventive action is the primary objective of any protection program.

Another benefit of the centralized investigative effort is the opportunity to foster better police/security relations by providing law enforcement agencies more direct access to organizational information. Law enforcement can develop a rapport with just one individual or unit rather than have to seek out the responsible security person in each facility. Likewise, if a law enforcement agency has information that would be helpful to all facilities in a given area, it is more likely to pass on this information to one contact than to contact many different facilities.

The central reporting of incidents leads to another advantage: the exchange of information. Matters of common interest can be compiled and distributed efficiently. The amount of time and money spent by each facility in sending a representative to security and safety meetings can be drastically reduced because a security person from the system can attend, thus representing all facilities. Information, ideas, and techniques can be shared with the system.

The systems approach also allows certain facility policies and procedures to be standardized. Standardized procedures such as package inspection, accident reporting, fire codes, incident reporting, and the like greatly benefit organizations as employees move from facility to facility.

The systems approach presents the opportunity to use more efficient security officer deployment patterns. Each facility has different and varied security requirements. The physical layout, the types of patients, the facility's philosophy, and other factors create unique assignments. Likewise, each security officer is an individual and fulfills his or her responsibilities uniquely. Regardless of the applicant selection process, it is difficult to predict job performance until the officer is actually working. Given the larger base of operations, officers can more often be placed in a position that closely fits their job expectations as well as the expectations of the organization. System officers can move to another facility within the system without the organization losing the cost of their training. Pre-service training will be required in the new facility; however, the required amount of training will be reduced to cover only specific facility requirements, as the officer is already trained in the systems general security program. Pre-service training is further reduced in relation to the extent that the system has been able to standardize forms, procedures, and policies.

The use of an officer who "floats" between two or three facilities is another important advantage of the systems approach. Many cases require an additional security officer on a temporary basis, but not enough to justify a full-time officer. In these cases, an officer can split his or her time among several facilities and thus be available for back-up and specific assignments for each.

In short, the systems approach allows security administrators and planners many opportunities to use dollars, labor, and equipment in new and innovative patterns not possible in individual facility programs.

HOW LARGE A STAFF IS NEEDED?

When a CEO or COO asks how much security is needed, it generally means, "What is the least amount of security needed to get by?" The number and types of security personnel required for an efficient security program is a fundamental question for every facility. It is indeed an individual facility question because the numerous factors that must be considered vary in scope from organization to organization. To arrive at the required number of security personnel, it is necessary first to analyze the security mission, to determine the organization's security vulnerabilities, and to identify the services to be rendered. The next step is to design a program that will address the mission, properly manage these vulnerabilities, and implement the intended services. Only then can the number of staff required to operate the program be determined.

Staffing is generally viewed from the two categories of staff positions (support) and line positions (field operations). The staff positions are those of training administrator, investigator, crime prevention manager, and documentation/communications supervisor. The line positions for field operations are fixed-post and patrol/response positions. Security systems monitors and/or dispatchers can be considered either support or field operations personnel.

Various approaches, or models, attempt to quantify the required staffing of a security program. The following five-factor approach will help an organization establish the size of its fixed-post and security patrol/response personnel. The number of security officers required will also vary according to the other security safeguards in place (alarms/closed-circuit television/access control) and the degree of security protection these safeguards provide as components of the overall protection system.

Factor I: Response Time
Establish the desired response time for requested services for:

- Emergency situations (assault, fire, disturbance, injury). This response time should normally be three to five minutes.

- Non-emergency situations (escorts, motorist assistance, patient assistance, deliveries, missing property). This response time should normally be within a five to eight minute window of time.

Factor II: Frequency of Patrol

Establish the desired frequency of patrol for specific areas. (Note: this frequency will vary by time of day). To facilitate planning, the following six general areas of a campus serve as a basis for analysis:

- Parking areas

- Inpatient bed areas

- Facility public areas

- Ancillary patient care areas (lab, x-ray, physical therapy)

- Support areas (food services, medical records, maintenance, and engineering)

- External grounds and outbuildings

The frequency of patrol should be the frequency required for routine day-to-day patrols and does not allow for an increase in patrols of a given area as a tactical response to a new or increased security vulnerability. Determine the length of time required for these patrols for each day of the week.

Factor III: Fixed-Post Assignments

Determine the need (philosophy and priority) of security fixed-post assignments and the number of labor hours required to fill these posts. Fixed-post assignments will reduce to some degree the number of hours required for patrol and response.

Factor IV: Scheduled Routine Functions

List all scheduled routine functions (excluding patrol and response) performed by security, categorizing them by the hour and the day. Determine the time required to accomplish this activity. Examples include scheduled cash escorts, locking and unlocking doors, picking up parking receipts, bank runs, routine deliveries, flag duties, and equipment checks.

Factor V: Nonscheduled Activities
List all activities that are not scheduled, but that are routinely performed by security personnel and determine the estimated time required to perform the activities. It may be easier to calculate the time required on each of three work shifts as opposed to the number of hours needed for scheduled activities. Examples of nonscheduled activities are preliminary investigation or problem resolution by first-response field officers, handling lost and found, unscheduled locking or unlocking of doors, assisting with patients on an emergency basis, accepting of emergency shipments, assisting in releasing valuables, acting as a witness, and preparing reports. It is not uncommon for this type of activity to take up to 50 percent or more of an officer's time.

By adding the time requirements for factors I through V, the number of hours required to accomplish field operations can be calculated. Although the personnel requirements are viewed on an hourly and daily basis, it is suggested that the required labor be projected to a weekly total in hours. The weekly total provides for easy conversion to a full-time equivalent (FTE) employee basis. It is not uncommon that labor needs vary with each different weekday. However, such needs generally remain fixed from week to week except for special assignments due to temporary planned or unplanned events. These types of situations may be handled by the redeployment of regularly scheduled personnel or may require scheduling of additional officers.

Healthcare organizations commonly make the mistake of hiring additional security officers and then determining what activities they will perform. In fact, some security planners answer every security problem by hiring additional personnel. More people are not always the answer, and in fact, numerous security programs have been upgraded by reducing personnel through improved management and the application of new preventive security concepts.

Unfortunately, sound planning and valid program justification often yield to emotion and easy solutions. More security personnel have been added to existing programs due to traumatic incidents than to sound planning.

Several basic guidelines can assist the security administrator in determining the allocation of security officers. A community facility located in a relatively low-crime area should provide, as a minimum, security officer patrol and called-for response capability on a 24-hour basis if the facility has 75 or more inpatient beds, regardless of its location or perceived vulnerabilities.

Twenty-four-hour coverage is also required in facilities with less than 75 inpatient beds when there are special vulnerabilities; for example, an extremely busy emergency room, a high outpatient treatment load, a large campus (property), and a location in or near a high crime area. For example, a children's hospital would require a higher number of security personnel per bed than a general acute care hospital would.

INCREMENTAL FACILITY SECURITY STAFFING

The very small facility may not employ any specifically designated security personnel. In these cases, required security activity is performed by maintenance, environmental services, or other facility personnel.

Seldom does an organization suddenly decide to employ security personnel around the clock if it has never had an organized security system. As the facility grows, or faces increasing security issues, it will face the need for security personnel. The first step in a security officer deployment plan generally involves coverage during the night hours. A coverage plan of 6:00 P.M. to 6:00 A.M. is a good first step. In organizations that are not required to pay overtime after eight hours, it is a consideration for officers to work the entire 12-hour shift. This deployment plan allows for two officers to each work three-and-a-half days each week, splitting the middle day, working 42 hours each week. The advantage of this deployment is that two officers cover the entire week, providing good continuity and consistency of program application. Some may argue that 12 hours is too long for one individual; however, it depends on the individual. In the case of an in-house program, at least one on-call or part-time officer would be required to cover scheduled or unscheduled time off of regular officers.

For the facility that currently provides night coverage, the next step in increasing personnel should be during the weekend. Although weekend days may on the surface seem peaceful enough, this is the time that general facility supervision is minimal, neighborhood street activity increases, and facilities are especially vulnerable to internal and external theft.

All too often facilities attain night and weekend coverage and then have a tendency to stagnate. Twenty-four-hour coverage increases the security posture of the organization two- or threefold. Instead of being forced to report property losses to security only during certain hours, for example, the organization can call on security officers at any time. When facilities assign another department or administrative person to pick up the security responsibility when security officers are not on duty, the system often does not function in a satisfactory manner.

When a program advances to providing one officer on duty around the clock, it begins to take shape and become much more productive. Security officer deployment during the day is geared to different activity than at night and on weekends. The day officer is usually the facility security supervisor. This officer takes part in committee meetings, works with various departments on planning and administration, and responds to called-for service. The day officer is the glue that solidifies all shifts of security into a unified program.

Facilities that provide 24-hour security officer coverage should consider one additional step: to provide 26-hour coverage. Under this plan, there should be a two-hour overlap of coverage during the primary night shift change period. One officer could remain on interior patrol while the second officer provides external coverage. It is recommended, however, that both officers be deployed externally. It is suggested that the arriving night employees need security preventive services more than the departing employees because the arriving employees are not grouped as well. In addition, employees leaving at off hours must be provided with an escort service. Healthcare organizations now use many different staffing shifts, and traditional shift change-times are becoming less distinct. This may negate the validity of the 26-hour deployment plan for some organizations.

To staff an in-house program with 24-hour coverage for one position seven days a week requires approximately five full-time equivalent employees. This number varies to some extent depending on the facility vacation, holiday, and sick time benefit. In the outsourced staffing model, the required number of FTEs would be approximately four and one half due to a lesser employee benefit package.

Staffing problems occur when the schedule goes awry due to sickness, accident, no show, or termination. Untrained managers or supervisors often overlook this costly area of program administration during planning processes. Although this problem is rather straightforward, it is often not fully considered when an organization analyzes the financial implications of maintaining its own security force or contracting with an outside agency.

REFERENCES

1. "Visions of Leadership," *Security Management*, June, 1998, p. 30.

2. "An Interview with: Joseph R. Coppola on Johns Hopkins Security Four Years Later," *Hospital Security and Safety Management*, August, 1998, p. 11–14.

3. *Security Magazine*, December, 1989, p. 42.

4. "Truax Parents to Get $500,000," *Rocky Mountain News*, November 18, 1998, p. 4A.

CHAPTER 7

Security Force Administration

The vast majority of security management plans require the use of security officers as a major component of the protection system. The development and preparation of the organization security force administrative plan is the basis for utilization of security manpower. The various elements or components of the plan must be addressed regardless of an in-house employment model or the use of out-sourced personnel. A major task is selecting the best applicants to fill the security department's staffing plan and to implement sound personnel management practices to achieve superior officer service. The three major components of the security force are thus **management, supervision** and **security officers**.

MANAGEMENT

The vice president, director, manager, or coordinator of the security program is the single most important person in terms of determining program outcomes. This statement does not infer that the person charged with the responsibility to manage the program can do the job alone. There must be upper administrative support as well as productive efforts of department line and staff personnel. The person charged with the responsibility of protecting life and property will, however, be the platform of program definition and implementation characteristics.

In the past, healthcare organizations have been rather vague in terms of defining the expectations and objectives of the security program. This organizational deficiency has in turn led to the hiring of inappropriate persons to lead this very important function of the healthcare delivery system. A person who simply has a law enforcement background, is an ex-fireman, has done government service (regardless of specialty), or is the number two person in the security department may not have the skills to properly manage a healthcare security program.

Organizations today are seeking individuals who are academically-prepared and who have relevant experience to direct their security programs. Relevant experience will, of course, vary depending on the organization's product or service. However, academically-prepared individuals will bring to the table business-related education. Many people believe that it is easier to learn the principles of security than it is to learn how to manage. Indeed, even the most experienced security administrators must continually seek further training, education, and self-development. There are at least six distinct activities that top-level security administrators must participate in as a professional:

1. **Review of the literature.** Healthcare security administrators must seek out pertinent healthcare security publications and video materials as they become available. Although it is impossible to subscribe to every periodical or newsletter, buy every book, or attain all the information available, security administrators should do their best to keep up to date on current literature. While most administrators maintain a personal library, healthcare and public libraries also are sources for this information.

2. **Networking with peers.** No one needs to reinvent the wheel. Chances are that someone has the information you need or has been in similar situations as you are. Interactions with peers are also beneficial in discovering possible problems or circumstances that can lead to proactive programming. One healthcare security administrator makes prearranged visits to healthcare organizations when he is in another city on business—or even on pleasure—in order to meet another peer and see another security operation firsthand.

3. **Credentialing programs.** There are two primary credentialing programs for the professional security administrator. The first, and specific to healthcare security, is the Certified Healthcare Protection Administrator (CHPA). The second is the Certified Protection Professional (CPP). These certification programs both require an extensive examination and a periodic re-certification process.

The CHPA program is offered by the International Healthcare Security and Safety Foundation (IHSSF). This foundation, which is closely affiliated with the International Association for Healthcare Security and

Safety (IAHSS), has been offering a management credentialing program since 1985. In this system, three levels of credentialing exist: Nominee, Graduate, and Fellowship. The Nominee status is conferred upon meeting established criteria submitted in an application to the foundation. Persons granted the Nominee status must take a graduate level examination within three years. The closed book examination, administered by the foundation, is based on a study guide and select reference material. Upon successful completion of the examination, the person becomes a Certified Healthcare Protection Administrator (CHPA). Each CHPA is required to re-certify every three years by submitting documentation of continuing self-development and education.

Once an individual has achieved the status of CHPA, he or she may become a fellow of the foundation, and is designated as a CHPA-F. In order to become a fellow, the candidate must have completed a research project, resulting in a publication approved by the IHSSF board of directors.

Although not a credentialing program, the American Society for Healthcare Engineering (ASHE) periodically conducts a three-day security and safety educational program. The program, "Fundamentals of Safety and Security Management," has five modules: Introduction to Healthcare Safety Management; Security Management; Environmental Management; Occupational Health and Safety; and Emergency Preparedness.

4. **Seminars and educational programs.** The opportunity to attend healthcare-specific security and safety programs is limited only by time and funds. These programs are offered by the International Association for Healthcare Security and Safety (IAHSS), American Society for Industrial Security (ASIS), the Joint Commission on Accreditation of Healthcare Organizations (JCAHO), state and local healthcare organizations, ASHE, and a whole host of other trade associations and educational organizations. Healthcare security professionals should have little trouble finding such programs in their general geographical area. A minimum of one such seminar should be attended on an annual basis, and such attendance can generally be utilized as a credit in the re-certification for CHPA and/or CPP.

5. **Contributing to the body of knowledge.** An essential element of self-development and keeping current is that of completing pertinent research.

Research in our context simply means the searching out of information in the study of a specific aspect of security for either general information or data analysis to indicate a course of action. This research may be of benefit to others in the field, and the true professional will seek opportunities to share this information with peers and students.

6. **Active membership participation.** Active membership is important to both the individual and the emerging field of healthcare security. Membership in a professional security organization can be the platform or catalyst for reviewing literature, networking with peers, and contributing to the body of knowledge through information sharing.

A common error in filling the top administrative position in a healthcare security program is falling prey to convenience. The convenience factor often comes into play when the department mission is not considered to be all that important, when there is an obsession with cost cutting, or when there is a sudden and unexpected vacancy at the top. A vacancy at the top, planned or unplanned, should be viewed as an opportunity rather than a crisis. It can be an opportunity to assess the direction and success of the program, and a time to examine the structure of the department, review position descriptions, evaluate the vacancy compensation package, and to reflect on program strengths and weaknesses.

There are at least two good ways to avoid the convenience factor of filling the "top job" too quickly. One is to appoint an acting administrative head while the review process stated above is being accomplished. The acting administrator would of course be invited to submit their application, or their intent to be a candidate for the permanent position. A second course of action may be the utilization of "interim management." An interim manager from outside the organization can bring fresh insight to the program and maintain stability for day-to-day operations.

There are several advantages to be gained by interim management. For one, the organization can obtain, on a short-term basis, the services of an individual who has the talent and skills not economically available to the organization on a permanent basis. This management arrangement can be utilized to perform a program evaluation while the process of recruitment is occurring. The interim manager can also assist in identifying candidates and be part of the selection process. The cost for such a manager may appear high; however, a short-term cost may be a very good investment in terms of program quality and long-term cost savings. This model of program transition typically lasts for a period of 45 to 90 days, terminating in a smooth leadership transition.

SUPERVISION

The security supervisor is the person in the middle. He or she represents the security administration to the security officers, and represents the security officers to the administration. The job of a first-line security supervisor has become increasingly complex. With the move away from the authority-obedience style of supervision, the application of many varied leadership factors must be applied. Unfortunately, healthcare protection systems are filled with people who have been hired as supervisors, but who lack the leadership skills to effectively fulfill their responsibilities.

To be a successful supervisor, one must acknowledge and put into practice basic leadership qualities. Leaders are expected to:

- Set a good example; they must motivate subordinates by showing them what is expected of them

- Not insist on agreement with everything they do or say

- Make allowances for inexperience and unintentional mistakes

- Be considerate of the personal needs of officers, but understand that the needs of the organization must receive the highest priority

- Give ground on small items, but never compromise on principles

- See those they supervise and be seen by them

- Have the courage to make objective decisions even when they know the decisions are not popular

In short, they must accept ownership of their responsibility as a supervisor. Successful leadership is characterized by involvement, participation, and commitment. Thus, supervisory responsibility is not for everyone.

Much has been written about what makes a good supervisor. The quality of leadership is the one factor that stands out. Basic leadership traits are intertwined with the practices of effective leadership. Basic operational signs reveal how well a supervisor has developed the traits and practiced the principles. These signs are evident in the proficiency of the operation, the state of morale, and the discipline of personnel.

Successful supervisors will analyze their strengths and weaknesses and work to strengthen the positive and overcome the negative. They resist the desire to be popular—a tendency that an officer promoted from the ranks must overcome. Supervisors can become well liked and get results by developing trust, confidence, and respect in those they supervise.

According to Bonnie Michelman, Director of Police and Security, Massachusetts General Hospital, "A supervisor must have a commitment to support the organization in all his actions and deeds. When the supervisor cannot do this, it is time to separate from the organization. This does not mean the supervisor will always agree with the directives and policies of the organization. And it does not mean that these directives and policies are always right. Working for positive change is always a goal and responsibility of the supervisor. These efforts must be directed in a positive manner within the structure of the organization and not through 'undermining,' regardless of how noble and right the goal."[1]

Selecting Supervisors

Filling a supervisory position requires a decision of the highest magnitude. No matter how well-planned a security program may be, its implementation is accomplished by people. How well these people are supervised is a key to the effectiveness of the program.

There are two basic sources of supervisors: they may be recruited from outside the organization or promoted from within. Each source has certain advantages. The advantage of one is generally the disadvantage of the other.

Supervisors selected from outside the organization can assume their role with a high degree of objectivity. They have no friendships or animosities that must be negated, and they can bring valuable new ideas and techniques to the security operation. Moreover, they can be selected on the basis of demonstrated ability. They must, however, accept the fact that they must learn new organizational goals and objectives.

On the other hand, most organizations prefer to promote from within to create a career ladder. Promotion from within provides motivation and incentive for security officers in working toward a personal goal. They must be able to perceive that hard work and knowledge can result in promotion. The dead-end job has little appeal for the types of people who should be filling the ranks of healthcare security officers. Further, there is a direct relationship between turnover and the avenues of job satisfaction and job promotion.

A problem often encountered is that few entry-level security personnel are qualified to be supervisors. It is a mistake to assume that a good security officer will be a good supervisor, because the tasks and functions of an officer and a supervisor simply do not correlate to any great degree. For this reason, a strong training program is essential to develop potential supervisors. Only a small percentage of healthcare protection programs are meeting this development need.

It is imperative that security administrators structure job promotion within a framework of objectivity. Position requirements and the method of selection must be established to ensure that personalities and prejudices are minimized to the fullest extent possible. The promotional structure should be fully understood by the rank and file to eliminate any possible misunderstandings and to allow officers to prepare themselves to participate in the selection process.

All officers possessing the prerequisites for promotion should be given the opportunity to take a written examination as the first step in the evaluation process. This examination should be designed to determine the applicant's job knowledge and general understanding of leadership principles.

After the written examination, a common selection element is the oral interview. The candidates for this stage may be all those who took the written examination, or in cases in which there are a large number of candidates, a certain qualifying score may be required for continuing participation in the selection program. The interview may be conducted by a panel or the interviewers may meet with the candidates on a one-to-one basis. If time and resources permit, the latter is preferred. The number of people to be included on the oral board is a matter of individual preference; however, the board must be limited to avoid overwhelming the candidate. No more than three people should interview a candidate at one time.

Regardless of the system used, the interviewer should evaluate the candidates according to the traits required of the position. Before the interview, the interviewer should review a copy of the job description and the pertinent candidate background information.

Who should serve on the oral panel? In the healthcare setting, numerous resources are available. A mix of persons from different disciplines provides a comprehensive evaluation process. The composition of the interview group will vary from time to time, but it often includes someone from the human resources department, a clinical supervisor or manager, and a security supervisor or officer. In most cases, the security administrator renders the final decision regarding the candidate.

Field Supervision

The need to maintain desirable levels of staff performance is not unique to healthcare security organizations. The very nature of healthcare protection, however, does present some unique factors that shape supervisory activities. The quasi-military structure of security operations generally dictates a high degree of direct personal observation and interaction.

One of the major problems in supervising the work of field security personnel is the lack of clear and concise criteria for measuring the performance of everyday activities. In addition, factors such as time (24-hours per day) and area (large complexes) generally require a high proportion of supervisors to the number of line security personnel.

Supervision essentially consists of three broad tasks: organization, delegation of responsibility and authority, and evaluation. Supervision is the process by which problems and vulnerabilities are identified, solutions planned, and programs implemented. Only in the smallest of security organizations can all this be accomplished by one person.

The patrol or field supervisory officer bridges the gap between the administrative officers, who develop and implement plans, and the field officers, who must carry them out. The supervisory officer must interpret the plan and instruct and assist the field officer in its execution, while evaluating the plan's effectiveness to provide administrative feedback.

The delegation of responsibility illustrates confidence in subordinates and creates a feeling that the organization, through the supervisor, has faith in their abilities. First, the subordinate must be properly trained and capable of carrying out the delegated task. Second, the supervisor must be able to detect mistakes that may occur as the subordinate performs the responsibility. Third, a system of controls must be available to prevent action that would seriously jeopardize the protection system if the subordinate is unable to carry out the task.

Inspection, one of the basic techniques of field supervision, determines the effectiveness of the security officers or the work being performed. Two different types of inspection, the line inspection and the staff inspection, interrelate and support each other.

Line Inspection

Line inspection is generally conducted by a supervisor who has control over the security operation. It is generally oriented toward people and things (vehicles, equipment, and conditions) rather than functions. This type of inspection concentrates on the field officer's appearance, attitude, and deployment, and it includes on-the-scene observation of the officer's incident handling. Many of the deficiencies encountered benefit by immediate, on-the-spot correction. Figure 7-1 shows a sample line inspection report.

Several techniques of the line inspection do not involve direct observation or contact with subordinates. One of these techniques is the random interviewing of people in contact with or served by the officer. These people—who may be complainants, victims, witnesses, administrators, or nursing supervisors—can be a source of information relative to the security officer's attitude and how he or she handled a specific situation.

Another means of inspection is the officer's written report. The completeness and timeliness of reports is more important for evaluating the officer's work than how well organized or well written they are.

Another useful technique is to conduct a review of an area that has been patrolled by an officer. An officer, of course, cannot be expected to observe everything, but much can be learned by supervisors who perform this type of inspection. Supervisors should be completely knowledgeable of all areas under their responsibility. A field inspection to deter-

SECURITY SUPRVISOR
FIELD INSPECTION REPORT

Date: Shift:

Post: Time: Officer:

    Officer Appearance:

    Post Conditions:

    Specific Element Inspected:
    Staff Contacted/Remarks:
    Corrective Actions/Remarks:

Date: Shift:

Post: Time: Officer:

    Officer Appearance:

    Post Conditions:

    Specific Element Inspected:
    Staff Contacted/Remarks:
    Corrective Actions/Remarks:

Date: Shift:

Post: Time: Officer:

    Officer Appearance:

    Post Conditions:

    Specific Element Inspected:
    Staff Contacted/Remarks:
    Corrective Actions/Remarks:

End of Shift Summary:
All posts covered: yes___ no___ explain:_____

Calls for Service (#): _____ Incident Response (#): _____

Total officer(s) shift time expended on: routine post activity ____(hrs) incident response ___(hrs) support services ___(hrs)

                 Use reverse side for additional post inspections.

Figure 7-1 Field Supervision Inspection Report

mine whether there are hazards or conditions that have not been corrected or reported by the patrol officer also benefits supervisors by maintaining their knowledge of the area.

Staff Inspection

The staff inspection is generally performed by those who do not have direct control over the employees or operations being reviewed. This inspection concerns a task or function and how well it is being carried out in terms of meeting the objective. The strengths and weaknesses of operations are reviewed to determine compliance with policies, to discover if the policies are current, and to decide whether there is continued need for the policies.

In most protection programs, the person in charge of security is involved in both types of inspection, often simultaneously. The security supervisor not only has line authority but must also inspect the performance of functions or tasks. Inspections conducted by high-level administrators usually focus more on total program effectiveness than on inspecting a post or determining an officer's skill level.

COMMUNICATION

Few management activities are more important in dealing with personnel than effective communications, both upwards and downwards in the organizational hierarchy. It has been said that the essence of security is communications. Hospital security officers must communicate with the people they serve each day, and there must be good communications between security officers and supervisors. Today's officers want more input into decisions that affect them than their predecessors did. If management fails to listen to employees, is unresponsive to their needs, or fails to deliver deserved recognition, employees will not perform in a satisfactory manner.

Field supervisors spend a good deal of time being agents of change. New directives involving field operations are invariably given to the field supervisor for implementation. Almost all changes are resisted by employees to some degree. The resistance to change is a protective mechanism of employees who may perceive the change as a threat to habits, job security, or relationships. Resistance can take many forms, such as lack of cooperation, slowdowns, wild rumors, and individual or group behavior aimed at discrediting the change. Recognizing that change will meet some form of resistance allows supervisors to plan ways to communicate that will minimize this resistance. Perhaps the key element in this respect is to communicate the reason for the change, if possible. The rationalization for all directives cannot—and out of practicality need not—be explained to all individuals, including supervisors. Security officers and supervisors must maintain confidence in the management of the security system and accept day-to-day directives without expecting detailed explanations for each and every change.

MOTIVATION

One of the basic responsibilities of supervisors is to motivate security officers to do their best. Motivation is very personal, and everyone will not respond to the same stimuli. Motivation also cannot be forced on an individual; thus the supervisor can only establish a climate in which employees can become motivated.

Motivating subordinates requires that supervisors be aware of and practice certain basic principles. Psychological studies indicate that recognition is one of the most significant factors in motivation, more important than responsibility, salary, advancement, or the work itself. Subordinates must not feel that they are just another face lost in the group, but rather that they are valued for their qualities as an individual. To motivate subordinates, supervisors must themselves be motivated. They must believe in the system and support all decisions handed down.

MORALE AND NEGATIVE ATTITUDES

The morale of employees is a frequent topic of concern for top management, and often centers around negative attitudes. Field supervisors play a major role in maintaining the morale of subordinates. Significant results cannot be accomplished solely by power, prestige, and authority. A supervisor's real power is achieved through a network of satisfactory relationships with subordinates and upper management.

Security supervisors must achieve the proper balance between meeting the goals of the organization, fulfilling the needs and interests of the security officers, and achieving their own personal goals.

A negative attitude of one officer can quickly become contagious. But because an attitude is difficult to define and explain, we will focus on negative behavior. Negative behavior cannot be ignored, and the sooner a corrective strategy is undertaken, the better.

HANDLING SUBORDINATE COMPLAINTS

In reviewing complaints by subordinates, supervisors should follow the five steps outlined by Barry E. Stotts and Albert J. Sweet[2]:

1. Remain calm and rational.

2. Take time to investigate and determine the relevant facts of the situation.

3. Analyze the facts to fully understand the complaint.

4. Discuss the complaint, and seek answers for each area of concern.

5. Take steps to resolve the complaint, and to the extent practical, eliminate the problem that was the basis for the complaint.

HANDLING PROBLEM EMPLOYEES

The following is a checklist developed by Dr. Leslie M. Slote that can help supervisors handle problem employees.[3]

1. **What is the employee's past record?** Always start any inquiry by assembling the facts to identify the problem. Has the employee committed this type of offense before? When? If punished now, should the employee receive a more severe penalty than a first offender?

2. **Has the employee had a fair chance to improve?** Review the employee's personnel record. Has the employee been given help in the past? Does the

employee fully understand what is expected? Did he or she possess this understanding at the time of the offense?

3. **When was the employee first given a fair warning of the seriousness of his or her behavior?** Is there a record of this warning? If so, who gave the warning?

4. **What action was taken in similar cases?** Review similar incidents that have occurred in the department.

5. **What will be the effect of disciplinary action on the group?** Is disciplinary action fully justified? What will be its effect on others?

6. **Are you going to handle this by yourself?** Will you need to clear your action with someone else? Will you need assistance? What about the timing?

7. **What other possible actions are there?** What is in the best interest of the organization? The employee? Is another warning appropriate? Suspension? Termination?

DETERMINING HOW MANY SECURITY SUPERVISORS ARE NEEDED

The number of security supervisors needed must be determined on the basis of the specific program. Important management principles such as chain of command, unity of command, and span of control must be recognized and applied to security, regardless of their size.

Chain of command refers to the levels of management control. The line of control divides at each level of authority in the structure, because at each level the authority of command is delegated to subordinates. Unity of command relates directly to the chain of command in defining the immediate supervisor of each person within the organization. Only one supervisor should be responsible for the direction of the individual at a given point in time to avoid friction resulting from duplication and conflicting direction. The supervisory position may be occupied by different individuals at different times of the day. In the absence of one level of supervision, the next higher level assumes control.

Span of control simply means the ability of one person to direct, coordinate, and control immediate subordinates. The factors affecting span of control are the ability of subordinates, the level of training, the complexity of tasks, and separation of the supervisor from subordinates by time or place.

Because most security programs operate on a 24-hour basis, the span of control is greatly affected by time. In small facilities with only one officer on duty during the night shift, the night administrator or nursing supervisor often assumes quasi-supervision of the officer.

Security organizations tend to become top-heavy. Too often, supervisory positions are used as a means of bypassing personnel and budget controls to compensate a specific individual at a higher rate of pay. An equally poor management practice is the designation of rank authority in lieu of monetary compensation. One relatively small organization had the following ranks: security guard, corporal, sergeant, lieutenant, captain, major, lieutenant colonel, and inspector. The objective is to keep the number of supervisors at a minimum while ensuring that security personnel are properly reviewed and have access to supervision.

THE SECURITY OFFICER

The security officer is the point of contact for the majority of security services and activities. A clear understanding of officer authority is a baseline of operations. The recruitment, selection, diversity of staff, compensation, motivation and officer discipline all interact to form an effective security force.

Security Officer Authority

Most healthcare security officers operate with no more authority than the ordinary citizen, which is generally the "right" to prevent or stop the commission of a criminal act in their presence. Security officers act as agents of the organization they have been engaged to protect, and thus their jurisdiction is derived from the organization. Jurisdiction, in this regard, is the legal power to exercise authority. The authority of officers to act on behalf of the organization should be clearly delineated in the security force administrative plan.

What can happen when a security officer does not act properly? In addition to organizational discipline, the officer may be liable for criminal or civil actions. Criminal charges may include assault, negligent homicide, and battery. A wide variety of civil actions (torts) exists; malicious prosecution, defamation, false imprisonment, and slander are among commonly alleged actions. Not only is the individual officer subject to legal sanctions, but the employer might also be vulnerable. Employers may believe they are protected if the employee acts outside the scope of his employment. It should be noted, however, that the scope of employment may extend further than expected. The case of Rivas v. Nationwide Personal Security Corp.[4] is one example. A security officer became involved in an argument with a store manager and began choking the manager. Rivas, a store employee, witnessed the incident and screamed for help. The officer struck her in the face in an attempt to silence her. Rivas sued the security officer and his employer. The court held that the employer was liable and that the assault on Rivas was within the scope of employment because the incident arose out of an argument concerning the service the officer was performing.

There are, of course, valid defenses for the actions of security officers, but officers should bear in mind that they may be more responsible for their actions than ordinary citizens. Citizens may be excused for their actions or inaction by reason of best intentions and lack of knowledge concerning the law, but security officers are expected to more fully understand the various provisions of the law. Security officers, by virtue of their training, experience, and responsibility, may be held to a higher legal standard than ordinary citizens. Thus security officers must understand their extent of authority and be well-versed in the legal implications of this authority.

Special Police Commission

In many jurisdictions, a special police commission may be conferred on healthcare security officers. These commissions often provide little or no additional authority beyond that of ordinary citizens. On the other hand, commissions that give security personnel the same legal power as regular police officers carry an increased exposure to civil liability. The actions of security officers with these special commissions are judged on the same level as those of regular police officers. The primary difference between special commissions granting full police authority to the security officer is that of time and location. These commissions generally restrict police authority to the property of the employer and to the actual time the officer is scheduled for duty. Security departments utilizing security officers with full police authority are often referred to as Departments of Public Safety.

Security officers can generally perform more efficiently without police powers. The advantage lies in their ability to interview and otherwise interact with organizational employees and visitors within the scope of the employer/employee relationship. Security officers have much more latitude than law enforcement officers. For example, courts have consistently held that private security officers are not held to the provisions of the landmark Miranda case and need not advise the accused of their rights.

As a general rule, whenever a private citizen, including a private security officer, acts as an agent of the police, all constitutional limitations against the police apply. At times, police and security activities are quite similar, and joint activities raise certain concerns. It is sometimes difficult to determine when private security actions cease and public law enforcement takes over. Some lawsuits have been predicated on a conspiracy between police and security to violate the constitutional rights of others. Security officers should thus have a basic working knowledge of the Fourth, Fifth, Sixth, Eighth, and Fourteenth Amendments to the U.S. Constitution and similar laws of other countries which concern the basic rights of the individual.

The exclusionary rule, which all states basically follow, is of particular interest to security officers. The exclusionary rule was intended to regulate illicit government conduct. In application, the rule excludes the introduction in a trial of evidence that a law enforcement agent has obtained illegally. On the other hand, when a private citizen seizes evidence, the evidence cannot be excluded from the trial no matter how illegal the seizure. Even though the evidence will not be thrown out of court, the citizen who seized the evidence illegally may not be free from criminal or civil actions. When security officers work in concert with a law enforcement agency, the exclusionary rule may well apply to any evidence seized.

Licensing

Licensing for security personnel should not be confused with police powers. Licensing refers to the regulation and control of persons performing certain types of security services. A common aspect of many licensing statutes and some special police commissions is that of producing revenue (taxes) while doing little to regulate the delivery of protection services.

Most states have licensing laws, and many U.S. cities have municipal statutes relative to security licensing. Many of these statutes appear to be directed at regulating the dress requirements of security personnel and the manner in which security vehicles are identified. These statutes, many drafted by law enforcement agencies, are intended to prevent confusion among the public regarding security personnel who look like law enforcement officers. This type of regulation is of course necessary; however, competent security administrators should make certain that security officers are not easily mistaken for police officers, regardless of the regulations.

Many licensing statutes border on the absurd and would probably not stand up under a test of constitutionality. One statute in a fairly large western city actually prohibits the use of the word "officer" in "any advertising or upon the premises within the limits of the City . . . or on any of its vehicles or equipment." The administration of some municipal security licensing laws does little more than foster a harassment atmosphere between security and law enforcement. Despite the acknowledged need for private security to protect life and property, many law enforcement officers continue to see security as some kind of threat. Their way of dealing with this "threat" is to put the security officer in their place under the guise of licensing requirements. These actions include limited processing availability, making it extremely difficult to hire new officers and to put the new security officer to work.

It is reported that one police agency allows for processing only two hours every two weeks, with substantial time after processing before the license and right to work is "approved." In yet another situation, a police officer threatened arrest of a security officer for impersonating a police officer. The security officer was working an emergency and construction access gate in a remote location. The city many months earlier had authorized security officers to work in navy blue jumpsuits due to the dirty post environment. This arrangement was verbal and worked well for months until 2 A.M. one morning, when a police officer ordered the officer off post, threatening his arrest, because the officer was wearing navy blue. It seems that navy blue jumpsuits were worn by range officers at the city police firing range. As ridiculous as this incident seems, the police officer's actions were upheld by police command officers and the city police detective assigned to the security-licensing bureau.

To upgrade and regulate the security function, good licensing laws are required. Professional security administrators can and should contribute to new statutes and ordinances that will eliminate the existing weak or misdirected laws, which are actually a detriment to safe environments. State licensing is to be commended and fostered, and municipal licensing should be actively discouraged. Meanwhile, there have been various attempts, through proposed legislation, to regulate security from the federal level of government.

SELECTING SECURITY PERSONNEL

A newly-hired security officer is generally a question mark for the first week or two of employment. In this time period it generally becomes evident whether the officer will survive employment past the probationary period. Some officers steadily improve, but unfortunately, some who are promising when they start, deteriorate rather quickly. Security work is not for everyone. Professional security managers review candidates from many different standards, but with one purpose in mind: to select an individual who is right for the job and to assign him or her to an appropriate job. Managers often hire the best-qualified person, but if the candidate is overqualified, job satisfaction suffers. Healthcare security work can be boring, routine, and monotonous, but within seconds turn into a situation that challenges the mind and body to the limit.

Perhaps no other position within the vast array found in healthcare has such a wide expectation level. The expectations for a security officer differ widely among staff members and specific departments. Emergency room personnel want a security officer the stature of a professional football player. The night nursing supervisor wants someone who will diligently check and recheck the exterior doors. The psychiatric department wants someone who can apply sound psychological principles to control a situation. The risk manager wants someone with good investigative skills coupled with good report writing.

Employees also see security officers in many different roles, some of which are created by security officers themselves. One day a security director received a call from a night nursing service employee who complained that the new officer assigned to the parking lot was not doing his

164 *Hospital and Healthcare Security*

job and certainly did not compare with the previous officer. Upon investigation it was found that the source of dissatisfaction centered around frost on the vehicle windows. The previous officer had taken it on himself to scrape the windshields of departing staff but the new officer did not perform this service.

Recruitment

There must be conscious effort to recruit security officer applicants. Viable applicants do not generally just drop out of the sky at the precise point in time a vacancy exists. Ideally, there should be between seven to ten applicants for each open position. Recruitment efforts will vary to some degree depending on the geographical unemployment rate. A recruitment program should be planned and be an ongoing activity. A very serious flaw of many in-house security departments is the time lag between the occurrence of a vacancy and the actual date the replacement officer is trained and ready for general duty. This delay is usually a result of the human resource department hiring process. This process can involve approvals required for replacement, posting of the position in-house, time delays in advertising schedules, preliminary screening, etc. This drawn-out process most often results in security shifts running short of staff and/or in excessive cost from the use of overtime.

Various methods and activities can be used to attract security officer applicants:

- **Recruitment brochure.** This brochure is distributed in a variety of ways, from organized job fairs, school placement programs, retirement groups, to current officers who are encouraged to pass them on to others. One program reports that their recruitment brochure is handed out to all applicants regardless of the applicant being hired. Their philosophy is that even the rejected applicant may know of another person seeking employment who may be an acceptable candidate for employment.

- **Signing bonus.** This recruiting incentive is also tied to a short-term retention objective. The basic concept is to pay a sum of money upon hire and then to pay an additional amount at some point of employment longevity. A 90-day period is common; however, many options are available within this concept.

- **Staff recruitment monetary award.** This type of recruitment pays a current staff member a sum of money for referring an applicant who is subsequently employed. As with the signing bonus, there is generally at least one payment at a later time provided that the referred employee is still employed by the organization.

- **Newspaper and newsletter advertising.** The newspaper advertisement remains the basic component for recruitment of healthcare security staff. Some organizations have also reported success by advertising in newsletters such as homeowners associations and church bulletins.

- **Open house and recruitment displays.** A well-advertised open house can attract a sizable number of applicants. This method of recruitment is more appropriate to the larger organizations with multiple positions available. Attracting too many applicants in a tight labor market can be counterproductive. Interested persons who are not hired or who do not get an interview are sometimes reluctant to return at a later time. This same problem may exist when utilizing a display booth at a job fair.

Selection Criteria

Previous security experience is not of paramount importance in the overall selection process. In fact, the amount of retraining required is often a significant obstacle and cost. Even applicants with previous healthcare security experience generally need to learn new methods and procedures to function in the new system. On the other hand, applicants with previous security experience usually realize that duties, even in a good security system, are usually routine, requiring diligence and self-motivation. Another advantage is that the applicant generally understands that security is a 24-hour, seven-day-a-week operation. Applicants who have not been subjected to this around-the-clock schedule often state they are willing to work nights and weekends, but later discover that the new job does not fit their particular lifestyle.

Communication skills are an important factor in selection. The security officer must be able to communicate effectively in both oral and written forms. Written skills can be upgraded; however, improving oral communication skills requires considerably more time and money. The security department as a whole is often judged on the basis of security reports. Not all reports stay within the security section. The incident report, for example, is often used by the facility administrator, risk manager, insurance company, and law enforcement and other government agencies.

Image is another factor of extreme importance. Many elements make up image, and a person either does or does not present a good image. Physical appearance and clothing are obvious items involved in applicant evaluation. Another characteristic of image often overlooked is the tendency to talk too much. Many times one is impressed with an individual until he or she begins to speak. It is not always what is said, but how much is said. Security officers who present a good image have learned good listening skills.

Attitude, image, and pride all fit together and should be a major consideration in any selection process. A positive attitude toward the job and the employer is a necessary first step in transforming a new officer into a seasoned security professional.

People are what healthcare is all about. Security officers must understand that their job entails a great deal of personal contact, and they must enjoy this aspect of the job or their performance will generally suffer. Good public and employee relations are an essential part of an efficient security program. I was once asked during an interview for the one word that best describes a good security officer in the healthcare setting. My answer was "caring." Officers must care about people, about their position, and about themselves.

Physical qualifications are controlled to some degree by government regulation. Federal legislation makes it unlawful for any person or agency covered by federal law to discriminate against any individual on the basis of race, color, religion, sex, national origin, or age. In setting physical standards, an employer must be able to prove that certain physical qualifications are required for the job. In a landmark Ohio case a court ruled on such aspects as physical strength and fitness, physical agility, height and arm's reach, ability to drive a car, and ability to impress others with psychological advantage of height. In each instance the court ruled against the defendants. It was unable to find rational support for the height and weight requirements. Although this litigation involved police officers, the implications concerning the hiring of security officers are apparent.

There is an increasing number of female security officers being added to the ranks of healthcare security forces. Not only have security administrators realized that women can do the job, but they have also recognized that women contribute an additional dimension to the protection effort. Because the security effort in the typical healthcare setting must deal with many women, it stands to reason that a female officer may be more effective than a male in many situations.

The first female security officers were assigned conservative positions, such as in residence buildings, behind desks, or at visitor control posts. Today women are assigned to general patrol duty, critical incident response, and other responsibilities previously held only by male officers. They can also be used effectively in surveillance, checking women-only areas, searching female prisoners, transporting women in vehicles, and other such functions that may be sensitive for the male officer.

Just as with gender diversity, cultural diversity is an important aspect of a well-rounded security staff. A medical care facility with a population of significant ethnic cultures requires a security staff mix that represents these cultures. Security staff members who are available to speak different languages and interpret basic customs of different ethnic groups can offer great assistance in the mission of the healthcare organization.

The Selection Process

It takes a great deal of experience to effectively interview security candidates, and even the best interviewers are often misled by applicants. The application is the basic selection document and is used extensively in conducting the interview. During the interview process, the interviewer must find out as much about the candidate, within legal limitations, as possible in a relatively short time.

In many cases the interview is simply an effort toward screening out the most undesirable applicants rather than on identifying the best applicants. The unstructured interview, the most often utilized process for screening applicants, has raised questions of validity. Lacking a modicum of validity raises questions about whether the unstructured interview method is a legally defensible employment practice.[5] Because a group of applicants rarely yields the one individual who possesses all the qualities required for the ideal security officer, especially in a time of low unemployment, the selection process is one of comparing one candidate against another.

The most important part of the selection process is the background investigation of the applicant. The first step is to verify as much information as possible concerning what the applicant has written on the application form and has stated during the interview. Is the applicant the person they purport to be? The most common and economical approach is through letters of confirmation, telephone calls, and personal contact. The best single predictor of what a person will do is what he or she has done. A criminal history record check and drug testing are important aspects of the hiring process. A more detailed process of applicant-checking is contained in another section of this text.

Federal legislation in 1988 prohibited most private employers from requiring polygraph examinations of employees or prospective employees. Some companies have replaced the polygraph test with so-called pencil-and-paper honesty (integrity) tests and now use these to screen applicants. Considerable controversy surrounds the value and the possible negative impact of the pencil-and-paper integrity tests. The results of a 1990 study by the Office of Technology Assessment, a research unit of the U.S. Congress, failed to produce any clear results on the credibility of these tests.[6]

The test questions utilized on the honesty test should be carefully constructed to avoid allegations of any bias. A security firm reached a $2.1 million settlement in a California class action suit brought by a rejected security guard applicant. The applicant sued under California Labor Code Section 1101–2 prohibiting employers from "tending to control or direct the political activities or affiliations of employees" or influencing employees "to adopt or follow or refrain from adopting or following any particular course or line of political action or political activity." The trial judge ruled with the plaintiff in that case.[7] Although this case was decided under California law, many other states have similar statutes.

The passage of the Americans with Disabilities Act of 1990 (ADA) has affected the security officer hiring process. In simple terms, an employer may not exclude hiring a person with a disability when the disability is not related to job requirements and the employer can make reasonable accommodations to fit the disabled individual into the work environment. As with most legislation, the law is rather straightforward; however, regulatory interpretations can be rather murky.

The ADA requirements do not ban the use of psychological tests for pre-employment screening. The tests, however, cannot be constructed to screen out individuals with disabilities unless the disability is shown to be job-related for the position and is consistent with business necessity. A distinction is made between personality traits and mental disorders. It is generally accepted that employers may seek out broad personality traits in the pre-employment process as long as the process does not disclose a mental or psychological disorder. A medical examination performed after a conditional offer of employment has been made is the proper avenue to determine any mental impairment of the applicant. In fact, a medical examination is often a statutory requirement for licensing security officers. The definitive resource on what constitutes a mental or psychological disorder is the Diagnostic and Statistical Manual of Mental Disorders (DSM) published by the American Psychiatric Association.[8]

RETENTION

Keeping good security officers and supervisors is a high-priority objective of management. The cost of recruiting, selecting, processing, and training new security officers is significant. The priority may thus not be retention but controlled turnover. The principle deficiency found in one healthcare security department program review was too *little* turnover. In this department of 14 officers, the average longevity was 17 years, with the newest officer being hired 6 years prior to the review. The department had merely gone to sleep. Security management must focus on maintaining a healthy turnover rate.

FULL-TIME VERSUS PART-TIME SECURITY OFFICERS

A security system cannot be effectively or efficiently operated with an overabundance of part-time security officers, nor can the program be operated with only full-time personnel. The appropriate number of part-time personnel depends on several factors. A highly structured system, with strong supervision and training, can successfully operate with a higher percentage of part-time personnel than can a program operating on an informal basis. It is a generally accepted rule of thumb that a healthcare security staff consists of no more than 20 to 25 percent part-time officers. An exception to this guideline would be officers who are regularly scheduled to work 32 hours per week. In some cases, an officer working 32 hours per week would be classified as a full-time employee.

A workforce consisting of only part-time officers cannot provide the continuity required of successful systems. Moreover, keeping the security staff informed requires constant attention, and full-time employees can generally keep better informed through greater frequency of system interaction. Officers who work 40 to 48 hours per week are generally better informed than officers who work 10 to 16 hours per week.

Ironically, although part-time officers often possess higher qualifications in terms of experience and education, they are generally less productive. This situation can in large part be traced to the fact that part-time employees usually do not depend on the part-time job for their main source of income. This does not imply that part-timers are consciously not doing their best, but they often do just enough to get the job done.

Another negative factor is the part-time employee's lack of availability for training and lack of flexibility in scheduling. The part-timer must generally schedule training and working hours around another job or other interests. One can only work so many hours in a day or a week, and moonlighters are often stretching themselves.

Part-time officers do fulfill an important need in most security departments, however, and should be viewed as a management tool. Just as overtime is an effective management tool, the part-time officer, when correctly used, can fill a void, especially in terms of cost containment. An important aspect of the part-time officer is flexibility. The ultimate goal is to employ part-timers who are not only competent, but who can readily extend the number of hours they can work in the week. Even better is the part-timer who can switch days or shifts on short notice.

The result of using only full-time personnel is almost always that of overstaffing. Rarely does the right staffing plan turn out to be divisible by 40 hours, or in other words, an even number of full-time equivalents. Thus an extra officer is often on a shift to provide the officer with a 40-hour week. Work always can be found for the officer, but it generally serves only to rationalize the schedule. Further, a staff of only full-time officers offers the department supervisor little choice but to operate short staffed or to use excessive amounts of overtime to fill shifts for vacations, holidays, sickness, and other absences. As a rule of thumb, the anticipated absences for each proprietary employee is 45 days per year, or 360 hours. Subcontracting the 360 hours from 2,080 hours (full-time equivalent) leaves 1,720 hours of productive service. Utilizing this formula, it would require 5.2 full-time equivalent (FTE) staff to maintain a deployment schedule of one officer on duty around the clock seven days per week. Staffing schedules become even more complicated as much of the projected 360 hours of non-productive time is not predictable in terms of when it will be utilized.

Thus, a proper balance of full- and part-time employees must be achieved. A program that requires one officer on duty 24 hours a day can be staffed with three full-time officers and three part-time officers. This system gives each part-timer 16 hours per week and provides a resource to cover additional hours as required. It is generally not productive to hire a part-time officer for less than 16 hours per week. It is also poor practice to employ only part-time staff on the weekends. As discussed, compared to the full-time officer, the part-timer may be less trained, motivated, and informed. Proper deployment of part-time staff is to intersperse their schedule with full-time officers.

WAGE COMPENSATION

The wage compensation received by security personnel is largely dependent on what the organization determines is the value of security services. Wages are often determined by a complex method of evaluation within a structured wage and salary program. A basic purpose of the evaluation is to compensate fairly all employees in relation to their contribution to the organization's objectives. In a simple example, if the security officer contributed the same effort as a radiological technician, the two wage rates would be the same.

One factor that affects compensation from a non-evaluation aspect is supply and demand. The healthcare organization may have to pay more for certain positions simply because there is a shortage of trained personnel to perform a particular function. In the structured system, the need to pay a higher wage than the evaluated worth is often referred to as a "red-lined position."

Among the major factors holding down wages for security officers in all fields of security service are the security personnel themselves. Their rigid ideas of what security services should be have worked against them. This is particularly true of security supervisors or security chiefs who have retired from other organizations. They may prefer not to rock the boat and just to drift along to another retirement. Fortunately, many exceptions to this generalization exist, and some of the best protection programs are being administered by individuals who have retired from other organizations.

Wage surveys in a common geographical area are often helpful in establishing the average compensation paid for protection services. Because cost of living differences and supply and demand produce wide salary fluctuations, comparing the wage rates of different geographical areas yields little valid information. In reviewing wage rates, one must be constantly aware that security functions differ from organization to organization, and job titles alone can mean very little.

A growing trend in healthcare security is to structure salary scales to training levels. This concept has been fostered in part by the training standards of the International Association for Healthcare Security and Safety (IAHSS).

SECURITY FORCE DISCIPLINE

Maintaining a strong degree of discipline is a high priority for security administrators who operate successful protection programs. Discipline must be exercised to develop a force amiable to direction and control. Security officers must set an example for the entire organization. Security officers are often deployed at the point of entry for patients and visitors and thus create a lasting impression. The organization must insist that security officers follow rigid regulations to maintain an impeccable image. Some security departments have shown such a professional approach by developing a code of ethics for security personnel or adopting the IAHSS Code of Ethics.

A security force with poor discipline exhibits the following general characteristics:

- Poor morale

- Lack of direction, objectives, and goals

- Inattention to duties

- Careless attitude toward the job, supervisors, and organization

- Common disregard for rules and regulations

SECURITY DEPARTMENT				
SERVICE PERFORMANCE RECORD				
NAME:			POSITION:	
Date	Entry Description	Absent	Late	Source
07/15/99		EU		Lt. Riles
08/09/99	Completed 90-day evaluation with satisfactory performance rating			Sgt. Mathis
08/27/99	Letter of appreciation from visitor to SLJH reference service			Lt. Riles
09/12/99			L	Sgt. Mathis
10/04/99	Officer commended for outstanding appearance during post inspection			Lt. Stones
10/14/99		PTO		Lt. Riles
10/21/99	Officer counseled regarding the need for more complete incident report preparation.			Lt. Riles

Legend: Absent   Late

- Paid Time Off (PTO)   - More than 15 minutes (M)
- Excused Unpaid (EU)   - Less than 15 minutes (L)
- Called Unexcused (CU)
- No Call/No Show (NS)

Figure 7-2 Example Security Officer Chronological History

Effecting a high degree of discipline in the security force requires an appropriate level of supervision and officer self-discipline. Unfortunately, the routine of the security operation provides ample opportunity for security officers to neglect their duties and to engage in dereliction, which reflects poorly on the entire security force.

Discipline can be both positive and negative. Positive discipline is the force that prompts the individual to do the right thing. Negative discipline is the force that restrains the individual from doing the wrong thing. Disciplinary action is intended to correct a deficiency and should not necessarily be regarded as a punishment. Regrettably, most discipline is negative in nature; however, both positive and negative practices are valuable in the development of a security officer.

Figure 7-2 illustrates a method of recording positive and negative data, attendance, and general information concerning a specific officer. This record is intended to be a work history summary and is a useful tool in evaluating the performance of an officer. It can also serve as a primary document in any unemployment cases or violation of equal opportunity cases that may arise.

RULES AND REGULATIONS

Rules and regulations concerning the conduct of security personnel must be in written form so that officers are apprised of the ground rules that apply. Unwritten policy is not an equitable method of operating a security program. The following prohibitions are generally included in most policies, along with prohibitions peculiar to specific organizations:

1. Security officers will not become involved in discussions of religion or politics while on duty or on the premises of the organization.

2. Security officers will not engage in lengthy social conversations with other employees. This is extremely important for the proper functioning of the organization and the security department.

3. Security officers will not criticize any employee or regulation except to the proper supervisor.

4. Security officers will abide by the organization's smoking policy and will not smoke on exterior patrol.

5. Except during break time, there will be no eating and no reading of material other than material applicable to the job unless it is specifically authorized by a security supervisor.

6. No radios or TV will be allowed on any post.

7. Security officers will not leave a security assignment until properly relieved.

8. The loaning or borrowing of money among employees is prohibited.

9. No member of the security department will solicit contributions for any purpose, except by permission of the security department head.

10. Security officers will not write notes or letters to employees or visitors concerning security problems, nor will they write personal notes to such persons.

11. Security officers will maintain strict confidentiality of information relative to all persons and organizations obtained during the performance of their duty.

The last item on the list is such an important issue that it is not uncommon for organizations to have each person in the security department sign a confidentiality statement as a condition of employment. Figure 7-3 is an example of such a statement.

PUNISHABLE OFFENSES

In addition to general prohibitions, a listing of punishable offenses for which the security officer may also be disciplined should be prepared. These offenses normally include the following:

1. Absence without proper notification.

2. Accepting any gift or bribe in the line of duty.

3. Conduct unbecoming a security officer or prejudicial to discipline of the security department either on or off duty.

4. Consuming alcohol or illegal drugs, being under their influence on duty, or reporting for duty in an impaired condition.

5. Bringing contraband to the workplace.

6. Enabling any person to secure stolen property.

7. False reporting.

8. Ignorance of rules and regulations after being duly informed.

9. Sleeping on duty or neglect of duty.

ST. PETER'S
COMMUNITY HOSPITAL
2475 Broadway, Helena, Montana 59601

CONFIDENTIALITY STATEMENT

I am aware while performing my duties at this facility I will have access to private and confidential information. Such information includes, but is not limited to, patient information, physician information, employee information, purchasing and financial information and computer passwords and is defined as anything I know (have seen or heard) as a result of my employment at the hospital. I realize, as an employee of this hospital, patients and their families, the medical staff, my fellow employees and hospital administration depend on me to conform to a standard of professional confidence. I will honor this trust placed in me and am aware that unauthorized release of confidential information is grounds for termination.

Signed this _____ day of _____ , 19 ____ .

_____
Witness

_____
Employee Signature

_____
Print Name

_____
Employee Number

051-619-N-2 (Rev. 10/92)

Figure 7-3 Confidentiality Statement (Courtesy of St. Peter's Hospital, Helena, Montana)

10. Excessive force or the improper display or use of a weapon.

11. Unnecessary harshness, violence, or profane language.

12. Willful disobedience of orders of a superior.

13. Failure to report any security incident either observed by the officer or brought to his or her attention by another person.

Written disciplinary policy should delineate the specific types of action that may be taken against an officer and the specific supervisors who may take that action. For example, the policy might include the following degrees of disciplinary action, all of which become part of the officer's personnel record:

- **Oral reprimand.** This action may be imposed by any security department supervisor.

- **Written reprimand.** This action is more serious than an oral reprimand, and it is a generally accepted practice for the security officer to sign a copy of this document. The officer's signature indicates he or she is aware of the contents of the reprimand but does not imply that he or she is in agreement with the reprimand. This form of disciplinary action may be taken by any departmental supervisor.

- **Probation status.** This action lasts for a specific period of time, not to exceed 60 days, during which the officer is evaluated to determine fitness for retention of employment. An officer on probation is not eligible for overtime assignment, and the officer's merit review date is advanced by the length of the probationary period. Probation status may be imposed only by the department head.

- **Suspension with or without pay.** This action lasts for a specific period of time, not to exceed five working days. It may be imposed only by the department head. (Note that an officer may be suspended for the remainder of the shift for any infraction of departmental rules and regulations, when in the evaluation of any security supervisor the continued duty of the officer may be prejudicial to the best interests of the organization. This suspension from duty should not be confused with the disciplinary

...ion of suspension as a form of punishment.) An officer may also be suspended for a period of time by the department head, pending an investigation of alleged misconduct.

- **Dismissal.** This action may be imposed only by the department head or higher authority.

EQUIPPING SECURITY PERSONNEL

The assigned responsibilities of and type of attire worn by security officers determines how they will be equipped. The vast majority of healthcare security officers are traditionally uniformed. Officers who do not wear uniforms may use much of the same equipment; however, officers wearing "soft cloths" should never carry a concealed firearm.

Uniforms

Most security professionals agree that the plainclothes security officer is of less value than officers who are more readily identifiable. The true plainclothes approach is practically nonexistent in the healthcare field today.

A more contemporary debate is whether security officers should wear a traditional uniform or a blazer and slacks. The traditional security uniform provides deterrence and commands control when it is necessary to regulate behavior. The blazer, on the other hand, denotes more of the management function. If blazers are worn, they should be designed so that security officers are readily identifiable. Without readily visible identification, poor public relations and unnecessary confrontations may result. The attire of security officers also influences their own attitude; attire that suggests an air of dignity and action tends to produce officers with those traits.

The style, color, and type of uniform are often controlled by local or state regulations. With or without regulation, the uniform should not be designed to replicate the uniform of any law enforcement agency. A hospital in Texas was accused by two legal aid groups of designing its security uniforms to look like the uniforms of U.S. Border Patrol agents. A representative of the Texas Rural Legal Aid claimed that the hospital used the uniforms to discourage Hispanics from seeking medical care and thereby avoiding any violation of the Medicare anti-dumping law.[9]

A traditional uniform can be softened in terms of color and style. For example, the visor cap, which strongly suggests a military and authoritarian role, is not part of many uniforms. Many programs prohibit hats within the facility, and some even prohibit hats outside the facility. Other organizations adopt both the uniform and the blazer in their programs: the regular security officers wear uniforms, while supervisory personnel wear blazers. Some job responsibilities may best be fulfilled by a uniformed officer, while for others, the blazer is preferred. For example, patrol and response officers might wear uniforms, while fixed-post officers who perform an access control function might wear blazers.

Supplying and Maintaining the Uniform

Because the uniform is such an important element in the operation of a security force, the organization should provide and, if possible, maintain the uniform. Ideally, officers should be required to report for duty in personal clothing and change to a uniform. In this system, the organization dry-cleans or launders the uniform and prevents officers from wearing the uniform off duty. This system is, of course, quite costly and is therefore not widely used.

Organizations that provide uniforms for security personnel have more control over the quantity and quality of the uniforms. All too often, newly hired officers who must provide their own uniforms find the initial outlay a burden. As a result, they sometimes do not purchase enough uniforms to maintain a proper appearance.

There are alternatives to the organization's supplying and maintaining the complete uniform. As a condition of employment, some organizations require that a certain amount of money be withheld to offset the cost of uniforms if the officer resigns or is terminated within a specified time, usually three months. Other organizations hold a deposit until termination. It is recommended that interest be paid on money held as a uniform and equipment deposit; in fact, interest may even be legally required. If money is withheld from an employee's paycheck to cover a deposit, the organization is limited in the amount that can be withheld from any given paycheck. The employee must be paid at least the minimum wage for the hours worked before a deduction can be made.

180 *Hospital and Healthcare Security*

Another method of cost control is to require that security officers purchase their original uniform, while replacements are paid for by the organization. This procedure is effective in eliminating applicants who are seeking only temporary employment. One facility reports that it has been able to contain costs by not purchasing an outside jacket for each officer. The facility maintains a supply of jackets in various sizes. Officers select their jackets from the supply at the beginning of the shift when they draw their weapons and other equipment.

Larger security forces can reduce uniform costs by making use of existing uniforms. Regardless of the size of the force, returned uniforms represent dollars, and the supply should not be allowed to build up excessively. It is much more economical to spend money on alterations than to order new uniforms.

Uniform rental firms also provide an alternative to hospital-owned and officer-owned uniforms. Uniforms should be clean when returned upon termination, and professionally dry-cleaned when appropriate. The failure to return hospital owned uniforms in the appropriate condition should result in a predetermined deduction from the officer's final wages.

Equipment Considerations: Firearms

Whether security officers should be equipped with side arms requires constant evaluation and reexamination. The answer is found in individual program needs, and the question cannot be answered with a simple yes or no. For program effectiveness and deterrent value, the preponderance of evidence supports armed security officers. However, armed officers may prove a detriment in various situations or functions rather than an asset.

Proponents of providing firearms for healthcare security officers argue that if an organization gives officers the responsibility of protecting life and property, it should provide them with the tools to do their job. Officers who can meet force with force can more efficiently carry out their responsibilities. Those against providing firearms generally cite the liability involved and almost always stress a case in which a firearm was used inappropriately. Some opponents argue that security officers guard property and need not use deadly force. The firearm does nothing more than allow officers to protect themselves and others while they protect property. The value of property is significant only to the extent that it invites intruders. If security officers are expected to confront strangers, their safety must be paramount regardless of property value.

At present, approximately 15 to 20 percent of U.S. healthcare security officers are armed. When the previous edition of this book was published in 1992, about 30 percent had firearms. Thus, the trend appears to be toward unarmed security officers. However, security managers must make the correct decision in regard to firearms for their particular circumstances, and must not simply follow a trend.

Considerations in Arming Officers

The correct decision on whether to arm security officers for a given organization requires consideration of many different factors. Among these considerations are personal safety, vulnerability, liability, deterrent value, environmental profile (status of the neighborhood, geographical setting, degree of crime in and around the facility), and quality of personnel.

Personal Safety

Personal safety is, of course, the central issue in whether to arm officers. The people at risk can be divided into the protection officers themselves and the principals (employees, patients, visitors) they are protecting. Armed security officers feel safer as their ability to protect themselves increases. No amount of judo or other alternatives can match an opponent with a firearm. Conversely, officers are sometimes safer without a weapon. If a security officer is obviously not armed, a foe need not use deadly force to accomplish his objective. The persons that the security officer protects have a greater feeling of security when the officer is armed. Thus firearms provide both officers and those they protect with a sense of security, regardless of the real need for firearms.

Vulnerability

The degree of vulnerability that the officer and the organization face is also an important consideration. In larger acute-care hospitals, the quantities of drugs and money and the number of serious assaults are considerably different that those found in small suburban or rural facilities. The degree of vulnerability also varies in relation to the environmental setting. For the individual officer, vulnerabilities also vary considerably. A security officer patrolling warehouses and parking lots at 3:00 A.M. is in a different position than that of an officer assigned to an access control point within the facility. Generally, fewer security personnel are armed in programs that are primarily internal than in programs that must deal with a campus and so-called street problems.

Liability

Potential for legal liability actions is greatest with armed officers. Officers who misuse their weapons can create a liability, as can nursing staff who misuse a needle when injecting a patient. However, an unarmed officer who cannot effectively prevent injury to a patient, visitor, or employee, might create a liability of a different nature. The problem is that one cannot know whether the firearm helped avert an incident that might have led to a liability claim.

To reduce liability while providing the security system with a limited weapon capability, some programs arm only the supervisory staff. This approach is predicated on the reduced exposure of weapons and the fact that supervisory personnel are generally better trained and more capable of properly handling weapons. Another approach is to arm those officers who are assigned to external patrol and to eliminate firearms for those personnel assigned to duty within the facility. One organization provides gun lockers, and officers put on their weapons when going outside and secure their weapons when entering the facility.

There is one approach to providing firearms protection to the healthcare center without arming any of the regular security staff: hire off-duty law enforcement officers. Although this is an expensive approach, the healthcare center can avoid the training issue and a certain degree of liability. What may be wrong with this approach is that training and liability may not be avoided at all, as the selection of the specific officer working the off-duty post is often outside of the control of the organization.

An example of what can go wrong when off-duty officers work at healthcare facilities can be found in the case of Melendez v. City of Los

Angeles.[10] In this case, two off-duty police officers working at the facility were involved in an altercation in which a person was shot. The healthcare facility that had hired the off-duty officers avoided a court decision by settling out of court for $550,000. However, a jury found the city liable for $10,212,500, in part because it thought the city was guilty of negligent retention of one of the officers, who had allegedly been involved in other incidents in which excessive force was used. In addition, the jury found that the police officers were acting within the scope of their employment as law enforcement officers at the time of the shooting, despite the fact that they were "off duty." This particular case is not unique. The issue of off-duty police officers working for private organizations deserves serious attention by private organizations and law enforcement agencies alike.

Deterrent Value

One of the strongest arguments in favor of arming security officers is the preventative value of firearms. One can only assume that most serious crimes are planned to some degree, and that part of that planning is to select a target in which armed security officers will not be encountered.

Environmental Profile

The type of neighborhood, together with the associated level and type of crime, must be analyzed in determining the need for armed security personnel. A quiet residential setting with an older population presents far different issues than a rundown commercial or transient community. In reviewing the crime status of the area, the number of crimes as well as the seriousness of the crimes is important. In this respect, a high number of minor crimes can suggest that more serious crime is foreseeable, providing there is a linkage. An example is a person stealing car parts in a parking lot that is interrupted and violence results during an attempted escape. An escalating level of minor crimes is often the forerunner of increasing violence and serious crime.

Quality of Personnel

Many times the problem is not whether a security officer should be armed, it is finding competent, well-trained security officers to properly arm. Perhaps as many as half of the security officers presently carrying weapons should be disarmed. No amount of preservice or in-service training can compensate for security officers who are untrainable.

Type of Weapon, Holster, and Ammunition

The decision to use firearms in a security program mandates additional management responsibility and adds to costs. The next decision that must be made concerns the type of weapon, holster, and ammunition to be used. These decisions are sometimes determined by licensing laws.

Whenever possible, the organization should furnish the weapon, and it is preferable that weapons be checked in and out for each tour of duty. Where economics and other operational factors preclude organizational ownership of weapons, basic standards must be established for officer-furnished weapons and ammunition.

The type of holster to be used is another important consideration. It must ride close against the body and must make it difficult for another person to remove the weapon from the officer. Too many security officers have been shot with their own weapons after losing them to an assailant. Healthcare security officers should never be allowed to carry concealed weapons while performing hospital services. Not only is this practice evidence of a poor management decision, it can also have serious consequences in terms of public relations and liability.

Whether to arm security officers or not is a grave decision that must be made with deliberation. There is always a risk, and the decision must be made on the basis of this question: Does the weapon provide positive benefits sufficient to offset the liability and cost involved?

MANAGING THE FIREARMS PROGRAM

A firearms policy is mandatory. The policy must be clear, concise, and understood by every officer. A firearms weapon affidavit should be completed by all officers who carry firearms. Figure 7-4 is an example of

HSS WEAPON USE AND SAFETY AFFIDAVIT

1. The weapon you carry in the performance of your duty is for the protection of life. Deadly physical force may be used only as a last resort if the Security Officer reasonably believes a lesser degree of force is inadequate, and; the Security Officer has reasonable grounds to believe, and does believe, that he or another person is in imminent danger of being killed or of receiving great bodily harm.

2. All weapons are dangerous, it is mandatory that the Security Officer treat his weapon with care, respect, and remembering that at all times handling the weapon safely is the most important requirement.

3. The person with a firearm in his possession has a full time job. You cannot guess-you cannot forget. You must know how to use, handle, and store your firearm safely. Do not use any firearm without a complete understanding of its particular characteristics and safe use. There is no such thing as a foolproof gun.

4. From the time you pick up a gun you become part of a system over which you have complete control. You are the only part of the system that can make a gun safe or unsafe.

5. Firearms will not be removed from the holster or otherwise drawn unless there is an immediate threat of death to the officer or other persons present. The firearm will not be removed from the holster for show or display or at the request of other security personnel. Security Supervisors are entitled to inspect the gun to determine the cleanliness of the weapon and whether you are carrying appropriate ammunition.

6. Warning shots will not be fired under any circumstances.

7. I will never leave a loaded firearm where someone else may handle it. When not on my person, my weapon will be secured. This includes at work, traveling to and from work and at home.

8. The officer must carry the firearm and ammunition that was approved by the local law enforcement agency. Carrying a weapon or ammunition other than that approved is forbidden and could result in termination.

9. The weapon must be cleaned after each shooting session, failure to do so could result in a malfunction of the weapon.

10. Alcohol, drugs, and guns don't mix. Do not handle firearms if you have been using alcohol or are under a doctor's medication containing narcotic derivatives.

11. Do not shoot at or from a moving vehicle. If you disable a driver you have now created a 3,000 pound missile capable of inflicting serious injury or death to an innocent party.

12. I understand that the license issued to me prohibits my wearing the uniform and/or weapon while off duty except to travel directly to and from home. The weapon must be secured in the trunk or placed in a container out of public view.

13. Don't be timid when it comes to gun safety; if you observe anyone violating any safety precautions, you have an obligation to suggest safer handling practices.

14. Any time you pick up a weapon you must adhere to the following practices:

    - Point the gun in a safe direction
    - Visually inspect the gun to be certain that the gun is loaded or not loaded. Count the cartridges.
    - When not in actual use, firearms must be unloaded.
    - Never touch the trigger on a firearm until you actually intend to shoot.
    - You must be able to identify your target and what's beyond it.

15. All security personnel shall strictly adhere to this order. Violations of policies set forth herein will result in disciplinary action. This policy shall be effective at all times regardless of location.

PRINT NAME_____ SIGNATURE_____ DATE_____

WITNESS_____ DATE_____

Figure 7-4 Example of a Security Officer Firearms Affidavit Training (Courtesy of Healthcare Security Services, Denver, Colorado)

such a firearms affidavit. The affidavit could be expanded to serve as the administrative policy.

It often is claimed that a weapon should not be taken from a holster unless it will be used, and that one should never fire a weapon in the air. However, a drawn weapon might be appropriate in some instances, for example when answering an intrusion alarm in a closed pharmacy or when interrupting a crime in progress and ordering suspects to put their hands up. Firing in the air is generally considered to be inappropriate, however.

Firearms training is an essential ingredient in properly managing an armed security program. This training must be an ongoing program of classroom instruction and firing range experience. All armed officers should fire on the range at least once—and preferably twice—each year.

Training instructors should be carefully selected for two reasons. First, the highest level of instruction possible should be provided. Second, the qualifications of the instructor and the quality of the instruction can be of prime importance in any litigation alleging misuse of a firearm by a security officer. The instructor should be qualified by the National Rifle Association (NRA) to teach the police and security program.

Other Equipment Considerations

A security officer can carry only so much equipment, and the security administrator must decide which equipment is most necessary for a particular system. Officers so loaded down with equipment that they have difficulty moving exhibit a poor image. The needs of each program will vary. The following equipment list is offered only as a guide:

- Communication device/radio/pager/cell phone

- Handcuffs

- Flashlight

- Rubber Gloves

- Chemical gas (irritant)

- Nightstick/baton

- Bullet-resistant vests

Although not categorized as equipment, a nameplate or other identification consistent with the facility's overall employee identification plan should be worn by all officers. Also, officers should never be allowed on a post or patrol without a notebook and writing instrument.

Equipment that is generally unnecessary includes whistles and extra rounds of ammunition. Items such as knives and novelty weapons should also be avoided.

Communication Device/Radio

The most important piece of equipment a security officer can carry is the two-way radio, which is part of the overall security communications system. A one-way pager is simply unacceptable. Not only does the radio provide an element of personal safety for the officer, but it is essential in achieving an effective security system. However, many facilities expend thousands of dollars for security personnel and fail to spend a small amount to achieve a 50 to 100 percent increase in effectiveness through improved communications. Archived reports attest to the success of radio communications in saving lives, preventing total-loss fires, and apprehending criminals of all types.

Radio equipment is available in all shapes and sizes and with varying states of sophistication. Radio systems now in operation allows officers in the field to link their radio to a telephone line, permitting them to dial any telephone virtually anywhere in the world. Likewise, anyone with a conventional telephone can call the officer in the field directly.

The low cost of cellular telephone units offers new options for healthcare security operations. For small security departments, cellular telephone service may be more advantageous than two-way radios. In large departments, the need for officers to communicate with one another and to hear broadcasts from the central station makes two-way radios the preferred communication device.

Good communications equipment is expensive; however, the cost has come down in recent years. Considering the life of today's equipment, the cost, depreciated over the number of usable years, is the best investment of security dollars that an organization can make.

Limited two-way radio codes in security operations can be useful in reducing valuable airtime. The 10 codes that were once popular have generally been found to be of limited value and have sometimes caused more problems than no codes at all. Most law enforcement agencies and security departments have eliminated the 10 codes except for a few basic ones.

Several problems are inherent in any code system; chief among them is the training required. With a constant turnover of personnel, the training issue assumes major proportions. Another problem is that the codes cannot cover the diversified and sometimes specific information that must be communicated. Field analysis has shown that departments that use extensive code systems do not necessarily use less airtime than do departments that have eliminated their codes. The main items of concern in radio transmission are minimal airtime and clarity (understanding) of the message being transmitted. Both of these goals can be adequately achieved by simply stating the message in concise, everyday language.

Handcuffs

Handcuffs are an important piece of equipment carried by the majority of healthcare security officers. Security officers may need to use handcuffs for maintaining custody and control of persons arrested, as well as for detaining persons who exhibit behavior that may be harmful to themselves or others. In restraining out-of-control patients, regular medical restraint devices will generally be utilized. On occasion, however, the officer's handcuffs may be the most expedient means of temporarily maintaining patient control.

The security officer will frequently use handcuffs when responding to major disturbances and other out-of-control situations. In one such situation, officers were called to a medical center parking lot on reports of a man kicking and screaming inside a parked vehicle. As the security officer approached the vehicle, the man exited it and charged the officer. A struggle ensued, and with the help of a second officer, the man was controlled with handcuffs. The man quit struggling as soon as the handcuffs were applied, and one of the officers discovered that the man had quit breathing. Medical assistance was immediately summoned and CPR was initiated. Unfortunately, in this case the man died, and the police began an investigation.

In the initial stages of the investigation, a little-known phenomenon called Sudden In Custody Death Syndrome (SICDS) was found. The majority of SICDS cases involve respiratory difficulties brought on by a variety of factors that lead to asphyxia. Asphyxia refers to either reduced oxygen or elevated levels of carbon dioxide and leads to the body tissue not getting sufficient oxygen.[11] Persons who are on drugs, abuse alcohol, have a mental illness, or are obese are at greater risk for asphyxia in stressful situations. In physically restraining persons, officers should not leave them on their stomach any longer than necessary or apply weight to their back or chest. In addition, officers should be cognizant that a person's resistance to physical control may be a struggle for oxygen as opposed to continued resistance to the restraint.

Quality handcuffs are a necessity. In some embarrassing instances, handcuffs had to be cut off a person due to a malfunctioning lock. All handcuffs carried by security officers should operate with the same type of key. Because handcuffs reinforce the police image, they should be completely enclosed within a leather case rather than carried exposed.

Flashlight

A flashlight should be carried by all security officers during night hours. It is the piece of equipment most often found lacking when reviewing officers in the field. The reluctance to carry a flashlight may be due in part to its size and weight. It is recommended that a small, two-cell "C" battery flashlight be used. This size is generally adequate for patrol activity. Larger flashlights or lantern-type lights can be stored for special use.

Gloves

The use of gloves in the healthcare setting has escalated in the past few years for all staff working in patient care delivery systems. One organization alone, the Mayo Clinic in Rochester, Minnesota, reports utilizing an estimated 10 million pairs of gloves per year. The advent of AIDS and mandates by the Occupational Safety and Health Administration (OSHA) have made the glove a major supply item in the healthcare environment. Gloves offer protection against the transition of disease and have, thus, become a primary item to be carried by the healthcare security officer.

The powdered latex glove is most widely used by all healthcare workers. However, it is reported that as many as 17 percent of healthcare workers have latex allergies—some so severe they have been forced out of their careers. In addition, powdered gloves create a source of airborne allergen that circulates freely through the air. The use of non-powdered gloves, gloves with a low latex level, or non-latex gloves should be considered in equipping security personnel.[12]

Chemical Gas

Aerosol sprays are quite popular in security work. There are two distinct types of gases: CN gas and CS gas. Both of these chemical irritants are designed to be sprayed in an assailant's face to produce skin and respiratory irritation and teary eyes. The use of these canister-type sprays is legal in most states.

Research indicates that the effectiveness of CS gas is somewhat limited by the need for direct eye impact to achieve a rapid reaction. Studies also show that severe skin pain starts in three seconds with CN gas and 60 seconds with CS gas. Both irritants last for about 5 to 6 minutes. In addition, there is some question as to the effects of chemical irritants on different types of people. In some cases, neither type of gas was effective on people under the influence of alcohol or drugs or on those who are mentally deranged. People must be able to feel or react to pain for the spray to be effective.

A relatively new chemical spray product, called capsicum, has recently been introduced, but there is little experience to document the manufacturer's claims. The chemical reportedly stops animals and those who are under the influence of alcohol or narcotics. The formula also contains a special dye that is visible only under ultraviolet light. This feature would assist in suspect identification.

Nightstick/Baton

The nightstick, or baton, is considered by some to be an alternative to firearms. As security equipment, it is not widely used. This weapon is often associated with brutality and has a more negative connotation for the public than firearms do. Another consideration is that a baton is a hindrance to officers in performing their routine duties. It constantly bangs into doorways, makes it awkward to sit, and makes it difficult to run. Those who favor the baton argue that it is a discriminating weapon that copes with the problem at hand and makes contact only with the intended person. It is difficult, however, to avoid head strikes in many cases. Paralysis or death may occur even days later as a result of subdural or bilateral hematoma.

The collapsible baton is gaining some favor and can be carried on the belt. The small compact size of this baton eliminates many of the arguments against the use of the regular nightstick or baton.

Bullet-Resistant Vests

The advent of the bullet-resistant vest used by many law enforcement agencies has spawned some interest for healthcare security programs. A survey of 79 hospitals, all in large U.S. cities, indicates very limited use of these vests. The hospitals surveyed averaged 318 beds; no hospital with fewer than 200 beds was included in the survey. Results of the survey indicated that 10 percent had formulated a policy on the use of vests. In most cases where vests are utilized, the policy provides that security officers buy their vest and that use is optional. The survey did not reveal any event or situation in the respondent hospitals in which a vest was a factor in preventing an injury.[13]

The Duty Belt

An important item in the security officer uniform is the duty belt, on which a good deal of this equipment will be arranged. The term "duty belt," in regard to this specific discussion, includes holsters, pouches, clips, and keepers. These items are often referred as the "leather," "gear," or "accessories." The traditional use of leather has given ground to the use of nylon. Nylon has certain advantages over leather:

- It is fairly easy to decontaminate

- It is durable and therefore lasts a long time

- It is lightweight

- It is scratch-resistant and won't stretch

- It is cost-competitive with leather

The duty belt should contain only the equipment needed to perform the job; thus, a strict policy of authorized equipment should be prepared. Security officers need not look like they are ready to wage battle.

Training

Deciding on the proper equipment to be used by security officers is an important first step, but it does not end there. The proper use of each item is essential. Initial officer training must be supplemented with periodic retraining. Equipping the officer with nonessential items needlessly increases the training time and the resulting program cost.

Security Operations Manual

The security operations manual brings together the security policy, standards, and general procedures. This manual should not be confused with the employee handbook, which basically contains the personnel policies of the organization. It is intended to furnish security officers with the information needed to perform their job effectively. The content of this manual varies from organization to organization. The typical manual includes the following general information:

1. Purpose and scope of the healthcare organization.

   - Table of organization

   - Key personnel (possibly with pictures)

   - Plot plans

2. Purpose and scope of the security program.

- Organizational chart
- Position descriptions (brief narratives)
- General and special orders
- Training program

3. Security records and reports.

- Types
- Intended utilization
- Distribution

4. General security information.

- Use and care of equipment
- Fire and safety information

The style, format, and content of the security manual are determined by individual program preference. A loose-leaf notebook is one style that permits the easy insertion of revised information or additional material.

TERMS

Interim Management: The temporary provision of day-to-day direction and control of departmental operations by either an acting organizational employee or an out-sourced individual.
Line Inspection: The review of actions of individuals by a supervisor having direct control over those individuals.
Staff Inspection: The review of function, procedures, policy, and outcomes of specified program components.
Special Police Authority: Legal authority (police powers) granted to an individual with certain restrictions. This authority is generally granted

in relation to specific job performance and while so engaged upon the property of the employer or in the performance of a specific function.

Full Time Equivalent (FTE): A unit of measurement related to employee(s) working the equivalent of 40 hours per week. One FTE could be an individual working 40 hours per week, two individuals each working 20 hours per week, three individuals each working 13.33 hours, etc.

RESOURCE INFORMATION

International Association for Healthcare Security and Safety (IAHSS)

International Healthcare Security and Safety Foundation (IHSSF)
Post Office Box 637
Lombard, Illinois 60148

American Society for Industrial Security (ASIS)
Healthcare Security Committee
1625 Prince Street
Alexandria, Virginia 22314

American Society for Healthcare Engineering (ASHE)
One North Franklin Street, #2700
Chicago, Illinois 60606

Presidents Committee on Employment of People with Disabilities
1321 F. Street NW #300
Washington, DC 20004

REFERENCES

1. Bonnie S. Michelman, "Supervisor Responsibilities," *Hospital Security Supervisory Training Manual and Study Guide*, International Association for Healthcare Security and Safety, 1988, p. 55.

2. Barry E. Stotts and Albert J. Sweet, "Employee Relations and Employee Appraisals," *Supervisory Training Manual*, p. 68.

3. Ibid., p. 88–89.

4. "The Spain Report: Rivas v. Nationwide Personal Security Corporation," 559 So. 2nd 668 (Fla. App. 3 Dist. 1990), 1991, p. G1–21.

5. J. Peter Leeds, "Structuring the Employment Interview to Select Medical Facility Security Officers," *Security Journal*, Vol. 10, No. 1, 1998, p. 30.

6. Office of Technology Assessment Staff, "Summary of Findings: Use of Integrity Tests for Pre-Employment Screening," *Security Journal*, Vol. 2, No. 1, 1991, p. 44.

7. "Security and Special Police Legal Update," Americans for Effective Law Enforcement, Inc., Thompson v. Borg-Warner d/b/a Burns Int. Security, No. C-94-4015 (MHP), U.S. Dist. Ct. N.D. Cal., 1998, p. 7–8.

8. David W. Arnold and Alan J Thieman, "Psychological Test in ADA's Wake," *Security Management*, January 1994, p. 44.

9. "Border Hospital's Guard Garb Ripped," *Modern Healthcare*, December 17, 1990, p. 8.

10. "Firearms Related Security and Special Police Update," Americans for Effective Law Enforcement, Inc., September 1996, p. 136.

11. Dennis McCauley, "Gasping For Breath," *Police*, July, 1996, pp. 56–58.

12. "Confronting and Dealing with Problems of Latex-Based Products," *Hospital Security and Safety Management*, Vol. 17, No. 11, March, 1997, pp. 5–7.

13. Brian Bakos, "The Utilization of Bullet-Resistant Vests in Healthcare Facilities," unpublished research study, July 1993, pp. 1–11.

CHAPTER 8

Training the Security Force

The need for adequate training of security personnel is vigorously espoused by management and line personnel alike. It is a subject that gets constant attention at security meetings and seminars, is probed during security reviews and audits, gets considerable space in magazines, newsletters, and journals, is sanctioned by consumers and providers, and is the basis of many lawsuits. However, this almost insatiable quest for proper training appears to break down at the design and implementation stage in many healthcare security programs. One of the most critical challenges—and one of the most basic responsibilities—of the security administrator is to provide the means for each person in the security department to achieve the skill-level required to perform the function as stated in the job description. A good security officer training program requires a plan that addresses everything from identifying needs to verification of skill levels and documentation. The proper training of the security staff is a direct reflection on the security administrator's commitment to quality.

Certain basic elements or steps in the training process must be addressed and tailored to each healthcare organization. There should be a combination of generic healthcare security training with training specific to the organization. An example of this blending is that of report preparation. The basics of how to collect information and prepare a report are somewhat the same for all organizations. However, the types of reports and methods utilized to accomplish the completion of a report are specific to each organization. For example, the International Association for Healthcare Security and Safety (IAHSS) basic training program provides a generic approach to healthcare security officer training as a foundation to be supplemented by training relative to specific facility security program tasks. Other important points to remember include:

- Job descriptions should provide the basic source of job task analysis to pinpoint specific skill levels required. Policies and procedures of the entire organization, not just security policy and procedure, will further identify skill level needs.

- Determine performance objectives, which in turn will be utilized to develop the knowledge required of the security officer to competently complete the tasks identified. The objective is what the trainee must know. Without clearly stated objectives, there can be no competency-based training.

- Develop measurement standards in order to determine whether the objectives of the training endeavor have been accomplished. The objective is to determine whether there was a sufficient transfer of information from instruction to actual situation performance.

- Develop curriculum and select training methods and materials.

The Wackenhut Training Institute, in Coral Gables, Florida, has taken an emerging adult learning model as its approach to training. This model is known as "andragogy," a term developed by Malcome Knowles, a widely known adult educator. Andragogy embraces the following four tenets of adult education:

1. Adults want to be self-directed as opposed to instructor-directed.

2. Adults bring unique life experiences to the learning process.

3. Adult learning is linked to what adults consider relevant.

4. Adults want an immediate application of learned knowledge.

This model is a very practical approach to healthcare security training; however, it is more difficult for both student and instructor. Students must stop thinking of themselves as students and realize they are adult learners with a responsibility in the training process. Likewise, instructors must think of themselves as facilitators of adult learning.[1]

Litigation has been a powerful driving force in the increase in healthcare security officer training. Claims that healthcare organizations have failed to provide necessary training are used with much success in lawsuits, especially those involving weapons, physical force, false arrests, and civil rights issues. The responsibility for the adequate training of security officers rests squarely on the organization. In fact, an increasingly common practice in public police agencies is for officers to file suit against their supervisors when they can show that an injury or an actionable mistake occurred as the result of inadequate training. This type of litigation is not yet common in healthcare security, but should provide food for thought.

Meanwhile, it seems there are never enough officers to really get the job done, and we often think more is better. The need for better-trained officers is expressed far less frequently. Ironically, although a trained security officer can be at least twice as productive as a well-intentioned untrained officer, it is usually easier to obtain money for an extra position than for training. The number of security personnel is often mistakenly used to determine the level of protection.

In healthcare facilities, extensive training is apparent in almost all departments, but security officer training generally lags. The medical care arena focuses on training and continuous in-service education at almost every level. Dietitians, medical technicians, medical records clerks, nursing assistants, registered nurses, and environmental services personnel undergo training in one form or another. Our demand for the highest quality healthcare requires ongoing education for healthcare providers of every description. Security should be no exception.

One of the basic hurdles that influences training programs is security officer turnover. In-house security programs, except very large ones, simply cannot provide extensive formal instruction for one or two officers. On the other hand, in-house programs generally have more funds for training than do contract security agencies, which are limited to providing services at a fixed cost. An organized security officer training program will reduce turnover and improve morale. Well-trained officers who know they are competent exhibit a higher level of job interest and job satisfaction than others do.

TRAINING CONCEPTS

The term "training" includes pre-entry training and, more importantly, continued training. Security officers are often classified as "trained" or "not trained." This concept should yield to the more appropriate idea of *level* of training.

There is a difference between training and education. Christopher Hertig, an instructor at York College of Pennsylvania, makes such a distinction. He states, "Training is an intensive process whereby an employee's job behavior is modified. Training prepares and enables a person to perform job tasks at a greater level of efficiency. Education is knowledge about something. It's the understanding of concepts and principles that enable a person to grow professionally; knowledge that provides one with an appreciation of various job functions. Education teaches the 'whys'; training teaches the 'hows.'"[2]

Training must be relevant. As simple and basic as this consideration seems, some training is given merely to fill the allotted time or because an instructor is available. An often-neglected area of training is the operational aspect of the healthcare delivery system. Security officers should learn how various departments and sections of the healthcare system operate to understand better what they are protecting. The better officers understand the operations, the formal and informal hierarchy, and the history, objectives, and goals of the organization, the better equipped they will be to carry out their responsibilities.

Types of Training

Considerable dialogue and printed materials are available relative to the type and content of training appropriate for healthcare security officers. There are three major types of training: basic training, specialized program training, and elective training. Basic, or generic, training is the basic security training applicable to virtually any healthcare security officer. The IAHSS training programs described in this text are considered basic areas of training that should be supplemented by specialized training. Both basic training and specialized training would be considered the organization-mandated officer-training program. Specialized training takes into consideration the function and responsibility of the officer in a specific organizational setting. Elective training involves training or education that is generally not mandatory. It is usually taken by the officer who has a personal interest or personal objective for participating in specific self-improvement activities. These training activities are generally pursued on the individual's own time.

Table 8-1 IAHSS Basic Training Standard, Program Subject Areas, and Units

The Healthcare Organization (2)	Pharmacy (1)
Security as a Service Organization (1)	Emergency and Mental Health Units (1)
Public/Community/Customer Relations (1)	Support Units/Ancillary Services (1)
Employee/Labor Relations (1)	Healthcare Vulnerabilities/Risks (1)
Patrol and Post Procedures/Techniques (3)	Access Control Concepts/Systems (1)
Security Interactions with Patients, Visitors, Employees (1)	Physical Security Measures (1)
Self Protection/Defense (1)	Equipment Usage/Maintenance (1)
Professional Conduct and Self-Development (1)	Basic Safety Concepts (1)
Crisis Intervention (2)	Fire Prevention (2)
Interview and Investigation (2)	Fire Control/Response (1)
Report Preparation/Writing (2)	Bomb Threats/Procedures (1)
Report Utilization (1)	Disaster Control/Response (1)
Judicial Process/Courtroom Procedure/ Testimony (1)	Civil Disasters (1)
Nursing Units (2)	Criminal and Civil Law (2)
Business Office (1)	Narcotics and Dangerous Drugs (1)
	Public Safety Interactions/Liason (1)

IAHSS BASIC SECURITY OFFICER TRAINING

The IAHSS has developed a 40-hour basic training program for security officers. The program, which is actually a standard, was developed in the mid-1970s and has stood the test of time, undergoing only minor changes. The standard represents a consensus of what healthcare security administrators felt should be included in a basic training curriculum. Table 8-1 presents the subject areas and the number of hours of instruction, or self-study, devoted to each.

The successful completion of this training program leads to basic certification by the IAHSS. Certification is granted after the candidate passes a closed-book examination, which is monitored by a senior member of the IAHSS. The examination is based primarily on the *IAHSS Basic Training Manual and Study Guide for Healthcare Security Officers* (2nd Edition, 1995). The examination currently consists of 100 true/false questions. (The IAHSS Education and Training committee is studying the feasibility of an on-line computer course instruction and examination.) One need not be employed as a healthcare security officer to become certified; the Association has certified well over 25,000 individuals.

The curriculum centers on understanding the healthcare environment and its relationship to security. This approach differs from police training, which exposes security officers to much irrelevant material and encourages a philosophy that is often at variance with the loss prevention management approach.

Several formats are currently used to prepare the student for the certification examination. One of the most popular is an IAHSS chapter project. This approach ensures a maximum number of students and utilizes chapter members as instructors and discussion leaders. A high level of training is ensured, costs are shared, and each organization need not devise a unique program. Another format is training through a community college or vocational college. Some colleges offer a regular credit course structured around the standard; others offer an institute-type course that may or may not award credit hours. The college assumes certain standards, which gives the instruction a certain amount of inherent credibility. The student must still successfully pass the IAHSS certification examination. In-house and contractor training formats vary from formal classes, to facilitated study groups, to supervised self-study or a combination of these approaches.

Figure 8-1 shows the layout and design of the current certification certificate.

IAHSS ADVANCED SECURITY OFFICER TRAINING

The most recent training program offered by IAHSS is the Advanced Security Officer course of instruction. A manual and study guide is available for this 20-hour program. It is intended that the student complete the basic certification program as a prerequisite to participating in the advanced training program. A certificate of completion is available only for the IAHSS basic certified officer. In order to obtain the advanced training certificate, a senior member of IAHSS must complete a training program record application form attesting to the successful completion of training by the applicant. Table 8-2 lists the advanced training program curriculum, with the number of hours for each subject.

Figure 8-1 IAHSS Basic Training Certification Certificate

Table 8-2 IAHSS Advanced Training Standard Subject Areas and Units

Security Awareness and Crime Prevention (2)	Enhanced Customer Service (2)
Premise Liability (1)	Methods of Patrol (1)
Investigative Techniques, Reports, and Procedures (2)	Off-Campus Security and Safety (1)
Workplace Violence (2)	Patient Risk Groups (2)
Security and Patient Interactions (2)	Special Security Concerns (1)
Security in Sensitive Areas (1)	Security Technology (1)
Critical Incident Response (1)	Advancing Professionalism (1)

Table 8-3 IAHSS Supervisory Training Program Subject Areas

The Supervisory training program is based on a twenty-hour (unit) IAHSS training standard as shown. The number shown in parentheses indicates the number of units for each subject area:

Introduction to Supervision (1)	Effective Communications/Management Skills (2)
Contemporary Issues in Healthcare (1)	Self Improvement (1)
Supervisory Responsibilities (2)	Civil Liability and the Supervisor (2)
Employee Relations and Employee Appraisals (2)	Safety (2)
Authority and Control (1)	Budgeting/Cost Control (1)
Leadership (2)	Principles of Customer Relations (1)
Handling Complaints and Grievances (2)	Professionalism and Ethics (1)

IAHSS SUPERVISORY TRAINING

The IAHSS also offers a 20-hour supervisory training program that includes a manual and study guide. This program is intended for persons who are in current supervisory positions or persons who want to prepare themselves for supervision. It has been reported that security officers have also completed this program so that they better understand the supervisory process. This program is separated into 14 different subject areas, as shown in Table 8-3. A certificate of completion is available for this program.

IAHSS SAFETY TRAINING

The safety training program offered by IAHSS is intended to provide an overview of healthcare safety as it relates to the security officer. This 20-hour program includes a manual and study guide. The program contains thirteen different subject areas, as shown in Table 8-4. There is also a certificate of completion available for this program.

Table 8-5 lists a summary of the IAHSS training programs.

Table 8-4 IAHSS Safety Training Standard Subject Areas and Units

The Safety training program is based on a twenty-hour (unit) IAHSS training standard as shown. The number shown in parentheses indicates the number of units for each subject category:

Regulatory Agencies (1)
Healthcare Safety Programs (2)
Accidents and Injuries (2)
Fire Safety (2)
Emergency Preparedness (2)

Equipment Management/Personal Protection (2)
Infection Control Programs (1)

Special Healthcare Settings (2)
Radiation Safety (1)
Construction/Renovation Safety (1)
Hazard Surveillance (1)
Hazardous Materials and Emergency Response (1)
Hazardous Materials/Waste Management (2)

Table 8-5 Summary of IAHSS Training Programs

Programs for Healthcare Security Officers	Hours	Certificate	Certification
Basic Training	40	No	Yes
Advanced Training	20	Yes*	No
Safety Training	20	Yes	No
Supervisory Training	20	Yes	No

* Basic Training Certification Required.

SPECIALIZED OR SUPPLEMENTAL TRAINING

The specialized training developed by the organization is intended to be specific to the needs, philosophy, and concerns of that organization. For example, weapons training would pertain to the weapons utilized in the security program. Specialized training may also build on areas of basic training. For example, the IAHSS basic training includes general crisis intervention; however, a specific organization may want to supplement training in this area by using a nationally recognized program or an in-house-developed program.

An example of developing specific programs to be part of the overall security training program can be found at Barnes-Jewish Hospital (St. Louis) and St. Louis Children's Hospital. There, the security staff

Table 8-6 Subjects and Topics of an Annual Security Officer Training Program at Barnes-Jewish Hospital (St. Louis) and St. Louis Children's Hospital

Annual Supplemental Security Training Courses

Workplace as a Whole	Security Concerns and Issues		Weapons
• Change Management • Cultural Diversity • Service Excellence	• Domestic Violence • Gang Awareness • Persons with Disabilities	• Environmental Issues • Gerontological Issues • Risk Management	• Enhanced Firearms • Impact Weapons

researches, designs, and teaches many of what they refer to as "supplemental courses." At the end of each course, the attendees grade the class and evaluate the instructor from an effectiveness viewpoint. A recent annual training program developed by the security staff consisted of some 11 different training areas, as shown in Table 8-6.[3]

Healthcare security officers who perform their job correctly spend more than 50 percent of their time providing general services. This is a key element of a successful security program. Thus, training for improved customer relations should receive high priority by the security department. The term "customer service" is just as appropriate in healthcare security as it is in any other security setting. Employees, patients, staff, and visitors are all customers that security serves. When providing service, security professionals have the opportunity to show their customers that they are part of the healthcare team and believe in its mission.

Sensitivity and de-escalation-type training is also important. Sensitivity training gives security officers alternatives to the use of force when dealing with people. It takes a humanistic—or sympathetic—approach to solving people's problems and tries to provide insight into why people behave the way they do. Some healthcare organizations develop and provide their own training programs to deal with disruptive behavior, while others utilize an outside source for this training.

ELECTIVE TRAINING

Elective training is generally considered to be for individual self-improvement, but may have some relevance to the employee's job. Healthcare organizations may offer classes such as general computer training or cardiopulmonary recessitation, neither of which may be required of the security officer's position. There are also numerous one and two-day workshops and seminars offered in communities in which the individual may wish to participate.

ON-THE-JOB TRAINING

The amount and quality of pre-service training for the new security officer is critical to the success of the officer and to the delivery of high quality services. Unfortunately, much pre-service training consists of on-the-job instruction of a new officer by another officer. The disadvantages of this method are obvious. New officers become only as proficient as their teachers, and they often learn the wrong way from the beginning. On the other hand, a formal 40-, 60-, or 80-hour course cannot be conducted for one or two newly hired officers.

This dilemma illustrates the difficulty of outlining a preservice training program where there are many variables, such as the size of the security force and the availability of resources. The most appropriate approach for a security force of three or four members must inevitably differ from that of a security department of 30 or more officers.

Although on-the-job training (OJT) has its shortcomings, it is necessary for providing officers with hands-on experience. There is no substitute for demonstrating the tasks that must be completed. A failing of many OJT programs is the lack of a formulated structure. The OJT trainer should use a checklist when providing instruction. Figure 8-2 is an example of an OJT pre-service training checklist. Both the OJT trainer and the trainee sign the checklist after the instruction is completed, and this checklist becomes part of the officer's permanent training record. This preservice training should be followed up by some form of competency testing.

	ON THE JOB TRAINING (OJT)		LPH	
Employee's Name	CHECK SHEET			Facility

Orientation and OJT are very important components of an overall training program. In order to assure that the vital components of a security/parking officer's position are adequately conveyed and adequately understood, the following check list is to be used for documentation purposes.

Please verify the training for each item is covered. The trainer, as well as the trainee, shall initial next to each item. Upon completion of the entire check sheet it shall be forwarded to the corporate office for inclusion in the employee's record.

AREA OF TRAINING	INITIALS TRAINEE	INITIALS TRAINER	DATE
FACILITY ORIENTATION: Outbuildings, Arapahoe medical plaza I, II, and III, alarm locations and access codes, trouble areas, PBX, emergency department, helipad procedure, hospital boundaries, vehicle location, introduction to facility representative, and to other key people.			
RADIO USAGE: When receiving a call or calling dispatch, if it is at all possible try and utilize a nearby telephone in order to limit air traffic for dispatch and other units who may have an emergency situation. Make sure that you abide by the proper radio protocol when answering a call for service as well as when transmitting information. (Refer to facility orders for proper protocol). Make sure that you properly charge the radio battery before using the radios. A battery should be charged once every 12 hours to help build the memory.			
COMMUNICATIONS CENTER: Facility direct dial number, master name index file, license plate information, emergency calls, call outs, and explanation of dispatch.			
BREAKS: A full time officer working an eight to ten hour shift, is allowed two fifteen minute breaks and a thirty minute lunch period. Bear in mind that your breaks are taken on the clock, therefore, any calls for service take priority. Breaks should be taken in authorized areas i.e., cafeteria, employee lounge, and Code 7. Do not take breaks in vehicles or other areas.			
FACILITY ORDERS: The facility orders are located in the security office. Facility orders detail specific procedures that are unique to Littleton Hospital. Please use the fourteen point plan to educate yourself and learn the hospital specific areas detailed in the orders. This will be supplemented with the hands on training received by a supervisor and a duty officer.			
SHIFT CHANGE: Location of shift change areas, times of coverage, proper visibility, and escorts.			
DAILY ACTIVITY REPORTS: DARs are daily logs that outline duties that need to be performed on a daily basis in addition to calls for service. If you cannot perform a duty at the time that is specified on the DAR, then make certain that it is logged down on the DAR or there is a report to justify the delay.			

Figure 8-2 Example of an OJT Preservice Security Officer Training Checklist (Courtesy of Healthcare Security Services, Denver, Colorado)

TRAINING RESOURCES AND RECORDS REQUIREMENTS

Training does not just happen—it requires considerable planning. The planning begins with identifying the curriculum and the resources available for training. Instructors, lesson plans, training material, methods of presentation, evaluation, competency measurements, and documentation are primary elements of the training program.

Instructors/Facilitators

Because continuing education is prevalent in almost all aspects of the healthcare delivery system, an excellent source of security instructors/facilitators can be found in the organization's staff. They are generally quite willing to assist other departments in training, and no one is better able to relate to a specific area's security problems than the person responsible for that area or particular function. Generally, an hour is sufficient to accomplish an acceptable level of general training for a specific operating department or function. One-third of this time might be devoted to explaining how the department interacts as a part of the healthcare team; one-third to the department as it relates to security (vulnerabilities, expectations, policy); and the final third to questions by security personnel. This allows security officers to question certain practices and to suggest ways to improve the security posture of the department. Often, a questionable practice can be explained by the departmental supervisor, giving security officers better insight into the rationale behind the practice.

The use of in-house staff as instructors has several important benefits. Staff instructors are forced to give some attention to their own work as it relates to security. It may be the first real look they have given to their security vulnerabilities. In addition, rapport often develops between the staff member and the security department and its officers. Finally, staff instructors may come to appreciate the security program more as they relate to the professional approach of a trained security force.

Instructors/facilitators from the community are also available to assist in the training program. Likely sources for instructors include insurance carriers, the Red Cross organization, the Occupational Safety and Health Administration, state safety agencies, fire prevention bureaus, community relations agencies, healthcare attorneys, and Offices of Emergency Preparedness, to name a few.

Training Materials

According to Richard Cook, president of Kottcamp & Young, Inc., a management consulting firm, all knowledge is gained through the five senses. Sight accounts for nearly 85 percent of learning; hearing, approximately 10 percent; smell, about 5 percent; feel and taste, negligible amounts. Thus, in training, one should not rely solely on lectures.

Technology has brought innovation to traditional training methods. Computers, videodiscs, and touch screens are now used to train personnel. Security trainers can effectively use relatively inexpensive, in-house-produced videotape presentations. With this medium, one can tailor the information to individual healthcare environments. Healthcare organizations have videotape equipment readily available. In addition, many commercial training tapes are available that cover a wide range of healthcare security topics. Interactive videodisc (VDI) technology, which combines these three tools, is also currently used for a variety of training applications.

A popular method of training is to include training topics in a periodic bulletin that also recaps past security incidents. This method can be used advantageously when security personnel are assigned to different facilities, as in a multi-facility security system. Meanwhile, an unusual system of training by telephone is used by various organizations. Security officers call a telephone number each week while on the job to hear a taped training message.

Computer-Based Training (CBT)

As computers become more and more a staple in healthcare security programs, their use for training is also increasing. Software is readily available that enables program managers to develop in-house CBT. Commercial training companies and associations also produce products utilizing the CBT approach. Among the advantages of this type of training are:

- It eliminates scheduling conflicts of getting a training group together for the classroom approach

- Trainees can progress at their own pace

- It reduces trainee stress since an instructor or facilitator is not present

- It facilitates learning through immediate feedback

- It saves money for training large numbers of personnel

- It gives consistent information to all trainees

On the other hand, CBT training is not suited for certain types of training, such as demonstrating competency in physically restraining a patient. In addition, there is no opportunity for a trainee to ask questions or benefit from group interaction.[4]

Records

No matter how simple or sophisticated a training program is, proper training records must be maintained. A record outlining the training accomplished by each officer is mandatory. A sample training record is shown in Table 8-7.

Training records can be entered into the computer and only printed on demand for a specific purpose. In one program the officers training record is brought up on the screen during the officer's periodic formal evaluation. In another program, each officer's training record is sent to the officer on an annual basis asking for the officers to review its completeness.

A standard of the IAHSS is that the healthcare organization maintains an individual training record. This record is to be provided to the officer upon termination of employment. Legal situations will often focus on the training provided individual officers. Complete and accurate records become very important in these situations.

TERMS

IAHSS Application for Basic Training Certification Examination: This form must be completed by individuals seeking to be examined for

Table 8-7 A Sample of a Security Officer Training Record

United Memorial Hospital: Security Training Record				
Name:		Employee #:	Position:	
Date:	Subject	Duration	Instructor & Affiliation	Describe Competency Measurement

obtaining the basic training certification status. A senior member of the IAHSS who has agreed to administer the examination must be designated on this form. The specified certification fee must accompany this application form.

IAHSS Training Program Record and Request for Certificate: This form must be completed by a senior member of the IAHSS or by a Certified Healthcare Protection Professional (CHPA) when requesting a certificate of completion for the Advanced, Supervisory, and Safety Training programs. There is a separate form for each of these programs.

REFERENCES

1. Michael E. Goodboe, "Should Security Practice Andragogy?" *Security Management,* April 1995, p. 65.

2. Christopher A. Hertig, "Education Teaches the 'Whys': Training Teaches the 'Hows,'" *Security Magazine*, August 1989, p. 29.

3. Fred J. Jackson, CPP, and Jeanne M. Locklear, "A Few Good Men," *Security Management*, September 1997, p. 89–91.

CHAPTER 9

Deployment of the Security Staff

Security operations are primarily concerned with security force deployment, which includes fixed-post assignments, patrols, response to requests for service, providing general services, and response to critical incidents. These areas often overlap, with considerable interaction. Each is dependent on the others for support, and their relationship combines the individual elements into a viable security staff deployment pattern.

How well the security department carries out its assigned responsibility will depend in large part on planning, controlling, evaluating, and modifying personnel in the field. Security operations require changes in operation, however slight, almost daily. The proper deployment of security personnel is a key element of an effective protection program and the cost of personnel mandates the efficient utilization as a major management responsibility.

Although many healthcare security programs are understaffed, the improper deployment of personnel is a major deficiency in many protection systems. Despite the professional growth of healthcare security—with the availability of written materials, multimedia information, seminars, and consultants—many programs still operate with excessive cost.

The objective method of determining how many security personnel are deployed is first to determine the functions and the activity to be accomplished. Reference to the number of personnel required is a rather inexact measurement; personnel requirements are better expressed in terms of full-time equivalents (FTEs) or hours of service.

Personnel should ideally be deployed on the basis of objective criteria; however, this is not always the case. A sudden rash of security problems, or a major incident, can pressure administration to respond quickly. The reaction is often the addition of security personnel, either because the security administrator does not know what else to recommend or because the decision is made by someone higher in the organization. It is generally the quickest thing to do. A short reaction time and visible action can be most important under many circumstances.

There is some misconception that adding elements of security following a serious incident will commit the organization to indefinitely continuing the added protection. This is not entirely true unless program deficiencies existed before the incident and the response merely put in place program elements that should have been part of the security program without regard to the incident.

Public, staff, and patients expect a responsible reaction to a serious incident. The decision to discontinue the added protection, such as additional security staff, must be made based on the current security risks and vulnerabilities. It is recommended that a formal review and evaluation be accomplished after the incident to determine the continuance of the reactionary elements of protection. It is quite possible that this review will result in a program change either on a temporary basis or on an ongoing basis. This review should be documented and should include the rationale for decisions made.

The skill level and degree of productivity of each security officer is a factor in determining the number of officers required for field operations. In addition, the number of security personnel required is often affected by security hardware applications and organizational policies. For example, the facility that secures its perimeter, designates street use of entry/exit points, and electronically monitors access needs fewer security personnel than does the facility that operates in a generally open environment.

DEPLOYMENT OBJECTIVES

The objective of deployment is to provide the right number of personnel at the right time and in the right place. In simplified terms, an officer should not be assigned to check the elevator penthouse when visiting hours are closing or shifts are changing. The four primary goals in deployment are to assign officers to times and areas of high risk; to provide rapid response to critical incidents; to cover peak workload times; and to provide high visibility.

Past incident report records and risk analysis data provide the information required to determine areas and times of high-risk potential. The computer has replaced the pin map in graphically portraying the types and locations of reported incidents. However, maps, plot plans, and building configuration documents are still useful in portraying certain information. The engineering or planning and construction departments usually have these types of documents already prepared. Incidents can be recorded by time period or type. The accumulated statistical data are useful for deployment planning and for patrolling officers, who can obtain at a glance a picture of the problems in a particular patrol area.

To understand the principle of risk potential, consider a pharmacy that operates between 8:00 A.M. and 10:00 P.M. If there have been no past incidents of armed robbery on which to base a patrol deployment, the risk potential is the guideline. The period from 5:00 P.M. to 10:00 P.M. presents a greater possibility of robbery than during the normal workday. After 5:00 P.M. fewer pharmacy employees are on duty, fewer patrons are in the area, and the hours of darkness naturally provide better escape opportunities.

A short response time relative to critical incidents is very important to the success of the security program. The entire complex must be patrolled in a manner that provides approximately equal response time for critical incidents from all areas of the facility. As response time is shortened, the probability of successfully handling incidents is greatly enhanced. Minimal response time is perhaps the most important factor that a security force can use to build confidence in the security system. Security and law enforcement groups are often judged more on how long it took them to arrive than on their appearance or handling of the incident.

Covering peak periods of requested and scheduled services is an important goal of deployment. This information is obtained from the facility's previous experience and depends on the functions of the protection program. The number of calls for service is an important factor in determining how the organization feels about the security service. A large number of calls for service indicates a high level of acceptance of and confidence in the security department. Response time to provide routine requested services is also important. This response will not be as immediate as that for emergencies; however, a good security force will provide service as soon as possible for even the most routine of services.

Another goal of deployment is high visibility of the security force. This practice provides a maximum protection image and a feeling of security and safety for employees, patients, and visitors alike. The importance of this factor cannot be overemphasized.

SCHEDULING THE SECURITY STAFF

A major administrative function of any security program is that of scheduling security personnel into work shifts. Scheduling of security staff does not mean merely putting down names to fill in the open spaces on a schedule. Scheduling and post assignment have somewhat the same basic objective of deploying the most appropriate officer to cover a specific assignment. Scheduling comes first and generally refers to shifts and days of the week. Post assignment is the utilization of officers who are scheduled for a particular shift. Thus, appropriate staff must be scheduled for a shift before a post assignment can be effected in the proper manner. Scheduling and post assignment are obviously synonymous when there is only one officer scheduled for a particular shift.

In both scheduling and post assignment, the factors for consideration include skill level; post specific training; appropriate image; gender; age; culture; language spoken; physical ability; and being properly licensed for the assignment if required. All these factors must be taken into consideration, without violating discrimination laws, to assign the best person for the specific assignment.

There are generally two types of schedules—the master schedule, which covers a specific time period in advance, and the working schedule, which is a day-to-day document that reflects the actual officer who filled the specific shift. The master schedule, when properly constructed, can be modified each day to reflect any changes in actual shift and/or post assignment. This record of persons actually filling an assignment, as opposed to the projected persons, becomes the official document of coverage and should be maintained for historical purposes. Compensation records become a backup record to prove validity of the schedule if such action becomes necessary.

The computer is quite helpful in maintaining scheduling assignments and in documenting all security programs, and is essential in large programs. The computer can, among other functions, search for open shifts, double assignments for a given officer, and assist in identifying officers available.

There is a contrast in the length of the work shift between in-house and out-sourced staffing models. In the common eight-hour shift, the in-house program typically utilizes an eight-and-a-half-hour shift, allowing one half hour for a meal break. The out-sourced model generally schedules officers for shift coverage for eight hours, allowing the officer to take a meal break during paid working hours. The latter approach is considered the best practice for two primary reasons. The most important reason is that the officer is on duty for the entire shift and, thus, is not allowed to leave the property except for work-related purposes. Thus, a meal break can be taken when the workload permits. The second reason is that the officer is available during the meal break to answer calls for service. In other words, the officer is always in service. This is very important when there is only one security officer on duty at the facility.

The basic reason most healthcare security personnel are uniformed is to provide visibility to persons being protected and a visible deterrent to would-be criminals. Those who are being protected develop a sense of well-being when they can see the security effort in action. In some facilities, employees will not go into certain areas or get out of their vehicles unless they can see a security officer.

Employees expect to see the security officer at certain times when arriving or leaving the workplace. A problem develops when that officer is called away from normal deployment to perform another activity, such as answering a call for service. Employees might then complain that security personnel are not where they are supposed to be and are thus neglecting their job—or worse yet a serious incident might occur. There are seldom sufficient security personnel to assure consistent preventive deployment patterns.

DEPLOYMENT PATTERNS AND CONCEPTS

Although vulnerabilities, the use of security hardware, the layout, size, and location of the facility, and its philosophies are factors that alter security officer coverage plans, some basic deployment patterns can generally be applied.

In extremely small hospitals that use only eight hours of security officer coverage per day, the hours from 6:00 P.M. to 2:00 A.M. generally provide the best coverage plan. In this coverage plan, the security officer reports for duty at about the time managers and supervisors are leaving for the day. The officer is present to cover the period of highest patient visitor load (7:00 P.M. to 9:00 P.M.), and after the visitors are gone, the facility access points can be secured. The officer is then available to assist in evening and night shift changes. The movement of personnel and the requests for services generally settle down shortly after 12:30 or 1:00

A.M., allowing the officer to conduct a thorough facility check before going off duty.

To cover a facility from 6:00 P.M. to 2:00 A.M. seven days per week, 56 labor hours are required. By extending this coverage by 32 hours per week, the facility can maintain continuous coverage from 6:00 P.M. Friday to 2:00 A.M. Monday, along with 6:00 P.M. to 2:00 A.M. coverage Monday through Thursday. Of course, this coverage pattern does not fit all facilities, and the available labor hours must be scheduled for the greatest benefit. If problems develop or new vulnerabilities present themselves, coverage must always be shifted to meet these needs.

One should not think only in terms of eight-hour blocks. A 10-hour shift from 6:00 P.M. to 4:00 A.M. or 5:00 P.M. to 3:00 A.M. would improve coverage significantly over the above-described 6:00 P.M. to 2:00 A.M. plan. The most advantageous deployment plan may require 4-, 6-, 10-, or 12-hour shifts. Split shifts may also be used to great advantage to provide the maximum coverage required.

Ten-hour shifts are becoming more popular for several reasons. Employees put a high premium on maximum leisure time. The 10-hour shift allows a four-day workweek, which in effect yields a three-day weekend. A four-day workweek also benefits employees financially by reducing work expenses, such as meals and commuting costs. The 10-hour shift also allows organizations to work an officer 50 hours per week if necessary and still give the officer two days off.

POST ASSIGNMENTS

Security officer deployment plans normally consist of a combination of post assignments. The variety of post assignments can be separated into four distinct categories: fixed post, modified fixed post, sectored or zone patrol, and unrestricted patrol. The latter two assignments are often referred to as roving patrols. Each of these post assignments has specific objectives and purposes; however, all are intended to provide a degree of activity accountability. The most accountable assignment is the fixed post.

The fixed post is a stationary post that is located at a specific location for a specific time period. A true fixed post requires the assigned officer to be relieved for any absence whatsoever. The fixed post is expensive and is generally used to provide a certain function, such as an access control point, operations center, communications control point, or other process center. It is also used to provide a presence, or visibility. Officers in fixed-post assignments obviously cannot be available to respond to calls for service. If fixed-post officers respond to calls, employees do not see them, which can lead to complaints and even legal problems should an incident occur while the officer is absent. Employees depend on this protection being in place, but on the other hand they have difficulty understanding why officers cannot leave the post to render routine assistance. For example, an employee who has locked his keys in a car must wait for a patrol officer to be dispatched to render assistance.

A modified fixed post is used in a number of programs. The post is left unoccupied at times to conduct patrol rounds or to answer a call for service. A good example is a modified fixed post located in an emergency department. The security officer may be responsible for the general area, including the parking lots outside the emergency area. The officer may at certain times leave the post to conduct a short security patrol or to assist patients or visitors within the general emergency department area.

Another variation of the modified fixed post is the random rotation to two or more fixed-post locations. For example, three areas of the facility—the main lobby, the emergency room, and the loading dock—may be designated as rotating posts. Security officers assigned to this type of post divide their time between the three areas on a non-patterned schedule. They are not free to patrol other areas of the facility; they must be in one of the three designated areas at all times.

Sectored (zone) patrol and unrestricted patrol are basic methods of deployment, but are still considered to be post assignments. The purpose of these roving patrols is to achieve security objectives through security officers who move within prescribed areas. Their actions can be divided into four primary categories: response to critical incidents, inspection services, routine preventive patrol, and response to provide courtesy or routine services. Sectored patrols, in which the patrol area is strictly defined, are used in larger programs when a patrol officer is assigned to a given area for a specific period of time. In unrestricted patrols, officers are free to patrol the entire complex. During any given shift, a single officer may be assigned to a variety of post assignments.

BASIC PATROL DEPLOYMENT PLANS

Security officers who perform patrol duties should be assigned to specifically defined areas. The officers are thus responsible for the protection of a given area and are held accountable for performing the prescribed activities.

Every facility has certain areas or sections that require a greater frequency of patrol. These more vulnerable areas can often be serviced by overlapping patrol patterns, shown in Figure 9-1.

Patrol area assignments may be altered for various shifts or during shifts in response to the number of personnel assigned to patrol an area or to variations in vulnerability. For example, a facility with two patrol officers on the 4:00 P.M. to 12:00 A.M. shift may deploy one officer internally and one externally, except for various times when parking lots and other external areas are vulnerable to assault, vandalism, or breaking and entering of vehicles. At these times, both officers may be deployed externally. The following schedule illustrates how such a deployment plan might work.

Patrol Officer One
4:00 P.M. to 5:00 P.M.: Entire grounds and parking areas
5:00 P.M. to 7:00 P.M.: North half of external area
7:00 P.M. to 10:30 P.M.: Entire internal area
10:30 P.M. to 12:00 A.M.: South half of external area

Patrol Officer Two
4:00 P.M. to 5:00 P.M.: Entire internal area
5:00 P.M. to 7:00 P.M.: South half of external area
7:00 P.M. to 10:30 P.M.: Entire grounds and parking area
10:30 P.M. to 12:00 A.M.: North half of external area

In this example, each of the officers patrols both internally and externally. This allows the officers to patrol the same area so that one may find a condition or problem the other officer may have missed. It is also desirable that the officers share in the exposure to adverse weather conditions.

Another method of providing increased patrol coverage is to assign to one officer a patrol area that covers two or more smaller patrol areas. This type of deployment is commonly assigned to a patrol

Deployment of the Security Staff 223

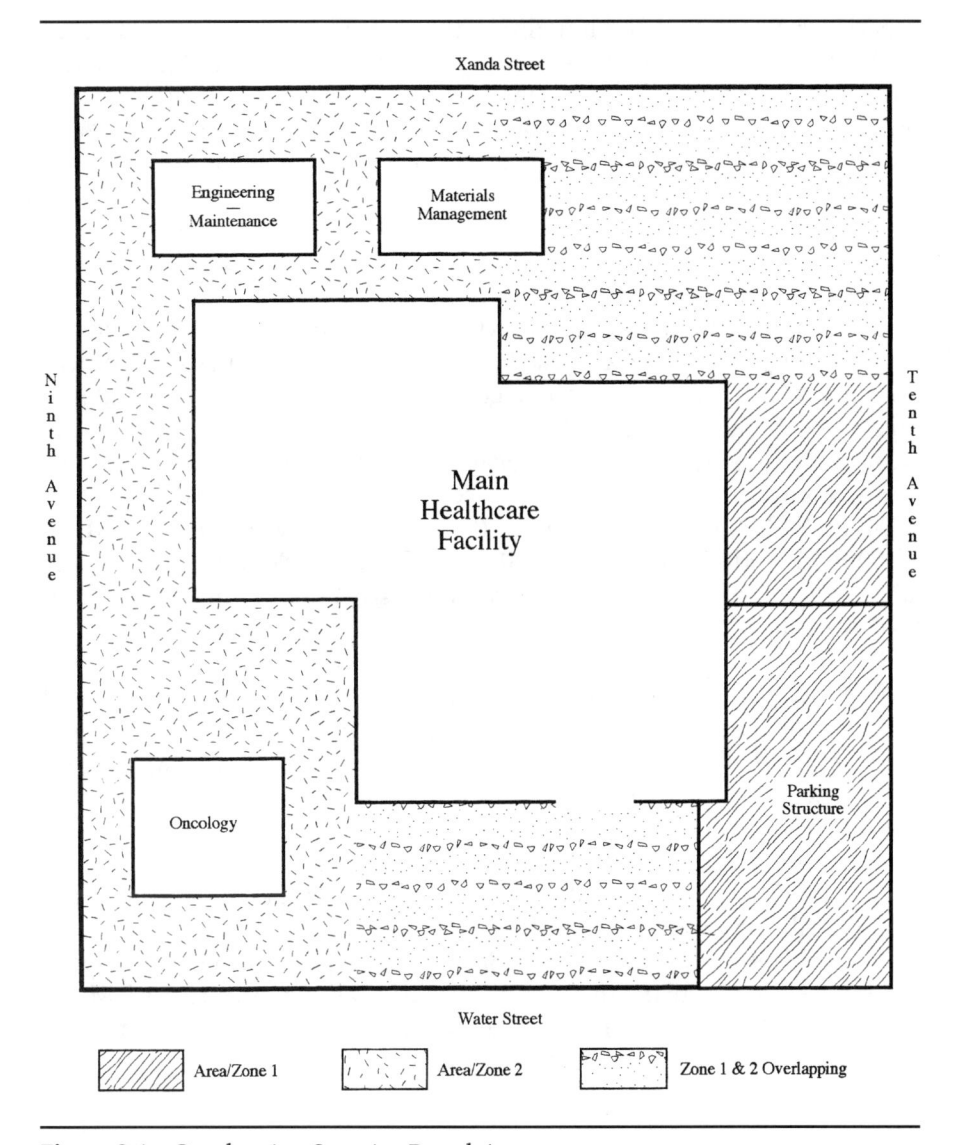

Figure 9-1 Overlapping Security Patrol Areas

supervisor; however, this is not always the case. The patrol officer assigned to the large patrol area not only provides extra patrol, but also acts as a back-up officer for each of the smaller patrol areas. Back-up assistance is provided without diverting another patrol officer from his or her assigned area and possibly leaving that area void of security coverage.

Double Coverage

A general principle in deployment is to maintain a 24-hour coverage schedule, seven days a week, before deploying more than one officer on a given shift. However, double coverage may be used to good advantage when building to a 24-hour program while the number of hours authorized is slowly increased. For example, a program authorizing 112 hours of coverage may find that a coverage pattern of 4:00 P.M. to 12:00 A.M. and 10:00 P.M. to 6:00 A.M. is more productive than 4:00 P.M. to 12:00 A.M. and 12:00 A.M. to 8:00 A.M. The double coverage during the late-night shift change may be more important than the two hours from 6:00 A.M. to 8:00 A.M.

In many medical centers, security officer shifts begin at 8:00 A.M., 4:00 P.M., and 12:00 A.M. These times work quite well in general hospitals or nursing homes because they follow the major shift changes of facility staff by approximately one hour. A change of security personnel is thus avoided when most facility staff are in the process of changing shifts. Today, there are fewer concentrated shift change times because medical center programs use many different shifts.

Table 9-1 shows a deployment plan for a medium size medical care facility utilizing all ten hour shifts.

Table 9-2 shows a deployment plan for a small medical care facility. In the staffing plan, there is double coverage for the 10:00 P.M. to 12:00 A.M. shift change. In this plan, which uses 182 hours of coverage per week, 8-, and 10-hour shifts are involved.

Operational Versus Non-Operational Times

Medical centers operate on a 24-hour basis. However, each facility can define an operational time period and a non-operational time period. As with so many other concepts, these time periods vary to some

Table 9-1 Sample Staffing Plan for a Medium-Sized Medical Center

Day of Week / Officer Assignment

Shift	Sun	Mon	Tuesday	Wed	Thursday	Fri	Sat
6 A–4 P	1	1	1	1	2	2	2
6 A–4 P	2	3	3	4	4	4	4
2 P–12 M	5	5	5	5	6	6	6
2 P–12 M	6	7	7	7	7	8	8
10 P–8 A	9	9	9	9	10	10	10
10 P–8 A	10	11	11	12	12	12	12
7 P–5 A	13	13	14	14	14	13	13

Table 9-2 Sample Staffing Plan for a Small Medical Center

Day of Week / Officer Assignment

Shift	Sun	Mon	Tues	Wed	Thurs	Fri	Sat
8 A–4 P	1	1	1	1	1	2	2
4 P–12 M	2	3	5	5	5	5	5
10 P–8 A	6	6	3	4	4	6	6

degree from organization to organization, with some quasi-operational periods falling between the operational and non-operational periods. These time periods have a direct implication for patrol deployment. During the operational time period, the patrol officer is a support element to be called on for assistance and to provide a general surveillance of public and general-use areas. The operating concept is that departments or sections require little if any internal patrol while fully operational.

During the non-operational time period, the patrol officer and the entire security function take on a custodial role in protecting the facility. Many departments are closed, and officers must check these areas to ensure that they are secured properly and to question strangers in the area.

One must first review the complex as a whole and then each area or department to determine the security officer's proper role for a given time period. For general hospitals, the operational period is usually from

6:00 A.M. to 5:00 P.M. The transition period between 5:00 P.M. and 9:00 P.M. may present some unique security vulnerabilities because some departments are less controlled than they are during the true operational time period. During this transition period, there is enough people traffic within the facility to provide would-be malefactors with anonymity and a possible "ruse purpos" for being in an area. After 9:00 P.M. facilities generally close their doors for the night. Of course, some departments do operate with reduced personnel on duty or on call.

Security officers must constantly monitor the status of their assigned area and alter their patrol activity in relation to this status. If a particular department is open after the normal time period, the officer checks the area more frequently to make certain the department is properly secured as soon after it closes as possible. Also, more frequent checks may be required due to the limited personnel on duty.

Weekends and holidays also present special problems. These periods can be categorized as quasi- or semi-operational periods for most facilities. Many departments are closed, yet visitors are numerous, and the routine of patient care continues. An added factor is that supervision and facility staffing are reduced to a minimum during these times. These considerations strongly suggest that increased patrol coverage is necessary on weekends to provide the required protection level. The assignment of too many part-time or inexperienced officers during weekends and holidays should be avoided.

PATIENT CARE UNITS/AREAS

Generally, no part of the facility should be off-limits to security inspection. On the other hand, a patrolling security officer has no business entering surgical suites, examination rooms, labor rooms, or other similar areas while they are in use. Security officers called to one of these areas should be knowledgeable about the proper attire to be worn and the procedures required for entering the area.

The need to patrol the corridors of patient units varies somewhat with the time of day. During the operational period, when units are fully staffed, there is generally little need for a security patrol. If security services are required, unit personnel should request the needed security support. During the non-operational period, the increased security patrol of patient units provides support to the limited staff, and the visibility of the patrolling officer creates a greater feeling of safety for staff. The deployment pattern for the patrol of nursing-care units should be planned in coordination with the nursing service administrative staff.

ENTRANCES AND EXITS

If all the people entering and leaving a medical care complex could be properly surveyed and controlled, the protection level would be quite high. It is virtually impossible to achieve this state of control, although some facilities with strong visitor control systems do control a high percentage of the people entering the facility and a somewhat lower percentage of those exiting. Most organizations do not impose this rigid control and instead provide numerous entrances and exits for the convenience of everyone—unfortunately this includes intruders. While relatively free access to hospitals may be the norm during the day, there is a need to reduce this uncontrolled access during the evening and night hours. A general plan is to lock designated entry points at 6:00 P.M. and to further lock down access points at the termination of visiting hours. All facilities should designate specific controlled night entrances for late night visitors, delivery, and others.

Greater patrol time should be allocated to the main entrances and exits and to external patrol than to internal areas when the entrances and exits are uncontrolled. Because officers cannot be in all places and see all things at all times, their patrols should be structured to view as much activity as possible. An officer who checks a busy entrance or surveys two or three exits from the exterior will be able to observe many more people than when patrolling in a far removed area of the facility. The distant areas are, of course, important in the total patrol deployment plan, but they should not receive attention out of proportion to the objective of surveying and controlling the general-use areas.

BASIC PATROL CONCEPTS

The backbone of the security effort is the security officer on patrol. A major objective of healthcare security is to manage the patrol responsibility so that officers maximize time spent on patrol and reduce time spent writing unnecessary reports or doing other nonproductive busy-work. Patrol can best be examined by the separation of patrol into external and internal considerations.

External Patrol

External patrol generally covers the grounds, parking areas, and streets surrounding the facility buildings. External patrol is intended to protect vehicles and people entering or leaving the grounds, to provide surveillance of people attempting to use unauthorized exits, to prevent the unauthorized removal of property from the facility, to prevent or discourage unwanted people from entering the facility, and to provide various courtesy services.

Officers on external patrol provide perimeter security protection. They can often observe much more activity than officers on internal patrol. Not only do the grounds typically offer a much greater area to be vandalized, but officers also have a view of a large area. For example, from a parking lot, an external officer may be able to see three or four hospital entrances and exits, while an internal officer can generally only observe one of these points at a time.

A major responsibility of external patrol is to ensure the integrity of facility access points by frequently checking doors, windows, and fire escapes to preclude unauthorized use. A common problem is emergency fire exits that are not intended to be used for entry. Although locked from the exterior, these doors often do not latch properly after an exit. In addition, employees and others sometimes place an object between the door and the frame to keep the latch from engaging. This is often done for convenience and not with the intent to compromise security. Nevertheless, this careless act can provide the access needed for an outsider to commit a serious crime. In addition, all fire emergency exits should be alarmed.

Vehicle Patrols

The basic types of external patrol are foot patrols, bicycle patrols, vehicle patrols, and a combination of the three. Many modern medical facilities occupy large expanses of property and require motor vehicle patrol to ensure proper coverage. Vehicles increase officer mobility, provide protection from the elements, and allow officers to carry the necessary equipment to provide an efficient and effective response to emergencies.

Various types of patrol vehicles have their own advantages and disadvantages. Facilities composed of many streets and roads, large and decentralized parking areas, and multiple buildings generally use an automobile or a four-wheel drive vehicle for security. Smaller facilities may find a small golf-cart-type vehicle suited to their purposes. Small electric and gasoline-powered vehicles are popular, especially in warm climates. These vehicles have several advantages: they are economical to operate, maneuver well in tight areas, and can generally be driven on grass or landscaped areas without causing damage.

Regardless of the type of vehicle used for patrol, they should be easily identifiable as security vehicles. To be an effective deterrent, it is not enough that the protection capability is present. It must also be highly visible to the people being protected and to those who might be contemplating a criminal act.

Although sharing a vehicle between the security department and another hospital department is usually a poor idea, it is possible to provide temporary markings for each type of use. Magnetic signs, available in assorted sizes, colors, and formats, are commonly used. When the vehicle is assigned to the security department, the security signs are applied, and when the vehicle is turned over to another department, the security signs are removed.

Battery Jumping Service

Every security department that uses vehicles for patrol service must decide whether battery-jumping service will be provided. Battery jumping is unquestionably a burdensome task. On the other hand, helping a stranded motorist with a dead battery can enhance good public relations.

A main factor to be considered is whether the service can be provided safely and without an appreciable decline in the primary protection effort. A nurse stranded in a parking lot at 12:30 A.M. presents a security vulnerability. The patrolling officer who provides a jump-start performs a good employee relations activity, while eliminating a security vulnerability.

Jumper service does appear to be in decline due to more and more costly claims of damage to the electronic computers now found in most vehicles. Improper charging procedures can result in substantial damage. If, however, an organization does decide to offer jumper service, the next step is to establish ground rules, including:

- **Charge:** Will there be a nominal charge for this service or will it be provided at no charge? Most programs do not charge for this service.

- **Hours:** During what hours will the service be provided? This may depend on the hours the patrol service is in operation; however, definite hours of service should be established. A general rule is to provide this service when commercial services (garages and service stations) are closed. In some facilities, the maintenance department provides this service during the day and the security department picks up the responsibility at night and on weekends.

- **Waiver of responsibility:** Motorists who need help should be asked to sign a statement waiving responsibility for any claim that may result from the service to be provided. The legality of the statement in court may be questioned; however, it does provide tangible evidence of intent.

- **Transportation of stranded motorists:** At times, a jump-start service is not sufficient to get a vehicle going. The security department should have a firm policy on providing transportation for stranded motorists.

- **Amount of service:** This service should not develop into a mechanic service, and a policy is needed to ensure that this does not happen. Any service can develop expectations in the mind of the recipient of the service that go beyond the intent of an emergency service.

- **Proper equipment:** The security department should not cut corners on the equipment used for the jumping batteries. Several commercial-type equipment hookups are available that are easy to operate and that minimize mistakes.

Transporting People in Security Vehicles

Guidelines must be established covering the use of security vehicles to transport people other than security personnel. Without a clear-cut policy, the security patrol may find that it has developed into a taxi service, and it is often difficult to cut back on this service once it has been established. In some circumstances, however, transportation is in the best interests of all concerned.

The transportation of people, other than through planned shuttle operations, should be properly documented. The names of those transported, the reason, the times and dates, and the mileage should all be recorded except where security is providing a routine shuttle type program.

Equipment for Vehicle Patrol

The type of vehicle used for patrol should be selected for the specific function to be accomplished. In the same manner, the security equipment carried within the vehicle should also be tailored to the function. All vehicles should have the following essential items:

- Communications device

- Spotlight (fixed or plug-in type)

- Fire extinguisher(s)

- Blanket

- Chain or heavy tow cable

- Rope and traffic cones

- Basic tool set (screwdriver, pliers, etc.)

- Small broom and dustpan

- Extra flashlights or hand lanterns

Optional items include a first-aid kit, flares, jumper cables, resuscitator, and air packs. As much equipment as possible should be affixed to the vehicle to keep it from rolling around and to provide a specific place for each piece of equipment. One security department mounts its equipment on a flat board with tie down straps and boxes constructed to hold specific pieces of equipment. The board can be easily removed and used in another vehicle if necessary. Equipment boxes are also quite useful.

Operating the Vehicle

Security personnel operating a security vehicle must generally observe all the rules and regulations that apply to private motorists. Rarely do ordinances or statutes classify security vehicles as emergency vehicles. Security officers may feel that their function gives them special driving privileges. Individual officers should be held responsible for any moving violation or parking ticket received while operating an organization-owned security vehicle. A state motor vehicle check of each officer who operates a vehicle should be accomplished on an annual basis. Many insurance companies require this type of periodic check.

Damage to the Vehicle

Security personnel should be held responsible for any damage to a vehicle in their care, custody, and control. Officers should completely inspect the vehicle before use. This inspection is often documented on the officer's patrol or daily activity log. All vehicle damage reports should be reviewed by an accident or property damage review board to determine whether the accident or damage was preventable and, if so, to recommend action. The action may be a change in procedure or a recommendation for further training for the individual responsible. In some review programs, the responsible party is required to pay for some or all of the loss.

Canine Patrol

There continues to be some limited use of canine units in healthcare facility protection programs. They have proven quite effective as a supplement to officers on foot or vehicle patrol, although their use for the internal patrol of buildings is necessarily limited. There is also an increasing use of dogs as an element in drug investigations or in an on-going drug prevention program. At least one firm, Drug Detection Dogs, utilizes Labradors and Golden Retrievers to discover narcotics in the workplace. These dogs are trained to simply sit when they locate an illicit drug and place their nose at the location. This "passive alert" is certainly less threatening and disruptive then loud barking or growling dogs. In a preventive mode, the dog is simply brought into a facility on a planned periodic basis to "sweep" it.[1]

Dogs offer several patrol advantages. They protect officers on patrol and generally make them more productive while they conduct their rounds. Dogs can often detect the presence of a person hiding when officers cannot observe them. Once trespassers or criminals have been observed, dogs have often been responsible for preventing an escape that otherwise would have occurred.

A basic argument against the use of dogs in security is the risk of the dog injuring someone. A few documented cases indicate that this can be a problem, although these are few in number. However, it is difficult to apply any meaningful security measures without assuming some degree of liability. One should always be conscious of the liability of protection system elements and should minimize the liability exposure as much as possible.

A canine program can be very expensive, especially in terms of cost benefit. In some programs, the dog is utilized exclusively by one handler, which has a variety of associated costs. In other programs, several different handlers utilize a single dog. An organization can purchase its own dogs or can lease dogs on an out-sourced basis. The out-sourced basis is a good method, as costs can be more readily projected and there is much less administrative support required. An organization that owns its own dogs and provides proper training (training is almost always out-sourced) can project an annual cost of $12,000 to $15,000 for each dog. This does not include the training cost of the handler nor department administrative time.

When all the advantages and disadvantages of using a dog on security patrol have been fully analyzed, there is little question that their presence produces a sharp reduction in security incidents. In terms of cost benefit, the use of dogs in the healthcare environment can only be justified in a very few programs.

Internal Patrol

Effective preventive patrol is the backbone of a deterrent program. Patrol is not just walking down a corridor or through an area; it requires being alert and checking and observing with all five senses. The security officer should always have a purpose for inspecting each department or area of the medical complex. This purpose will vary from area to area, but generally the security officer will:

- Check to see that the people assigned to an area are not in need of help (that is, sick, injured, or being victimized)

- Practice conservation (check water or fuel leaks, unnecessary lights or windows left open, unfamiliar equipment noises)

- Look for safety hazards (moisture on the floor, holes, protruding hazards, or malfunctioning lights)

- Inspect for fire safety (undue accumulations of combustibles, blocked exits, extinguishers that are out of place or show evidence of use, doors opening in the wrong direction, sticking or malfunctioning locks, and smoking violations)

- Watch for evidence of unauthorized people or unusual physical factors

- Watch for signs of theft or unauthorized removal of property

- Be alert for acts of malicious destruction, horseplay, consumption of intoxicants or drugs, boisterous conduct, and secure items or equipment that may have been inadvertently left unattended

- Ensure that all doors are secure at the appropriate time and follow through with periodic inspections

- Check out-of-the-way places and know where each door leads and how to reach every part of the medical care complex

- Answer questions for visitors, employees, and patients; direct and escort them

- Be available for service; if an officer is in doubt as to appropriate action, he or she should check with a security supervisor or perform the duty and check afterward for future clarification

- Frequently check locker rooms and public washrooms

- Enforce hospital rules. To enforce rules properly, it is essential that security officers always abide by the rules and by security department regulations (authority is easily abused, and nothing creates resentment as quickly as the misapplication of authority)

It is impossible to list all the areas or conditions that should be inspected. Every facility has unique characteristics that require special patrol activity. The one common area that should be patrolled in all facilities is the stairwells, storage areas, and other out-of-the-way areas. A woman being treated for a stomach ailment disappeared from her seventh-floor room in a Nashville, Tennessee, hospital. Sixteen days later, a nurse noted a foul odor; the missing patient's decomposing body was found on the 10th floor in a storage area.[2] In another case, a man was missing for five days after failing to show up for a hospital medical appointment. He was later found dead in a stairwell by a housekeeping employee.[3]

The trash collection system is an important aspect of security patrol that is too often overlooked by patrol officers. All aspects of the trash collection system should be constantly inspected. Trash carts are a common means of moving stolen or contraband material.

Importance of the First Patrol Round

The officer's first patrol check of an assigned area is extremely important. During this round, the status of the patrol area is determined. The first patrol thus provides a basis for comparing all subsequent patrol activity. Professional security officers carefully check their assigned areas to determine whether the necessary doors are locked, whether lights are on or off, and whether fencing is intact. They note general conditions, such as the number of people in an area that may require special attention, and special conditions, such as areas that create different safety hazards. Patrol checks on the second and subsequent rounds are geared to observe any changes in the environment. These changes signal conditions to be evaluated to determine whether security has been compromised or whether there is cause for action. A standard operating procedure is to vary rounds so that they do not occur on a recognizable schedule.

It is important to recognize that every security officer patrols with a unique point of view based on his or her background and previous experience. Some officers are persistent door checkers but observe little detail while on rounds. Others are less inclined to spend much time checking locked areas, but take careful note of all people encountered on their rounds. Some officers check out-of-the-way places more frequently than others. All officers tend to establish a pattern by which they conscientiously patrol their areas.

Security administrators take advantage of this knowledge by frequently rotating personnel and changing their assigned patrol areas. These changes can occur during a shift or at periodic shift assignments. If possible, changes in assignment should occur during shifts to provide the best possible patrol coverage and to avoid security officers becoming bored.

Not all patrol is generalized and random. There will always be a need for certain intensified inspection of a closed area or of an area that has been the object of security problems. An example would be a parking lot that has experienced many breaking and entering incidents. This theory of patrol variation might also be called a selective or concentrated patrol. It is the same concept that traffic enforcement agencies have used to assign extra patrol coverage to areas subject to many accidents or violations.

Officers reporting for work must properly prepare themselves to effectively provide security service during their tour of duty. Some security programs schedule a 15- or 30-minute overlap of security officers during shift changes to allow incoming and outgoing security personnel to exchange information. Unfortunately, in actual practice, most of this time is used for socialization. The result is a waste of labor both in terms of coverage and economics.

Incoming officers can quickly prepare for duty by reviewing the activity (including incident and condition reports) that has occurred since their last tour of duty and by reading any information entered in the pass-on book. Incoming officers should relieve officers going off duty in the field rather than in the office. Any necessary discussion or exchange of equipment can be accomplished in the field without losing field patrol time.

In large security programs where several officers report for duty at a specific time, a formal incoming officer-briefing period can be conducted. Essentially the same material is disseminated as when a single officer reports; however, it is presented by a briefing officer. This briefing period can also be effectively used for training. A short period devoted each day to training is an extremely effective method of instruction.

Shift Rotation

Security personnel are subject to all human frailties, including complacency and boredom. When one performs the same activity every day, one tends to develop a routine. Even though security personnel are called on to perform many varied activities during a shift, the basic work is routine and subject to patterned activity.

Just as important as the rotation of work assignments during a shift is the periodic rotation of shift assignment. Security officers must be knowledgeable about the security duties and the general activities of every shift to provide optimum protection services. In other words, each officer must be exposed to the total protection system and environment. The protection effort changes hour-by-hour and shift-by-shift in all organizations.

Systems that rotate security officers between different shifts and facilities automatically provide new and challenging situations. Security officers faced with a change in environment, including new people and activities, generally provide a higher level of protection. Officers who are not completely at home with this new challenge will read directions in more detail, ask more questions, be more objective in dealing with personnel with whom they have not had time to develop friendships (or animosities), and follow directions in more detail. Officers who are rotated to new shift assignments often discover security deficiencies or initiate improvements not perceived by their predecessors.

One of the strongest objections against rotating shift assignments is that officers do not get to know who belongs and who doesn't belong in the facility or in a particular area. This argument has only limited validity; it is often personal relationships among employees and others that provide a strong rationalization for shift rotation. The overly friendly or adverse relationships that have evolved are terminated, at least for a time.

Security officers can usually determine whether a person belongs by checking with known personnel or by simply making a positive inquiry or contact with the individual.

How often should personnel be rotated? There is no established timeframe; however, a cycle of six months to one year works well. Too-frequent rotation does not give officers adequate time to adjust their personal lives.

Rotating all the security personnel on one shift at the same time is also not advisable. Security officers should work with other officers who have been on the shift for some time, thus rendering a continuity of service. Officers should be rotated individually. Some officers need to be rotated quite frequently, and others can remain quite objective for a long period of time.

The individual rotation plan also allows officers to work with different security supervisors, which provides two benefits. First, officers are exposed to more in-depth supervision and development because each supervisor has a different point of view and a different method of supervision. Second, supervisors are stimulated to some degree by assuming responsibility for new officers. In explaining the system and procedures to a new officer, the supervisor also benefits by program review. As a general rule, supervisors should be rotated less frequently than security officers. The shift supervisor is considered the thread of continuity for the program.

Patrol Verification

In all programs it is necessary to supervise patrol officers to determine whether objectives and standards are met. The best method of patrol verification is the field supervisor, supplemented by secondary methods. In small programs, no direct field supervision may be available, and thus secondary methods are used to verify patrols. One such method is the mechanical watch-clock, which has been in use for many years and have largely disappeared from most programs. However, with this system, checking in at the clock station can become the officer's primary objective, with little observation or inspection activity occurring between stations. Another problem encountered with the watch-clock system is the clock itself. When security officers are already laden down with equipment, the clock can become quite burdensome.

Some programs have overcome this problem by installing electronic reporting stations. Officers carry a key or other means of activating a signal at the designated reporting station rather than a clock. The signal is transmitted to either a proprietary monitoring point or to a commercial monitoring station. The officer must normally report at each station within a certain time. If the signal is not received within the required time, the dispatcher or monitor initiates a field check to determine why the officer failed to report.

Computer tour-reporting systems are also being used increasingly. Several companies manufacture this equipment, which reads bar codes or magnetic strips located throughout the patrol area. The officer carries a small handheld computer that reads "the point." Most systems also permit officers to enter data into the computer during patrol rounds. At the end of the shift or at some other designated time, the computer is placed into a charger, which also downloads the data and prints it on a personal computer.

Another type of patrol verification system is an adaptation of the regular telephone system. This system permits each facility's touch-tone telephone to become a reporting system. Patrol officers simply key in an identification number, the extension number of the telephone they are using, and a condition code. The information is downloaded to a personal computer for analysis and documentation. An obvious advantage of this system is that officers do not have to carry any recording equipment.

The Patrol Officer's Key Ring

Patrol officers must carry certain keys to effectively carry out their responsibilities and to provide necessary services. Officers do not need to carry keys that grant access to every locked door within the facility. Conventional wisdom holds that officers must be able to gain instant access to any area in case of fire, but professional security administrators recognize that there must be a balance between total access and an overly restrictive access policy. Security personnel are subject to error and human weakness and should not unduly be put in a position of temptation. Just as security administrators strive to reduce the opportunity for incidents in general, they must also protect the security officers and the integrity of the protection program.

Each locked area of the facility must be evaluated and a plan developed regarding access requirements. For example, consider the need for security officers to carry a key to the general storeroom. (Note the term "carry"; access to a key for a particular area is not at issue here.) The general storeroom is particularly vulnerable to pilferage and theft. Most storerooms are protected against fire by sprinkler systems, or at least by an automatic fire detection system, negating the need for a security officer to conduct periodic internal inspection. If a fire alarm were activated in this area, the security officer would likely have sufficient time to obtain the necessary key before the fire department arrived. If necessary, the fire department could enter forcibly, which is acceptable compared with the risk incurred by officers who carry keys to be used "just in case."

Various methods allow access to areas without compromising control. In small facilities such as nursing homes, and even for certain areas in large facilities, the double-lock system is quite effective. This system requires two people, with two separate keys, to gain access through a particular door. This solution was effectively applied to a maintenance storeroom in a facility that had experienced a loss of electrical and plumbing supplies attributed to the maintenance personnel themselves. The maintenance personnel obviously needed access to this area. Each maintenance person now carries a key to one lock and the security officer carries a key to the second lock. The double lock prevents either person from gaining entry to the storeroom without the other.

Another simple way to eliminate the need to carry a key is to make the key available at a location controlled by another department. The key can be released to certain predesignated employees after a record is completed that includes the name of the person receiving the key and the date and time of checkout. A common holding area is the switchboard room, the cashier area, or a central security office in larger operations. Collusion between employees can always result in a compromise; however, the probability of this occurring is quite low.

A system currently in use in one facility appears to handle the access problem very effectively. The keys to all areas are maintained in the central security office, which is operated 24 hours per day. There is a key envelope for each key in the facility; it contains two keys. One key is for temporary use; the second never leaves the envelope except to be reproduced. The envelopes are filed by lock number, which correlates with the room number, with a letter following the key number to indicate multiple locks within a given room or area.

Critical keys, such as for the gift shop, pharmacy, cashier, and storage areas, are contained in special envelopes that remain sealed. When a critical key is needed, the envelope is opened and the reason for its use is recorded in the daily log and in the key checkout register. The director of security keeps the supply of special envelopes. When a special key is used, the key and the opened envelope must be forwarded to the director's office to be returned to the system. A list of the keys in the special envelopes is maintained in the central security office. Each incoming shift supervisor must inventory these envelopes and attest that they are all accounted for and properly sealed. In this system, patrol officers carry only a security perimeter key that fits all exterior doors and security locks, a door exit alarm key, and a handcuff key.

Another advantage of this key control system is the ability to eliminate the security officer as a possible suspect when a problem occurs in an area that was locked. The people who control problem areas often prefer to direct their suspicions to people outside their department. This phenomenon prevails when the housekeeping department is blamed for leaving doors unlocked, a situation with which security practitioners are familiar.

Also on the market are electronic key boxes that require a Personal Identification Number (PIN) to access a certain key. This system records each use providing for system audits.

By eliminating the need for patrol officers to carry many keys, the accidental loss of the key ring, which has proven to be costly and embarrassing, is also eliminated. A key identification tag, indicating a reward for the return of the keys, should be part of the key ring. The return address and telephone number should not be that of the facility, however. Nothing on the ring or on any key should indicate that the keys fit locks for a specific facility.

The Officer's Notebook

Most security administrators recommend that security officers carry a notebook at all times when on duty. It should be small enough to be carried easily and eliminate bulges in the officer's uniform. (A three-by-five inch notebook usually works well.) The notebook contains only the information necessary for handling field situations. Too many notebooks contain such information as the purpose of security, post assignments, disciplinary policy, and regulations for uniforms. This type of information should be set forth in a manual issued to each officer, or in the general orders located at specific security posts, rather than in the officer's notebook.

The notebook should be used to record observations and facts concerning incidents or conditions. Certain guideline information is useful and does have a place in the notebook. Examples include emergency telephone numbers, fire alarm location codes, basic interrogative questions for specific incidents, and incident classifications.

SECURITY OFFICER RESPONSE

Security officers on patrol are the first to respond to calls for service and will most likely encounter situations that require intervention, from simple inquiry to the use of physical force. The healthcare environment presents many situations requiring response to routine calls for assistance, response to crisis situations, and critical incident response.

Routine calls to provide an escort, to unlock a door, or to assist a motorist require an efficient—that is, timely and knowledgeable—response. The term "timely" should need no explanation, but officers often give these calls low priority. To the department and the person seeking assistance, they are no less important than emergency calls. Thus, all routine patrols should be suspended and the officer should proceed where required as quickly as possible. Knowledgeable response means not only having enough information to complete the task, but having the proper equipment. For example, officers should know every key on their key ring, including which locks require special procedures.

Response to a crisis situation demands extra preparation and an adequate skill level. Crisis has been defined as a significant emotional event or a radical change in one's life that has reached a critical stage. Proper security intervention requires a working knowledge of basic de-escalation principles, including verbal communication, nonverbal communication, personal space, and territory.

Officers also must know what to say and how to say it. Words are important, and the tone and volume of voice can also carry different meanings. A fast rate of speech may convey that the officer is afraid, uneasy, or lacks confidence. Tone can indicate such messages as anger, resentment, assurance, and attitude.

Nonverbal communication consists of posture, eye contact, facial expressions, hand gestures, and appearance. Everyone uses body language and must be aware of the messages being sent. Body language can convey comfort, concern, sympathy, hate, disrespect, disbelief, authority, and confidence, among other things. Security officers need to practice positive body language as part of their training, not only for handling crisis situations but also everyday personal interactions.

The issues of personal space and territory are closely related. Space is generally related to physical area, and territory is related to environment, such as the workplace and home. Security officers generally work more with the aspects of space. In general, personal space is the area around the individual that others are expected not to invade. This area is different for different individuals and is affected by personal traits, habits, environmental factors, culture, and gender. Although it is hard to be specific, personal space can range from 18 to 20 inches for intimate contact, and four to five feet for public contact. Intruding in this space can escalate a crisis. This does not mean that security officers cannot enter this space to resolve a situation. It merely means that they must be aware of the concept and the ramifications of their actions.[4] The rule of treating others as you would like to be treated is prudent and practical in all situations.

Security officers responding to a critical incident should follow these guidelines:

- Upon receiving notification, proceed quickly and safely to the scene. Do not run. Arrive in a composed manner, cautiously proceeding into the area.

- Perform a quick assessment, gather basic information, and determine an initial course of action.

- Alert other appropriate resource personnel (dispatcher, additional security personnel, police, fire, etc.) with succinct and pertinent facts.

- Direct action at the scene. Minimize danger to yourself or others and limit further damage if possible.

- Secure the scene, identify witnesses, and preserve evidence.

- Take notes, obtain statements, and complete an incident report.

PATROL PROBLEMS

Several common problems involving patrol officers in medical care settings require close supervision and repetitive training, regardless of how basic these problems appear on the surface.

The first major concern is excessive socialization. Because many security personnel are male and most healthcare personnel are female, frequent socialization is an inherent problem. It's true that it takes two to socialize and that the problem involves both employees; however, the nonsecurity employees are generally in their assigned work area. When officers linger too long in a particular department, they are not only neglecting their duty, but also hindering others from doing their job.

A second major problem is the tendency of security officers to talk too much. This tendency relates in part to the previous issue; however, the main concern is discussing confidential security information with nonsecurity personnel. One hospital administrator reported receiving more security information from the telephone operator being briefed by security than directly from the security department itself. Security officers should not be overly secretive, but they should discuss security plans, programs, and problems only with appropriate people.

When looking for a security officer, some people automatically check in the coffee shop or cafeteria. Security personnel gravitate toward these locations and consequently spend too much time there. Uniformed officers sometimes go to the cafeteria or coffee shop before or after their tour of duty. The problem is that the officers are the only ones who know that they are off duty. To others, the officers appear to be on duty and wasting time.

Perhaps the biggest problem in patrol deployment involves keeping officers separated when more than one is on duty. Of course, officers should back one another up on a call and give other legitimate assistance, but they should not congregate simply to pass the time. When more than one officer is on duty at a time, it generally means there is too much area for one officer to cover adequately. When two officers are together, the effective coverage is reduced to that of a single officer.

Reading while on post is most prevalent in fixed-post assignments. This situation reflects rather poorly on the entire security effort. Reading should be limited to material pertaining to the job and supplied by the program.

Although these concerns cannot be considered to be in-depth supervisory problems, they are real, and they occur in all security systems to some extent. Such minor problems have had a significant impact on keeping security officers in the low-status position that they are so desperately trying to rise above.

TERMS

Fixed-post assignment: The fixed-post assignment is the most restrictive of all deployment methods. The individual assigned to a fixed post generally has no discretionary autonomy in terms of geographical location and generally cannot leave the post unless relieved by another individual.

Modified fixed-post assignment: In this deployment assignment, the officer is mandated to be in a rather close geographical area, such as an emergency department, lobby, or staff entrance. The person may or may not be available to answer calls for service depending on the individual program directives.

Sectored or zone post assignment: In this type of deployment, persons are assigned a specific geographical area of patrol and are generally dispatched to calls for service. These persons may also be dispatched out of their zone to provide back up and support to another zone officer. A specific healthcare facility may have a different number of zones for different hours of the day.

Full Time Equivalent (FTE): The number of full-time equivalent persons required for any staffing plan is the total weekly hours of scheduled coverage divided by 40. In some cases, an organization will consider a person working 32, 34, or 36 hours as full time for benefits purposes; however, those numbers are seldom utilized to calculate the number of FTEs. The FTE number is commonly utilized for budget purposes and does not indicate the number of persons employed (that is, the number of full-time versus part-time or contingent employees).

REFERENCES

1. "Dog Detectives Combat Workplace Drug Use," *Security*, April 1995, p. 65.

2. "National News Briefing," *Rocky Mountain News*, Denver, Colorado, July 23, 1997.

3. "Late Patient Found Dead in Hospital," *Denver Post*, May 8, 1999, p. 7A.

4. Wayne C. Church, "Keeping Crises Cool," *Security Management*, March 1989, pp. 143–146.

CHAPTER 10

Records and Reports

The foundation of a successful program is a comprehensive documentation system. The efficiency of a security operation is directly related to the quality of its records and documentation procedures. Such documentation includes budget and fiscal documents, personnel records, policies, procedures, correspondence, bylaws, contracts, reports, and a whole host of specific records. In this chapter we will limit our discussion to the operational records and reports utilized in healthcare security programs.

PURPOSES OF RECORDS

The use of and necessity for security records varies from organization to organization, but the primary reasons to maintain records remain the same. Records provide a memory system, permit the exchange of information, fulfill various administrative needs, and assist in security activity planning. Within each of these primary reasons are many subcategories designed to provide operational efficiency and effectiveness for the healthcare protection system.

Memory System (Permanent Record)

The need to retrieve information contained in a report may occur within hours, days, or even years after it was written. A quick and effective technique for evaluating a security system is to determine how many questions concerning past activity are answered by personal memory and how many by documented facts.

One of the inherent problems of security operations is that it is difficult to anticipate today what information contained in records and reports will be required tomorrow. Although the statute of limitations for litigation proceedings varies from state to state, all are measured in years rather than months. It is often the so-called minor incidents for which information is later required. Lawsuits are sometimes filed at the last minute in the expectation that supporting defense information will be lost, forgotten, or incorrectly interpreted due to the time lapse.

Not only do civil lawsuits illustrate the need to preserve facts, but the overloaded criminal justice system in the U.S. also makes the need readily apparent. The term "continuance" is often heard in criminal actions. Delay after delay can result in a considerable period between the time action was initiated and the time adjudication is completed.

The use of recorded facts as a memory system is a major tool in the investigative function. Records are as important to the investigator as the scalpel is to the surgeon. Trends, modus operandi, and the facts of past incidents can be instrumental in successfully concluding an investigation.

Obviously, records should not be maintained merely for the sake of maintaining records. A record should be retained with a specific purpose. Unfortunately, healthcare security programs tend to collect and store data that has no meaningful purpose or intended use.

Exchange of Information

The exchange of security information takes place among members of the security department, organizational management, and various outside agencies. The interchange of information among security personnel allows each officer to be knowledgeable about field conditions. This information is necessary for officers to effectively carry out their responsibilities. Security protection could be increased by perhaps 100 percent if all the bits of information known by all members of the security force could be assembled and organized in a meaningful manner. While some exchange of security information is verbally transmitted, the vast amount of such information is exchanged via some type of record or report.

Reports are also necessary to record questionable activities and security deficiencies; they can then be transmitted to an appropriate person for follow-up action. General information that affects an organization must be effectively conveyed through the appropriate channels.

Information transmitted to local, state, and federal law enforcement agencies has often supplied the link that allowed the agency to successfully conclude an investigation. Progressive law enforcement administrators and professional security administrators have established working relationships that recognize the positive contribution that each can render. Security information can be transmitted to not just law enforcement agencies, but to insurance companies, planning agencies, fire departments, offices of emergency preparedness, and many other similar organizations.

Administrative Records Need

Security records fill many needs in the administrative control and effective operation of the protection program. Although each security department needs specific records peculiar to its own operation, certain administrative records are needed by all operations, regardless of size, to provide a viable service.

One of the basic uses of records is the location and identification of security needs through the statistical analysis of security records. Once a need has been identified and a possible solution devised, the technique for measuring the effectiveness of the solution is the analysis of the same security records that first identified the need. In addition to identifying problems, security records are useful in projecting trends; early warning of a possible problem allows preventive measures to be taken.

The deployment of security force personnel is predicated on existing or projected security needs. On the basis of records, security administrators can objectively deploy security personnel at the times and in the places that are most effective.

Security officers usually execute their duties without being directly observed by a supervisor. A security officer's evaluation must include a comparison of individual activity with that of other members of the security department. Records list assignments, assign responsibility, and verify the accomplishment of tasks. Adequate records measure an officer's relative capacity for work and indicate special abilities and aptitudes.

Department records are necessary to account for security property and to ensure the proper maintenance of equipment. Preventive maintenance is a cost-effective management tool that depends on proper record keeping. A history of maintenance and repairs can be used to justify equipment replacement.

DOCUMENTATION POLICY

Documentation systems should be implemented and controlled according to detailed policy. Norman Bates, president of Liability Consultants, Inc., suggests a five-point document policy that includes presentation, content, correction, review, and retention:[1]

- **Presentation:** The report conveys a nonverbal image to the reader. The visual appearance of the report provides the opportunity to present a professional image.

- **Content:** The report should be clear and comprehensive to the point that it is understood by a reader unfamiliar with the event or situation.

- **Corrections:** A review of a report by a supervisor or manager can find errors, including spelling and grammatical mistakes and structure deficiencies. The original author should make the necessary changes, which may require that the report be rewritten.

- **Review:** Document review is an essential tool in proper program management. Information obtained from document reviews is the basis for program planning, helps to assess training needs, initiates disciplinary actions, supports litigation considerations, and measures activity.

- **Retention:** In terms of litigation, documents may either subject the organization to liability or protect it from liability. A document retention policy should ensure that documents are retained as long as the time frame of the statute of limitations for negligence requires.

REPORT FORMATS

Whenever a new report form is considered, the security administrator should ascertain whether the form is absolutely necessary. The next consideration is simplicity. Needless and overly complicated reports make for tedious and time-consuming paperwork and result in reluctance on the part of security officers to complete their reports. The excessive time required to complete the form reduces valuable time in the field. Regardless of format, the guiding principles for all types of reports should be accuracy, simplicity, and efficiency.

Security reports come in all sizes, shapes, colors, and designs. The design of report forms falls into three basic classifications: (1) narrative style; (2) check-off, or block style; and (3) a combination of narrative and check-off styles. These three types of forms have certain advantages and disadvantages; however, the combination style is in predominant use.

Narrative Form

The narrative style can be used to create virtually any type of security report, and it is the least expensive of all styles. Stocking and supplying the form is logistically uncomplicated. The basic disadvantage of the narrative form is that it requires a higher level of training than other types of reports. The preparation of a narrative form can also be very time consuming.

Check-Off Form

In contrast to the narrative form, very little training is required to complete the check-off form because all the necessary information is shown. The check-off form is highly specialized and is the most expensive type of form to create and use. The high cost is largely due to the check-off format, which requires many different forms to cover different types of incidents. It can be difficult to have the proper form in the field when needed. A common problem with check-off forms is that more than one page is often necessary because so many alternatives must be listed for each question.

Combination Forms

Because the nature of security incidents in the healthcare setting is so widely varied, the most popular and the most functional type of reporting form is the combination report, a form that uses both narrative and check-off formats. The combination report can be used for virtually any situation that requires a report.

Other Format Considerations

In addition to report format design, other considerations include color-coding, the number of copies required, and size. Two systems for color-coding reports are popular. The first is to color-code by type of report, and the second is to color-code for distribution or filing. The latter is the most common approach. The number of copies required for a specific report is determined by the organization's structure and needs.

The use of no-carbon-required (NCR) paper has many advantages when multiple copies are required. When preparing a report printed on NCR paper, one must take care to separate the sets of forms from the supply before writing. A single-sheet draft form for officers to outline their reports is worth considering. Even the best report writers begin a report and for one reason or another must start over. A single-copy draft report identical to the multiple-copy NCR form will save money.

Some forms can be printed on both sides of the paper to save money. This logical approach is often overlooked. Forms that lend themselves to this practice include logs, activity sheets, maintenance records, and other single-copy records.

The use of computers for report generation may mean that a hard copy of a report is never generated. It is simply stored, reviewed on screen, and only printed when a hard copy is needed.

BASIC RECORDS

Basic administrative and operational records must be maintained in all healthcare security systems. Administrative records include employee time records and pay records, management reports, property accountability records, employment and training records, lost-and-found logs, visitor logs, statistical analyses, vehicle registration records, key control records, and the like. The most important operational records are security incident reports, security condition reports, daily activity reports, and various vehicle reports and records. Individual security programs will have requirements for records and reports unique to their specific programs. A few of the most basic records and reports will be discussed in this section.

Security Incident Report (SIR)

The basic record found in all security operations is the security incident report (SIR). This report should not be confused with the unusual incident report (UIR) that is commonly utilized to report medications errors, patient falls, and other clinically related situations. These two types of incident reports should be maintained separately and not combined into a single multi-use form. In some systems, the SIR is known as *case reports*, *offense reports*, or *investigative reports*. These terms are basic police nomenclature and should be avoided. Figure 10-1 shows a sample security incident report.

A widely accepted but general definition of a security incident is "any security-related situation not consistent with the routine of normal operating procedures or conditions." The following list of incident classifications is typical and allows the easy tabulation and analysis of incidents.

- **Alarms, False:** Any alarm activated as the result of negligence, mechanical malfunction, accidental use, or extenuating circumstances. This classification is separated into fire and security alarms. Any alarm that was answered and proved to be real is entered in another appropriate classification (fire, breaking and entering, missing property, etc.).

- **Assault:** Any threatening or physical attack on a person, other than a sexual assault.

- **Auto Accident:** Any incident that results in damage to a person, vehicle, or property by a vehicle.

- **Breaking and Entering:** Unlawful entering of a vehicle, building, or premises—with or without force—with no evidence of property loss. This classification is separated into vehicle and building.

254 *Hospital and Healthcare Security*

1999 Norton Healthcare, Inc.	**SAFETY AND SECURITY OCCURRENCE REPORT**	*Report Number*

Facility: ☐ *NOR* ☐ *KCH* ☐ *NHP* ☐ *NAB* ☐ *NSB* ☐ *NSW* ☐ *NHC*

COMPLAINANT:	
COMPLAINANT CLASSIFICATION:	AFFIX PATIENT LABEL HERE
ADDRESS:	
PHONE NUMBER:	
REPORT TYPE:	
INJURY/NON-INJURY	POLICE NOTIFIED: ☐ YES ☐ NO ☐ N/A
DATE OF REPORT:	POLICE OFFICER:
TIME SECURITY NOTIFIED:	POLICE REPORT NUMBER:
REPORTING OFFICER:	
EVENT TIME FRAME:	
EVENT LOCATION:	
AREA STATUS: ☐ SECURED ☐ UNSECURED	
OCCUPIED: ☐ OCCUPIED ☐ UNOCCUPIED	
ITEMS INVOLVED:	
REPORTED BY:	
EXTENSION:	

EVENT DESCRIPTION:

Signature of Reporting Officer: _____

DO NOT PHOTOCOPY COMPLETED FORM   CONFIDENTIAL   PAGE 1

Figure 10-1 Sample Healthcare Security Incident Report Form (Courtesy of Norton Healthcare, Inc., Louisville, Kentucky)

- **Disturbance:** Disruptive behavior by employees, patients, or visitors that requires the intervention of staff to neutralize the situation. This classification is separated into employee, patient, and visitor categories for reporting purposes.

- **Drug Abuse:** Incidents that involve the misuse of any drug.

- **Fire:** Any burning or evidence of damage by fire.

- **Found Property:** All property recovered or turned in to security.

- **Information Only:** Any information received from staff, visitors, security, or an outside agency regarding a situation, incident, or crime. Examples include pharmacy alerts, professional patients, information from law enforcement agencies, supplemental reports with additional information, and injury reports.

- **Missing Property:** All items belonging to or in the possession of the healthcare organization, patients, employees, or visitors that are unaccounted for or have been stolen, including all vehicles, regardless of ownership. This classification is separated into facility-owned property, personal property, and property missing from a vehicle.

- **Patient Assistance:** Requests for security to render assistance to patients as needed, including restraining, locating, watching, and handling property. This classification is separated into two categories: emergency department and all other locations.

- **Robbery:** The unlawful taking of property from a person through the use of actual or implied force. This classification is separated into armed and unarmed robbery.

- **Sex-Related Incident:** All incidents that are sexual in nature. This classification is separated into sexual assault, obscene call, obscene or lewd remarks, and an "all other" category.

- **Suspicious Person:** Any individual on the premises who does not appear to have legitimate business at the facility or persons observed acting in a strange or suspicious manner. This classification is separated into those contacted by security officer and those not contacted by security officer.

- **Threat:** A verbal or written statement expressing an intent to hurt, destroy, punish, or intimidate. This classification is separated into bomb threats and all other threats.

- **Vandalism:** Malicious or senseless destruction or defacing of property. This classification is separated into facility, personal, or vehicle property.

These categories were established to standardize field-reporting procedures. The categories permit ready analysis and define incidents for periodic statistical reporting. Figure 10-2 shows a sample security incident statistical summary report.

Every healthcare security program must define the parameters or conditions that require an incident report. There are gray areas to be sure, and the reporting of every incident is virtually impossible. When officers successfully conclude a minor incident, they tend to avoid preparing a report. In addition, different security programs have different reporting procedures for minor incidents. For example, suppose a security department receives a report that a patient is missing a ring, but when the security officer arrives, he or she is advised that the ring was found in the narcotics drawer. In some programs, the officer would not be required to report such an incident; in others, he or she would simply note the incident in the daily activity log; and in other programs, an incident report would be required. In this scenario, the daily activity log would be preferred as the most efficient approach. One program defines the necessity of completing an incident report in terms of the number of sentences required to record the event. If the occurrence has been successfully concluded and can be described in three sentences or less, the information is recorded in the officer's daily activity log, and no incident report is completed.

The basic rule is, "When in doubt, write it out." In other words, if an officer is uncertain whether an event should be reported, an incident report should be completed. Progressive security officers develop skills in observation and investigation. However, it is not enough to develop these skills unless the results can be recorded accurately, clearly, and succinctly in written form.

HUNTINGTON MEMORIAL HOSPITAL MEDICAL CENTER
MONTHLY INCIDENT REPORT
CURRENT MONTH, YEAR-TO-DATE
CURRENT YEAR COMPARED WITH PREVIOUS YEAR

1998-1999	JAN		FEB		MAR		APR		MAY		JUN		JUL		AUG		SEPT		OCT		NOV		DEC		TOTAL	
	98	99	98	99	98	99	98	99	98	99	98	99	98	99	98	99	98	99	98	99	98	99	98	99	98	99
DISTURBANCES																										
Patient Rooms	0	0	0	0	0	0	1	0	1	1	2	0	0	0	0	0	0	0	1		0		0		5	
Emergency	0	0	0	0	0	0	1	0	2	0	0	0	0	0	0	0	0	0	0		1		0		4	
Other	0	0	0	1	1	0	2	0	1	1	0	0	1	0	1	1	0	0	0		0		0		6	
Assault on Staff	0	0	0	0	0	0	0	0	0	0	0	0	0	0	0	0	1	0	0		0		0		1	
Assault on Patient	0	0	0	0	0	0	0	0	0	0	0	0	0	0	0	0	0	0	0		0		0		0	
Assault - Other	0	0	0	0	1	0	0	0	0	0	0	0	0	0	0	0	0	0	0		0		0		1	
SUB-TOTAL	0	0	0	1	2	0	4	0	4	2	2	0	1	0	1	1	1	0	1		1		0		17	
THEFTS																										
Patient Rooms	0	1	0	1	1	3	1	1	0	3	3	0	2	1	5	2	3	3	2		1		1		19	
Offices/Locker Rm.	0	2	2	2	0	5	1	2	4	3	0	0	0	3	1	0	1	2	0		1		3		13	
Vehicle Burglary	1	1	0	0	1	1	1	1	0	0	0	0	1	2	0	0	3	1			1		0		7	
Vehicles	2	0	0	1	0	0	0	0	0	0	1	0	0	0	0	1	0	0	0		0		0		3	
Robbery	0	0	0	0	0	0	0	0	0	0	0	0	0	0	0	0	0	0	0		0		0		0	
Other	0	0	1	2	0	0	2	1	1	2	0	1	0	1	2	0	1	0	0		0		1		8	
SUB-TOTAL	3	4	3	6	2	9	5	5	5	8	4	1	2	6	10	3	5	8	3		3		5		50	
MISCELLANEOUS																										
Trespassing	0	1	0	0	0	1	1	0	1	0	0	0	0	0	1	0	0	0	2		2		1		8	
Vandalism	0	0	0	0	0	0	0	0	0	0	0	0	0	0	0	0	0	0	0		0		0		0	
HMH Prop. Vandal.	0	0	0	0	0	0	0	0	1	0	0	0	0	0	1	0	0	0	0		0		0		2	
Vehicle Vandalism	0	0	0	0	1	0	0	1	0	1	0	0	0	0	1	0	1	0	0		0		0		1	
Threats	0	0	0	0	0	0	0	0	0	0	1	1	1	1	0	0	0	1			1		0		4	
Traffic Collision	1	1	0	1	4	2	4	1	4	2	3	1	1	3	2	2	1	6	2		1		3		26	
Other	5	3	2	0	2	1	1	1	1	0	1	1	4	3	0	2	3	1	4		1		3		27	
SUB-TOTAL	6	5	2	1	7	4	6	3	7	3	4	3	6	7	5	5	4	8	9		5		7		68	
VISITOR FALLS/ INJURIES																										
Patient Rooms	0	0	1	0	0	0	1	0	1	0	0	1	1	0	0	0	0	0			1		0		5	
Offices	0	0	0	0	0	0	0	0	0	0	0	0	0	1	0	0	0	0	0		0		0		1	
Parking Lot	0	0	1	1	1	0	0	0	1	0	0	0	0	0	0	0	0	0	0		0		0		2	
Stairs/Steps	0	0	1	0	0	0	1	0	0	1	0	1	1	2	2	0	0	0	0		0		1		6	
Sidewalk	0	0	0	2	0	1	1	1	0	0	0	1	1	1	1	0	1	0	0		0		0		4	
Other	1	1	2	1	1	2	2	0	2	1	0	1	1	2	4	2	1	1	1		0		1		16	
SUB-TOTAL	1	1	5	4	2	3	4	2	3	2	1	3	4	4	8	4	2	1	1		1		2		34	
MONTHLY TOTALS	10	10	10	12	13	16	19	10	19	15	11	7	13	17	24	13	12	17	14		10		14		169	

Figure 10-2 Sample Security Incident Statistical Summary Report (Courtesy of Huntington Memorial Hospital, Pasadena, California)

Even the most seasoned officers find report preparation the most difficult part of the incident process, and the most difficult part of reporting is often the beginning. The key to completing an incident report is to record information in a logical sequence. If the report is written in a logical sequence and the writer has adequately answered the basic interrogatives (who, what, when, where, and how), the report will be essentially complete.

A report must be objective and must include both favorable and unfavorable facts. If a report contains an estimate, such as distance or size, it should be identified as such. Personal opinion should generally not be included in reports; however, an opinion can often be valuable in evaluating the facts. It is not necessarily wrong to include an opinion if it is clearly identified. For example, an officer who reports information from someone who seems vague, inconsistent, or contradictory may wish to note that the person did not appear completely rational and might have been under the influence of drugs or might be senile. However, it is generally accepted that opinions or suppositions be recorded on a separate sheet of paper and attached to the formal report.

In some security departments, handwritten field reports are later typed by a department clerk. This is a poor practice for a variety of reasons, not the least of which is cost. A few departments use dictating equipment, and this system can work quite satisfactorily. Although officers require training and practice to dictate complete reports, they may be better able to verbalize than to write. In still other programs, officers enter their reports directly into the computer. This method is generally considered to be very inefficient and is often an attempt to appear high tech. The degree of training required and the need to access a terminal, which is generally in the security office, is not cost effective. This method of report preparation is actually contraindicated in the opinion of many professional security administrators.

Security officers should never be allowed to go off duty before completing their required reports. Reports should be completed as soon as possible after the facts are collected. In cases where a security officer initiates an investigation just before going off duty, the incoming officer can assume responsibility and relieve the first officer. Incident reports can be begun by one officer and completed by another. The report must identify where the relieving officer took over; this can be simply stated in the body of the report.

Most organizations implement a review process. The administrative review of field reports has several distinct purposes. One is to provide feedback to the officer who prepared the report on how the writer could have prepared a better report. This task is an example of how training and supervision are interrelated. We all learn through our mistakes; however, no learning takes place if our mistakes are ignored, and we are not made aware that a mistake, error, or substandard performance has occurred.

The administrative review also ensures the completeness of the report. Officers should be encouraged to prepare a rough outline of the report to make certain that they have the proper information organized in good form before they begin to write. This method helps eliminate false starts and reduces the waste of costly multiple-copy forms.

Security Supplemental Report

The supplemental report form is used to record additional information not included in the original report. Supplemental reports are generally used in conjunction with security incident reports, but they may also be used as a follow-up to other records or reports. This form is often used to record follow-up investigative information. For example, after reporting a case of missing property, a security officer will often discover that the property was recovered. If the original report has not been distributed, the facts can be added to the original report indicating the new time and date of the information being added. However, if the original report has been distributed, a supplemental report is prepared to be matched to the original loss report at a later time. It is also common practice to use supplemental report forms if additional pages are required when preparing an incident report. Figure 10-3 shows an example of a blank sample supplemental report.

Filing Security Incident Reports

Once an incident report has been completed and distributed through administrative channels for information, recording, or follow-up, the report must be filed so that it can be efficiently retrieved. One of the

Security Department   **Healthcare SECURITY SERVICES**   **Supplemental Report**

Facility _____ Date _____ Time _____
Supplemental information to original report of:
Facility _____ Date _____ Time _____

Nature of Original Incident: _____

_____
_____
_____

Security Officer _____ Police called at _____ Arrived at _____ Officer _____

Figure 10-3   Sample of a Supplemental Report Form (Courtesy of Healthcare Security Services, Denver, Colorado)

Healthcare				
SECURITY SERVICES	**Security Condition Report**	Attention _____ Date _____ Time	Facility _____ _____ (AM) (PM)	

The following condition was noted during patrol rounds and is brought to your attention for information or corrective action

_____
_____
_____
_____
_____
_____
_____

Security Officer _____ Cond. Corr. (yes) (no)   Copy left (yes) (no)

Figure 10-4 Sample Security Condition (Violation) Report (Courtesy of Healthcare Security Services, Denver, Colorado)

simplest methods of filing incident reports is by date. Only in very large security departments is it necessary to use a system of serial numbers. In some departments, copies of the incident report are filed as cross-references; however, this system tends to create more paperwork than necessary. Data-processing systems work well when cross-references are deemed necessary and reports can be searched in many ways.

Security Condition Report

The sample security condition report, illustrated in Figures 10-4 and 10-5, is used to advise others in the organization of a security condition rather than a security incident. It takes the form of a memorandum that describes unsafe conditions, security vulnerabilities, malfunctioning security equipment, areas found unsecured, and other situations that may require action. The form can also be used to relay general information to responsible parties.

An example of a security condition that should be reported is an office door found unlocked during a late evening security patrol check. Suppose that a security officer is aware that the door is usually locked around 5:00 P.M. and that it had been secure on the last round. Upon

MISSION HOSPITAL
REGIONAL MEDICAL CENTER

A Sisters of St. Joseph of Orange Corporation

VIOLATION REPORT

☐ SAFETY ☐ SECURITY ☐ FIRE

TIME _____ DATE _____

LOCATION _____

DEPT. _____

NAME _____ EXT. _____

☐ UNLOCKED DOOR
☐ UNSECURED WINDOW
☐ UNATTENDED KEYS
☐ FAILURE TO DISPLAY ID BADGE
☐ BLOCKED AISLE
☐ BLOCKED EXIT
☐ BLOCKED EXTINGUISHER
☐ BLOCKED ALARM BOX
☐ SMOKING IN UNAUTHORIZED AREA

REMARKS: _____
_____
_____

S/O SIGNATURE

C 8420

Figure 10-5 Sample Security Condition Report (Courtesy of Mission Hospital Regional Medical Center, Mission Viejo, California)

internal inspection, the office appears to be intact and the security officer assumes that someone who had legitimate access failed to lock the door. A housekeeping, maintenance, or office employee might have inadvertently failed to lock up. However, the possibility that an intruder gained access does exist.

The security condition report serves a couple of purposes in this situation. First, the officer records the date, time, and the action taken, and leaves an information copy of the report in the office to inform the occupants on their return. Their response should be to determine whether anything is missing or another security problem exists. Second, a copy of the report goes to the director of security or the person responsible for review for possible follow-up action. This report may fit a pattern that suggests that housekeeping does not always lock up, and a follow-up with the housekeeping department may be indicated. Some security programs forward a copy of the security condition report to the maintenance department to serve as a work order.

Security condition reports also serve to advise other security officers that a condition has been reported. For example, officers who note that an officer on the previous shift prepared a condition report about a burned-out parking lot light will not duplicate the report. The condition report thus serves as a communication tool and helps to coordinate the protection effort among officers.

Daily Activity Report

As a basic rule, all field officers should be required to complete a report of their activities during their tour of duty. There are as many different types of daily, or tour, activity reports as there are security departments. Figure 10-6 shows an example of a security officer's daily activity report.

Figure 10-7 shows a different type of officer activity report, which uses an electronic patrol verification system. Total reliance on computer input is not realistic, and all activity reports should allow the officer to add narrative to the report.

In some larger departments that have a 24-hour central security control center, each officer does not complete an individual activity record. Instead, the officer assigned to security control makes all assignments and directs the activity of individual field officers. A chronological

WELLSTAR HEALTH SYSTEM
SECURITY SERVICES
OFFICERS ACTIVITY LOG

NAME	DATE / /	SHIFT	RADIO	KEYS
CASE NUMBER	LOCATION		INVOLVED PERSON	

NUMBER OF CALLS FOR SERVICE: _____

TIME CALLED	TIME CLEARED	CODE	LOCATION	COMMENTS

ENTERED ON COMPUTER	YES___	NO___

Figure 10-6 Example of a Security Daily Activity Report (Courtesy of Wellstar Health Systems, Marietta, Georgia)

```
                    MORSE   GUARD   TOUR
                         Tour  Report
    Report Time: 14:04:09
    Report Date: 04/01/91

    Tour Number: 1
    Facility: Water Treatment Site
    Recorder serial Number: 00005749
    Tour Began: 03/27/91, 0:35:33
    Tour Status: Incomplete                              Page 1
    ------------------------------------------------------------
    No. |    Station                  |   Time    |  Tour Errors
    ------------------------------------------------------------
    004    Initiate Tour A               0:35:33
    013    Ops Bldg-Photo Lab Area       0:36:38
    015    Ops Bldg-Reception Area       0:38:44
    011    Ops Bldg-Hallway by 46-55     0:39:09
    018    Ops Area 56/S Entrance        0:39:26
                                                    Sequence Error
    012    Pole at N end of Property     0:42:01
                                                    Sequence Error
    014    Ops Bldg-N Entrance           0:43:35
    017    TV Bldg-N Entrance            0:44:38
    005    TV Bldg-NE Office Area        0:45:38
    006    Barns-Cntr Bldg-E Cntr Ga     0:47:46   Missed Station
    010    TV Bldg-W Garage Entrance               Missed Station
    009    Ops Bldg-E Center Door                  Missed Station
                                         0:51:24
    008    TV Bldg-W Entrance
                                         0:56:23
    007    Pole Bldg-S Door/SE Gate
    016    Maint Bldg-E Entrance
    END REPORT
```

Figure 10-7 Sample of an Electronic Patrol Verification Report

activity log is thus maintained centrally. Entry directly into the computer program is completed at the time of each activity. This system reduces paperwork and makes it much easier to review activities performed by the entire security department.

The chronological computer entry record can also be used for various administrative purposes. For example, by recording the time a call was dispatched and the time the officer arrived, a response time profile can be maintained. Likewise, the time expended on each service activity can be recorded and collated to produce a profile of the times required for each type of activity.

One of the pitfalls of the central security control system is that not all requests for service are directed to the security control desk. Much activity is originated by field officers and by direct customer contact with field officers. In these instances, officers are required to call the dispatch center to initiate the record.

Parking Violation Notice

The purpose, size, shape, and format of the parking violation notice varies from program to program. The design of the form is obviously dependent on the system of parking control used by the organization. Generally, the violation notice is intended to be a friendly reminder that orderly parking benefits everyone. In parking systems where specific areas are designated for different groups (physicians, visitors, employees, outpatients, etc.), the violation notice takes on a stronger connotation. Some jurisdictions issue citations that include a punitive-action, government-code violation.

The size of the form should be determined to some extent by the uniform or attire worn by security officers. The notices should fit neatly into a pocket or special holder because officers must carry a supply while on normal patrol duty. The copy of the notice to be placed on the vehicle should be printed on card stock. If an additional copy is required, a lighter paper may be used.

Pass-On Record

Every security department must have a system for transferring information from shift to shift or from officer to officer. In some programs this system is known as the party line. Various procedures are used to handle this important aspect of protection operations. A bound or loose-leaf book is widely used. All officers reporting for duty must be required to read the information added to the book since they were last on duty and to sign each page to signify that they have read the information. The computer is also a useful tool in which the officers coming on duty can simply access this information.

The information that is recorded on the daily pass-on record originates from many different sources, including administration, department heads, security officers, and various elements inside and outside the organization. For example, the information entered in a pass-on record might include a vehicle granted special permission to park in a particular area; a new key that has been added to the patrol officer's key ring; a special shipment of products expected during the night, with disposition instructions; the need to block off a certain area of the parking lot for special parking or construction; and a meeting in the facility for which special security activity is required. The pass-on record should include timely information officers need to perform their responsibilities efficiently and effectively.

The security administrator must review all pass-on information periodically to determine whether the post orders, policies, or procedures must be modified or deleted. For example, if a key is added to the system, the post order that identifies all keys on a specific key ring and the procedural use of such keys must be updated.

The bound book works well for single-facility organizations; however, for organizations with multiple facilities that are widely separated, the computer is recommended. Security administrators should consider including a short training message for each day on the pass-on record.

Master Name Index

The master name index is a very simple, but extremely useful security device. A record is prepared about anyone who has had a significant interaction with a member of the security department or about whom information has been received. The intent is to provide a ready historical reference for inquiries and investigations.

Names to be included in the master name index are obtained from security incident reports, which include names of complainants, victims, suspects, and witnesses. Exactly which names will be included in the index is a matter of individual philosophy. Some departments include names of their security officers, employment applicants, people who have corresponded with the department, and individuals named in newspaper articles concerning the healthcare facility.

The index lends itself to computerization and may be cross-indexed. Small departments without computerization will find the three-by-five index card the most economical approach. The record may simply refer to an incident report, a piece of correspondence, or other records, or it may contain all the information known. Figure 10-8 shows a sample format for a typical master name index.

Monthly or Periodic Security Report

All healthcare security systems should prepare periodic activity reports. A great many security departments prepare monthly, quarterly,

```
                        MASTER NAME FILE

CONTACT DATA        Last Name
                    First Name
                        Gender              Race
                    Birth Date  / /      or Age
                        Height              Weight              Hair

FACILITY DATA           Name

INCIDENT DATA           Date   / /       Time    :   Location
                      Category
                    Description

                Were Police Called?
```

Figure 10-8 Sample Master Name Index Format

and annual activity reports. The Joint Commission on Accreditation of Healthcare Organizations (JCAHO) requires security reports to be sent to an organization multi-disciplinary review committee. This committee, often referred to as the Safety or Environment of Care Committee, is charged with the review and evaluation of security data. This committee generally meets on a bi-monthly basis, although some meet on a monthly basis. Committees that meet on a less frequent basis must justify the rationale for their meeting schedule.

The content and organization of the activity report reflect the style of the person responsible for the protection program unless the organization specifies a standard format. Reports should cover major department functions and should include comparative data measuring changes in activities and effectiveness. The following are some meaningful general areas that activity reports can cover:

- Current and comparative incident information designed to gain management support for new programs

- Assessment of workload by units

- Timely identification of specific problems requiring planning and safeguards

- Status of equipment, including projections concerning cost of maintenance or replacement

- Performance evaluation of the program in general terms

- Status of goals and objectives

Many healthcare programs prepare monthly Quality Improvement (QI) reports. One format is to prepare the report as a two part document. This report is usually a statistical summary of security incidents and secondly a narrative relative to security issues. This part of the monthly security report is also forwarded to the multi-disciplinary committee for review and appropriate action. It is suggested that the statistical format include the number of security incidents for the month, in various categories, with comparisons to previous months and cumulative totals. Figure 10-9 shows a sample security incident QI statistical and issues report.

The second part of this monthly security report should deal more with activity, planning, and program status information. This section of the report is prepared more for the administrative review process as opposed to the trending of information.

Annual Security Management Plan and Program Evaluation

There should be a formal review of the security program on an annual basis. This review should address the objectives, scope, performance, and effectiveness of both the security management plan and the operational implementation of that plan. In short, the review should look at how the program measured up to expectations. The security management plan as well as the periodic reports prepared throughout the year for the multi-disciplinary review committee make up the basic sources of information for the annual evaluation. The annual evaluation does not need to take place on a calendar-year basis; however, the calendar year is utilized by most healthcare security administrators.

Performance Improvement Records

A primary goal of the healthcare security program must be to seek program improvement. Improvement requires setting standards

HUNTINGTON MEMORIAL HOSPITAL

Safety Program 1999

SECURITY MANAGEMENT/QI PLAN

Reporting Period:
Reporting Date:

STANDARD	Threshold	Jan	Feb	Mar	Apr	May	Jun	Jul	Aug	Sept	Oct	Nov	Dec
Huntington Hospital shall assure the manpower and processes necessary to provide a reasonable environment in which individuals are safe from harm.	95%												
Risks will be minimized as appropriate to incident	Event Falls base Theft												

SIGNIFICANT ISSUES IDENTIFIED	CORRECTIVE ACTIONS TAKEN	FOLLOW-UP REQUIRED

Figure 10-9 Sample Monthly Security QI Incident Statistical and Issues Report (Huntington Memorial

for measuring, monitoring, and setting improvement goals. Records maintained for these purposes ultimately document program quality. The performance standards vary widely according to program needs. An example is the security alarm system. An alarm system only provides an element of quality when it is operational. A system of periodic documented tests measures the reliability (quality) of the system. Testing may merely indicate whether the system is operating as intended or it may go a step further and measure an operational response to an alarm.

Figure 10-10 lists a number of performance standards that may be considered for healthcare security programs.

Daily or Weekly Security Bulletin

The daily or weekly bulletin is a communications device that summarizes the incidents or major activity that has occurred during a given period of time. This record is generally used by larger security departments and programs with multiple facilities that are far apart. The bulletin advises security and administrative personnel of the incident profile on a timely basis. The information may be used to alter protection planning in anticipation of certain problems or to provide efficient and useful tours of duty.

KEEPING DEPARTMENTAL RECORDS CURRENT

In addition to basic records, a protection program may require many different records and reports to meet its particular needs. Regardless of the number of records and reports used in a security program, a periodic review of every form is mandatory. Each form should be analyzed to determine whether it is necessary and whether it is being utilized in a satisfactory manner. Do not hesitate to change a form if it does not meet the organization's needs in every detail. The most common error encountered is that forms call for more information than is really necessary. Either time is wasted in obtaining and recording the information, or officers tend to ignore certain details.

**HEALTHCARE SECURITY
PERFORMANCE STANDARD/MEASUREMENT/IMPROVEMENT**

Activity/Process: The Security Department investigates all reports of patient missing property. A security incident report (investigation) is completed for each reported loss.

Performance Standard: There should be a 50% resolution of all cases of patient property losses. Resolution includes recovered property, identification of perpetrator, arrest, careless discard, and unfounded reports.

Measurement/Indicator: The Director of Security will maintain an ongoing status review of each incident to include statistical data relative to location, time frames, property categories, and resolution/non-resolution.

Performance Improvement: A performance review committee, consisting of the Director of Security, Investigator, and Risk Manager, will meet each month to review the statistical data and formulate activities/plans for resolution improvement as appropriate.

Activity/Process: The Security Department provides for 24-hour security officer response to critical incidents.

Performance Standard: The response time for a critical incident shall be under five minutes from the time security is notified until an officer arrives at the scene.

Measurement/Indicator: Security dispatch logs which indicate notification times and officer arrival times, will be utilized to track this information and create a monthly statistical report.

Performance Improvement: A performance review committee, consisting of the Director of Security, Dispatch Supervisor, and Security Operations Supervisor, will meet each month to review the statistical data and formulate activities/plans for response time improvements as appropriate.

Figure 10-10   Sample Healthcare Security Performance Standards

RECORDS RETENTION

The retention of records should be controlled by policy, subject to any state law, which ensures that needed records are retained and unneeded records are discarded. As a general rule, most departments retain too many records for too long a time. Each operational form used by the security department should be assigned a specific retention period. When litigation arises months or years after the actual incident, the plaintiff will generally demand all business records relevant to the claim during the discovery process. The absence of a document retention policy could lead to an accusation of destroying evidence if a particular document cannot be located. This is commonly known as "spoliation" of evidence and could constitute an obstruction of justice criminal offense.[2] The following are offered as general guidelines for record retention:

- Security incident reports: five years

- Monthly or annual activity reports: five years

- Annual security evaluation reports: five years

- Parking violation/reminder notices: one year

- Security condition reports: six months

- Security officer daily activity reports: six months

TERMS

JCAHO environment of care management areas: The seven management areas are Safety, Security, Hazardous Materials and Waste, Emergency Management, Life Safety, Medical Equipment, and Utility Systems.

JCAHO environment of care multidisciplinary review committee: A committee—comprised of representatives from administration, clinical services, and support services—that analyzes and seeks resolution of management safety issues in all seven environment of care management areas.

JCAHO-ICES: An organization-wide information, collection, and evaluative system utilized to evaluate and improve conditions in the environment of care.

REFERENCES

1. Norman D. Bates, "The Power of Paperwork," *Security Management*, May 1995, pp. 79–82.

2. Ibid. p. 80.

CHAPTER 11

The Interrelationship of Security with Patients and Visitors

There must be a clear understanding of how security interrelates with various groups and individuals within the healthcare environment in order to properly fulfill the security and organizational mission. These individuals include patients, visitors, employees/staff, and public safety and regulatory personnel. This chapter focuses on patients and visitors, while Chapters 12 and 17 deal more directly with outside agencies and general employees.

The relationship, or degree of security interaction, with various groups will vary not only according to the group but also according to the location of the interaction. As an example, the security officer may have a greater need and responsibility for interaction with patients in public areas of a facility, but have rather limited contact with patients in their rooms or in clinic-type treatment areas. Likewise, security officers have a greater responsibility in dealing with visitors in parking lots than in patient rooms.

Patients and visitors can each be viewed in two distinct groups. The patient may either be an outpatient or an inpatient. The vast majority of our discussion of healthcare security focuses on the latter. In terms of visitors, some people are visiting an inpatient, while others are accompanying a person seeking or receiving short-term medical treatment, such as in an emergency room or clinic. Types of visitors may be very diverse and includes people visiting employees, people visiting a department for educational, information, or business purposes (salespersons, vendors, delivery persons, etc.), and people who have no legitimate reason for being on the property (transients, loiterers, criminals, etc.).

PATIENTS

The Joint Commission on Accreditation of Healthcare Organizations (JCAHO) has various standards that refer to "patients rights." Although for the most part these standards refer to patient care services directly, all security personnel should be cognizant of these rights as they pertain to the delivery of security services.

The healthcare organization exists for the patient. Thus, all of the security program's activities must directly or indirectly support patient care. As such, security officers must keep the patient foremost in mind, and must always observe a patient's rights. Security officers must remember that the patient

- is the most important element in the healthcare business

- is not an interruption of the security officer's work but the reason for it

- does a favor by calling security; security does not do a favor by serving the patient

- is part of the healthcare business and not an outsider

- is not a cold statistic but a human being with feelings and emotions

- is not someone to argue or match wits with

- is a person with wants; the security officer's job is to fill those wants

- deserves the most courteous and attentive treatment possible

- makes it possible for the security officer to be paid

- is the life blood of every hospital

Inpatients

The basic protection for inpatients comes from the nursing unit staff, which consists of nursing personnel, unit clerk, data entry persons, and ancillary staff. It is extremely rare that security personnel routinely interact with patients on a pro-active security basis.

The nurse assigned to a patient is responsible for his or her total care, which includes the security and safety of the patient. Nurses do, however, receive support from the security system in protecting the patient, just as they receive support from other disciplines in administering medical care.

During non-operational periods, nurses must be acutely aware of who enters the unit and for what purpose. Just as the security role becomes more custodial during the night hours, the nurse assumes a more custodial role for the patient's safety. Of course, nurses have a responsibility during operational periods to challenge strangers on the unit or in patient rooms at any time. In terms of strangers, it is also the responsibility of all staff to inquire of persons in their work area if they or their business is unknown. The need for this inquiry is greatest during the evening and night hours, and it increases the nearer the stranger is to patient care areas. During the late night hours, the nursing unit often becomes very quiet, which in a sense aids unit personnel in their custodial responsibility. The quiet atmosphere means that even minor noises, such as a stairway door opening or closing, will be detected. Nurses must always be sharply attuned to the status of the unit.

The nursing staff is the largest group of employees in the hospital and one with which security must continually interact. According to Kathleen Pedziwiatr, former director of nursing at Alexian Brothers Hospital in Elk Grove, Illinois, one of the difficulties encountered between nursing personnel and security officers is the difference in their general perception of people. On the whole, nurses are generally trusting and sympathetic, while security officers are generally suspicious. Security perceives that nurses do not always attend to security to the degree expected, due to their casual and trusting attitude. Nurses perceive that security officers often look for trouble because of their suspicious attitude. The need for both groups to communicate and understand one another is vital to good patient care and a good protection effort.

In addition to nurses and other unit staff, a variety of groups enter the patient unit areas to carry out their work. They include environmental service employees, volunteers, maintenance workers, physicians, therapists, and technicians. Each of these people also helps to protect the patient. They must investigate or report any suspicious or unusual activity that they observe. Ironically, some of these individuals have been responsible for perpetrating crimes against patients, ranging from petty theft to homicide.

Assisting with Patients

Security officers routinely assist in moving patients about the facility. More frequently, however, security is asked to assist with irrational patients. In some security programs this is a planned function; in others it is considered a necessary evil to be discouraged whenever possible.

Responding to requests for assistance with patients is a valid and necessary function of any protection system; however, the scope of this assistance should be clearly defined. Security personnel should not take the place of medical care personnel. When emergencies occur, security officers should respond as part of the total resources available. This response is best considered a support role, and security should not assume responsibility for the situation or the patient.

The frequency of calls for assistance varies from organization to organization and depends on many factors, including the types of patients the facility serves and the availability of nursing personnel. There is a tendency for security to be called too frequently and thus serve as orderlies. Ironically, the better trained and more responsive the security operation, the greater this tendency becomes. Healthcare security administrators must review and evaluate patient-assistance activity very closely. Interestingly, psychiatric centers make fewer calls for assistance than do general medical facilities of the same size. This is most because psychiatric centers are programmed to care for difficult patients as a routine activity.

The Missing Patient

Missing patients are one area in which patients and security personnel interact. In many cases, this interaction will test the interpersonal skills of the officer. The accountability of patients is not always as exacting as one might expect. Patients may leave the unit to take a walk, go to the cafeteria, find a place to smoke, or even visit other patients without informing unit personnel. Others may be away for tests or treatment, which may not have been properly communicated to all staff. Still others decide they do not want to remain in the facility and leave without informing anyone of their intention. Whatever the case, unit personnel cannot automatically sound an alarm whenever they cannot readily account for a patient. However, when a patient is clearly missing, or there are extenuating circumstances, the unit staff should notify security. Extenuating circumstances may involve the mental state of the patient or situations in which the safety of the patient may be in question.

The two most important factors relative to security involvement in the missing patient incident are timeliness and thoroughness of the search. The probability of a successful search decreases as time increases.

Specific guidelines should cover the actions and responsibilities of the security officers in investigating missing patients. Officers should thoroughly search the common and support areas of the facility, including food service areas, corridors, lobbies, lounges, public washrooms, parking areas, and the grounds. Unit personnel and other staff should search other patient and treatment areas.

When missing patients are located, officers should attempt to persuade them to return to the unit voluntarily. Hospitals bear responsibility for patients who may be irrational. Security officers should use extreme caution in chasing or yelling at patients, because an irrational patient can easily be panicked and might fall or run into a street. Officers should also try to summon medical personnel to assist in returning the patient to the unit. Officers should not use physical force unless they are so directed by a competent authority or, in their judgment, the patient is clearly endangering his or her life or the lives of others. This is a delicate judgment. Officers can be held liable for false arrest or assault and battery if they detain patients against their will. In all instances, officers must complete a detailed incident report describing all the facts of the situation and the action taken.

As a general rule, security should begin their search on the perimeter of the grounds and work inwardly, while other hospital staff begins searching on the unit floor and expands outwardly. It is important also to address questions as to how far off the property the search should be conducted and at what point law enforcement should be notified. Facility property lines should not be used as a "line in the sand" in terms of searching. The search should include blocks surrounding the property; however, this off-property search is generally conducted as a secondary phase to the initial search. A missing patient incident that took place in Pennsylvania illustrates this point. An intensive care patient left his bed at approximately 3:00 A.M. The responsible caregiver notified security within minutes of the situation as she heard the monitoring alarm sound while she was caring for another patient. Security searched the facility and grounds to no avail. At approximately 6:00 A.M., the police were notified by passers-by of a man in a hospital gown lying in the middle of the sidewalk approximately one block from the hospital. The patient, with Foley catheter still in place, was dead.

All healthcare facilities should have the capability to conduct an appropriate search of the premises within 30 minutes of a missing persons report. At the time the initial search is completed, and certainly within 45 minutes of a negative search, the police should be notified. Special circumstances would reduce this time frame appropriate to the information available.

If the search is unsuccessful, officers should report back to the patient care unit to detail their actions and state the outcome of the search. It is not within the general scope of the security program to assume responsibility for anything more than the search. Notifying the administration, the physician, or the family is not the responsibility of the protection officer.

A common medical record form used in many hospitals is the against medical advice (AMA) form. It is normally used for patients who, after admission, decide they do not want to stay in the hospital. If unit personnel cannot persuade these patients that it is in their best interest to remain, the patients are asked to sign the form stating that they understand that they are leaving against medical advice. Patients can refuse to sign the form and should be allowed to leave.

Sometimes when security officers are advised of a missing patient, they discover the patient leaving the facility and getting into a cab or parked vehicle. Officers should, of course, try to persuade the patient to return to the unit. Reluctant patients can often be convinced to go back to the unit, supposedly to sign out. This gives unit personnel an opportunity to talk further with them. Once back on the unit, patients may be more easily persuaded to remain, or to at least to wait until their doctor can be contacted.

Patient Risk Groups

Certain patient risk groups require specific attention relative to security. These basic groups are identified by patient type and include the

VIP patient, the infectious patient, the combative patient, the forensic patient, the wandering patient, and the infant/pediatric patient.

The VIP Patient

The VIP patient is any patient that poses special security problems and may require certain security precautions to be taken. For celebrities and high profile politicians, strict visitor control procedures may be required. In some cases these patients are accompanied by their own security personnel. The hospital's protection service thus has little responsibility for the patient's security. This is especially true when a government figure is involved. Special telephones, quarters for protection personnel, special visitor passes, and the like may require consideration.

The second major type of VIP patient requiring security precautions is the patient who has been threatened or beaten, is a victim of a crime or a witness, or is involved in an activity that puts them a risk of being harmed during treatment. Once the treating organization is aware of such potential danger, there is a responsibility on the part of the organization to take preventive steps. These steps will vary according to the degree of risk and include:

- Removing the patient's name from the general patient population data base. That way, if someone inquires after the patient at the telephone information center or information desk, the operator will indicate that there is no such patient.

- Disconnecting all telephone service to the patient's room.

- Moving the patient to a room that provides maximum surveillance by unit care staff.

- Restricting or denying visitors.

- Providing a patient companion, or sitter, to be with the patient at all times.

- Providing a security guarding arrangement. This would involve the patient who would not be under police control or custody. (The handling of the forensic patient is considered to be in a different patient risk group.)

Figure 11-1 shows an example of a security VIP policy.

The Infectious Patient

When assisting with patients, security personnel have always been concerned about inadvertently contracting an infectious disease. This concern has been heightened by the advent of AIDS and the increase in hepatitis-B infections. AIDS patients are in the final stages of a series of health problems caused by a human immunodeficiency virus (HIV), which can be passed from one person to another through unprotected sexual contact with an infected partner, the sharing of intravenous drug needles and syringes, the exchange of body fluids, and, less frequently, blood transfusions. There is no known risk of infection in most of the situations encountered in daily life and no evidence of transmission of the AIDS virus by everyday contact.

By nature of their occupation, healthcare workers, including security officers, are likely to come in contact with people infected with AIDS or hepatitis-B. The major occupational risk for healthcare workers is the contact of their skin or mucous membranes with infected body fluids or tissues. Exposure can occur from needle stick, cut injuries, and splashes of blood. The virus has also been linked to other body fluids, including semen, amniotic fluid, saliva, tears, urine, vaginal secretions, cerebrospinal fluid, and, possibly, human breast milk.

For security personnel, the risk of exposure to AIDS or hepatitis-B in the course of normal duties is extremely low; exposure could occur only under unusual circumstances. It is possible that security officers might sustain cuts or puncture wounds or be stuck by a needle while assisting with patients or dealing with suspicious people. The risk of infection from being bitten by an infected individual is low.

The first step security management should take is to fight fear with facts. Employees should be reassured that there is little reason to fear that they will be exposed to infection. Continually educating security personnel about the nature of AIDS and how it can be transmitted and informing them of the availability of any emergency equipment will do much to alleviate fear.

<u>Example</u>

**HEALTHCARE SECURITY
POLICY AND PROCEDURE
FOR
THE VIP PATIENT**

GENERAL

The VIP patient is any patient who requires special protection measures during outpatient or inpatient medical services. This patient may be a high profile public figure, a celebrity, or a patient that circumstances or information indicate the patient may be in some elevated degree of danger.

PUBLIC FIGURE/CELEBRITY

Except for emergency treatment or admission the protection of this type of patient is generally preplanned. In many cases the security department will coordinate protection safeguards with the VIP's personal security staff or a public safety agency such as the police, secret service or FBI.

PATIENT IN DANGER

This patient may be in danger due to threats to the family or directly to the patient, the result of a gunshot wound, stabbing, or victim of gang or criminal activity, or being a witness to a major crime.

PROCEDURES

The same type of security safeguards and procedures will be utilized for each type of VIP however the degree of the security precautions and activity will vary with the specific patient situation. In general the security precautions and safeguards could include the following actions:

1. Notify appropriate organization personnel including Risk Management, of patient identity and circumstances requiring increased VIP security measures.
2. Notify public safety agencies if deemed appropriate and/or coordinate efforts with these agencies.
3. Assign a patient room that is away from elevators and fire stairwells or exits.
4. If security officers, bodyguards, or forensic staff will be utilized assign a patient room at the far end of a dead end corridor. If this type of personnel is not utilized assign the patient a room close to the nursing station where good surveillance of the room can be maintained.
5. Remove the patient name from the patient information system, Front Desk, and census reports substituting an assumed name for the actual patient.
6. Maintain the patient's chart in the patient's room.
7. Brief the nursing unit staff of general information and/or specific action items required of medical care staff.
8. Determine if any visitors will be allowed.
9. Obtain name and telephone number of person(s) coordinating security for the VIP who can be contacted as questions arise or if there is an emergency. This contact person may be a family member.
10. Utilize security officer briefing procedures to communicate information to all security personnel.

Figure 11-1 An Example of a Hospital Security-Related VIP Policy and Procedure

Legal issues should not be overlooked when educating personnel about AIDS. A suit was filed against Kings County Hospital in Brooklyn by a doctor who contracted the AIDS virus when she was stuck by a needle left among gauze on a patient's bed. The suit claims negligence and breach of contract because a safe workplace and safety equipment should have been provided and the defendants should have warned and trained staff members about the dangers of AIDS-infected needles.

Another legal element that must be considered is invasion of privacy. If a staff member released information about an AIDS patient and that patient lost his or her job, the value of the lost income would certainly be sought in a lawsuit. Security supervisors can protect such information by

- Reporting known infractions of organizational policies regarding patient information

- Reminding security officers to keep all security reports and other organizational documents confidential

- Taking appropriate steps to discourage talk among employees about any patient

The Combative Patient

Security personnel assist with combative patients most often in four areas of the facility: the emergency department, mental health areas, and the general nursing unit and medical clinics. To provide patient assistance regarding combative patients, all security personnel should be well-trained in verbal and non-verbal de-escalation measures and restraint procedures.

Emergency Department

The emergency department requires frequent security assistance, especially in facilities that treat many drug overdose patients, patients with injuries due to shooting or stabbing incidents, and patients with mental health or drug impairments. This section primarily concerns the security officer's interactions with patients and staff in the emergency department. Other security concerns for this department are discussed in Chapters 15 and 17. Belligerent and intoxicated patients may also require security assistance, particularly when they are brought for medical care against their will. These patients are often brought to the medical care treatment facility by law enforcement authorities, ambulance crews, or friends/relatives; often the transporters are more aware of the treatment needed than the patient is.

When friends or relatives are present, there is an added concern for the protection officer. If the accompanying people are intoxicated or drug impaired, they will require control or at least surveillance. They can easily become annoyed or angered at delays in treatment, or they may have their own ideas of what treatment is required. Emergency department physicians have estimated that more than 75 percent of patients and visitors to some inner-city emergency departments are under the influence of drugs.

Emergency department clerks and triage nurses are generally the first staff members to interact with people entering the department. They must be stationed to observe people entering the department, to provide service and directions, and to keep the area under surveillance to detect people in distress.

Only in very large security operations or in areas with a demonstrated history of frequent harmful situations is it necessary to station a security officer in the emergency department 24 hours a day. The emergency room staff must be alert for impending disruptions. When they suspect trouble, they should call for a security presence. The only preventive action required may be for a security officer to patrol through the area or to stand by unobtrusively.

In smaller security operations, a security officer may be assigned to the emergency room during peak periods. In one small hospital, an officer is assigned every Friday and Saturday night between 7:00 P.M. and 3:00 A.M.

When security officers are in a support role as members of a team managing a combative patient's behavior, these guidelines, developed by the American College of Emergency Physicians,[1] should be followed:

- Do not use the word "security" or "police" when calling for assistance

- The most experienced medical staff member should assume a clear leadership role

- Each member of the response team should be given specific instructions about their role

- Search the patient after he or she is restrained

- Only trained staff should apply restraint devices

- Never leave the restrained patient alone

- The patient chart should be updated with information about why restraints were used, what type, and for how long

In all instances in which security has assisted with patient restraint, officers should complete a report detailing this assistance. Figure 11-2 shows a sample of a patient restraint form. Depending on the degree of interaction involved, a security incident report may also be required.

Mental Health Unit

A call to the mental health unit generally indicates that an emergency exists and that additional help is required to deal with the problem. In some facilities, the standard operating procedure is for uniformed security officers to don a gown before entering the unit. This procedure is intended to minimize the officer's authority in the eyes of the problem patient and the other patients on the unit. A more common procedure is for uniformed officers to respond as they would to any other call for assistance. The rationale for this response is that mental health treatment should provide experience and therapy so the patient will be able to function in society. In society, someone who causes a disturbance should expect the police to be called.

Armed officers, as opposed to unarmed officers, must use a different response to problems in the mental health unit. Each organization must develop its own approach. In one large facility, the first security officer to arrive waits outside the unit and collects equipment from the other officers who respond. Other hospitals have installed gun lockers just outside the unit. Of course, circumstances will prevail, and in a non-medical emergency, such as a fire, a different response is indicated.

As a general rule, security officers should not patrol mental health units. Regular medical care personnel provide surveillance and control of patients and visitors as part of their routine activity. However, security may be part of the access control system for locked units and they may also be required to patrol under special circumstances.

The Interrelationship of Security with Patients and Visitors

WellStar Health System
Security Services
Seclusion/Restraint Checklist

Patient_____ Patient ID#_____ Date_____

Type of Restraint_____ Seclusion (Room_____)

Facility_____ Dispatcher (KH)_____

Officer Transport from ED to Security Holding_____

Time started (from Emergency Dept.)_____ Time called SO_____

Time left hospital with SO_____ Total time_____

Name of SO picked-up patient_____

Time	Visual Alert/Sleeping Belligerent, Confused	Pt. Obsv 30 Mins	NV 2 Hrs	Fluids 2 Hrs	Elim 2 Hrs	Vital Signs 4 Hrs	Food 6 Hrs	Comments	Initials

Other Comments_____

_____

_____
(Initials)

Figure 11-2 An Example of a Security Patient Restraint Form (Courtesy of Wellstar Health System, Marietta, Georgia)

Elopement is always a concern when treating the mental health patient. It is reported that 3 to 15 percent of all patients admitted to mental health units elope each year. Certain sources suggest there are identifiable characteristics of the patient who is prone to elope. Such sources indicate these patients are generally male and usually verbalize a desire to leave prior to elopement. Often they have eloped on prior occasions and have a diagnosis of schizophrenia or a mood disorder.[2] Security and the mental health unit must work closely with each other to manage the preventive aspects of elopement.

General Nursing Unit

Another category of patients who require assistance is the so-called "normal patient" on the nursing unit. In some cases, patients not previously diagnosed as possible combative patients may suddenly and unexpectedly develop irrational behavior. Generally, the nursing staff is not prepared to handle this unpredicted behavior and must seek off-unit resources.

Regardless of the situation, security officers should not be forced to render medical judgments. They should base their actions on specific instructions from a nurse or a physician at the scene. If these instructions are not forthcoming upon their arrival, officers should determine who is in charge and inquire about their role and necessary actions. At all times, security officers should act to assist and support rather than assume primary responsibility. The more responsive security is in providing patient assistance, the more often they will be called.

Medical/Dental Clinics

General medical/dental clinics can be an area of disturbances caused by both patients and visitors. There are at least two factors creating conditions for such problems: the large number of people who frequent these facilities and the length of time patients must wait to be served. It is not unusual for a clinic patient to have four or five persons accompanying them. These "visitors" are often infants and small children, which can add to confusion and frustration. Extended clinic hours have reduced instances of disruptive behavior as parents are less likely to bring their children as sitters become more available in the evening hours.

The Forensic Patient

The forensic patient is a patient under police, court-ordered, or correctional institution custody. The forensic patient may either be brought to the medical care facility for emergency or outpatient treatment or for a planned hospitalization as an inpatient. In all cases, the forensic patient must be viewed as a potential threat to the facility.

An added security dimension associated with this type of patient is due to a very questionable practice on the part of the police. This practice occurs when police discover that an arrested person will be in the hospital for a number of days, and, therefore, "un-arrest" the patient to avoid the time and expense of furnishing a 24-hour police guard. In these cases, the police ask the provider to advise them on the planned discharge of the patient so that they can show up and re-arrest the individual. In other cases, the arrested patient is simply issued a citation to appear in court.

Confusion and conflict can take place when caring for the forensic patient. Law enforcement or correctional personnel often do not understand the procedures of medical care, while medical care staff do not always understand the implications of the custody of the patient.

The JCAHO also views forensic patients—especially those patients who are shackled to their beds—as being at some risk should there occur a fire or other emergency situation. The commission has issued a standard regarding the training of guarding forensic persons. This standard can be found in the Human Resources section of the accreditation manual. The current commission standard (H.R.4.1) requires that any person guarding a forensic patient receive training on how to interact in the medical care setting, on procedures for unusual events (fire, disasters, medical emergencies), on proper channels of communications, and on the distinction of the administrative/clinical restraint/seclusion elements of control.

There are a number of ways to accomplish this training. The most common method is to furnish written information to the forensic staff (guard) upon admission of the patient. In this method, the first guard is asked to make this information part of the agency's post orders and to pass on the information to all other guards. Figure 11-3 shows an example of a security-briefing card for forensic staff.

Health First

Forensic staff is defined as correctional agency or law enforcement personnel assigned to guard a patient-prisoner. This information is provided to all forensic staff.

1. Forensic staff shall remain in the room with the patient-prisoner, in the anteroom when the patient-prisoner is in isolation, or in a designated area when the patient-prisoner is in an intensive care unit or in the OR and shall accompany the patient-prisoner at all times when they must be transported to areas outside their room.

2. Administrative restraints must be worn by all patient-prisoner at all times, except to facilitate patient care. Whenever restraints are removed, forensic staff must remain in visual contact.

3. Patient-prisoners shall not be allowed visitors.

4. Patient-prisoners shall never be informed of follow-up appointments. Return appointment/follow-up care shall be received by forensic staff in writing and in a sealed envelope.

5. Questions, complaints or problems involving patient-prisoners or other issues should be directed to Hospital Security (CCH x0, HRMC x7380, PBCH pager 634-8582) or to the patient's nurse for clinical issues.

6. During a fire alarm or other emergency, forensic staff shall prepare the patient-prisoner to be moved, if necessary, and await instructions from hospital staff.

7. Applicable patient rights shall be reviewed with forensic staff.

– Over –

Figure 11-3 A Security Briefing Information Card Furnished to Forensic Guard Staff (Courtesy of Health First, Inc., Melbourne, Florida)

Code Red	-	Fire/Smoke
Code Blue	-	Cardiac/Arrest
Code Black	-	Bomb Threat
Code White	-	Crisis Assistance
Code Green	-	Missing Patient
Code Yellow	-	Disaster
Code Alert	-	Infant/Pediatric Abduction

Code Red - Fire reporting procedures - Notify the nearest hospital staff member.

Chemical/Bio-Hazard Spill - Notify the nearest hospital staff member.

Figure 11-3 *Continued*

A rather unique program developed for training law enforcement agencies in guarding inpatient prisoners was developed jointly by three hospital systems in Brevard County, Florida. This program, spearheaded by James C. Kending of Health First in Melbourne, Florida, consisted of developing a 10-minute video relative to guarding the forensic patient. This video was distributed to some 20 area criminal justice agencies to be used as a roll-call training activity. The video is also being utilized by the Brevard County law enforcement and corrections academy in their recruit training program.

The guarding of a prisoner by a governmental agency can be costly and may deplete needed street coverage. It has become quite common for governmental agencies to contract with private security companies to perform prisoner guard services. Healthcare Security Services of Denver, Colorado, has been providing this type of service for the past twelve years, serving such clients as police, state correctional institutions, and the U.S. Marshall's office. Since the company provides day-to-day security in the majority of facilities in Colorado, the prisoner guard service is a natural extension of its services. The fact that one company can offer both services mean that the guarding officer is already trained as a healthcare security officer. However, the day-to-day and prisoner guard service are kept separate, with the only link being the radio system and emergency support. In this respect, facility-assigned officers do not provide prisoner guard assistance in their day-to-day deployment.

The following is a list of prisoner guard instructions utilized by Healthcare Security Services.

Prisoner Guard Service Instructions

General

The Prisoner Guard Service (Service) is offered to a Law Enforcement Agency (Agency) on a contract basis. The Agency contracts with Healthcare Security Services (HSS) to guard a prisoner while he/she is a patient in a healthcare facility.

Responsibility

The officer's responsibility is to prevent the prisoner from:

- Injuring him/herself, visitors, other patients, security staff, or the medical staff
- Escaping
- Gaining access to contraband or a weapon
- Communicating with an unauthorized person

The officer is in charge of ALL non-medical care of the prisoner. The officer controls the prisoner's movements inside and outside of the room, as well as visitations and telephone access.

The prisoner does not have input into the security measures used and restriction applied. Hospital staff also does not have input into the security measures used.

Stay alert. Pay attention to details. Do not be lulled into a false sense of confidence that the prisoner or visitors will always cooperate.

Confidentiality

Do not discuss the prisoner's specific criminal history with *anyone*. If the staff is concerned about safety, assure them of your competence.

Refer *all* medical questions to the medical staff.

Do not discuss service procedures with the prisoner or his/her legal representative.

Confidentiality continues after the prisoner has left HSS custody.

Service Paperwork

Form numbers 1, 2, 3, 4 and 5 are described as needed.

The Assigned Officer Log (PGS Form #3) is the time-keeping record for the service. Record the date, time on duty, time off duty and your name each time you are assigned to this case. Also record your time on your regular time card.

The Activity Log (PGS Form #4) is to be completed by each officer assigned. Record the following:

- Issue/retrieval of the prisoner's personal belongings
- All telephone communications
- Any out-of-room trips by the prisoner
- All non-medical visitations
- Periodic checks of the prisoner and restraints

Use a Security Incident Report (SIR) for unusual events described in these orders. Do not distribute any log, report, or SIR from the service to the facility administration or facility security staff.

Prisoner Property

As few items as possible should accompany the prisoner. The prisoner may have the following personal items:

- Writing materials
- Legal paperwork
- Books/magazines
- Money to purchase television privileges
- Candy (if not medically restricted)

All personal items will remain in the control of the security officer when not in use. Keep the items in an area of the room out of reach of the prisoner.

Record all personal items given to and taken from the prisoner on the Activity Log.

Refer to special instructions on the Prisoner Information page (PGS Form #1)

Communications

The Agency may issue a radio and instruction for its use.

HSS may issue a radio. Do not give the prisoner's room or phone number over the radio. The Operations Center will provide other pertinent instructions for radio use.

Notify the Agency and then the Operations Center in case of emergency. An emergency will always be documented on a SIR. All report copies will be retained by HSS. No documentation is available to the hospital.

Refer to special instructions on the Prisoner Information page (PGS Form #1).

Admission to Facility

The prisoner will stay in transport restraints until placed in the room.

An assigned security officer or the Agency will stay within a controlling distance during the admitting process.

An assigned security officer of the Agency will observe exists, hallways, and other persons in the area.

The prisoner should be kept in an unused admitting room, private office, emergency room treatment area, or a transport vehicle if a room (without another patient) is not available.

Initial Room Search

Search the area the prisoner will have access to while lying in bed (prior to placing the prisoner in bed). Items of risk or contraband will be removed from the area.

Look for the following items during the search:

- Medical instruments left by accident or not in use
- Metal eating utensils
- Metal, wood or any items that could be used as a weapon
- Glass items

After the area is clear the following should be completed:

- Place the prisoner in the bed
- Apply holding restraints
- Remove transportation restraints

The rest of the room will be searched *after* the prisoner is properly restrained in bed.

All questionable items will be removed from the room, unless specified in writing by the attending physician.

Ongoing Room Control

Only plastic eating utensils are to be provided with each meal tray. Count and keep track of the utensils to insure none are retained by the prisoner.

Follow these procedures at all times:

- *Never* leave the prisoner alone
- Always keep your firearm away from prisoner, if you are armed
- Maintain your position in the room to control the door and the prisoner
- Immediately document any breach of policy or confrontation on a SIR. All report copies will be retained in the room until the prisoner is discharged.

Prisoner movement within the room is allowed only under the following conditions:

- The prisoner may use the bathroom in the room (if medically approved)
- The officer will place himself between the prisoner and the door
- The prisoner may sit in a room chair (in leg restraints) if ordered by a physician and the prisoner is not a threat
- The prisoner may not wander in the room or hallways
- The door to the hallway should be kept open

At the time of a shift change in security officers, the on-coming officer will:

- Check restraints for application and security
- Account for all supplies and equipment; document any missing item on an SIR and notify the Agency and the Operations Center

At the time of a change in security officers, the off-going security officer will:

- Brief the on-coming officer of change in medical status, threats, breaches of policy, and all information concerning the prisoner watch

Refer to special instructions on the Prisoner Information page (PGS Form #1)

Security Officer Break

Each officer is on-duty the entire assigned shift. Bring a lunch and other comfort items with you. Do not "switch" duties with any HSS or other facility security officer. Do not request a security supervisor to provide "relief."

Request the duty nurse to be present with the prisoner when you take a restroom break. Insure restraints are in place. Use the prisoner's restroom.

Do not watch television, read, or engage in personal telephone conversations, which limit your ability to guard the prisoner.

Do not sleep or become over-relaxed.

Medical Visits

Medical treatment personnel will be allowed unlimited access to the prisoner. An identification check may be required if the officer is in doubt about the identification of the staff member.

Record the time and general activity performed by each medical staff member on the Activity Log. The name of the staff member is not required to be logged unless unusual activity or circumstances warrant such documentation.

Non-Medical Visitors

Record each visitor on the Activity Log (PGS Form #4). Visitor procedures are as follows:

- The Agency must be aware of and pre-approve each visitor

- Only one visitor is allowed at a time

- Other visitors must wait in a facility waiting area; not in the hallway

- No more than two visitors per 24 hours are allowed

- Visits will last no longer than 15 minutes

- The prisoner must stay restrained

- The visitor will not bring a coat, purse, package, or any other item into the room in which any weapon(s) could be hidden

- The visitor will *not* make physical contact with the prisoner

- Security must remain in the room during all visits and observe all activities in the room (including attorney visits)

- Security can terminate a visit any time the prisoner or visitor is not in control. Notify the Agency and the Operations Center of the terminated visit and document the information on a SIR.

Refer to special instructions on the Prisoner Information page (PGS Form #1)

Phone Calls

The prisoner may not accept incoming calls.
    The prisoner may make outgoing calls to Agency approved persons *only*. The security officer will dial the telephone number and confirm the correct person has been reached.
    Record each call on the Activity Log.
    Refer to special instructions on the Prisoner Information page (PGS Form #1).

Media Contact

All requests by the media to contact the prisoner will be referred to the Agency.

Movement Outside the Room

Notify the Operations Center whenever the prisoner leaves the room. Provide the dispatch with the destination and estimated length of stay. Record the time and destination on the Activity Log (PGS Form #4).
    Transport the prisoner in a wheelchair or on a gurney.
    Restrain the prisoner during transport and, if possible, during treatment. If this is not possible and the escape risk warrants, summon additional security or law enforcement to ensure that control and custody is maintained.
    Keep the prisoner in a private office or empty treatment area, not in a public area. Maintain a low profile so that other patients and visitors do not become unduly alarmed.
    Accompany the prisoner in the treatment area or remain outside the treatment area but in a controlling position. Notify security or the local police agency if additional manpower is required to maintain control.
    If unable to return to the room in the estimated time, re-contact the Operations Center with an update.
    Notify the Operation Center upon your return to the room. Record the time and general activities that occurred on the Activity Log (PGS Form #4).

An officer may refuse an out-of-room non-emergency treatment, if prisoner control cannot be maintained. Notify the Agency and the Operations Center of the refusal and document the information on a SIR.

Refer to special instructions on the Prisoner Information page (PGS Form #1).

Subsequent Room Search

Use extreme caution upon re-entering the room after a movement within the facility. Before the medical staff removes the prisoner from the wheelchair or gurney, search the bed area and the room, as outlined in the *Initial Room Search*, unless the room was in full view by the officer at all times.

An in-house security program administrator may wish to consider the prisoner guard service as a revenue source. The provision of this service would generally become an assignment within the deployment plan and relief would be provided as a normal rotation deployment. There should, however, be a formal agreement with the agency having jurisdiction over the prisoner with the cost of the service clearly spelled out.

The Wandering Patient (Dementia- and Psychological-Related)

Wandering patients are a security concern presented by certain types of dementia patients, most frequently those with Alzheimer's disease. It is estimated that each week at least one resident of the nation's nursing home facilities wanders away from a facility and dies. The wandering patient is of course not limited to nursing homes. The mental health facility and even certain patients in the general medical/surgical category can be wandering patients. Intensive care staff have long recognized psychological responses of patients, which include delirium, catastrophic reaction, and euphoric response. The most frequent of these responses is delirium, which has been described on a continuum from slight clouding of consciousness to a full-blown psychotic reaction. In this respect, patients experience varying degrees of cognitive impairment.

A patient movement control system utilizing an electronic tag is a fairly common safeguard for suspected wandering patients. The patient wears a tag that contains a radio frequency circuit; this circuit communicates with a detection sensor usually installed at the exit door or elevator opening. Some systems do not use multiple-detection sensors at doors, but have a radio receiver installed at a central location instead. In these systems, the distance between the tag and central monitor is constantly measured with an alarm, which sounds when a pre-determined distance is exceeded. Electronic systems can be installed as standalone systems at each door or as centralized computer-controlled systems. Computerized systems are capable of identifying the individual patient and can display the alarm information as either text or a graphic map. Individual tags can be de-activated in a number of ways to allow family or staff to take a patient out of the defined secured area.[3]

A rather extensive radio frequency tag system for managing long-term care patients is currently being used at the Sunnybrook Health Sciences Center, which is part of the University of Toronto (Canada). The Sunnybrook Health Sciences Center is a 1,300-bed facility, with 550 beds being occupied by long-term care patients. There are, thus, varying degrees of control depending on the unit and type of patients. In addition to the radio frequency system, the hospital has what they refer to as the "Blue Shirt Program." In this program, the at-risk cognitively impaired patients wear a blue shirt with the Sunnybrook Health Sciences Center logo emblazoned in yellow across the back. All staff members—and even members of the immediate community—are educated on the Blue Shirt Program and are asked to report any observed wandering patients.[4]

An effective approach to managing the problem of wandering patients requires proper facility design and physical security safeguards, good control policies and procedures put into practice by staff, and ongoing staff training in the management of the wandering patient.

The Infant and Pediatric Patient

A great deal has been written about preventive steps that can be taken to avoid the abduction of newborn infants. A facility birthing unit is generally classified as a security sensitive area in terms of JCAHO standards. As such, the security issues surrounding the abduction of infants will be more fully addressed in Chapter 17.

The possibility of discharging an infant to the wrong parents is a concern that requires proper clinical management. Security is not typically involved in developing clinical policies and procedures, but may well become involved should an actual event occur.

The pediatric patient presents several security risks, including the possibility of abduction and of physical abuse while in the hospital. In addition, pediatric patients may wander off the unit. The possibility of abduction is somewhat higher for the pediatric patient than the newborn infant. This higher risk is the result of a greater length of stay, generally less security precautions, and the number of custody battles that involve children. In pediatric abductions, the perpetrator is almost always known, and in many cases there is significant early warning that allows pro-active security measures to be put in place.

In recent years, medical care providers and healthcare security administrators have become more and more aware of a form of child abuse referred to as Munchausen Syndrome by Proxy (MSBP). It is a form of child abuse wherein a parent (usually the mother) intentionally fabricates illness in her child and repeatedly presents the child for medical care, disclaiming knowledge as to the cause of the problem. Child victims of MSBP are at risk for serious injury or death. The security department therefore plays a critical role in investigating and managing MSBP. The following are the "symptoms" of MSBP:

- Illness in a child that is simulated (faked) or produced by a parent or other caretaker or both.

- Presentation of the child for medical assessment and care, usually persistently, often resulting in multiple medical procedures.

- Denial of the knowledge by the parent as to the cause of the child's illness.

- Subsiding of acute symptoms and signs when the child is separated from the parent.

- Typically, but not always, the mother spends a good deal of time in the hospital with the child and exhibits a remarkable familiarity with medical terminology. She may be "confidentially friendly" with the hospital staff, although she may show frustration with her child's chronic illness and anger at the medical staff's inadequate vigor in pursuing her child's problems. She may insist that she is the "only one" for whom the child will eat, drink, or swallow medicines. The syndrome often persists for years and can result in death.

Bonnie Michelman, CHPA, CPP, Director Police and Security, and a leading security expert in MSBP, suggests that a multi-disciplinary child protection team should become involved the moment MSBP is suspected. The team should include medical personnel, security management, the primary care nurse, social services, mental health professionals, and an epidemiologist (a person who, in part, specializes in figuring out the cause of a disease). Together they must determine whether the child's medical condition can be attributed to MSBP, warranting civil proceedings to remove the child from the perpetrator's care and, possibly, criminal proceedings. Police and security personnel should become involved early in the case, collecting evidence collection, making timely arrests, and helping to develop a case for prosecution. Once the child is assumed to be at risk, a customized protection plan for the child must be designed and implemented.

Patient Property

A highly visible and troublesome security problem is missing patient property. The average financial loss is quite small; however, large losses do occasionally occur. The impact of property loss on a sick patient and the negative public relations that result indicate a concern far more important than the value of property involved.

Most hospital facilities engage in a program commonly referred to as pre-admission registration, which obtains certain information from the patient before admission. The pre-admission information, or instruction, form should state that the hospital does not have adequate storage for personal property and should instruct the patient to leave jewelry, wallets, radios, and similar items at home. The statement should also note that the hospital cannot be responsible for personal property brought to the facility by the patient. Bold type should be used to highlight this policy.

When patients are admitted, the person who signs the admissions form should be required to initial a statement that the hospital is not responsible for personal property not in its possession or control. The patient should be advised to surrender for safekeeping any keys, credit cards, jewelry, watches, and money over an established limit. There have been numerous instances in which a patient's purse has been stolen from the bedside or closet and the keys and identification used to set up a burglary at the patient's home.

General Principles for Handling Patient Valuables

Property being checked with the hospital requires a sound handling procedure. Hospital security administrators should check the following principles against their current procedure:

1. The primary responsibility for the accountability and storage of patient valuables belongs to the business office.

2. A heavy, numbered envelope is used, which, when sealed, must be torn open to remove the contents.

3. Receipts are written out in triplicate. One copy stays with the patient (sometimes affixed to the chart), one copy is placed inside the envelope, and one copy is sent to the accounting or security office.

4. A numerical listing of envelopes with patient names is recorded for accountability. The property stored in the envelopes is not listed on this record.

5. Each envelope is inspected when shifts change.

6. Specific hours have been established concerning the withdrawal of stored property. This usually coincides with the cashier's hours. There is no need to provide withdrawal service on a 24-hour basis, and, in fact, this practice is detrimental to the security effort. Envelopes should be secured after hours, and the new envelopes should be dropped into a non-retrievable night depository box by two employees.
Patients discharged when the cashier is closed should not be able to retrieve their valuables. This does not mean that patients, or their representatives, must return to the hospital during regular business hours. Some hospitals make arrangements to mail the envelope and its contents to the patient.

7. When the patient requests the partial withdrawal of property, a new envelope and receipt are prepared, and the number of the original envelope and the original receipt are included.

Regardless of how well admissions personnel perform their job, some patient will always end up with too much personal property in the room. The nursing staff should assume some responsibility in eliminating this vulnerability. They should encourage the patient to send property home or to permit the hospital to hold the property for safekeeping. Otherwise, an admission clerk must respond to the unit; in some cases, the responsibility is assigned to the security department to obtain the property and transport it to the safekeeping area.

Outpatient property can also present security problems. Outpatients are presumed to be better able to care for their property than inpatients. Small signs in clothes-changing areas should indicate that the organization is not responsible for lost or missing property.

Hospitals should deny all claims for missing property that was not held by the hospital. Weak-hearted administrators or risk managers who pay these claims will find that a monstrous and costly situation may develop. Each claim must be evaluated on its own merits.

VISITORS

In contrast to limited patient contact, security officers will often initiate contact with visitors, vendors, and suppliers. In regulating parking, loading docks, ambulance entrances, and building access, security officers take on the task of regulating visitors. Once visitors reach their intended destination, such as a patient room or the outpatient department, the regulating task is transferred to the facility personnel responsible for the specific work area or unit.

In all contacts, whether with a patient, visitor, or employee, security officers must bear in mind that they are representatives of the hospital administration. They must make every effort to ensure that their interactions are carried out with tact and diplomacy. Security officers are often the first people encountered upon entering the healthcare system. Impressions made at this point are lasting, and security officers should capitalize on this opportunity to act professionally.

It is generally agreed that sick or convalescing patients need visitors as part of the recovery process. On the other hand, visitors sometimes interfere with medical care, refuse to leave when asked, steal, complain, sleep in patient rooms, litter, engage in loud and boisterous conduct, and leave patients exhausted or in a state of tension, which can be detrimental to the recovery process.

Many factors affect visitor control. Chief among them is the philosophy of the administration. Some administrators feel strongly that visiting is the right of the public and should not be controlled or discouraged. Others feel that good patient care requires strict visitor control. The trend toward more liberal visiting policies peaked in the mid-1990s. Today, there is a noticeable shift toward more restrictive visiting, brought on, in part, by the greater awareness of workplace violence.

A second major factor affecting visitor control is that the poor layout and design of many healthcare facilities greatly hinder meaningful visitor control, at least in terms of the cost of overcoming the design deficiency.

Six areas of the hospital present special visitor control considerations: the medical/surgical patient units, pediatric units, obstetrical units, psychiatric units, intensive care units, and isolation units. The discussion here focuses on the overall visitor control problem because these units generally rely on special procedures and unit personnel for control.

Some people question whether visitor control rightfully belongs in the realm of security operations. This view may have merit when the concern is for legitimate visitors during designated visitor hours. However, overall access control that includes visitors during late-night hours is a protection responsibility.

An adjunct to access control is the questioning of persons, including visitors and employees, who appear to need help, or persons who are acting or looking suspicious. People who are stopped by security and questioned concerning their business can often become annoyed or hostile regardless of the approach or intent of the security officer. Security officers at New York University Medical Center carry cards that are handed to persons who are stopped by the officer making the inquiry. The card, as shown in Figure 11-4, has been beneficial in explaining the general policy of the medical center and in de-escalating negative behavior.

Time Periods

To properly view access control, three distinct time periods, each presenting different security ramifications, should be considered:

NYU MEDICAL CENTER
A private university in the public service

Thank you for your patience. As part of our expanded effort to protect you and the property of NYU Medical Center a security officer has stopped you to request identification or a package pass. We appreciate your cooperation.

Security Department - Ext. 5038

Figure 11-4 Information Card (Courtesy New York University Medical Center Security Department)

designated patient visiting hours; operational, non-visiting hours; and non-operational hours.

Patient Visiting Hours

The time designated by the facility for visiting patients can vary from 24 hours (no restrictions) to specific hours. Normally, patient visiting hours are during the afternoon and early evening. Most facilities limit patients to no more than two visitors at any one time. Specialized units may be even more restrictive.

The majority of hospitals do not provide visitor identification during regular visiting hours. For those that do, there are two basic types of visitor control currently in use: a card system or a badge system. Both systems operate in basically the same manner, and the passes can be color-coded for various areas or according to the day of the week. The general procedure is to prepare two cards or badges for each patient. These passes are issued when the visitor enters the facility. When both cards or badges have been given out, the next visitor is told to wait until a pass is returned to the control point. To promote good public relations, the clerk often calls the room to let the patient know that another visitor is waiting. Some facilities provide house phones in the waiting area to permit the visitor to call the patient's room.

The details of these systems can be tailored to meet a facility's specific needs. Some facilities use a self-adhesive disposable badge, while others use a re-useable laminated visitor badge. A limited number of facilities custom-make badges for visitors using PCs and video-imaging techniques. The latter is very costly, and the question of cost effectiveness is a serious consideration.

Badge and pass systems can work; however, numerous elevators and stairwells leading to patient units can tempt visitors to bypass the entire system. A visitor control plan used during regular visiting hours should be considered as minimal protection for the patient and as a screening procedure at best.

Regardless of the procedures used, the ultimate responsibility for patient visitor control must remain with the personnel assigned to the patient care units. They must determine whether a patient has too many visitors, or whether the visitors will have an adverse effect on the patient or the facility as a whole. A uniformed nurse or nursing assistant can generally correct a visitor without adverse public reaction. If unit personnel cannot resolve the problem, a security officer may then be called for support. Security officers should not be called on until other options have been unsuccessfully exercised.

In some programs, security officers make the rounds of patient rooms when visiting hours are over and tell people it is time to leave. This is not a good practice. Unit personnel should handle this responsibility because they know who has been granted extended visiting time. It is considered poor public relations for security officers to perform this unit management responsibility.

Operational, Non-Visiting Hours

The second period for which visitor control must be considered is when the facility is operational but outside of the designated visiting hours. There is always the person who is leaving town and wants to visit before leaving, or the out-of-town visitor who was delayed and could not get to the facility during regular visiting hours. These and other extenuating circumstances—some legitimate and some contrived—must be managed in the visitor control plan. An overly strict policy will cause endless problems for the hospital, and an overly lenient policy renders the visitor control program ineffective.

Regardless of the system in effect, someone must be available to make decisions regarding exceptions to the visitor policy. Many facilities refer after-hours visitors directly to the nurse in charge of the unit. This is a very time-consuming function for the nurse, and as might be expected, there is a tremendous lack of consistency. Some nurses honor virtually any request, and some take a very restrictive course of action. However, the charge nurse is in the best position to evaluate the appropriateness of the request or finding the unexpected presence of visitors in a patient's room.

Non-Operational Hours

The non-operational period is generally the most manageable of the three time periods. Non-operational hours vary among hospitals. Most facilities close down after visiting hours, but many unlock various entrances and exits for shift changes in the absence of electronic locking systems, providing controlled employee access points. Whenever possible, the facility should close down one-half hour after the night visiting hours and remain in the non-operational (access control) status until 5:30 or 6:00 A.M. each day.

When a facility is in the non-operational mode, access should be tightly controlled. All people entering the facility should be challenged, their purpose for entering the facility should be established, and their entry should be authorized. Obviously, the integrity of the access control system can be compromised by many means. Compromises can occur when a visitor or employee opens an exit door to permit entry and when exit doors do not latch properly. Security patrols and alarm hardware at emergency exit doors are helpful in preventing breaches of the security system.

During the non-operational period, the entire complex should be locked except for public (visitors/patients) entrances where a visitor control person is in attendance. The most common night entrance is the emergency department entry; in facilities that do not provide emergency care service, it is generally the main entrance. All general-use doors available during the operational period should have signs directing the public to the designated night entrance when these general-use doors are locked.

In many facilities, all entrances are locked, and controls vary from night doorbells, to closed-circuit television, to security officers. A growing trend is to develop a vestibule or waiting area with a security officer controlling a second set of locked doors with a manual or electrical release system. Also in wide use are portable desks that can be moved to a control point during the controlled access hours.

A current design concept in medical center construction is to connect physician office buildings to the hospital proper along with connected parking decks. These connecting corridors usually have a major entrance, which provides a good access point for effecting control.

All who enter the facility during the non-operational period must be cleared for admittance. The control point should be supplied with resource data. A computer database listing all patients and any restrictions, such as "no visitors," "family only," and "wife may visit anytime" is a common resource. A pre-surgical visitor list is also helpful, because many of these visitors arrive quite early in the morning, before the night access control systems are terminated. A computer reduces paperwork and is generally more accurate.

When a patient's condition deteriorates, the physician often asks the family to come to the facility. Unit nursing personnel are almost always aware of this situation and should notify the public access control point so that access can be expeditiously handled. It is poor public relations when family members have been called and are unnecessarily delayed because no one notified the person at control point.

All access control personnel must exercise extreme caution, so that legitimate access to the facility is not denied. A person who appears to be intoxicated may be a diabetic in shock seeking medical care.

After-Hours Badging (Non-Operational Time Period)

A system of badging after-hours visitors should be established even if there is open visiting during the day and early evening hours. A system of pressure-sensitive adhesive paper badges can be used quite effectively. After a person is cleared for access, the date and destination can be written on the badge. A log should be maintained that includes name, time, destination, purpose, patient to be visited, and the visitor's signature. The signature is helpful psychologically because it implies stricter control. In some control programs, personal identification, such as a driver's license or social security card, is required; however, this requirement is somewhat superfluous as legitimate visitors will not be denied entry just because they cannot produce such identification. If such identification is an element of the access control program, the identification itself should not be held by the facility to be returned upon exiting.

One of the pitfalls of an after-hours badging program is legitimate visitors who enter the facility during regular visiting hours when no pass or badge system is in effect. If they are given permission by unit personnel to remain after visiting hours or even for the entire night, the charge nurse should be required to send them to the access control point for badging. In this way, all late-night visitors will be badged—not just those entering after the night-access control system goes into effect.

Night outpatients and people accompanying them often present a control problem. It is not uncommon for someone who requires emergency room treatment to arrive with numerous friends or relatives. Because treatment is not instantaneous, these non-badged people often leave the waiting area to explore. The proper layout and design of the emergency department is covered in Chapter 17.

Large Acreage Facilities

Visitors to healthcare facilities with extensive grounds (often government facilities) can be effectively controlled at a single vehicle entrance. These facilities generally have some form of perimeter barrier, and all traffic can be channeled through a central access control point. Most control systems record the visit on a log and issue a pass to be displayed on the dashboard of the vehicle. The pass is retrieved when the vehicle leaves. This system of vehicle access control does not preclude another system of visitor control at any of the units within the perimeter.

Conclusion

All medical care facilities require a system of visitor control tailored to the specific needs of their facility. Systems cannot simply be transplanted; however, a review of other hospital visitor control programs can help to eliminate the pitfalls that may jeopardize a new or reorganized visitor control program.

REFERENCES

1. "Emergency Department Violence: Prevention and Management," *American College of Emergency Physicians*, 1988, pp. 38–46.

2. William E. Platts, "Psychiatric Patients: Promises Liability and Predicting Patient Elopement," *Journal of Healthcare Protection Management*, Vol. 14, No. 2, Summer 1998, p. 75.

3. Dan M. Bowers, "Closing the Door on Wanderers," *Journal of Healthcare Protection Management*, Vol. 15, No. 1, Winter 1998/1999, pp. 109–117.

4. George Partington, "RF System Keep Up with Long-Term Patients," *Access Control and Security Systems*, November 1997, p. 1 and 23.

CHAPTER 12

Security and Public Safety Agencies

Healthcare organizations must ensure that they provide proper medical care to patients while protecting the legal rights of patients and expediting the legitimate activities of public safety agencies. The primary objectives of healthcare organizations and of public safety agencies can be quite different with respect to patients. The relationship of the patient to the law enforcement agency determines the procedure to be followed. In other words, a patient who is the subject of an investigation or is a witness should be handled differently than a patient who is actually under arrest or for whom an arrest warrant has been issued. Cooperation and understanding by both parties are required in every instance. The problems or potential problems between public safety and healthcare employees are less acute; however, objectives and policies must be mutually respected.

The majority of interaction between security and public safety agencies is with local and state law enforcement authorities and correctional officers. In addition, fire service, emergency preparedness, and federal law enforcement agencies also have frequent business with healthcare organizations.

REQUESTS FOR LAW ENFORCEMENT SERVICE

A greater demand continues to be placed on security services as the traditional law enforcement response becomes less able to answer requests for service. The high cost of law enforcement officers is forcing most communities to alter the method used to respond to requests for nonessential police services. Thus, the police can provide only a minimal amount of investigative support for misdemeanor crimes and many property-related felonies. It is now the standard for victims to report property losses by mail or to go to the police or sheriff's station to report losses.

The burden on 911 dispatchers is increasing, and they often must make decisions on whether a physical response is necessary.

Professional security programs must respond to scarce law enforcement resources in different ways, including limiting calls for police service to the extent possible. Of course, pitfalls always exist. When the police are not called as soon as someone would like or when they are not called at all, the action or inaction is often criticized. This criticism comes not only from the population being served, but also from the police agency that wants it both ways. The answer to whether police service was needed in a specific circumstance is often decided after the fact by "Monday morning quarterbacks" who have the benefit of hindsight.

The security department must attempt to formulate policies that comply with the local law enforcement methods and procedures of doing business. Often, however, the official administrative protocol is not followed by or reflected in the actions of street officers. Another player is the prosecuting attorney, who may also follow a protocol that is not in complete synchronization with the law enforcement agencies. This situation requires constant liaison with the police jurisdiction involved to avoid misunderstandings.

General policy should prohibit employees from calling for police service as a representative of the organization. In organizations with a full-time security effort, a security representative should make the call for required police service. In organizations without full-time security service, the policy should designate an administrator who will not only approve the call for routine police service, but also generally initiate the call. In times of extreme emergency, the general policy will by necessity be bypassed.

The reasoning behind this general policy is basically just good business practice. An organization cannot tolerate employees calling the police for organizational problems without administration or security being aware of the problem and determining whether police service is actually required. For organizations with a security department, the objective is to protect patients, visitors, staff, and facilities whenever possible without assistance from, or intervention by, a law enforcement agency. This objective does not imply that information will be withheld from the police or that necessary police action will not be instituted. It does mean that when the police are called, it must be for a legitimate police problem and not for a management problem that does not warrant police action.

Another reason for centralizing the responsibility of calling for police service is to assist the police agency in responding to the proper location. A poor situation is created when, after the police respond to a call, they must spend considerable time tracking down the source of the call to determine where they are needed.

A general exception to this policy is cases where the emergency room or other treatment area is reacting to a reportable injury or death of a patient as a matter of business.

The administrative policy should not stop at governing calls for police service. The policy should also channel law enforcement officers to report to the security officer or other administrative office when the police have initiated the contact. Obviously, the police are not bound by an administrative policy, but staff contacted by a police officer must determine that proper administrative procedure has been followed. This central reporting assists law enforcement officers in efficiently contacting the proper person to obtain the information they seek, and it makes the organization aware of the activity taking place. This procedure is also helpful in preventing the disclosure of information to persons fraudulently representing themselves as police officials. Healthcare staff are not always aware that they should require proof of identity before releasing information, or they may accept invalid identification.

The policies and procedures just described are intended to benefit both the organization and the law enforcement agency. Because these procedures are mutually beneficial, police agencies should not balk at following these simple, courteous steps. Of course, emergency situations will preclude following a specified procedure in every instance.

POLICE INTERACTION WITH PATIENTS AND EMPLOYEES

The police frequently need to obtain information from patients. If there are no visiting restrictions for the patient, the police will generally present themselves like any other visitor. When visiting is restricted, the security department may be able to assist the police. Hospitals employ at least two different types of visiting restrictions. The first, for non-medical reasons, is generally requested by the patient or the family. The second restriction, due to a medical factor, is generally imposed by the attending physician. In either case, security can assist the police by furthering communications with the hospital staff.

The request by a law enforcement officer to question a patient must always be referred to the nursing supervisor, who will determine whether the patient is well enough to be interviewed. The nursing supervisor may sometimes need to consult with the attending physician before making this decision. This should not be construed as an indication that the medical care personnel are being uncooperative. It is simply a medical decision that must be made in the best interest of patient care. If medical personnel decide that the patient is too sick to be questioned, the hospital can show its cooperation by notifying the law enforcement agency when the patient's condition improves enough to permit an interview.

If the police have a warrant for a patient, the general procedure is to seek medical opinion before allowing the police to serve the warrant, to avoid any medical complications.

The police do not always come to medical care facilities to contact patients. Employees may also be the subject of a police interview or arrest. Most police jurisdictions recognize that interviewing people at their place of employment may not always be welcomed by the employer or the employee. In some instances, however, time may be an important factor or the police may not be able to make contact elsewhere. The proper procedure is for the police representative to contact the hospital security representative or Human Resources department, who should produce the employee without delay. The normal protocol is to call employees away from their work area rather than interview them in the presence of coworkers.

The facility should also work with the police agency when they have an arrest warrant for an employee. Depending on the seriousness of the charge, the arrest can sometimes be delayed until the work shift has been completed. If an immediate arrest is necessary, employees should be called away from their work area, as in the case of the police interview.

EMERGENCY ROOM ACTIVITY

The emergency room is usually the scene of considerable police activity. Hospitals are required to report cases concerning gunshot wounds, knifings, rape, etc., as specified by law. This should be the responsibility of the emergency room staff and not the security department. However, the security department should be notified if trouble is expected with a person being treated within the facility. The need for security service may involve patients or people who have accompanied them to the facility.

Hospitals that render a large volume of emergency medical service, including police-related cases, generally provide accommodations to help the police complete their work, including a room for interviews that is equipped with a telephone. If the security department maintains an office in the emergency treatment area, the police should be permitted to use or share the space. This combination of use not only conserves space but, if coordinated properly, can promote good relations between the police and the security department.

In Albuquerque, New Mexico, the police department has a system of mini-substations. One station is located at Presbyterian Hospital at the request of the hospital. The hospital was required to furnish the space, a telephone, a pushbutton office lock, and signs. It is designated the Albuquerque Police Department Southeast Mini-Substation. This unique concept holds promise for other facilities.

The security operation is sometimes required to interact with law enforcement agencies, which frequently need to obtain the clothing and personal effects of injured people. If the injured person is under arrest, the police agency is legally entitled to take custody of this property. The hospital should obtain a receipt for all property released. The personal possessions of individuals who are not under arrest may be released only by the patient, an authorized agent, or pursuant to a valid search warrant. If the patient is dead on arrival at the facility and the circumstances of death fall under the legal jurisdiction of the coroner or medical examiner, no property should be released until that office grants authorization.

Another area of interaction in the emergency room that may involve the security department is photographing patients for evidential purposes. In these cases, the same basic guidelines prevail as in the release of clothing. The patient who is a police prisoner has little to say in the matter, and the hospital cannot stand between the police and the patient unless a competent medical authority decides that the medical well-being of the patient is at stake. Patients who are not under arrest may be photographed with their approval or, in the case of a minor, with the family's approval. A written photograph consent form should be executed.

Some hospitals in large municipalities have problems with law enforcement officers who bring patients to the emergency room and then abruptly leave. Some of these patients create disturbances; others may have no means of transportation home. The hospital ends up with a problem that has little to do with medical treatment. Calls for police assistance with abusive patients are often answered by a different police unit than the one that left the problem on the doorstep. In some cases, police officers must get back in service without delay, but all too often police are simply getting rid of a problem. If a facility experiences this difficulty, it should be handled at the administrative level.

DETAINING PATIENTS

Related to security's involvement with patients and law enforcement is the telephone or radio request to detain a patient. Neither private security officers nor medical personnel can legally detain patients against their will. The law enforcement agency that requests that a patient be detained should be made aware that patients cannot be legally held. At the same time, stalling tactics are certainly in the best interests of all concerned, particularly if police personnel are en route to the facility.

Often if the police do not request that a patient be detained, they may request that security ask the patient to wait for the police. If the patient does leave, information such as a license number and direction of travel can be obtained to assist the police.

PRISONERS AND POLICE HOLDS

With the large number of people being cared for today in all types of medical care facilities, it stands to reason that there are many wanted felons among the patient population. Most come and go, and their criminal status is never discovered.

There are numerous occasions, however, when a patient is under arrest or serving jail or prison time. The responsibility for ensuring detention belongs to the criminal justice agency having jurisdiction. Hospital security officers should not assume any role other than to offer mutually beneficial, non-custody assistance, unless the security department has been hired to provide specified service. It is becoming quite common for law enforcement and correctional agencies to contract with private security to guard prisoners.

Prisoners being treated in Joint Commission on Accreditation of Healthcare Organizations (JCAHO)-accredited facilities present a standards compliance issue. There is a requirement that individuals guarding forensic patients be given specific training pertaining to certain healthcare policies, procedures, and protocols. This JCAHO standard was discussed in detail in Chapter 11.

An important service that security officers can and should render is to brief the law enforcement representatives about the layout of the area, pointing out escape or intrusion possibilities. Security officers may also take steps to eliminate or minimize these vulnerabilities. A simple step would be to place the patient in a room that can be secured. If intrusion by others is a concern, locking the doors leading from the stairwell would provide added protection. In brief, security officers should do everything possible to assist the criminal justice agency.

Although rare, hospitals have been the scenes of tragic incidents that resulted from forensic patients. A Denver County Sheriff's Deputy was about to check the leg irons of a forensic patient at Denver General Hospital when the patient, who had freed himself, jumped the deputy and was able to obtain the officer's weapon. After killing the deputy, the prisoner fled down a stairwell. Through a good radio communication system and trained security personnel, the prisoner was arrested and disarmed before he could flee the facility.

It is imperative that hospital admitting personnel notify the security department of every forensic patient admitted. In conjunction with the agency, a decision should be made regarding visiting and the release of information concerning the patient's location.

REQUESTS FOR INFORMATION

All requests by law enforcement agencies for information about patients being treated should be referred to the security department, or to medical records for information regarding discharged patients. The facility representative must always make certain that the person requesting the information has been properly identified. If the request for information is made by telephone, extra precautions must be taken. One method that may be used is to return the call to the person making the request. If the telephone number is not that of a law enforcement agency, further verification is in order.

In most cases, information concerning a patient's name, address, birth date, date of admission or discharge, and diagnosis and the name of the attending physician can be given freely to law enforcement officers. If patient records must be reviewed or copies released, the law enforcement officer can readily obtain a court order, which will protect the officer as well as the facility. Because medical and employee personnel records are increasingly being used as a tool for solving legal suits, settling insurance claims, conducting medical research, and other purposes, there are often conflicting opinions on what information can be released. When the guidelines are not absolutely clear, the medical records department and hospital administration should be involved in the decision.

Releasing of Information

General guidelines for the release of information by healthcare organizations were developed by the Colorado Hospital Association in cooperation with the Denver District Attorney's office and the Denver Police Department. They are offered as guidelines for all hospitals. Some modifications may be required for certain jurisdictions.

For the purposes of these guidelines, the following definitions are used:

- **Employee Health Record:** The record containing the employee's health-related information, such as the employee's physical and medical history. In some hospitals, these records are maintained separately in different locations from other employment information. In other hospitals, these records are combined and typically stored in the Human Resources department. The distinction is important because information from the personnel record is not privileged and can be released pursuant to criminal investigations, but the employee health record contains privileged communications, and should only be released pursuant to a search warrant or grand jury subpoena.

- **Patient Medical Record:** A documentation of medical services performed at the direction of a physician or other licensed healthcare provider on behalf of the patient. Patient records do not include notes made by a physician about observations of the patient made while the patient was in a non-hospital setting; these are maintained in the physician's office.

- **Personnel Record:** The record or portion of the record maintained in the Human Resources department, which contains information regarding an employee's employment history and performance evaluation. It can be released to law enforcement agencies during criminal investigations without a search warrant or subpoena.

- **Privileged Communication:** Communication between a physician and an employee or a physician and a patient that is recorded in the employee's health record or in the patient's medical record. Privileged communications occur while the physician is attending the patient or employee and are necessary to enable the physician to prescribe or act for the benefit of the patient or employee.

- **Search Warrants:** Court orders issued and signed by a judge. Confidential information and privileged communications must be provided pursuant to a search warrant at the time it is presented.

- **Subpoena:** In these guidelines, a grand jury subpoena. Grand jury subpoenas can request that confidential information and privileged communications be presented to the grand jury on a specific date. They are signed by the clerk of the courts.

Recommended Guidelines Regarding the Release of Information from Personnel Records Pursuant to Criminal Investigation

A. The hospital should designate the individuals to whom requests for information from law enforcement agencies will be referred. The identification of this person(s) should be made known to the appropriate law enforcement agencies, the hospital information desk, the admissions department, medical records department, or others deemed appropriate. The individuals designated by the hospital should have the authority to provide the information to the requesting law enforcement officer.

   Law enforcement agencies should make requests for information from the personnel records during regular business hours. Access to records outside normal business hours is extremely difficult. If it is an emergency, the hospital should contact the administrator or his designee to resolve the matter.

B. Information should be provided only to a properly identified representative of a law enforcement agency. When picking up a record, the representative should complete a written request for the information. It should be recognized that the provision of information pursuant to criminal investigations is legal and there is no legal requirement to notify, or not notify, the employee of such information. The provision of the release of information to a law enforcement agency does not expose a hospital to any civil liability, if done in good faith. It should be noted that most law enforcement agencies prefer that the employee not be notified of the investigation. It is, therefore, recommended that the hospital not notify the employee unless the law enforcement agency indicates that it has no objection. If the designated individual at the hospital who is supplying the information to the law enforcement agency has any doubt as to the validity of the request, the name of the law enforcement officer's supervisor should be obtained, and the agency that employs the officer should be called, using the telephone number listed in the telephone book.

C. If the employee's personnel record also contains employee health or medical information, such as the employee's physical, this information should not be made available to the law enforcement agency without a search warrant or subpoena. If medical information is released by court order, the employee should be given notice of this release of information.

D. All hospitals should amend their employment application forms to advise the applicant that while personnel files are not open to the general public, the hospital is required to give access to authorized agencies such as law enforcement agencies and other regulatory agencies, including the Board of Nursing and the Board of Medical Examiners.

Recommended Guidelines for the Release of Information from Patient Medical Records

A. See Section A of previously discussed Guidelines for Release of Information from Personnel Records.

B. The patient's name, address, telephone number, and birth date can be released from patient medical records without requiring a search warrant or grand jury subpoena. Other information may also be appropriate for release. As an example, in a criminal investigation pertaining to drugs, it is possible that information pertaining to the charting of administered medications and the hospital's checkout sheet could be released. The person designated to handle the release of requested information must use his good judgment regarding further release of information, taking into account that law enforcement agencies can get the information by obtaining a court order. The search warrant and grand jury subpoena become public information, subject to public dissemination. It is suggested that an effort be made to work with the local district attorney and law enforcement agency, to voluntarily provide appropriate information and minimize the necessity of obtaining search warrants and grand jury subpoenas. Law enforcement agencies should recognize that the point at which a hospital will require a search warrant or grand jury subpoena for further release of information may vary slightly from facility to facility.

When Providing Information from Personnel, Employee Health or Medical Records Pursuant to Search Warrants or Grand Jury Subpoenas

A. Legible copies of the requested record should be provided and should be acceptable to the law enforcement agency. The original can be made available for comparison purposes, but should not be removed from the hospital premises unless in the custody of a hospital employee.

B. Determine that the search warrant or subpoena is authentic. All search warrants must be signed by a judge. Grand jury subpoenas for criminal investigations will be signed by the clerk of the court.

C. Carefully review the warrant or subpoena to determine the specific information requested and supply only that information. Record the name of the individual who was supplied with the information and maintain a copy of the warrant or subpoena.

D. If "privileged communication" is being sought by a law enforcement agency pursuant to a search warrant, it must be provided when requested and the individual notified thereafter. When privileged communication is requested pursuant to a subpoena, there will be time to notify the individual before the communication is made available to the grand jury. Notification will allow the individual an opportunity to take appropriate steps to protect the "privileged communication."

Key Considerations for Information Release

1. The law enforcement agency must obtain its evidence in a legal manner or it will not be admissible in court, so they must follow certain guidelines.

2. It is desirable, and in the best interest of all concerned, including those under investigation, to ensure fairness and to protect the integrity of the investigation, to keep the information within the investigating agency.

3. If the information requested by law enforcement agencies can be supplied voluntarily within the law by hospitals, it will be unnecessary for the law enforcement agencies to obtain search warrants or subpoenas. It should be noted that once a search warrant is filed for or a subpoena requested, the case becomes public information.

4. If there is disagreement between the law enforcement agency and the hospital as to the information to be released, it is recommended that the hospital contact the local district attorney's office that is involved and attempt to resolve the problem.

5. It should be understood by law enforcement agencies that there may be some instances in which the hospital would prefer that a search warrant or subpoena be obtained prior to release of the information. This request should not be viewed by law enforcement as the hospital being uncooperative.

6. Police investigation files are confidential; therefore, release of information to a law enforcement agency is not a release to the public. Also, if the information is information to which the law enforcement agency can compel access through the courts, there would seem to be no basis for liability against the hospital just because it made the information available voluntarily.

SECURITY AND LAW ENFORCEMENT LIAISON

The discussion thus far has revolved around the security department's operational relationship with law enforcement. In addition, security administrators must foster good formal and informal law enforcement relationships. The most common method is direct, good-will contact with agency personnel. In addition, one of the best methods of fostering law enforcement liaison is to show various agencies that the security program is a professional one that supports the law enforcement mission at every opportunity.

One example of this support is that of enhancing public responder safety. Private security is increasingly forming a vital link between the citizen and emergency service providers. As part of this link, security officers are often the ones to report emergency situations or crimes in progress. The information they report and their support at the scene can be very instrumental in providing an extra measure of safety to the responder.[1]

Meanwhile, various national initiatives are being developed which are intended to form a closer working relationship between law enforcement and security. For example, the Bureau of Justice Assistance of the U.S. Department of Justice has funded a project called Operation Cooperation. This project is intended to establish cooperative relationships between law enforcement agencies and private security organizations through guidelines and practical working examples.[2]

The International Association of Chiefs of Police (IACP) have also worked on guidelines pertaining to the selection, training, and hiring of security officers. This work has been accomplished through the association's Private Sector Liaison Committee (PSLC), which includes representatives from large guard force providers and from others outside the IACP organization, including the American Society for Industrial Security (ASIS). As one PSLC committee member states, "ASIS is working with the IACP to raise minimum standards for private security officers." One major objective of formulating those guidelines is to provide guidance to lawmakers in developing more uniform standards in place of the variety of laws affecting private security in some 40 states. One recommendation is to require a National Crime Information Center (NCIC) "insta-check" for armed security officers.[3]

Various local programs also work toward security/law enforcement liaison. An example of such an effort is the Hospital Employees Assisting Law Enforcement, or HEAL, program at the Tarrant County Hospital District in Fort Worth. HEAL, in effect, is a hospital crime watch program. This program revolves around a base of crime watch coordinators. By its very name, it shows its support of the law enforcement community.

It isn't always security administrators who initiate or foster a good relationship with law enforcement. Progressive law enforcement agencies often take the lead in this endeavor. An example is the Dallas Police/Security Joint Information Committee. This committee, formed by the Dallas Police, offers an effective and innovative approach to the overall protection of the community. In essence, the committee's purpose is to create an atmosphere of mutual understanding, cooperation, and coordination between the police and private security programs. As part of this program, every student at the Dallas Police Academy takes a class on how private security programs and the police work together to reduce crime and improve community safety.

In Edmonton, Canada, the Edmonton police department appoints a special hospital liaison officer. This officer meets frequently with hospital security staff and is the point officer for communications between the hospital security program and police services.

It is projected that police and security operations will work together to a greater extent in the future. On the basis of study research, William Tafoya of the FBI Academy predicts that by the year 2035, half of all law enforcement duties will be assumed by private security companies. In 1990, it was estimated that police officers spend 80 percent of their time performing services rather than law enforcement duties. In many communities, police and security are already sharing training programs and information, and private industry is training police officers in such areas as computer systems and corporate security.[4]

SECURITY AND NON-POLICE LIAISON

The fire department is a public safety agency that has frequent contact with healthcare organizations as a whole, and specifically with hospitals. These contacts take the form of fire prevention and inspections and emergency response. In most cases, the interaction of the organization with the fire department is more in the arena of safety as opposed to security.

Security does, however, play an important role in emergency fire response. This role pertains to providing efficient access to the facility and guiding the first responders to the alarm locations. Proper actions by security personnel can save valuable time, which is critical in fire situations. Although infrequent contact may be made with the office of emergency preparedness on local, state, or federal levels, the security department is vital to their planning efforts.

REFERENCES

1. Theresa L. Martin, "Security's Role in Public Responder Safety," *Access Control & Security Systems Integration*, September 1998, p. 59.

2. "Initiative to Increase Cooperation Between Law Enforcement," *Security, Access Control and Security Systems Integration*, February 1998, p. 10.

3. Ann Longhorn-Etheridge, "ASIS Aids IACP in Formulating Guidelines," *Security Management*, June 1998, p. 103–104.

4. "Future of Security-Shared Resources," *Security Magazine*, June 1988, p. 16.

CHAPTER 13

Human Resources and Staff Contributions to a Secure Environment

The protection system in medical care facilities interfaces directly with the human resources (HR) department. The security program is charged with enforcing rules and regulations that in all probability were promulgated by the HR department. Furthermore, security incidents often involve employees, and the HR department may be involved in determining the action to be taken against the employee. Also of extreme importance to the security function is immediate access to personnel records for investigative purposes. Conversely, in doing their job, HR personnel are often dependent on security department records and expertise in obtaining pertinent data from sources inside and outside the organization. The security and HR departments, like all other departments in the organization, must support one another in providing a system of protection beneficial to the entire organization.

CONSIDERATIONS IN HIRING AND MANAGING EMPLOYEES

There are various human resource activities and functions that bear directly, or indirectly, on the security posture of the organization. Included in this area are: access control of applicants, staff identification systems, background investigations, disciplinary actions, and maintaining proper employee conduct.

Human Resources Office

The location of the HR office is an important security consideration. The objective should be to keep applicants out of the main facility.

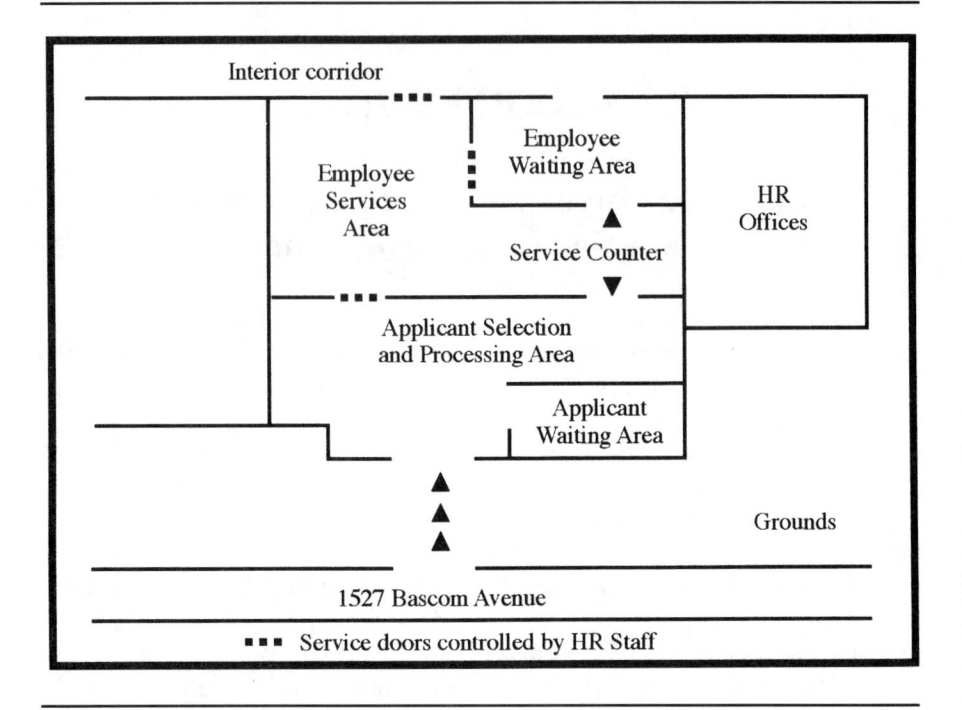

```
┌─────────────────────────────────────────────┐
│  Interior corridor                          │
│  ─────────■■■──────┬──────────┐             │
│                    │ Employee │             │
│        Employee  ■ │ Waiting  │   HR        │
│        Services  ■ │ Area     │   Offices   │
│        Area      ■ └──────────┤             │
│                        ▲      │             │
│                   Service Counter           │
│        ─ ■■■ ──────────▼──────┤             │
│           Applicant Selection │             │
│           and Processing Area │             │
│                    ┌──────────┤             │
│        ────────┐   │ Applicant│             │
│                │   │ Waiting  │             │
│                │   │ Area     │             │
│                    ▲                        │
│                    ▲           Grounds      │
│                    ▲                        │
│        ──────────────────────────────       │
│            1527 Bascom Avenue               │
│        ■■■ Service doors controlled by HR Staff │
└─────────────────────────────────────────────┘
```

Figure 13-1 Example of Design of a Human Resources Department

Not only may applicants interfere with clinical care, but they also have been known to commit various security infractions while looking for a job. Further, applicants—who may also be potential malefactors—should not be given the opportunity to become familiar with the facility's layout and design. The employment portion of the HR department should either be in a separate building or have its own entry and an individual address to discourage access to the main facility. Figure 13-1 shows a layout for a human resources department that has a street entry point for applicants and a separate internal entry point for employees.

The offsite screening of applicants has very positive security implications. Organizations that use state or local employment commissions to screen positions that draw a large number of applicants have reported success with this method.

Selecting Employees Through Due Diligence

Healthcare organizations must search out new and better ways to effectively reduce the incidence of employee misconduct. The best place to begin this effort is to exercise a reasonable standard of care in the selection of new staff. The selection process is an area in which the healthcare industry as a whole receives poor marks. HR departments have simply been deficient in properly screening applicants.

It has become difficult indeed to seek information relative to hiring appropriate staff with the restrictions imposed by legislature constraints. The problem is further attenuated by the courts in holding employers liable for negligent hiring. The current state of these controls and sanctions is directly responsible for much of our workplace violence and the billions of dollars lost to employee defalcations, which must be paid either directly or indirectly by all of society.

Despite legal constraints, there are ways to reject dishonest and dangerous applicants. The HR department must therefore provide due diligence in the applicant selection process. Unfortunately, however, there will always be some flawed hiring decisions, though the number of bad decisions will decrease when more in-depth information regarding the applicant is sought.

Information relative to an applicant's suitability for employment can be developed through various methods, including a properly constructed and completed application form; contacts with previous employers; verification of information through official public records, a variety of tests; and information from friends and previous co-workers.

Employment Application Forms

A good employee selection process begins with the proper design of the application form. The form must be designed with security in mind along with the primary objectives of the organization. All applications must ask whether the applicant has been convicted of any crime (misdemeanors and felonies, excluding traffic offenses). Employees should be required to formally update application information annually, including criminal convictions. This can be accomplished as part of the formal employee evaluation process.

Conditions of Employment

Although every applicant accepted for employment is required to comply with the policies, rules, and regulations of the organization, many organizations have found it helpful to use conditions of employment, or employment agreements. These conditions are usually attached to the application form, although in some instances the conditions are incorporated into the application itself.

Background Investigations

Personnel specialists, security professionals, and top management continue to agree that much more must be done in the area of applicant background investigation to properly protect patients, staff, and property. The courts generally support this view.

The problem that presents itself is that the courts render judgments for inadequate hiring processes, yet in other decisions they make it virtually impossible for organizations to obtain any significant background information. It is the opinion of many security and police administrators that the Federal Privacy Act has done great harm to employers and has, in fact, encouraged greater criminal activity. If, in fact, negative information about an applicant is discovered, the government bureaucracy prohibits any intelligent use of this information. Many believe that the rights of employers and society in general have been negated to the point that effective applicant screening is more of a myth than a reality. As a result, many protection systems are geared to reacting to problems involving employees rather than preventing such situations through good hiring practices.

Although the courts and most government agencies set up to protect employees' rights have indicated insensitivity to the cost of crime and the suffering of victims, medical care facilities must continue to do everything possible to employ individuals who contribute to excellence in patient care.

An increasing number of medical care organizations rely on their security departments to assist in screening applicants. In some cases, only applicants for the so-called sensitive positions are subject to security input, but in other organizations, all applicants are the subject of security background investigations.

Because unfit employees tend to move from one medical care facility to another, new and improved methods of facility interaction must be put into place to prevent these employees from repeatedly victimizing healthcare organizations. The advent of large healthcare systems provides an opportunity to at least consolidate employee information within the system.

Employee Photographs

Healthcare security practitioners generally agree that all employees should be photographed. In some facilities, this responsibility is assigned to the security department, and in others, the personnel department handles this task while processing new employees. The picture identification badge has become almost standard for healthcare organizations. Video imaging has replaced the film camera for creating and maintaining a picture file of employees. When a hard copy is needed, it can be readily produced from the videotape file.

EMPLOYEE IDENTIFICATION

Healthcare organizations must provide each employee with identification. It is a common practice to combine the identification card and the name badge into a single unit, creating a picture identification badge to be worn by all staff. A picture identification badge is a stated standard of the International Association for Healthcare Security and Safety (IAHSS). The rapid increase in the use of card access systems in healthcare facilities has resulted in one badge that has multiple uses.

The identification badge utilized in healthcare provider organizations has two basic purposes. The first purpose is to function as a basic element of the access control system. Secondly, it serves the purpose of compliance with the Joint Commission on Accreditation of Healthcare Organizations (JCAHO), which requires that all patients have the right to know who the person is involved in their treatment.

Administering the Badge Program

There are several key security issues relative to the administration of staff identification systems. First, the system must provide for expeditious replacement of lost or stolen cards or badges. However, replacement procedures often make it simple for employees to obtain two badges if they desire. They can then turn in one badge at termination and still retain the second badge for various purposes. Even organizations that make a substantial effort to control employee identification badges can easily fail to retrieve as much as 20 to 30 percent of the badges issued. Fortunately, in most cases, the uncollected cards are not used for negative purposes. One of the major advantages of the electronic card access identification system is that a badge can be immediately invalidated at the computer keyboard.

Another issue pertains to funding. All badge systems cost money, and while the cost of the materials needed to produce the cards is a rather small percentage of the total program cost, in projecting material costs, there is a tendency to underestimate the number of badges that will be produced. The number of badges an organization will require annually is generally at least two-and-a-half times the number of actual employees. This estimate allows for lost cards, name changes, position changes, cards ruined in the production process, and turnover. One organization reports that it used 2,850 cards the first year for an average of 880 employees during the year.

Although badges normally contain only name and departmental or position information, the reverse side of the badge can be used for other pertinent employee information. The reverse side can also be used to display the security telephone number, code information, or even a brief description of emergency procedures. Since space on the badge is limited, it is not uncommon to find a second laminated information card attached to the primary badge. Recently, the JCAHO surveyors have not looked with favor on these cards containing emergency response information.

The most common problem in any employee badge identification system is getting employees to wear the badge as prescribed. A certain number of employees will always resist, and organizations that initiate a badging program must be prepared to provide strong administrative support.

Organizations can take actions to promote voluntary compliance. Chief among these is to make the badge useful to employees. In other words, the more often employees must have their badges to engage in certain activities during their shift, the more apt they are to wear them. Also of paramount importance in promoting compliance with the program is for top administrative personnel to set a good example by wearing their badges. In one program, the badge system was initiated by issuing badges to supervisory personnel two weeks before they were distributed to the other employees. Not only did this procedure set a good example, but it also generated interest among employees, who wanted to know when they were going to get their badges.

In another program, the badge had a designated place to affix employee longevity award logos. When employees reach their fifth year of service, for example, they are issued a new employee badge with the award logo. This system provides a practical means of recognition; other award pins often end up at home in a dresser drawer. In some programs, so many stickers and other items are attached to badges that the whole purpose of identification badging is defeated. A strict policy should be in place to address this issue.

Identification Badge Design Considerations

The name of the individual must be of sufficient size so that it can be read from a distance of at least two or three feet. An 18-point type allows the name and position to be read from a distance of approximately 8 to 10 feet.

It is important that the organization be able to produce the badge in-house so that it is ready for an employee's first day on the job. This capability is also important in preparing a new badge in the event of a loss or name or status change. When badges can be quickly produced by the organization, employees will not be without a badge, and the entire process can be completed in only one trip to the processing station.

The use of specific job titles on the badge will necessitate considerably more changes than the use of a more general title or department designation. For example, it would be better to include "Food Service" on all badges issued to that department, rather than "Head Cook," "Dishwasher," "Tray Attendant," etc. In clinical areas, more precise titles, positions, and/or credentials are required to more properly identify the employee for purposes of patient treatment and interactions.

A system of issuing temporary badges must be established. Employees should not be allowed to work without a badge if it was left at home or misplaced; they should receive a temporary badge. In some systems, the temporary badge must be checked-in when employees have completed their shift. In other systems, the temporary badge is issued for a given shift or a specific number of days.

Employees should be given a choice of a pin clip or other means of affixing the badge. Some organizations allow the badge to be affixed to a chain worn around the neck. Giving employees this choice is intended to enhance compliance with wearing the badge.

In some badging programs, contractors, salespeople, students, and others who perform a service within the facility are badged as well as employees. These badges can be permanent issue or, in the case of a contractor or salesperson, can be issued for one day only.

Using color codes to denote the various authorized areas that the bearer may enter does not usually work well within medical care facilities. All employees should be issued the same type and color of badge, except for staff assigned to a mother/infant unit. Different types or colors may be helpful for temporary badges to identify contractors, salespeople, clergy, and others.

Physicians should be required to wear identification badges, just as other staff. In order to promote wearing the badges, there must be strong medical director support. As a general rule, physicians will resist badging. House staff (interns and residents), who usually receive training by rotating among several facilities, are often able to utilize a single medical school or teaching hospital identification badge in multiple facilities. In these cases, all participating facilities must be party to a structured, formal agreement regarding this type of arrangement. Since the staff of any specific organization are responsible to challenge other caregivers who are not properly identified, there must be a communication link in regard to *accepted* identification from other organizations.

SECURITY-ORIENTED PERSONNEL POLICIES

A major function of the protection system is to control employee losses and protect the organization's well-being by enforcing organizational rules and regulations. Concise, written personnel policies provide a solid foundation on which to regulate employee conduct. Vague, unwritten policies benefit neither the employee nor the organization.

Commonly, personnel policies are contained in the employee handbook or administrative policy book. Although policies for sick leave, vacation time, wages and hours, disciplinary action, etc., are always carefully spelled out, security policies are often ambiguous or omitted entirely.

Policies affecting employees must be tailored to the type of facility and to what is expected of employees in that facility. However, certain basic security policies are germane to every medical care facility. The most important of these are discussed here.

Employee Security Responsibility

A unique aspect of healthcare security is the important role every employee plays in providing an adequate level of protection for the facility. It is important that every organization clearly set forth the employee's responsibility for security. A typical policy, which should be part of every healthcare organization's policy, is as follows:

> It is the responsibility of every employee to be aware of anything observed that may affect the welfare of the patients, other people on the premises, or the physical property of either individuals or the organization. When any such observation is made, employees will take steps to investigate further, intervene if time is of the essence, and report the circumstances to their supervisor and the security department. Further, it is the responsibility of every employee to report any and all threats to staff, visitors, or patients in accordance with the hospital threat policy.

Off-Duty Employees

Many facilities face serious problems with off-duty employees who remain in the facility after their shift ends or who return on their off-time to visit other employees. These visits not only waste the time of employees on duty, but also often result in other problems, such as disturbances, loud and noisy activity, drinking, and drug use. The following is a typical policy pertaining to this problem:

Employees who are not on duty should not be on medical center property more than 30 minutes after their work shift or more than 30 minutes before the start of a scheduled work shift. Employees who are off duty may return to the facility to receive medical care or to visit a patient, or they may return with the specific authorization of an administrator or supervisor for a specific purpose.

Employee Weapons

Unfortunately, many healthcare employees carry weapons to their place of employment. Whatever the purpose, the possession of weapons on facility property should be prohibited. Because almost anything can be construed as a weapon, the policy established should define which weapons are specifically prohibited. The following is an example of a weapons policy:

Employees are prohibited from bringing weapons or explosives onto hospital property. For the purpose of t\his policy, *weapon* is defined as any gun, loaded or unloaded, any knife with a blade longer than three inches, or any weapon it is illegal to possess.

Package Inspection

The control of packages and equipment entering or leaving the facility is a major security responsibility. The primary concern is for egress; however, at times, ingress is also an issue. Effective control requires the compliance and cooperation of all employees, as well as the control of various entrances and exits.

Unfortunately, most healthcare security programs are not adequately staffed to enable them to control all egress points. As a result, package inspection is conducted as a spot-check or is incidental to patrol services. Good control programs depend largely on the ability to designate and enforce a policy that authorizes only certain doors for staff use.

The property pass is widely used, but faces varying degrees of success. Although they differ considerably from facility to facility, pass programs have the common objective of discouraging theft and providing property accountability. These systems establish a sound basis for security officers to inquire about employees observed carrying an item from the facility. In some programs only organization property is subject to the pass policy. This creates the problem of determining what is personal and what is organization property.

A package inspection policy should cover not only packages being taken from the facility, but also those being brought in. The following is a typical policy:

> All property being taken from or brought into medical center buildings or upon medical center property is subject to inspection by security officers or medical center administrative personnel. Any medical center property, regardless of value, being taken from the property shall be accompanied by dated, written permission that contains a description of the property and the name of the person authorizing its removal.

All property pass systems should be well organized to eliminate as many weaknesses as possible. If reasonable compliance appears doubtful, it might be better not to implement the pass system at all. One commonly cited weakness is the lack of feedback to department management. In too many programs, passes are simply collected and discarded. Collected passes, or a copy of such passes, should be returned to the authorizing department for review and audit purposes.

Figure 13-2 is an example of a property removal pass.

Of course, an organization can maintain a property inspection system without a formalized property pass. In other words, security personnel may still inspect property to determine whether its removal has been authorized.

The following policy is offered as a sample of an inspection system:

I. GENERAL

    A. Cause to Believe that Contraband or Stolen Property Is Being Transported. On occasion the security officer will receive information that a possible theft will occur; receive a request to inspect by a facility administrator or supervisor; or observe extremely suspicious activity. In the case of the first two circumstances, the officer should confer with a security supervisor if time and extent of the problem permit. In the case of activity in progress, good officer judgment will prevail.

    B. Observation of Exposed Equipment. Often, an item of possible medical center property is observed being removed from a facility and does not fall under the suspicious activity category. Open-view removal

UNITED MEMORIAL HOSPITAL
PROPERTY REMOVAL AUTHORIZATION

Date: _____ Time: _____

Name: _____ Staff ___ Visitor ___ Patient ___

Has permission to remove the following property from the UMH campus (Describe fully: amount, color, type of property):

Property: Surplus _____ Obsolete _____ Loan _____

Other (explain): _____

Authorization Signature: _____ Position: _____

Department/Service: _____ Tel. Ext. _____

Prepare in Duplicate – Forward Copy to Security Services

Figure 13-2 Sample Property Removal Pass

generally indicates legitimate removal; however, the security officer should make tactful inquiry as to ownership. The legitimate person will seldom take offense, and the procedure helps to solidify the image that the facility is concerned about the safety and protection of its environment.

C. Concentrated Package Inspection. Such package inspection is a planned security operation under the supervision of a security supervisor per direction of the Security Director. Security personnel will be assigned to a specific exit and check property being removed by any person. In this regard, purses and lunch boxes will be excluded unless the purse is extremely large.

II. HANDLING PERSONS REMOVING PROPERTY

A. Identified Medical Center Property. The person removing the property should be identified. If the person is a medical center employee, the person should be allowed to proceed after a list of the property has been prepared and the employee's department verified. The department will be called to verify authorized removal if the officer deems such action necessary. If the person removing the property is not an employee, the employee authorizing removal should be contacted.

B. Suspected Medical Center Property. The security officer should prepare a list of the property and identify the person, who may then proceed on his way.

Complete documentation of package inspection is of course mandatory. Also, employees should be reminded periodically of the policy concerning property inspection. Two methods are the hospital newsletter and handbill-style notices. Figure 13-3 shows an example of the latter. During a concentrated package inspection, security officers may hand these notices to employees who are surprised by or express ignorance of the policy.

Cooperating with Investigators

Investigation is a continuous process in healthcare organizations. Although the concern here is for security-related investigations, healthcare organizations conduct other investigations to collect and analyze facts for various business and patient-care situations. To efficiently and

---

PACKAGE INSPECTION

With hundreds of persons coming and going daily, the need to inspect property being taken from the hospital is readily apparent. This inspection, by security officers or hospital supervisory staff, is a protection for everyone's welfare. Inspection applies to all persons and employees should not take this precautionary measure personally and are expected to cooperate fully.

Property losses cost you and the patient money!

Security Division — Hospital Shared Services

Figure 13-3 Example of a Handbill Notice Given to Employees Regarding Property Inspections

thoroughly carry out this activity, employers must have the full cooperation of all employees. A policy such as the one that follows is highly recommended:

> All employees are required to cooperate fully with any medical center supervisor, manager, or member of the security department who is conducting an investigation or inquiry on behalf of the medical center. Failure to cooperate may be considered as insubordination and may subject the employee to disciplinary action.

Employee Lockers

A frequent concern for healthcare organizations is the employee locker. Lockers furnished to employees for use in connection with their employment should be inspected periodically. Two supervisory employees, one from security and one from a relevant department, should conduct the inspection.

To maintain proper control of employee lockers, personal locks should not be permitted. If the facility does not furnish locks and employees must provide their own, the organization must still retain access to the lockers. Employees must furnish a duplicate key or the combination to the department responsible for the employee locker program.

The following is a typical policy for employee lockers:

> Employee lockers are the property of the medical center and are subject to inspection at any time for sanitary or administrative purposes. No medical center property will be stored in an employee locker, except such property issued to the employee for which he or she is responsible.

Solicitation and Distribution of Products Policy

Virtually all healthcare facilities have a policy on solicitation, which generally pertains to both employees and people from outside the organization. However, many organizations do not include in this solicitation policy the free distribution of products or materials. In one sense, this distribution could be viewed as indirect solicitation, but not always. One hospital reports that an author of a paperback book came to the hospital and began visiting patients at random, leaving them a complementary copy of his book for their reading pleasure. The hospital did not know anything of this situation until one patient complained that the book was pornographic. After a review of the book, the hospital visited patient rooms with an apology and hastily retrieved the books. The author was contacted and he stated that his purpose was to simply provide reading material to help cheer up the patients. He was asked to cease and desist. Medical care organizations cannot carry out their work efficiently while permitting solicitation or the distribution of materials to staff or patients.

The following is an example of a solicitation and distribution policy:

> To protect employees and patients from annoyance or disruption, no solicitation or distribution of products or materials of any kind by employees or outside persons is permitted on medical center property without the express permission of the medical center administration. This prohibition includes circulating petitions, selling merchandise, selling chances for a lottery or drawing, or distributing products or literature. All employees have an obligation to report any solicitation or distribution to their immediate supervisor.

Gifts from Patients or Family

Employees should be prohibited from accepting gifts or gratuities from patients or their families. Employees are paid to provide their services, and the acceptance of any form of gift fosters possible abuse such as favoritism, special treatment, and fraudulent practices. The enforcement of this policy rests with departmental supervisors and rarely becomes a security issue.

Employee Time Recording

The concern for the loss of tangible hospital assets often overshadows the loss of employee time. However, organizations lose money every day by paying for time that employees do not work. Although the improper recording of time is a supervisory problem, the security department may become involved in an investigation of fraudulent time-recording activities.

All organizations should maintain a policy that strictly prohibits an employee from recording time for another employee. An example of such a policy follows:

> No employee will record time on a time card belonging to another employee or through electronic means. No employee will allow another person to record time on his or her behalf.

The problem of fraudulent recording increases as organizations grow in size. The larger and more impersonal an organization becomes, the better the climate for the theft of time. Virtually every department and section of the organization is vulnerable to this often-ignored source of financial loss.

The concept of flexible work schedules (flex time) renders the control of time records and the surveillance of employee traffic more difficult. Within certain defined parameters, flex time programs allow employees to report for work on their own schedule, after which they are required only to work the designated number of hours. Flex time does not lend itself well to the delivery of healthcare, because most medical facilities must be geared to appointments, timetables, and specific work shifts to ensure adequate staffing.

Surplus or Damaged Property

Medical care facilities of all sizes continually accumulate surplus property that is damaged, obsolete, or for various reasons unsuitable for use. A policy must be prepared that defines a procedure for the proper disposition of such property.

The following is an example of a policy covering the disposal of surplus or damaged property:

> All medical center equipment or products deemed by an employee to be unusable for any reason will be returned to the Director of Materials Management. No employee will have the authority to sell or give away any medical center property, regardless of value, unless authorized by the Director of Materials Management on a case by case basis.

Contraband

In this context, the term "contraband" includes not only illegal items, such as weapons, drugs, and explosives, but also alcohol. Alcohol must be included in a hospital policy banning employees from bringing contraband items onto facility property. The following is an example of a policy covering contraband:

> No medical center employee will possess or knowingly assist another person in possessing any contraband, including illegal drugs, explosives, weapons, and liquor of any kind, unless authorized by a supervisor for a specific medical center purpose.

Drug Testing

Testing employees and applicants for drugs is a commonplace procedure in healthcare organizations. The Drug-Free Workplace Act, contained in the Anti-Drug Abuse Act of 1989, spurred many organizations to action, even though the act does not require a drug testing program.

The act applies to any contractor who has federal contracts for the procurement of goods or services valued at $25,000 or more or who receives federal grants, regardless of the amount. The act requires these contractors to publish a policy statement prohibiting the unlawful manufacture, distribution, dispensation, possession, or use of a controlled substance in the workplace and specifying penalties for violations; to establish an education program on drug abuse; to provide policy statements to each employee; and to require employees to report any conviction for a criminal drug violation that occurred in the workplace.

When considering drug testing, all aspects of such a policy must be covered, including the type of testing and the conditions under which employees will be tested. The details of the policy must be presented to all affected individuals. Organizations should document the relationship between job performance, health and safety, and drug usage. The results of drug tests are confidential and generally should not be maintained in the personnel files.

EMPLOYEE ASSISTANCE PROGRAMS

Most healthcare organizations have an employee assistance program (EAP) of one sort or another. A direct relationship exists between security and EAPs. Many instances of employee wrongdoing can be traced back to personal problems. Stealing to support a drug habit is an obvious example where theft could be averted by helping an employee with this problem. Employees who steal because they do not understand how to manage their personal finances are a less obvious example. Even marital problems may lead to wrongdoing that otherwise may not have occurred. An in-depth EAP effort is a way to prevent crime among employees. Progressive security administrators may wish to explore this concept further with the administrator of the healthcare EAP program.

LOSS OF EMPLOYEE PROPERTY

Unfortunately, the loss of employee property is a continuous problem for protection systems. The provision and use of employee lockers is a primary safeguard against employee property losses. This problem usually evolves from a lack of proper storage facilities, carelessness, or the misuse or failure to use the facilities provided. An inspection of virtually any healthcare facility—hospital, nursing home, clinic, or physician's office—will usually reveal purses sitting in open view, simply inviting a loss. The mandate for the security function is to provide an adequate means of storage. Failure to use the storage provided gives employees little cause for legitimate complaint if their property is stolen.

EMPLOYEE SECURITY ATTITUDES

Healthcare organizations have found it extremely important to determine employee attitudes concerning their work environment. A positive attitude of support and appreciation of the security effort is essential to providing a safe and secure environment. A common method to assess such employee attitudes is to hire an outside firm that specializes in employee surveys. These firms generally use standard questions, but allow the organization being surveyed to develop some specific attitude questions. When security questions are used in these surveys, they should be very specific. If a survey produces a slightly positive or a neutral response, it should be considered extremely good because many employees have been victims of incidents, have received parking violation notices, or have a general disregard for the authority that security represents.

Another method of measuring the attitudes of employees is to conduct an in-house survey. One hospital obtained good results by approaching a local college and having the survey conducted by students as a class project. The class acted as a third-party surveyor and tabulated and analyzed the results.

Surveying the attitudes of employees must be an ongoing endeavor. Figure 13-4 is an example of a form utilized in one program in an ongoing effort to measure the performance of security personnel. In this program, completed Security Incident Reports and Security Condition Reports are utilized to send a random survey form to a recipient of a specific service or incident. This form is a pre-stamped mailer that is sent back to security for analysis and the formulation of improved service plans if appropriate.

EVALUATION REQUEST

Our records indicate you recently requested a security service as described below.

It is our intent that you receive prompt, courteous and professional service.

Please complete this form to help us evaluate our performance.

INSTRUCTIONS: Upon completion, refold the form with the stamp showing, tape closed and mail.

Thank you,
Security Services

_____ at _____

on _____ at _____. Rate Officer(s):_____

[circle one word per line]

public relations/courtesy:	Poor	Fair	Good	Excellent
appearance:	Poor	Fair	Good	Excellent
communication skill:	Poor	Fair	Good	Excellent
response time:	Poor	Fair	Good	Excellent
overall helpfulness:	Poor	Fair	Good	Excellent

Comments _____

_____
_____
_____
_____
_____
_____

Figure 13-4 Security Services Performance Survey (Courtesy of Healthcare Security Services, Denver, Colorado)

Survey results are the basis for recognizing outstanding service, the need for training, and a review of operating procedures. This measurement tool can be very useful in comparing one facility with another. This type of performance measure fits in with the Joint Commission on Accreditation of Healthcare Organizations (JCAHO) accreditation standards and is ready-made to help security personnel develop a performance improvement program.

EMPLOYEE SECURITY EDUCATION AND MOTIVATION

The strategy of preventing crime is a key concept of the protection system. In the United States, the Crime Prevention Coalition, formed by 19 organizations in 1980, provides strong leadership for national programs. Today, the coalition is stronger than ever, and it consists of over 130 national, state, and federal organizations and agencies.

"Crime prevention" has been defined in many ways. The definition found in the coalition's handbook, *Foundations for Action*, seems to be the most appropriate for the purposes of this discussion. Crime prevention, it says, is "a pattern of attitudes and behaviors directed both at reducing the threat of crime and enhancing the sense of safety and security, to positively influence the quality of life in our society, and to help develop environments where crime cannot flourish."[1] This is a tall order and a challenge for even the most professional healthcare security administrator.

A primary function of any protection system is to educate, stimulate, and motivate the first-line protection resource: employees. The protection level of a medical care facility is directly related to the extent to which employees participate in the security effort.

This participation varies from overt to covert activity. This is not to imply that all employees are engaged in overt security activities. Rather, some employees may participate by obeying the rules; for example, not taking property that does not belong to them. Other employees participate overtly by reducing inventory and thus reducing the opportunity for theft, maintaining key control, marking property, reporting losses and suspicious activity, tightening procedures for identifying people in their area, and properly locking their areas. All these activities, occurring simultaneously, are what a security system is all about. No one should be so naive as to think all employees will do their share. However, education and direction by the security department certainly increase employee participation.

Employee education begins with new employee orientation. New employees can be channeled into the protection system with a minimum of effort. They seek the norms and want to know what their employer expects. The moment employees first enter the workplace is the prime time to develop a positive protection attitude. Employees will not remember everything that is presented, but they will form a basic opinion, either consciously or unconsciously, of the importance that the organization places on security. There should be a handout for the new employee emphasizing the importance of security to themselves and the organization. The more progressive security programs will distribute a small book or pamphlet that describes the basic elements of the security program, including employee expectations in terms of providing safety and security.

Healthcare organizations are traditionally heavily involved in a continuous program of in-service education. Professional security administrators take advantage of every opportunity to involve protection services in these educational programs through departmental meetings or small group meetings. At one medical center, the entire workforce is subjected to a general in-service program on a quarterly basis.

A security slide/sound presentation was successfully used in one large facility. The program was designed to explain to employees how everyone fits into the protection system. The presentation equipment was taken directly to employees in their own work areas. Videotapes and computer presentations are increasingly being used. They can be produced in-house or bought from a national company.

Posters are another method of educating employees about security. In medical centers, posters have traditionally been used for safety messages, but they can be used to convey other messages as well.

Handbill notices are another way to deliver short messages to employees. Handbill notices can be distributed at employee orientation sessions or at periodic employee in-service programs. Figures 13-5 and 13-6 show examples of handbill notices.

Medical center newsletters are also a good medium for educating employees. Most newsletter editors are continually looking for new material. Because the protection effort is of general interest to employees, the security administrators generally find that such material is welcomed. Security information may be published randomly or in a regular column.

Human Resources and Staff Contributions 349

WE'RE HERE WHEN YOU NEED US....

SECURITY ESCORTS

During normal shift change hours officers are regularly assigned outside to offer maximum protection for all employees. If you leave work either before or after these times, call for an escort.

To request an escort call security a few minutes prior to your departure. An officer will be dispatched to escort you as soon as possible. However, response time may vary due to other responsibilities.

Please utilize hospital parking lots as off-property escorts are limited to one block.

WE CARE ABOUT YOU!

Healthcare Security Services

Figure 13-5 Example of a Crime Prevention/Security Awareness Handbill

ARE YOU KEEPING PATIENTS GUESSING

your support helps patient, staff, and security identify authorized personnel and suspicious persons

WEAR YOUR NAME TAG!
IT SAYS IT ALL

HEALTHCARE SECURITY SERVICES

Figure 13-6 Example of a Crime Prevention/Security Awareness Handbill

Special classes provide another opportunity to tell the protection story. Because medical care facilities employ many female personnel, personal safety and self-defense classes are popular. A broad range of security information can easily be included in special classes.

The security fair is another popular crime prevention activity. They have proven quite successful and generally draw more than 75 percent of the total employee workforce when organized and promoted. Pens and pencils carrying various security themes are distributed with scratch pads that have the security telephone number. Door prizes and food always boosts attendance.

Professional security administrators must seek new ways and new opportunities to communicate with employees. This activity yields a high return for the time and money expended.

HOSPITAL WATCH

The term "hospital watch," which refers to an approach to hospital crime prevention, was adopted from the neighborhood watch programs promoted by local police agencies. Hospital watch can take on many different forms. It is a generic approach to involving the hospital community in observing, reporting, and dealing with suspicious activity. Because there are no specific guidelines or program elements, the activities of this program are limited only by the ingenuity of the security administrator.

REFERENCE

1. "Foundations for Action," Crime Prevention Coalition, 1990.

CHAPTER 14

Investigative Activity in the Healthcare Setting

Investigative activity is a major component of any security system. It involves gathering and evaluating facts (including evidence) for either criminal or business (corporate) purposes.

The techniques and purposes of a business investigation often differentiate it from a law enforcement investigation. In addition to investigating crimes, security personnel may gather information regarding the violation of organizational rules and regulations; a job applicant's background; alleged harassment; alleged discrimination; conditions that may lead to criminal violations; the need for new security controls and procedures; liability claims or potential claims; unsafe conditions; or evidence needed to prove or disprove certain allegations against the organization. A law enforcement investigation, on the other hand, is conducted basically for the purpose of apprehending the perpetrator of a crime and obtaining the evidence required to successfully prosecute the case. In short, healthcare security investigations are much broader than law enforcement investigations. Also, the objective may be different even when the healthcare organization has a strong policy of prosecuting those who violate the law; the result may be an administrative remedy rather than a court proceeding. The style of an investigation is shaped by organizational philosophy, the purpose of the investigation, risk to the organization, as well as the background and traits of the investigator.

In general, investigators use two types of reasoning in conducting their inquiry: deduction and induction. Deduction is evaluating the meaning of verbal and physical clues, while induction is a basic scientific process to assign credibility to a generalization by setting up and observing a test.[1]

The many types of security investigations required in the healthcare facility can be as complex as the function of medical care itself. Most conditions or incidents that require investigation are non-criminal or of such minor criminal status that law enforcement agencies are virtually unconcerned with them.

If every incident legally classified as a crime were reported to a law enforcement agency, a crime wave would appear to take place. The number of crimes reported to the police is many times less than the actual number committed. However, the so-called minor crimes that are not reported to the police are of concern to a medical care facility for a variety of reasons. Even minor crimes may give a healthcare organization a poor public image. Further, such crimes may be only the surface of a larger crime problem and thus always deserve an investigative response. Also, not all incidents reported to security are crimes. In fact, many property losses can be traced to the loss of accountability or false reporting rather than actual theft.

Consider some specifics. An all too common problem in healthcare facilities is the loss of personal property of patients. Although many losses of patient property do occur, most incidents involve small items or cash amounting to less than $10. These losses are generally not reported to the police because it is simply unrealistic. On the other hand, the loss of patient property is a major problem for the organization.

Another type of loss of little or no interest to law enforcement agencies is the disappearance of a key to a critical area of the facility. The police do not become involved until the key is used to commit a crime. On the other hand, the security investigator should conduct an inquiry to ascertain whether the key was misplaced, lost, or stolen. If the facts point strongly to the latter, the investigator might recommend changing the locks or setting up a surveillance of the area. Neither of these alternatives would normally relate to law enforcement involvement.

A significant part of a security investigator's work is determining whether a crime has actually occurred. In addition, investigators examine procedures or operational areas to determine whether there is potential for loss. This broad area of investigation activity could also be labeled an *investigative audit*. If a major loss were uncovered during such an audit and an arrest were effected, it would merely be a byproduct of the audit investigation from the organizational point of view. An investigative audit is a major activity of a sound preventive security program; investigation should not be limited to the follow-up of reported security incidents.

TYPES OF INVESTIGATIONS

We have already discussed the general aspects of healthcare security investigations. These investigations can be divided into operational investigations and the more sensitive, or higher-level, investigations. The operational investigation typically begins when the security officer is dispatched to respond to a specific situation (vandalism, theft, property damage, disturbance, threatening behavior, etc.). The second type of investigation involves significant and/or ongoing conduct, such as embezzlement, sexual abuse, drug abuse, fraud, kickbacks. It may also involve the activity of high-level management personnel.

Planning for higher-level, and possibly sensitive, investigations should take place before the need arises. The basic question is, "Will this type of investigation require the services of an outside investigator, or can it be handled in-house?" Except in very large security programs, all investigations will be handled by in-house personnel. There are, however, various advantages to using an outside investigator, including added expertise, resources, and time. In addition, an outside investigator tends to be more objective and impartial.

The healthcare security administrator should seek out at least one outside investigative resource as part of a sound strategic plan. It takes time to interview investigative firms, check out references, assess capabilities, explore pricing and methodologies, determine a "fit" to the healthcare environment, and to understand organization philosophies of both the buyer and the provider. Selecting a vendor ahead of time will save time when the need arises.

In any investigation, the goals and objectives of both the organization and the healthcare organization must be mutually agreed upon and clearly documented. Details to be agreed upon include projected costs, reporting protocols, timetables, and the means of maintaining control of the investigation. The investigation should be continually monitored and managed with accurate and timely feedback relative to the investigative effort.

Incident Investigations

Incident investigations generally have two distinct phases. The first phase, generally referred to as the *preliminary investigation*, is usually conducted by field security officers. A preliminary investigation is conducted up to the point at which postponement of further investigation will not jeopardize the successful completion of the case. O.W. Wilson, one of the greatest police executives the U.S. has known, defined preliminary investigation over a quarter of a century ago. It is a definition that remains current today.[2] He defined it as follows:

- P Proceed to scene with safety and dispatch
- R Render assistance to injured
- E Effect arrest of perpetrator
- L Locate and identify witnesses
- I Interview complainant and witnesses
- M Maintain scene and protect evidence
- I Interrogate suspects
- N Note all conditions, events, and remarks
- A Arrange for collection of evidence
- R Report fully and accurately
- Y Yield responsibility to investigators or higher authority

One of the most important considerations during a preliminary investigation is to proceed to the scene as quickly as possible. How well the preliminary investigation is conducted and how quickly it is initiated have a direct effect on the probable outcome of the investigation. A prompt arrival enhances the possibility that evidence will not be tampered with or destroyed. Witnesses will still be present, and they will have less chance to compare what they saw, which in turn decreases the possibility for error.

Security officers should remember that a report is only the documentation of action taken and the collection of information (facts) concerning the incident. Thus, a security officer goes to the scene to conduct an inquiry and take appropriate action.

The second phase is the *follow-up investigation.* It may begin immediately after the preliminary investigation, or it may be days before further action is taken. Regardless of the time interval, a follow-up to the initial report is generally required. Supervisory review may be all that is required of some information-only reports. In small security organizations, the follow-up activity may be conducted by the same person who handled the preliminary investigation, or the security administrator may also function as the department investigator.

The follow-up investigation often produces additional information; at the same time, it creates a favorable image for the public and employees. Another aspect of the follow-up investigation is that it shortens the preliminary investigation required and allows security field personnel to return to patrol, making them available for further service. Follow-up investigators generally have access to records, files, and sources of information not available to preliminary investigators. Because follow-up investigation is centralized, specialized techniques may be used and past incidents that may have a relationship to the incident under investigation may be analyzed.

An examination of a typical hospital incident—the loss of patient property—illustrates these points. A patient informs the charge nurse that she cannot locate her gold wristwatch, which was in her bedside cabinet at 5:30 P.M. Although it is now 10:30 P.M., the charge nurse notifies security, and a patrol officer is dispatched to conduct a preliminary investigation. After a thorough search of the room and the soiled linen collection area, the officer completes the report, addressing all the basic questions. Several possibilities exist concerning the whereabouts of the watch:

1. The patient misplaced the watch, even though the search failed to locate the property.

2. An employee found the watch and has, against hospital policy and procedure, locked it up for safekeeping.

3. An employee, another patient, or a visitor has stolen the watch.

4. The patient's family or friends have taken the watch home for safekeeping.

5. The watch was discarded unknowingly by the patient or staff.

6. The watch was checked in with the admissions office.

7. There was never any watch in the patient's possession.

Because of the hour, the security officer does not have access to admitting records. Good judgment would preclude contacting the family late at night and the police would probably not be called until most of the above possibilities could be eliminated, providing a stronger indication that a theft had, in fact, occurred. Thus, the security officer must gather all the information readily available and forward the report to the appropriate person to initiate a follow-up investigation.

The follow-up investigator should start by re-contacting the patient. The investigator can obtain additional information from the patient and can find out whether the watch was found. This contact allows the investigator to begin with current information or, if the watch was found, to close the complaint. The follow-up contact assures the patient that the hospital is concerned, and that the matter is not being ignored. In facilities with poor investigative response, patients frequently complain that their concerns are not heard and the hospital does not really care.

In some hospitals, the nurse prepares an unusual-incident report. This is an unacceptable practice and generally results in reporting that is not timely and lacks sufficient information. In the case of the missing watch, it is doubtful whether the nurse-prepared report would include the last time the watch was seen, whether the patient received visitors, and which unit personnel were on duty. Unless unduly delayed, the unusual-incident report passes through the nursing service office and reaches the appropriate administrative person several days later. Frequently, no follow-up action is taken. The report may also end up with the risk manager, who again generally lacks the resources for a thorough follow-up. In short, security should conduct the inquiry and prepare the report.

Patterns of Wrongdoing and Suspects

A major reason to encourage employees to report all wrongdoing is that sometimes incidents cannot be resolved individually, but they can be resolved in combination. Skilled investigators seek out and recognize emerging patterns that point to suspects or the probability of a repeated act. The investigation then shifts somewhat from gathering facts to setting up a plan of action, which may include surveillance or even a covert operation. Investigators often use electronic equipment (closed-circuit television, video recording, alarm devices, etc.) and various dusting powders or ultraviolet light techniques.

The "planting" of an object that has been the subject of theft is also a common method of resolving problems. A possible disadvantage to this procedure is that it may induce a person to steal, but it may not be the person who has been responsible for the incidents under investigation. Regardless of the methods used, the resolution of incidents not only identifies perpetrators and detects system failures, but it also sends a strong message to future malefactors.

Background Investigations

Good security programs go a step further than incident investigation, and conduct various other types of investigations or audits. One such activity is the background investigation. In some security systems, a criminal history record check is a routine step in the employment process. In others, security is called on to perform a background check only for particular positions or when there are specific background questions that need to be explored in more detail. This type of investigation is almost always performed in collaboration with the Human Resources department.

Audits

Another type of investigation is sometimes referred to as an *audit*. One type of audit is a check of certain areas or activities to determine whether crimes are occurring or to determine the level of security safeguards and their effectiveness. Another form of security audit is to determine whether policies and procedures are being followed. Simply having a policy and procedure does not insure compliance. In fact, noncompliance, or partial compliance, may be false security.

Spot-Checks and Surveillance

Spot-checks of operations and investigative surveillance activities are closely related to audit investigations. These types of investigations are almost endless; they are limited only by the imagination and resourcefulness of the investigator. Care should be taken that the scope of the activity is coordinated with the hospital's internal auditors, even though security checks investigate areas that are not considered within the scope of internal auditing.

An example of this type of activity is to conduct unannounced checks on incoming shipments of goods and supplies. One security investigator decided to check a fuel oil delivery being made to the hospital. He discovered that the load was short by more than 200 gallons, and subsequent investigation revealed that the driver had been making short deliveries for some time. Because no one had ever checked the metering device to see that it registered zero before unloading, the driver was free to unload some of the fuel before he arrived at the hospital.

A surveillance investigation is usually initiated as a result of information received, although it may be just a "fishing expedition." One hospital security department plants purses or trousers in high-loss areas. The wallet inside is attached to a magnetic contact/transmitter, which sends a signal to an FM radio receiver when the contact is broken. Another method is to use a light-sensing device to activate the transmitter. This device is particularly useful in moneyboxes, desk drawers, and file cabinets.

General surveillance of critical areas can also produce results. Although no losses had been reported in the facility, one investigator set up a surveillance of a general storeroom and discovered that an employee was helping himself to supplies after hours with a key that was not known to be in existence. Loading docks and trash collection areas are also good places for the general surveillance investigation.

Unemployment and Worker's Compensation Investigations

There is a great need for the investigation of fraud in unemployment benefits and worker's compensation. Healthcare organizations should become more involved in these areas because government administration and controls are largely ineffective. These frauds have cost organizations, and ultimately the patient, billions of dollars.

The known cases probably amount to less than 1 percent of the actual cases. The cost of fraudulent worker's compensation claims is many times that of fraudulent unemployment claims. In the former, not only do employees receive their wages, but there are also physician charges and other unnecessary medical care treatment costs.

Undercover (Covert) Investigations

Undercover operations are widely used in the healthcare setting. The most common activity is to infiltrate a department where a specific or suspected problem exists. The concept of utilizing an undercover operative in a patient care facility may seem extreme to some and somewhat frightening to others, but professional security administrators consider it good business procedure. The operation is intended to protect trustworthy and faithful employees and to ferret out those who are detrimental to the organization. The undercover operation may in deed seem extreme; however, so are the stakes and the responsibility to properly manage the healthcare organization.

A successful undercover investigation requires that as few people as possible in the organization know about the operation. Department heads and supervisors generally should not be involved in the plan or privileged with the information that an operative has been placed in their department. In a few cases, it may be essential that the department head be part of the effort in order to obtain the proper position for the operative or because of special circumstances or the type of information being sought. More often than not, however, information leaks begin with the department head and result in a wasted effort.

A major objective of a covert operation is to severely limit the number of people who know about the operation. The failure to comply with this simple concept has compromised more operations than any other factor. Generally, if more than two people in the organization, other than the security director, know about the investigation, it should not be initiated, and if it is already underway, serious consideration should be given to aborting the project.

In addition to specific investigations, undercover operatives are used as a check on operations to determine whether security policies and procedures are meeting their objectives. It is a method to determine whether the funds spent for security are providing the desired results. Information derived from the investigation need not be negative. Operatives who find that all is going well produce valuable management feedback. After operatives have done their job in one department, they can transfer to another department to continue the audit operation. Department transfers are sometimes easier to effect then bringing the operative into the organization as a newly hired employee.

When an organization commits itself to an undercover program, it must be prepared to fund the program for a considerable period of time. Many undercover programs fail because results were expected too soon. This is especially true of operatives working on a significant problem where those involved are extremely cautious. New people are always treated with a certain amount of suspicion, and operatives must slowly build positive relationships with fellow employees. Of course, the skill and competence of the investigator play a significant part in how much time is required.

In large organizations, newly hired security personnel are a possible source of undercover operatives. There are, however, two basic disadvantages to this approach. No matter how thorough the background check and the selection process, the abilities of new employees are always unknown. Another drawback is that not everyone is suited for undercover investigation activities. The wrong operative may produce not only an ineffective investigation, but embarrassing problems for the organization.

Another source of undercover personnel is the loan of an officer or investigator from another security healthcare organization. The mutual aid approach can be economical, and the abilities of the personnel are not as unpredictable as may be the case of a newly hired employee. Borrowed and newly hired operatives can do a good job because they have more at stake than do operatives from the outside who move on to other unrelated assignments. The new hire is seeking a good employment beginning and continued employment. The employee on loan seeks positive feedback on his work to reach his employer.

Undercover operatives should be required to report their activities and observations periodically. This communication should take place at a location outside the organization and is best accomplished in face-to-face meetings rather than over the telephone. Daily logs of all activity should also be required. Information collected by the operative should be broad in nature and should include any information that might help improve organizational management. To be more specific, information on morale, how well a new policy was received, the falsification of time records, cleanliness, and other items that will help the organization be more efficient should be included in the feedback information. Reports should also include positive information on which systems are functioning effectively.

INVESTIGATORS AND THEIR TOOLS

Good investigators have a firm understanding of human relations, a natural aptitude for inquiry, and are intrigued by the investigative process. Investigations always offer a challenge and often succeed or fail in direct relation to the investigator's competence and enthusiasm. A good investigator must have the following traits:

- The ability to remain objective
- Energy and alertness
- Knowledge of the law
- The ability to set realistic objectives
- A methodical nature
- Knowledge of human nature
- Observation and deduction skills
- The ability to maintain meaningful notes

It is generally accepted by the security industry that all investigations are limited by the investigator's reasoning ability. One of the greatest threats to reasoning ability is a lack of objectivity. The excessive influence of subjective feelings, prejudices, or interpretation also severely affect reasoning. Although it is not possible to be 100 percent objective, professional investigators are able to exert the necessary control over subjective influences to understand any effect they may have on the investigation.

The investigative process must be considered to be a major element of the successful protection program. The investigations of many current healthcare security programs need to be upgraded. Administrators should remember that an investigator is called on to determine the facts and not necessarily to solve the problem.

Investigators must at all times conduct investigations within the guidelines set out by the law, and they must always exercise proper employee relations procedures and conduct. The investigation must be conducted to avoid:

- Compromising a criminal case
- Compromising an arbitration
- Creating a damage action
- Violating the law

In respect to violating the law, the areas of entrapment, invasion of privacy, eavesdropping, and self-incrimination deserve careful attention. Legal actions against investigators and the organizations they represent are fairly common.

Detection of Deception

The polygraph (lie detector) is an important tool of the investigator. Although federal legislation passed in 1988 has curtailed the use of the polygraph in industry, it still may be used under certain circumstances. Because the device's use by law enforcement agencies is not restricted, security administrators may do well to promote the use of polygraphs through police investigations. As with undercover operatives and informants, the polygraph is used to accomplish various objectives.

In investigation, the polygraph test is used to determine whether specific people possess knowledge of a specific set of circumstances. It often assists investigators in eliminating suspects.

Another electronic device for detecting deception is the psychological stress evaluator (PSE). This device records and measures stress in the human voice. The PSE and the polygraph both measure emotional stress to determine whether the subject is telling the truth. The PSE uses a voice print in which the vocal response can be analyzed in 32 different ways. The polygraph measures respiration, blood pressure, and galvanic skin reaction. Debate over the accuracy of these two devices continues.

Hypnosis

Another tool for investigators is hypnosis. Hypnosis is more widely used in law enforcement than in security. The most accepted theory of hypnosis is that the hypnotic trance subdues the conscious mind and allows the subconscious mind to dominate. Because memory is a function of the subconscious, subjects under hypnosis can access their memory without the constraints of the conscious mind. Hypnosis must be viewed as a means of discovering information. Its effectiveness varies from person to person, and it can also vary from one trance to the next in the same person. Hypnosis has not been reliable in obtaining the truth from a reluctant witness. Information obtained through hypnosis has resolved many crimes and security problems, but like the polygraph and the PSE, it is only a tool to be used in the investigative process.

Employee Informants

A corollary to the undercover operation is the development of employee informants within the organization. Employee informants are developed in a number of ways. Certain employees naturally develop a good rapport with security during routine contacts. Employees may report possible wrongdoing due to loyalty or moral motivations. Generally, employees provide just enough information to indicate a problem because they are hesitant to get too involved. These people can often be drawn into on ongoing and productive reporting system.

Informants must satisfy a material or psychological need. The most common motivation is financial. Information is sometimes provided in return for a payment. These payments should always be made when information is received, and the amount of the payment should be based on the value of the information. In the early stages of developing a source, payments may be withheld until the information can be verified. Informants should not receive retainers or regular payments.

Another method of obtaining information about employees from other employees is to establishment telephone hot-lines. These systems provide a means for employees to report wrongdoing while maintaining their anonymity. Various national companies offer this service. The service includes providing materials and presentations to employees on how the system works and the employee's responsibility to report wrongdoing. Organizations using these systems report good success.

REFERENCES

1. Carl Stanton Klump, "Taking Your Cue from the Clues," *Security Management*, September 1997, p. 124.

2. O.W. Wilson, *Police Administration*, McGraw-Hill Book Co., 1963, p. 282.

CHAPTER 15

Physical Security

The security of a healthcare facility can be considered as a system of interrelated safeguards. These safeguards can be divided into overlapping psychological and physical components. A protection system must combine the many physical and psychological safeguards that are available into a meaningful program that efficiently manages the defined organizational security vulnerabilities. Psychological safeguards were discussed in Chapter 3; this chapter discusses the physical components.

The most common physical security controls—barriers/fences, alarms, lighting, locks and keys, electronic sensors, and closed-circuit television—are basically dependent to various degrees on personnel to operate them or to render them effective. The purpose of these physical controls varies; they might be used for traffic control, surveillance of an area, in summoning help, or in access control. Now more than ever, healthcare facilities are placing a greater reliance on physical security.

Physical security controls can be divided into electronic security systems and non-electronic hardware components.

ELECTRONIC SECURITY SYSTEMS

Electronic security safeguards have been around for some time; however, their use has recently grown at an accelerated rate with the introduction of new and upgraded technologies. Electronic systems can be broken down into the basic categories of alarms, closed-circuit television (CCTV), and access control. These three categories are often referred to as sub-systems with a certain amount of overlap. For example, alarms and CCTV are often integral to the overall access control plan. In addition to the physical electronic safeguards, there are other electronic subsystems utilized for program management purposes, such as guard tours, vending equipment, and communication devices.

A term endemic to any discussion of electronic security safeguards is *systems integration*. Prior to the 1990s, many subsystems were purchased and maintained as standalone technologies; however, these were difficult and expensive to "marry" with one another. The 1990s saw a move toward designing these multiple subsystems to work together as a master or integrated system. Systems integration, thus, entails either that the subsystems operate from a single platform, or that the subsystems work together to achieve efficient monitoring and cost-effectiveness. The security administrator should make sure the system is flexible, and that it will meet current and future needs.

And while integration can be carried beyond the security level to include engineering, fire, and energy management, it is not recommended except in very small facilities. There are, however, opportunities for dual, or redundant, monitoring between separate security and engineering systems.

THE CENTRAL SECURITY STATION

The efficient operation of a protection system requires that there be a hub, or center of operations. In smaller facilities, this hub is likely to be the telephone operator, which is only marginally satisfactory but a necessity in the small organization. Generally, communications personnel resist the addition of security to their responsibilities. Without a central security station (post), the functions of lost and found, key control, alarm monitoring, personnel clearance, central records, and security officer deployment, to name a few, are difficult to manage.

Advantages

One of the basic functions of the central security post is to handle security communications. To maintain a high level of protection, each employee must report problems and suspicious activity to security. The easier it is to contact security, the more the employees will be motivated to participate in reporting. When a security officer answers the telephone, the communication is quite direct. Not only is quicker response time obtained for emergency calls, but also inquiries can be promptly handled

Figure 15-1 Example of a Central Security Station (Courtesy of New York University Medical Center Security Department)

without relaying messages. The monitoring and linkage with public safety organizations can also render their service more efficient.

The functions assigned to the central security post vary from organization to organization, depending on the elements of the security program. In any case, the potential for a 24-hour post expands the alternatives for program planning. Figure 15-1 shows an example of a hospital central security station. The station monitors security, fire, and critical electrical/mechanical building functions, and also serves as the operational center for a variety of security and management services.

Design

When a central station will involve many process control functions, such as alarms, CCTV, radio, and general monitoring, the design of the station requires considerable planning. One area that is often neglected is the human factor, which must be integrated with the physical aspects of the equipment. There are considerable differences in the size of the personnel who will operate the center; thus some averages must be determined. For example, a person who is 60 inches tall has a line of sight when standing of 56.5 inches; a 72-inch person has a line of sight of 69 inches.

In general, the following distance averages, which assume a seated shoulder height of 35 inches, can be used for planning sit-down consoles:

Keyboard/controls	25–26 inch reach
Benchboard height	25 inch minimum
Keyboard/counter depth	18 inch minimum
Benchboard to chair seat	7.5 inch minimum
Horizontal sight	45 degrees maximum
Vertical sight	75 degrees maximum

The horizontal and vertical sight recommendations are measured from a straight-ahead, level line of sight. Temperature, humidity, ventilation, illumination, background noise, and sound absorption are also important factors to consider in the design planning process.

Cost

The basic problem encountered in operating a central security post is the expense, particularly for the labor required to maintain the post 24 hours per day (this requires at least 4.5 full time-time equivalent employees). Even though significantly increased protection will result, the required funding can be difficult to obtain. In addition to labor costs, the implementation of a central station can involve an extensive capital budget increase over several years. Prioritizing the services to be provided and realistically projecting the implementation of those services will help in justifying the cost and obtaining the necessary funding.

Proper planning can reduce the cost of a central station by reappraising the entire system and considering certain trade-offs. The first consideration is location. It is neither necessary nor feasible to find a basement room that can be fortified against attack or severe storms just because it is available and is space no one else really wants. Instead, the post should be located in an area that requires the presence of a security officer and is accessible to employees and the public. Good locations include the entrance to the emergency room, the employee entrance, the loading dock, and even the front lobby. Central security posts situated in these locations perform a double duty. The officers assigned to the post can perform a traffic control and surveillance function while fulfilling the responsibilities normally assigned to the central security station.

If the station is located in an area that already has 24-hour security coverage, it might perhaps be established without additional personnel. Another approach is to look for an area that requires a part-time or full-time clerk performing a function in another facility department. It may be possible to integrate the clerk's role into the security function and divert more funding into the security budget.

ALARMS

A basic component of most protection programs is an alarm system. Alarm systems have many fire detection and warning applications; however, the discussion in this chapter is limited to the application of alarms for security surveillance, response, and control purposes.

The use of security alarms in the healthcare environment is increasing, as it should. Properly planned, installed, and used, the alarm system is a very cost-effective component of the proactive security system. Cost-effectiveness is greatly enhanced when alarm systems are designed and installed as part of new construction.

The factors that have limited the use of alarms include limited availability of capital funds, lack of monitoring capabilities, lack of knowledge, absence of administrative or physician acceptance, imagined or real employee morale problems, and the lack of innovative thinking on the part of protection administrators.

The security costs and the need to justify the budget force security administrators to recognize that the proper balance between labor and physical security is mandatory. *Proper balance* is the key phrase because alarm applications are primarily designed to render security personnel more effective. It is true, however, that alarms and other security hardware components can reduce the total number of security personnel required for a given complex by increasing the productiveness of the security system.

In planning alarm systems, the concept of security as a system of perimeters may be helpful. The first concern is the outermost section of the building. The *perimeter protection* includes fences, windows, doors, roofs, and the like. Working inward, the next concern is *area protection*, which may be a room or a series of rooms, such as a pharmacy, general storeroom, or medical records area. The next concern is *point protection*. The point may be a safe, vault, office machine, or even a piece of art. One hospital had so many thefts of artwork that it installed magnetic alarm switches behind each picture.

Alarm System Components

An alarm system is composed of three interrelated parts: the sensory device, the transmission medium, and an annunciator. The sensory device determines that a potential problem exists, generally through an electrical circuit that is either open or closed. The types of change that an alarm system can detect include vibration, sound, and motion; a break in an electrical circuit; a change in pressure; the interruption of an energy beam; and a capacitance change due to the penetration of an electronic field. Each type of alarm has various applications in the healthcare setting. Each sensory device is often referred to as a *point*, and an alarm system monitors or supervises a number of these points.

The transmission of the sensory's device signal to the annunciation point is usually accomplished by hard wire, telephone lines, or radio waves. The transmission medium must be monitored for line trouble or attempts to circumvent the alarm system. The security of the transmission medium must not be overlooked in the proper application of an alarm system.

The third component of the alarm system is the annunciation, or reporting, point. The annunciator, sometimes called a *monitor*, is a visual or audio signaling device that indicates the condition of the alarm circuits. Annunciation is usually accomplished by the activation of a signal lamp, visual display, print-out, audible sound, or any combination of these elements.

Annunciation may occur in several places. A local alarm announces the signal in the immediate proximity of the area or item being protected. This announcement may be by bell, horn, light, or other means. For example, a local alarm might have a bell placed next to the door, protected by an electromagnetic switch. This type of annunciator is used more as a deterrent to scare off intruders than as a system to apprehend intruders. Some systems activate a voice message that tells intruders that they have entered a secure area and warns them to turn back. Of course, any message can be generated in this type of system.

A central station installation transmits the signal off the property and may be coupled with a local alarm annunciator. The central station is a remote, off-premises monitoring point. This system, generally provided by a commercial service, is specifically applicable to the medical office buildings, retail pharmacies, and clinics, which, when closed, do not have the benefit of onsite security personnel. Central stations today are seldom located in the community where the alarms originate. There has been a tremendous consolidation of central stations, resulting in very large operations in various cities. It is not uncommon for an alarm system to be monitored a thousand miles or more away from the point or origin.

Some central station systems are approved by Underwriters Laboratory (UL). The central station of an alarm company that offers a UL-approved system must be located and built to fairly rigid UL specifications. UL approval is not necessarily required for most healthcare alarm applications, and the services of a non–UL-approved alarm company may even be superior to those of a UL-approved central station.

Basic Alarm Applications

The two basic security alarm applications found in healthcare facilities are the *intrusion alarm* and the *holdup alarm*, or *panic alarm*. The intrusion alarm is used for sensitive areas within a healthcare facility that are closed for certain periods, including clinics, pharmacies, laundries, general stores, medical records, libraries, and gift shops. The intrusion alarm is also a primary safeguard utilized for offsite satellite facilities and physician office buildings.

The holdup alarm is frequently used in cashier's offices, pharmacies, and gift shops. This type of alarm is more often used to summon security personnel to observe suspicious people or activities rather than solely as a holdup alarm. Thus, in the healthcare facility, the term would more appropriately be referred to as a panic alarm. Panic alarms are used in psychiatric areas, emergency departments, and remote work locations to summon both security officers and medical help.

Most panic buttons (alarms) are attached to a wall or desk at a fixed location. There is, however, a portable product that allows an individual to move about a given "protected area" so that the activation device can be carried or worn on the person. This system generally operates using a radio frequency.

Few would argue against the intrusion alarm as a necessary component of a security system. Common agreement does not exist concerning the panic button utilized as a holdup alarm, however. Some people believe that in holdups the perpetrator is likely to have a weapon, and a response by the police or by security personnel will likely create a situation that could result in injury or death. This theory advances the premise that if a holdup is in progress, the security system has failed to prevent the crime, and it has become a law enforcement situation.

The essence of this question revolves around the response to the alarm rather than the existence of the alarm. An alarm warning might signal security personnel to observe an area or to adopt positions that will be advantageous in a confrontation or for general surveillance. The safety of those in the area is the foremost concern, and it is far better to obtain a good description of the event than to risk injury or death.

Proprietary Alarm Systems

The proprietary annunciation system is similar to the central station system except that the monitoring function and sometimes the installation and service are provided by the organization that is being protected. In this system, the alarm terminates on the property, and organizational personnel handle response to the alarm. This response may be to notify the police or the fire department or to notify onsite security personnel. In many healthcare facilities, this function is assigned to the telephone operator because the switchboard is a 24-hour service. In larger facilities and multiple-facility systems that operate a 24-hour central security post, this post is the terminal point for the alarm system.

Duress Codes

Some healthcare security administrators support the use of duress codes. A duress code is simply a word or phrase that alerts the person being called that the caller is in some kind of danger. However, the high turnover of healthcare personnel suggests that such codes may do more harm than good. Their use depends largely on their application and the number of people involved. If a protection system includes a central security station that receives alarms and the personnel in the alarmed area are limited in number, duress codes might be a part of the system. On the other extreme, gift shops are often operated by volunteers; it is therefore generally difficult to inform everyone involved about a panic alarm and its use, let alone teach them about duress codes.

False Alarms

False alarms should be analyzed to determine the validity of an alarm system. False alarms result more often from personnel errors than from malfunctioning equipment. Proper installation is a key element in preventing false alarms, and alarm activation devices should be well-planned to avoid the false alarm problem. Having too many false alarms tends to decrease the protection level. In some situations, alarm systems have been simply disconnected because the high number of false alarms rendered the system ineffective. Where the police are called, it is quite common for fines to be imposed when false alarms occur. A high number of false alarms will often alter the type of police response.

CLOSED-CIRCUIT TELEVISION

Closed-circuit television (CCTV) continues to be an element in most healthcare security programs. There has been a switch to different applications in recent years, from large central systems to a more decentralized approach. Even in the large central systems, the utilization of a systems integration approach has greatly reduced the ratio of the number of monitors to cameras.

CCTV has two basic security uses: access control and surveillance. In healthcare security programs, CCTV has primarily been used for surveillance; however, access control applications are increasing. These access control applications may be found at emergency room entrances, receiving dock gates, physician offices, computer rooms, pharmacies, and basic building or parking access points.

Closed-circuit television and alarms have much in common, and they often work together as an integrated system. They both help to render security personnel more effective, and they generally require monitoring and response. Some CTV systems, however, are intended to only capture (record) images to be utilized later if necessary. In these systems, there may or may not be any screen monitoring involved.

Live monitoring of CCTV is a greater problem than monitoring alarms, at least for general surveillance. A person generally cannot view a monitor for more than 30 minutes without becoming bored and ineffective. Many CCTV systems are thus integrated into protection programs so that constant viewing is not required. Other security duties break up the monotony of continuous viewing and considerably extend personnel effectiveness. "Smart" CCTV systems are coming into greater use. This monitoring equipment alerts the operator when the monitor must be viewed. In these systems, the monitor to be viewed will often be a larger screen that has the ability to activate recording equipment.

The basic CCTV system consists of five components, or subsystems. The *lens* collects light and forms an image on the sensitized *camera*. This image is then electronically transmitted over a *transmission line* via coaxial cable, microwaves, fiber optics, or regular telephone lines to the *monitor*, which translates the signal back into a visible image. A *recording device* preserves the image for review and storage.

Applications

The challenge for hospital security professionals is not to fully understand the electronics of CCTV, but to be innovative in applying this physical safeguard to the management of vulnerabilities.

Hospitals usually lock all entrances during the late-night hours, except for designated night entrances. A closed-circuit television camera with an audio capability and electric-strike door latches allows a person far removed from the entrance to screen visitors and delivery or service people, and to grant access as required. When necessary, a security officer can be dispatched to the location to verify authorization for entry. Authorized persons can bypass the need for an operator to release the lock by using electronic push-button, card access devices, or biometric technology.

Physical Security 375

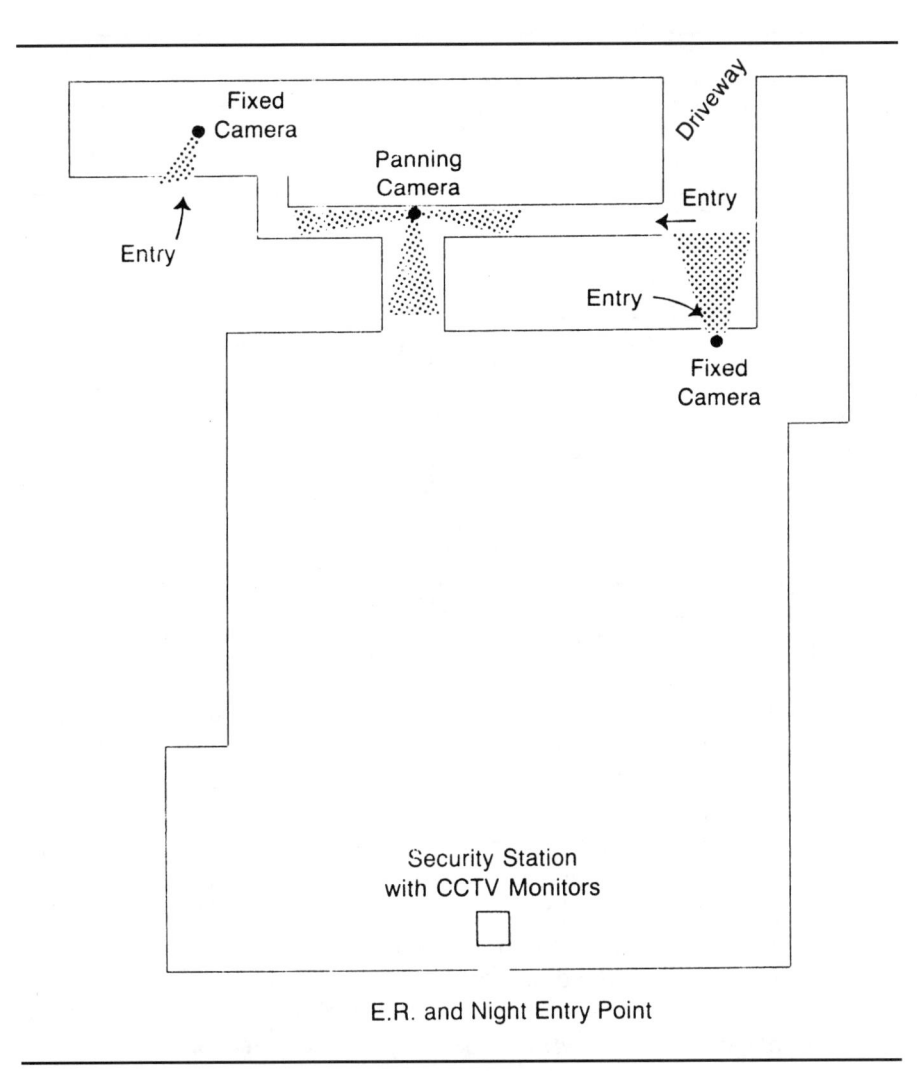

Figure 15-2 Example of Using CCTV to Protect One Side of the Facility with a Security Officer Controlling Access and Monitoring Cameras on the Opposite Side

General surveillance is one of the basic uses of CCTV. When used for this purpose, the system is perhaps more of a psychological control than an actual physical control. The configuration of the three cameras in Figure 15-2 was designed to protect the access points of the west side

376 *Hospital and Healthcare Security*

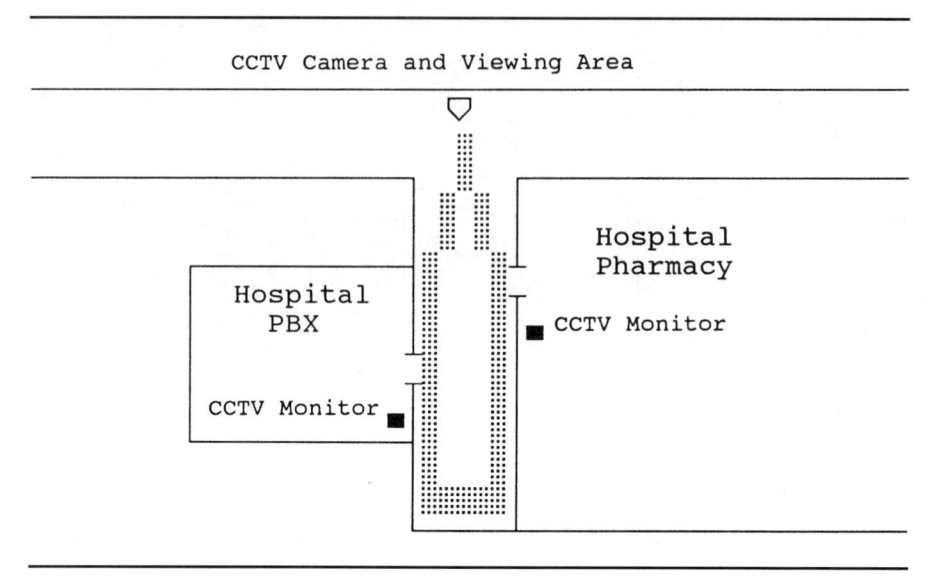

```
                    CCTV Camera and Viewing Area
                                 ▽

                    ┌──────────┐     ┌──────────────┐
                    │          │     │  Hospital    │
                    │ Hospital │     │  Pharmacy    │
                    │   PBX    │     │              │
                    │          │  ■ CCTV Monitor   │
                    │ CCTV Monitor ■ │             │
                    └──────────┘     └──────────────┘
```

Figure 15-3 An Example of the Use of CCTV for Security Purposes in a Decentralized Configuration

of the facility while a security officer at a monitoring station physically controlled access on the east side of the facility. The east side has the emergency room entrance and the night employee entrance.

CCTV is increasingly being used for security in decentralized systems. The responsibility for certain aspects of security are returned to the operating or functioning level of a department. An example would be a loading dock that requires surveillance during receiving hours to determine who is coming and going and to address the vulnerability of unattended merchandise on the dock for short periods of time. The materials management department could monitor the dock with CCTV. A monitor could be placed on a secretary's desk or at another point within the department. This type of installation is quite economical as compared to transmitting the signal back to a central security station.

Another example of the decentralized approach is to place a camera in the corridor just outside the main pharmacy employee service door. The monitor is placed inside the door, permitting pharmacy employees to view the corridor before opening the door to exit.

In the decentralized design shown in Figure 15-3, one camera can be viewed by two different operating departments. Employees working in both the telephone switchboard room and the pharmacy can view the common corridor before exiting from their respective workstations.

Equipment

The most important consideration in a CCTV system is the quality of the image received, and this is largely dependent on the camera. The major factors crucial to picture quality are amplitude response, signal-to-noise ratio, resolution, horizontal aperture correction, sensitivity, and transfer smear. Comparing these qualities in relation to the price will provide the right camera for a specific application.

The transmission of the signal to the monitor also affects image quality. Although coaxial cable is widely used, the use of fiber optics is growing. Fiber optics can eliminate line-loss problems and camera synchronization problems. The use of regular telephone lines is also increasing, particularly for applications where clearness of image is not the major factor.

The size of the monitor should be based on the purpose of monitoring and individual preference. A general rule is to increase the size of the monitor as operator-viewing distance increases.

The charge-coupled device (CCD) is a widely used chip camera. Chip cameras generally do not need heaters, consume much power, or need large housing. Despite some drawbacks in resolution and sensitivity, they have replaced tube cameras.

Another major advance is the use of microprocessors and microcomputers in video systems. This technology allows systems that were formerly operated manually to be preprogrammed and automated. Digital video technology has also progressed rapidly. Digital processing, which plays a significant role in almost every aspect of video security, is a more effective method of processing signals than is analog processing. The continuing development of high-definition television (HDTV) with multiplexing, and improved digital processing equipment will provide new and improved CCTV security applications.

Dummy Cameras

No discussion of closed-circuit television would be complete without some mention of the so-called dummy camera. There is no question that some of the value of CCTV for security applications is the psychological deterrent it creates. Malefactors are never quite sure how many cameras there are and who is watching their movements. It therefore stands to reason that a fake television camera would provide this deterrent.

Unfortunately, it is extremely difficult to avoid revealing that the dummy camera is not real. Opponents argue that because the dummy camera cannot be kept secret, it implies to employees that the organization is "playing games" with them. If security controls are to be administered on a positive rather than a negative basis, there is little use for fake cameras.

The strongest argument against the use of the dummy camera is that it can create the expectation that one is being protected when in fact no protection is being provided. This may produce a situation in which a person takes chances or invites trouble based on their false sense of security. A false sense of security can also exist when real CCTV systems are not monitored or do not function as intended. The concept of false security has been the basis of many lawsuits, for example, Cisky v. Longs Peak Association, et al. (84 CV 5668) District Court, Denver, Colorado, wherein the plaintiff was awarded more than $6 million by a jury. The issue in this case was, in part, the question of a camera that did not provide the protection that was indicated.

Accessories

One accessory that can be added to a CCTV system is an electronic switcher, which expands the system's capability. Switchers shift the image being received to a given monitor or a recording device, and they can limit the number of monitors required. Sequential switching can be set for various intervals; however, operators can at any time override the sequence if they need to hold the image of a specific camera or transfer it to a large screen.

Time and date generators can be added to a CCTV system to record the time and date on the images being recorded. Camera identification numbers can also be recorded and displayed to identify the source of the picture. Pan and tilt controls and zoom lenses are utilized in some CCTV systems. Pan refers to the horizontal rotation of the camera, and tilt controls allow the camera to move up and down. Pan and tilt can be set to function automatically or can be manually controlled by a joystick or computer.

One area often overlooked when installing cameras is the security of the camera itself. Cameras must be mounted to preclude theft of the camera or the lens. In addition to the cost involved, the loss of a security camera can be extremely embarrassing. Theft-proof enclosures are readily available and should be considered in all installations. In addition, camera housings protect cameras from the elements. Indoor and outdoor housings are fabricated from metal or high-impact materials.

Videotape Recording

CCTV monitoring can be greatly enhanced by incorporating a videotape recorder (VTR) into the system. The price of a VTR has dropped significantly over the past few years, and it is now economically feasible to include a VTR in virtually any CCTV security system. In some applications the VTR is used without anyone monitoring the live picture. A videotape can be scanned at a faster speed than real time. If there have been no significant problems, there may be no need to review the tape at all. In systems that monitor closed areas or areas with very light traffic, a sensor can be used to start and stop the recorder; the tape is thus shortened to just the periods when movement occurred in the camera field.

One of the best applications of the VTR is as a supplement to live viewing. The VTR captures the scene, and regular photographs may be taken of the video picture for permanent documentation purposes.

As a general rule, all CCTV cameras utilized in a security system should be recorded and the recording retained in a seven-day library as a minimum. It is not uncommon to maintain this information for 30 days.

Monitoring

A major question regarding the use of any closed-circuit television is how the cameras will be monitored. The answer, of course, depends on the application. There are many combinations of monitoring, from a dedicated security person centrally monitoring the system on a full-time basis to no live monitoring at all. In the case of no live monitoring, the cameras are simply recorded for future viewing if necessary. There are partial viewing and redundant (two or more viewing locations) monitoring models as well. Redundant monitoring is generally reserved for specific strategic cameras and is most often found in CCTV systems that utilize both a centralized and decentralized design model. An example of redundant viewing would be the facility birthing area. It is common to install a completely self-contained system for this area being monitored on the unit. Only certain cameras would also send signals back to a centralized security monitoring point.

In programs that do not have fulltime security officer monitoring, it is common to locate the CCTV monitors at the facility telephone switchboard. In this application, the monitors should be set on a shelf that is tilted down and faces the operators. They should not be so high that the operators must constantly strain to look upward. This positioning saves space and allows the operators to make normal eye contact with the monitors while they carry out their primary duties. In some programs, security alarms and the security radio system are also controlled from the main switchboard. A problem arises when the operators are reluctant to take on this additional responsibility. Telephone operators, who are on duty 24 hours a day, are often given many extra responsibilities and therefore tend to be overloaded.

Another area for monitoring is the engineering control room found in many modern physical plants. Electrical, mechanical, water conditions, and other functions are monitored in this room. This location may also provide an acceptable place for monitoring security equipment. This location is used for monitoring and dispatch at St. Joseph Medical Center in Towson, Maryland. In this program, the dispatch and monitoring is accomplished by the hospital facilities department.

NON-ELECTRONIC PHYSICAL SECURITY SAFEGUARDS

The securing of a facility is often described as a system of perimeters in which each succeeding perimeter is closer to the most critical areas of the facility than the preceding one. The grounds, including the parking areas, are the first perimeter for security consideration because the natural environment rarely provides adequate security; in fact, the environment can create additional security needs.

Some older healthcare facilities have extensive brick, stone, or concrete walls enclosing the facility. These barriers, which were generally patterned after European facilities, were probably built more to provide privacy than to provide protection. The cost of construction today has practically eliminated the wall as a form of protection.

The outer walls of modern facilities are often the first line of perimeter protection in urban areas. As new facilities have been built in suburban areas, they have often adopted spacious grounds. Some level of security must be implemented at the outermost perimeter line to serve the functions of deterrence, delay, detection, access discrimination, and boundary identification.

Fencing

Fencing is one of the oldest forms of physical security. Although it is a meaningful protection element for many facilities, it may not be a practical application of control for specific situations. The proper application of fencing as a safeguard is largely dependent on the layout and design of buildings and grounds, and the organizational philosophy.

Fencing need not always completely surround an area. It can be effectively used to control traffic patterns and to define property lines for only certain areas or parts of the complex.

Healthcare administrators often object to fencing from a public relations and aesthetic standpoint. A fence might imply to the community that the facility is sealing itself off from its neighbors. For this reason, if fencing is required, facilities should consider installing it in segments to minimize its negative impact. Fencing can be ugly, or it can be somewhat pleasing.

Fencing is generally installed (or considered) in healthcare facilities as a result of various protection problems that arise; it is rarely part of the original design. The exceptions are government and private facilities with large amounts of land; in these cases, fencing is often planned in the design stage. Fencing a large tract of land usually produces no adverse effect on public or community relations.

Parking areas are prime locations for protective fencing. The basic premise behind fencing parking areas is that criminals generally do not want to engage in their activity where the means of escape is limited. On the other hand, fencing also limits the victim's escape route. General experience demonstrates that properly fenced areas are considerably safer than unfenced areas.

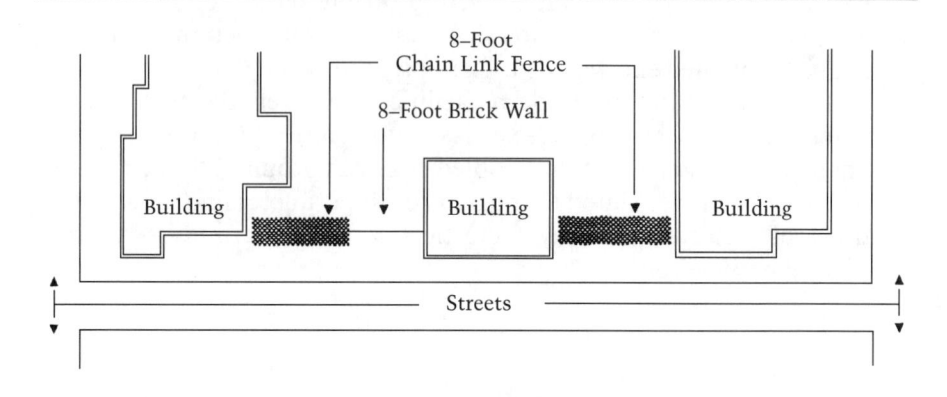

Figure 15-4 Example of the Use of Fencing for Security

Many types of fencing barriers exist. The basic type used in the security industry is the galvanized steel, chain-link fence, which permits visibility from both sides. The protection offered by this fencing is directly proportional to its height. A short fence is basically a psychological barrier, but a high fence with barbed-wire outriggers or a razor-ribbon topping is a physical barrier. When barbed wire and other types of topping are offensive to members of the healthcare organization, increased height is a good alternative. If an area requires fencing, the minimum height of the fence should be seven feet for security purposes.

Barbed wire support arms (outriggers), if required, should be placed at a 45-degree angle to the upright posts. The arm should face toward the direction that penetration is to be denied. In the healthcare setting, situations rarely require support arms on both sides.

Additional protection can be gained by burying the bottom of the fence below grade. In addition, electronic devices, such as infrared, taut-wire, laser, and seismic technology systems, can be used in high-risk areas.

Fencing has many applications in healthcare facilities in addition to parking areas and property lines. Among the most common enclosures are oxygen storage, outdoor equipment storage, and bicycle storage areas. Figure 15-4 is an example of utilizing fencing to provide a barrier between buildings.

The stark appearance of fencing can be minimized with landscaping. However, the landscaping design must exclude any heavy foliage or shrubs, which can provide a hiding place for contraband and intruders. Thorny foliage may serve as an effective barrier by itself or in combination with fencing.

Lighting

Security professionals generally agree that exterior lighting is one of the best protection bargains available. Exterior lighting serves two distinct purposes: safety and security. Safety lighting provides an efficient, hazard-free environment. Security lighting, on the other hand, is designed to discourage criminal activity and to provide light for surveillance purposes. It is important to note, however, that lighting also creates a feeling of safety and can thus conceivably create a false sense of security.

When installing external lighting, the security administrator must consider the potential for vandalism of the light fixtures. The proper design and location of the lighting fixtures reduces the probability of malicious destruction. One method is to install light fixtures as far inside the property line as possible and to use break-resistant cover guards. Lighting fixtures should also be designed so that the failure of a single lamp will not leave an area unprotected or reduce the light below acceptable standards.

The following are the six most common types of lamps used in security applications. Their output is given in lumens per watt.

Incandescent	20
Mercury vapor	63
Fluorescent	83
Metal halide	115
High-pressure sodium	140
Low-pressure sodium	183

The quality of exterior lighting is often reduced by tree foliage. Pruning the foliage or altering the position of the lighting fixture may correct this problem. Security personnel should ensure that lighting operates at maximum effectiveness by regularly checking the foliage and reporting any lights that have burned out.

The amount of night lighting required varies according to the area's vulnerability and the security administrator's judgment. More light is required at entryways than in parking lots. Figure 15-5 shows the lighting requirements that are considered to be a standard of the security industry.

Trees and Shrubs

Trees and shrubs can be used to create physical barriers or to enhance other barriers and increase security protection. On the other hand, trees and shrubs also provide a convenient hiding place, a place to dispose of or hide contraband, and a place to store stolen property for later retrieval.

Landscaping need not be sacrificed for security purposes; rather, the landscaping should be planned and maintained to meet security objectives. The word *maintained* is important. A small shrub that does not present a security hazard when planted can grow into a problem in a relatively short time.

LOCKS AND KEYS

Locking devices of all kinds are a primary element in virtually all security systems. Electronic locking systems are rapidly replacing the traditional lock and key systems for many areas of a facility. However, there will always be the need for the traditional key applications.

Locks come in all sizes and shapes, and they function in a wide variety of ways. In most applications, the lock is intended to serve two basic purposes. The first is to delay a compromise of the security system. Different locks will delay compromise for different lengths of time, and the selection of the lock should be based on the protection level required. A sturdy lock will discourage an amateur and will force a professional to work harder to compromise the locking system. The second function of the lock is to provide visual evidence that the lock was compromised when such compromise occurs as the result of physical force.

The level of protection a lock is designed to provide against someone who does not possess a key, a combination, or other information is fairly easy to calculate. The protection level drops significantly, however, when the lock and key program is poorly administered. The initial risk is that an unauthorized individual will obtain a device or infor-

SECURITY NIGHT LIGHTING STANDARDS

Lighting standards are grouped into the following four zones:

ZONE I
- 2.0 FC for building entrances and exterior walls, to a minimum height of 8 feet, for vital locations or structures
- 1.0 FC for roof surfaces requiring surveillance

ZONE II
- 1.0 FC for parking lots
- 0.4 FC for roadways
- 0.2 FC for storage areas
- 0.2 FC for walkways

ZONE III
- 1.0 FC for parking lots
- 0.4 FC for roadways
- 0.2 FC for walkways
- 0.1 FC for storage areas
- 0.05 FC for open areas

ZONE IV
- 2.0 FC for pedestrian entrances
- 1.0 FC for roadway entrances
- 1.0 FC for rail entrances
- 0.2 FC on vertical plane, at points 3 feet above the ground plane, for "Glare Barrier"
- 0.1 FC for fence line (non-isolated)
- 0.1 FC for water approaches
- 0.05 FC for open areas
- 0.05 FC for boundary line (isolated fence or no fence)

SOURCE: IES Lighting Handbook, 5th Ed., and American National Standard Practice for Protective Lighting. Published by the Illuminating Engineering Society, 345 East 47th Street, New York, N.Y. 10017.

Figure 15-5 Commonly Used Standard for Security Lighting

mation to operate the locking mechanism. The second risk is the unauthorized use of the device or information by an individual who has obtained it. In both cases, a false sense of security prevails because an intruder can gain entry for unauthorized purposes without leaving any evidence that the system has been compromised. Locks used in conjunction with alarms or recording devices are necessary in preventing and detecting both break-ins and unauthorized use.

Administering the System

It is an unfortunate fact that the lock and key systems in over 90 percent of healthcare facilities are inadequate. This widespread inadequacy is more often the result of lax administrative controls rather than improper hardware. However, the improper use of hardware, which either defeats the purpose of the lock or fails to provide the protection level assumed, contributes to the problem.

Facilities spend large sums of money on locking hardware, but many fail to provide the funding and administrative control required to properly manage the system. In any hospital of at least 300 beds, a security administrator who is given full responsibility for the lock and key program can reduce the number of required locks, lock changes, and keys issued to such a degree that the money saved will be enough to pay for the personnel required to properly administer the program.

It is generally recommended that the security department administer the lock and key control system. Just as checks and balances are required in cash accounting, with one individual performing a certain step and another individual performing another step, the principle of separation of responsibilities applies to key control. The person who controls the key-cutting equipment (often someone in the maintenance department) should not control the key blanks. The authorization for keys and the key blanks required should be forwarded to the person who will actually perform the work.

An effective system might work along the following lines: The security representative receives a request for a key, a lock change, or a new lock. After establishing the validity of the request, the security person forwards a work order (perhaps the original request form) to the person or department that will perform the work. The key is then returned to the security department for issue. In some large systems, the locksmith function may actually be part of the security department. This is a good arrangement, but in most facilities there is not enough work to keep an employee busy with this responsibility. It is not uncommon, even in some large facilities, to contract out all lock and key work to a local locksmith. If this is the case, the control system should still remain a specific facility individual or department.

A key may be issued to an individual, or a group of keys may be issued to a section or a department. Individual key issue by the security department is the preferred method. This system provides a central record, and the status of the system can be accurately assessed at any time.

This method of security department control requires a rigid system of procedures to ensure that terminating employees are routed through the key control center. A substantial key deposit should be required as an incentive for individuals to return keys, even if the key is returned by mail or by other means if they do not go through the regular termination process. Deposits of $25 to $50, which tend to render the key control program effective, may be necessary.

Fragmented key control may be unavoidable due to the distance between facilities or the failure of the administration to recognize the value and cost/benefit of a centralized key issue system. In the fragmented approach, the security department still remains responsible for authorizing lock and key work. The difference is that the keys are released to sections or departments rather than to individuals. The departments then have the responsibility for issuing the keys, maintaining the records, and retrieving the keys before or during the employee termination process.

A point in favor of the fragmented system is key retrieval. Individual departments are the first to know of terminations for cause and voluntary resignations; this knowledge should enhance key retrieval. However, proper records must be maintained to determine the number of keys that have been issued to each individual.

Computer programs are commonly used in lock and key systems today. Many excellent software programs are available at a very low cost that are applicable to a system of any size.

Master Key Systems

An important decision that must be made when designing a lock and key system concerns master keying. Many security professionals are reconsidering the actual need for and the limitations of the master key system. Master key systems require a considerable investment in hardware and labor, and often the master key becomes a status symbol rather than an effective security safeguard. Master key systems actually reduce the security capability of a lock by providing fewer usable combinations. Master keying is generally a matter of convenience rather than a security safeguard.

When planning a master key system, a growth rate of 300 percent over 10 years should be assumed to avoid prematurely outgrowing the system. Ten to 12 years should be regarded as the practical limit of the system.

The obvious disadvantage to the master key system is the complete compromise of the system when the master key is lost or when unauthorized duplicates are produced. A typical progression in a master-keyed complex is to remove an increasing number of locks from the master key system as the result of security problems that indicate the master key may have been used.

Certain locks should not be placed on the master key system. The number of exceptions depends in large part on the number of master keys distributed. Examples include certain pharmacy areas, some storerooms, and perimeter doors that should be controlled by an electronic access system.

Many security administrators cling to the concept that security officers must carry a master key in case of emergency. This view is not necessarily valid. In numerous facilities that are not master keyed, the security function is still accomplished. Security officers should have the means to obtain timely access, on a controlled basis, to any part of the complex, but neither a master key nor a big ring of keys is an absolute necessity.

Lock Installation

No type of locking mechanism is totally effective unless it is installed correctly. All too often a facility spends a good deal of money to buy the proper lock but fails to install it properly, resulting in a degree of protection no better than a less expensive and less suitable lock would have provided.

A common problem encountered in lock installation is that the bolt does not penetrate the doorframe sufficiently. The throw of the bolt should be a minimum of one inch. If there is a wide space or a gap between the edge of the door and the doorframe, the bolt throw may have to be longer.

The door and the frame must be substantial enough to resist physical attack. If they are of doubtful strength, it would be uneconomical to install an extremely resistive locking device. The weakest part of all the components determines the resulting level of protection provided.

Lock Changes

No matter what, keys will be lost and unaccounted for. It is, thus, a matter of judgment when a certain lock should be changed. This decision generally takes into consideration the number of lost keys for a particular lock, how critical the area protected by the lock is, and what additional safeguards are used in protecting the area.

All organizations should have a schedule of changing locks as on ongoing program. The schedule should be developed so that the locks in each area of the facility are changed approximately every five years. The ongoing program avoids a high cost all at one time, permits higher priority areas to be selected, and is much simpler to manage.

Push-Button Locks

Electrical and mechanical push-button locks have gained popularity over the past 10 years. These locks are particularly advantageous where a large number of people require access. The major advantage is the ability to change the lock combination instantly without incurring the cost of changing the lock and reissuing keys. Common areas of use in healthcare facilities are nursing and doctor lounges, small storage rooms, and restricted areas.

These locks can be quite simple and inexpensive, with single combinations, or they can be high-security locks that require a push-button combination and an access card. Some electronic locks require no wiring and permit hundreds of combinations and time schedules.

Another advantage of push-button locks is that authorized personnel need never be locked out. There is no key to lose, and no access card to leave in another coat or purse.

Padlocks

When planning lock systems and security controls, padlocks should not be overlooked. In areas where aesthetics are not important, a case-hardened padlock can provide a high level of protection at a reasonable cost. As with door hardware, proper installation of the hasp is paramount.

Security departments should maintain several padlocks for temporary use. One department paints a red stripe around the body of its padlocks. A plastic tag, which moves freely on the shackle, clearly identifies the lock as a security padlock and states that the central security control desk must be called to open the lock.

Key Making

There are various preliminary steps to establishing a key control program. First, each lock location must be identified. For door locks, each room must be numbered or identified, and any doors within these rooms likewise must be identified. The number or other reference given each door need not appear at the actual location and can be identified on a lock control drawing. However, the doors or rooms should be numbered at their location as a means of identifying these areas for other purposes, such as maintenance work orders, deliveries, and visitor information. All rooms should be identified, regardless of whether the doors currently have locks, because locks may be installed later.

Another element of key control is marking or identifying the keys themselves. For obvious reasons, keys should not be marked with the specific lock number or room number to which the key belongs. Numerous codes have been devised by specific organizations to fit their purpose. It is suggested that letters of the alphabet be substituted for numerals, either selected randomly or through ten-letter code words. The latter system is advantageous when many individuals need access to the code, because the code need not be written down. Written codes are subject to a greater degree of possible compromise.

Keys fitting multiple locks require additional code markings, and the method used for cross-referencing is based on the security administrator preference.

Consideration should also be given to marking keys with the words *DO NOT DUPLICATE*. The effectiveness of this practice is unknown. Many places that provide key-cutting services ignore this stamp; however, many professional locksmiths will honor it. Furthermore, this marking may deter employees who want a key, but are reluctant about trying to have the key duplicated.

Locks from numerous manufacturers come with key blanks that are not generally available except to the organization that purchased the lock. Security is further enhanced when keys must be cut at the factory to fit a particular lock. One lock manufacturer, Medeco, provides a lock with one set of keys, and beyond this original set no keys may be duplicated. The keys are marked to identify each key and the total number of keys in the set. For example a set of three keys would be marked *1 of 3*, *2 of 3*, and *3 of 3*. This type of lock enhances security.

Periodic Inventory

Regardless of whether the key distribution system is centralized (keys are given directly to individuals) or decentralized (keys are given to departments, which pass them out), a procedure must be established for periodically inventorying the keys in the possession of individuals. This responsibility should be assigned to the security department. In the decentralized system the security department must first check the records of the various departments to determine whether all keys issued from the security department can be accounted for. The next step is to contact each employee who has been issued a key and to check the existence of the key.

The security officer must also see each key in the central system. Various methods can be instituted to make this an ongoing program. The processing of identification badges and the inventorying of keys can occur simultaneously. In one system, identification badges expire on the employee's anniversary of hire. When employees are processed for new badges, the security department checks the records to determine whether they have been issued any keys. If so, the keys must be accounted for before the new badge is released.

Seals

In the absence of an alarm system, a wire, metal band, or plastic seal may be used to aid in determining whether an area has been entered. These seals also help to discourage unauthorized entry.

The system is simple but effective. The security officer applies a seal on the doors to an area after all access requirements are over for the day. Examples of areas that might be sealed include the main storeroom, gift shop storage area, laundry, library, electronic data processing department, and maintenance storage area. On each patrol, the security officer can check the seal to determine whether access has been gained. The seal can be removed by the officer at a preset time or by the first department employee to arrive the next work day.

In most cases, the maintenance department will have to install eyelets on the door and the doorjamb to provide a means of looping the seal. Because the seal can be easily broken and thus does not provide any real physical protection, the eyelets need not be overly secure. Extra long seals can be used to loop through fire exit release devices and for similar applications.

WINDOWS AND GLASS AREAS

After doors, the second most common openings into rooms or buildings are windows. Doors with glass are also plentiful and, when regular glass is used, invite easy compromise of the locking device.

Although illegal entry is a prime security vulnerability, glass windows and doors with glass windows also present a potentially costly vandalism problem. Another problem associated with windows is vulnerability to an arson attack by means of a Molotov cocktail or a flammable liquid poured through a broken window.

An alternative to using regular glass is acrylic plastic (sometimes called *polycarbonate*) or a glass laminate with an acrylic core. The latter is the most expensive, but it offers the best protection against physical force, blowtorches, and projectiles. Acrylic plastic has the benefit of being lightweight (approximately one-half the weight of glass). Until recently, the greatest problem with the acrylic sheet was its tendency to scratch easily and to lose its transparency from even routine cleaning. Most manufacturers of acrylic sheets now produce a coating product that stands up very well. The acrylic sheet may be labeled "bullet resistant"; however, this resistance is dependent on the thickness of the sheet. To provide protection from medium-power small arms (.38 caliber), the material should be 1.25 to 1.5 inches thick.

Protective screening and decorative ironwork have been used effectively over the years to protect windows and other openings. This type of protection is often utilized at small freestanding clinics and physician office buildings.

FASTENING DOWN EQUIPMENT

The familiar saying, "They'll steal anything that isn't nailed down," is certainly true in healthcare facilities. Items that should be "nailed down" include computers, audio-visual equipment, microscopes, and other expensive pieces of equipment. With the many relatively inexpensive locking devices that are commercially available today, there is little excuse for any organization to suffer the loss of essential and expensive items. Tagging equipment with sensors that sound an alarm when there is an attempt to remove the equipment from the "protection field" are also becoming increasingly popular.

Some facilities still prefer to bolt down equipment. If this is the case, equipment service representatives should perform this work rather than in-house maintenance personnel. Undue stress on equipment and the use of bolts that are incorrect can result in damage to equipment.

Insurance companies are reluctant to provide incentives for organizations that protect their own property, but it does seem that locking devices would be effective in reducing insurance costs. The high deductibles of most insurance policies, however, translate to hospital out-of-pocket loss rather than to insurance company–paid claims.

MARKING PROPERTY

Conspicuously marking organizational property is a cost-effective means of reducing property loss. Asset number tags, although important, do not deter theft to any extent and can generally be easily removed. Marking hospital property serves the following purposes:

- It identifies the ownership of the property in case of theft

- It assists with management accountability controls (inventory)

- It provides a visible sign that the property being removed is hospital property

- It serves as a deterrent to theft

The wheelchair is a good example of an item that should be marked. Many privately owned wheelchairs are brought into medical facilities every day. When security officers or other staff observe a wheelchair being folded up and placed in a vehicle, they must be able to determine whether the wheelchair belongs to the organization.

How should a wheelchair be marked? First, the fabric should be a special color, ideally one that is not popular for private wheelchairs. Next, the back of the fabric should have the organizational logo or initials stenciled in at least a 10-inch square. The location, department, and wheelchair number may also be useful in the day-to-day use and accountability of the equipment. Finally, small bands should be painted or taped on certain tubular parts of the chair to further distinguish it from personal property.

SAFES

Safes are often the target of criminals because the mere existence of a safe engenders visions of valuable items. The safe is a formidable-looking piece of equipment, but it does not always afford the protection assumed by its owners.

Healthcare facilities use safes, or vaults, to protect records, certain drugs, cash, patient valuables, and negotiable paper. Regardless of the item being protected, the best protection is to reduce the quantity of stored materials and examine the storage container to see that it is designed to furnish the protection required.

Safes are similar to locks in that a false sense of security can be created when the equipment is misused or misunderstood. Perhaps half of the healthcare professionals who use safes do not know the difference between a safe designed for fire protection and one designed for the storage of cash and valuables. Facility surveys often reveal a record safe being used for valuables.

A record safe is designed to protect against fire only. Wet insulation is poured between two very thin steel walls. Water is retained in the insulation, and when a fire occurs, the water creates steam within the safe. The steam acts as a cooling agent and holds the internal temperature below the flash point of paper (350°). These safes are designed to withstand only one fire; after that, the insulation no longer provides protection. The UL label inside the safe indicates the length of time the safe will provide protection during a fire. The construction of the walls of the record safe are so thin that they offer little protection against forced entry.

The burglar-resistant safe is constructed of heavy steel plate, and some are reinforced with ceramic or metal filler to increase protection against torches and burning bars. The UL ratings indicate the length of time the safe can withstand attack. Because fire will cause heat to build up inside, burglar-resistant safes should not be used to protect paper records. Multipurpose safes are also available; these are basically fire safes that have an inner protection liner to render it a burglar-resistant safe.

Safes should generally be bolted to the floor. It is not uncommon for a safe to completely disappear from the premises—and often the safe is worth more than the contents. Placing the safe so that it can be regularly inspected and providing proper lighting are additional commonsense safeguards. Safes containing high-risk materials may also need the added protection of an alarm system. Several types of alarms are designed specifically for safes.

Safes must always be used properly, and there is no substitute for storing as few items as possible.

CHAPTER 16

Managing Workplace Violence

Ever since it became a hot topic in the 1990s, the term "workplace violence" has referred to violence involving one or more employees. Despite the thousands of pages written on workplace violence, there is no concise definition for it. The heightened level of interest in workplace violence has broadened the definition, and to some extent has created a backlash of skepticism about the true proportions of the problem. In fact, an October 1994 article in the *Wall Street Journal*, titled "A False Crisis: How Workplace Violence Became a Hot Issue," cites an August 1994 federal census of workplace violence homicides that found that only 59 employees were murdered on the job in 1993, or one murder for every 2.1 million workers.[1]

Today, the term has been expanded to include any act of violence in the workplace regardless of the connection of the victim or perpetrator to a specific business or employer. The California Department of Industrial Relations, Division of Occupational Safety and Health (DOSH), divides events of workplace violence into three categories: Type I, Type II, and Type III. In a Type I event, the perpetrator has no legitimate relationship to the workplace. A Type II event is committed by someone who is the recipient of a service provided by the workplace or the victim. A Type III event perpetrator has an employment-related involvement with the workplace, such as current or former staff members, or spouses, lovers, relatives, and friends who have a dispute involving an employee. In other words, the term "workplace" has been defined as simply a location without regard to the relationships of persons involved.

One of the first in-depth reviews of violence in the healthcare industry was published in 1984 by James T. Turner. His book, *Violence in the Medical Care Setting: A Survival Guide*, has served as a basic resource for healthcare security administrators.[2] In addition to Turner's book, another authoritative book on the subject is Sandra L. Heskett's *Workplace Violence: Before, During, and After*. Although it is not exclusive to healthcare settings, Heskett does open her book by describing a violent hospital incident that occurred on June 20, 1994, at Fairchild Air Force Hospital in Spokane, Washington. In the incident, a recently discharged man from the military used a Chinese-made MAK-90 to kill five people and injure 23 others.[3]

The majority of people generally associate violence in the workplace with assault and homicide, not with intimidating postures or expressions of mild anger. Yet many studies that report workplace violence count such situations as incidents. It is important that the healthcare administrator thus break workplace violence down into *actual* violence and the *threat* of violence. In this breakdown, the healthcare industry rates fairly low on the number of actual violent acts compared to other industries, but quite high in terms of threats of violence. This is not to say that there are not a large number of severe violent acts in the healthcare setting; violence is a major problem in all healthcare settings. However, it is important to keep in mind that healthcare professionals are not among the top ten occupations who are killed or injured at work.

A brief look at some study statistics reveals:[4]

- Between 1980 and 1990, 27 pharmacists were killed at work

- Between 1983 and 1989, 69 registered nurses were killed at work

- Nursing staff at a psychiatric hospital sustained 16 assaults per 100 employees per year, which compares to 8.3 injuries in all industries

According to the Occupational Safety and Health Administration (OSHA), healthcare and social service workers face a high degree of work-related assaults due to the following risk factors:[5]

- A high number of guns being possessed by patients, families, and friends

- Increasing use of hospitals by criminal justice agencies for criminal holds and the care of acutely disturbed persons

- The early release from hospitals of acute and chronic mental health patients who have not received follow-up care and who can no longer be involuntarily hospitalized except in extreme situations

- The availability of drugs and money at hospitals, clinics, and pharmacies, which makes them targets for robbery

- Situational factors such as open facilities with basically unrestricted movement, as well as the presence of drug abusers, trauma patients, distraught family members, and frustrated clients

- Low staffing levels at various times

- Isolated work situations during client examination or treatment

- One-person workstations in remote locations

- Lack of staff training relative to recognizing and managing escalating hostile behavior

- Poorly lighted parking areas

It should be noted that the OSHA guidelines (OSHA 3148, 1996) address only the violence inflicted by patients or clients against staff.

There are various ways of looking at violence in order to understand its impact on healthcare organizations. In this chapter, we will approach the subject from the basic categories of who, what, why, when, and where.

THE WHO (PERPETRATORS/VISITORS)

There are four basic groups of perpetrators and victims in the healthcare environment: staff, patients, legitimate visitors, and illegitimate visitors. Figure 16-1 shows the many combinations of perpetrator to victim. The illegitimate visitor (trespasser/intruder) often is involved in stranger-to-stranger situations, while in the other groups, the perpetrator and victims are known. In the vast majority of situations, both parties know each other, and their relationship has provided the motive for the violent act.

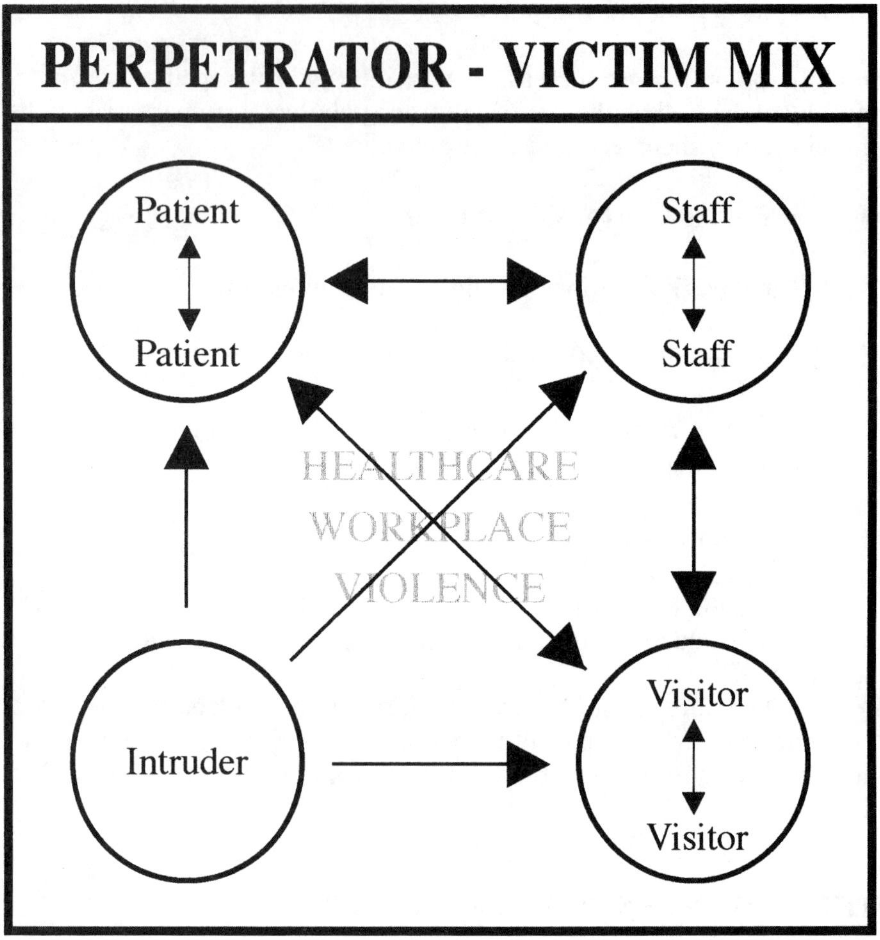
PERPETRATOR - VICTIM MIX
Patient
Patient
Staff
Staff
HEALTHCARE
WORKPLACE
VIOLENCE
Intruder
Visitor
Visitor

Figure 16-1 Healthcare Workplace Violence Perpetrators and Victims

Visitors

There is a high potential for workplace violence caused by individuals or groups who are from outside the organization (that is, visitors). The illegitimate visitor is one who has no legitimate business being on the property. This type of visitor includes criminals contemplating or committing a crime (robbery, abduction, assault); gang members intent upon causing injury or harm; unwelcome friends or family members of staff or patients; protestors; terrorists; transient persons; and former patients and employees. It is almost impossible to discern the presence and intent of these persons until an overt act occurs. In fact, they often blend right in with the legitimate patient, staff, or visitor.

The legitimate visitor is one who is visiting a patient or staff member or one who is accompanying a patient seeking treatment or being treated. It also includes outside service workers, construction workers, and vendors. While on occasion these people are responsible for violence, they do not present a major danger. Violence regarding these individuals is generally related to situational events occurring within the facility.

Patients

We have previously discussed some situational events in both the outpatient and inpatient setting in which the perpetrator of violence is the patient himself. The clinic patient is often the source of confrontation, largely due to the volume of patients, long waits, and disputes relative to services being rendered. Hospital emergency rooms, along with mental health evaluation and treatment areas, have a high potential for violence. There are cases in which patients have attacked other patients or staff ostensibly without warning or provocation.

Employees

Employees and staff members have been the source of many violent acts, especially against other employees or staff members. The day-to-day supervision, work evaluations, disciplinary actions, and terminations all set up situations that can be confrontational and that can provide the motivation of employee and ex-employee violence.

There is common agreement among human resource managers and security administrators that individuals who have committed violent acts in the past are potential perpetrators for further violence. Persons prone to instigating workplace violence share common characteristics and warning signs:

- They are usually loners
- They place blame for problems elsewhere
- They have an unusual fascination with weapons
- They have a history of intimidating or threatening others
- They have frequently been described as "a bomb ready to go off"[6]

A preventive approach to employee workplace violence requires recognizing that acting out may be the end result of an invisible process. An individual may perceive that he has been unfairly treated, discriminated against, harassed, or purposely exposed to stress by a supervisor. Other mental factors such as stress, discrimination, and harassment can have a cumulative effect on the individual and lead to a traumatic event.[7]

THE WHAT AND THE WHY

The what of violence pertains to the specific act itself in terms of the severity or type of crime. The type of crime can be viewed on a continuum, as shown in Figure 16-2.

There are at least three different categories of a violent act viewed from the causation or perpetrator viewpoint. These are the targeted victim, situational event, and the spontaneous event. The targeted victim is tied closely to stalking and generally involves a previous conflict between the perpetrator and the victim. The most common scenario in this regard is related to a domestic or intimate relationship. Violent acts in many of these cases are somewhat predictable, thus providing an opportunity to implement a number of possible prevention strategies.

The situational event generally results from a conflict between the perpetrator and the victim in the course of their interacting with each other. In the medical care setting, such conflicts often revolve around delivery of care issues. Patients may feel they are not receiving the treatment they deserve or that their treatment is not timely. Sometimes it is not the patient, but visitors who perpetrate the violence, whether it is at a hospital, clinic, physician's office, dentist's office, or long-term care facility. Violent acts resulting from such situational conflicts are often fueled

ACTS OF WORKPLACE VIOLENCE

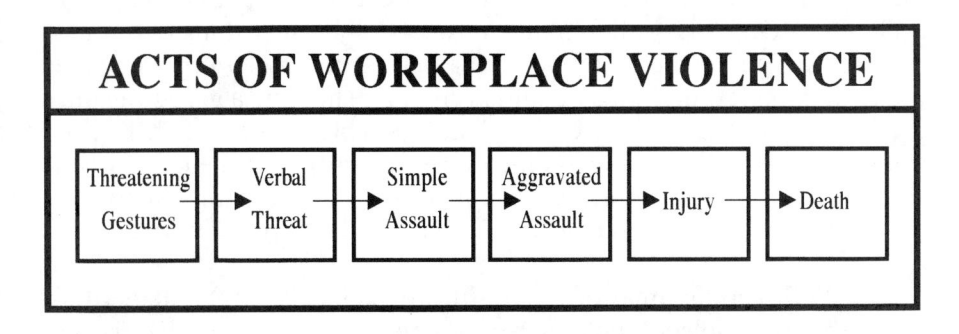

Threatening Gestures → Verbal Threat → Simple Assault → Aggravated Assault → Injury → Death

Figure 16-2 The Acts of Violence in the Healthcare Workplace

by drugs or alcohol. The mental health patient may be involved in confrontational situations that lack an apparent, or outward, rational motivation.

In spontaneous acts of violence, victims generally do not have a direct relationship with the perpetrators, and there is no forewarning of the danger. The act is premeditated and many have involved weeks, months, or years of planning or thought. The motive for these acts is usually general in nature and directed toward a cause, organization, or controversial issue. Unfortunately, the open healthcare environment is conducive to providing the opportunity for carrying out spontaneous violent acts.

One example of a spontaneous violent act occurred when a gun-welding 57-year-old woman entered an eye clinic at the Henry Ford Hospital in Detroit, Michigan, and started shooting, severely wounding two technicians who she thought were physicians. Investigations revealed that she blamed physicians for the death of her mother, which had occurred over four years earlier. There was no evidence that she had complained of wrongdoing in her mother's death, had ever visited or been in Henry Ford Hospital, or had ever met the two technicians she shot.

THE WHEN AND THE WHERE

Of course, there is no way to get inside the minds of violent persons so that we can predict the time and location of an act. We do know that in the medical care setting, there are certain times and locations in which acts are more likely to occur. The most severe acts generally occur during the regular business day, when things are busy, facilities are open, and many potential victims are in close proximity to each other. For example, a disgruntled employee holding a grudge against the Human Resources office would not be able to act out his anger against department staff unless the office was open. On the other hand, employees and patients in the mental health ward and the emergency department are possible targets of violence 24 hours per day, seven days a week.

While certain areas of the healthcare facility present a higher risk than others for violence, no area can be considered immune. History has provided examples of violence in hospice units, admitting rooms, physician offices, stairwells, business offices, intensive care units, other patient care areas, cafeterias, materials management areas, and even in surgery areas. In the latter, an estranged husband shot and killed his former wife, a surgical technician, in the surgery area of a Louisville, Kentucky, hospital. In Miami, Florida, a hospice patient beat two nurses at a nurses' station so severely that both were hospitalized with serious injuries; neither returned to their careers in nursing.

THE MANAGEMENT OF HEALTHCARE VIOLENCE

Not all violence occurring in the healthcare environment can be prevented; however, many acts can be prevented and managed to minimize injury, death, and damage to property. The three phases of managing violence in the workplace are before, during, and after. The after phase provides information and lessons that help healthcare professionals to consistently improve preventive measures and intervention.

Preventive and Management Steps

There are three specific steps of preparation and response that organizations must implement to properly address workplace violence. The first step is to provide a reasonable level of security for the overall environment and especially to areas of probable conflict. This includes an organized security program that includes access control plans, proper physical security safeguards, enforced security policies and procedures, staff training and empowerment, and an effective critical incident response capability. To adequately plan and implement these essential elements, there must be strong commitment from top management and the board of directors to provide a high level of philosophical and management support, including adequate funding of the program.

The Threat Policy

The foundation of a successful violence prevention program is the organization threat policy, which is an everyday working document. The policy should state clearly that threats of any kind are not tolerated, that the staff is responsible for reporting all threats, and should indicate the procedures for reporting such threats. In small organizations, the Human Resources department may be the central reporting point; in larger organizations, this is the security department's responsibility. Regardless of size, there should be a central reporting department that has responsibility for initiating follow-up actions.

In very large organizations, there may be two or three different threat policies with some limited fragmentation for reporting and follow-up. For example, there may be a policy specifically for threats to employees and another one for threats to patients, visitors, and others. It is suggested that organizations preparing threat policies seek out such policies from other organizations as resources. In general, threat policies should include the following key points:

- Zero tolerance for threats against anyone on the property

- Mandated staff reporting of threats and reporting procedures

- Responsibility for immediate response and/or investigative action (24 hours per day)

- Staff obligation to report any application or knowledge of protective/restraining order naming the property of the organization as a protected area

- Statement of confidentiality of reporting party

Response to Threats

There will be two distinct types of threats in terms of response and follow-up action. The first type of threat is one in which time is of the essence and immediate response is required. The organization's critical response element should be empowered to take whatever steps are necessary to protect life and property in an immediate intervention.

In most situations of reported threats, there will be a window of time for planning, developing, and implementing actions required. The degree and severity of the threat will be somewhat of a subjective judgment in terms of actions to be taken. All threats must be taken seriously, however; it is better to err on the side of taking too much action than doing too little too late.

Threat Response Team

There should be a specific response team that evaluates and plans actions concerning all threats. The team should be comprised of the security administrator, director of Human Resources, nursing administrator and in some cases the risk manager. The coordinator or leader of this team should initially decide the team member or combination of team members responsible for the management of the threat. A minor dispute between employees, resulting in a mild threat, might be handled by the director of Human Resources and the affected department supervisor. In the case of a threat to a patient by a person outside the organization, there would possibly be a need to involve the entire team. In some emergency situations, a team member may immediately implement preconceived action protocols relative to the specific type of threat. A typical preconceived protocol may involve the domestic violence patient who has reason to believe that his or her assailant will come to the facility to cause further physical harm. Common steps in this regard may include:

1. Removing the patient's name from the list of inpatients (specifically from the switchboard and information desk and nursing station).

2. Assign room away from a stairwell.

3. Restricting patient visitation.

4. Changing room location so that the patient can be seen from the nursing station.

5. Using a private duty nurse.

6. Hiring a special security guard and/or requesting law enforcement services.

In extraordinary situations, the team would develop a specific plan for the situation. There should be a definite authority for increasing, modifying, and ending the specific precautions implemented.

Another common threat that presents itself is the threatened staff member. These threats are often domestic-related and require preventative steps such as escorts to and from parking areas, work shift and/or location reassignment, restraining orders, or a change in work functions.

PREVENTING VIOLENCE IN THE WORKPLACE

All organizations need a strategy and plan to deal with workplace violence so that they can reduce the number of violent incidents and minimize the severity of these incidents to a large extent. The best means of managing workplace violence is to have a strong protection program in place that can be expanded to include specific facets of workplace violence. A program of preventing and managing workplace violence, in addition to a sound day-to-day security program, will include:

- A strong commitment from top management that preventive workplace violence is a priority both in terms of administrative and funding support

- Organization threat policy and procedures

- Staff training and education relative to staff responsibilities, early warning signs of escalating danger, de-escalation techniques, and general security awareness

- The identification of criminal justice agencies, social agencies, and other community services as a resource to managing potential violent incidents

- The utilization of in-house resources such as employee health and employee assistance programs

- Proper screening of employee applicants

- Consistent enforcement of organization workplace rules and regulations including the facility access control policy

Restraining Orders

In dealing with targeted victim situations, the utilization of court-ordered restraining orders is a fairly common safeguard. These orders may be available to the individual and to the organization. The restraining order has two specific purposes. One is to prohibit specific conduct by a specific individual and to order the individual to maintain a specific distance from the victim. In some cases, an organization may be able to obtain a restraining order without legal action. In these cases, the organization must prove the conduct caused the individual to believe there was a threat of death or serious bodily injury. In all cases, a restraining order is only one element of managing a potential incident and should not be overly relied on in the course of business. Some of the most major crimes of workplace violence have been perpetrated by individuals who were under a restraining order.

REFERENCES

1. Harvey S. Waxman, "Putting Workplace Violence in Perspective," *Security Management*, September 1995, p. 123.

2. James T. Turner, *Violence in the Medical Setting: A Survival Guide*, Aspen Systems Corporation, Rockville, Maryland, 1984.

3. Sandra L. Heskett, *Workplace Violence: Before, During, and After*, Butterworth-Heineman, Boston, Massachusetts, 1996.

4. "Guidelines for Preventing Workplace Violence for Health Care and Social Service Workers," U.S. Department of Labor, Occupational Safety and Health Administration, OSHA 3148, 1996, p. 1.

5. Ibid. p. 1–2.

6. J. Branch Walton, "Violence in the Workplace Is Not the Exception Anymore," *Security Technology and Design*, January/February 1997, p. 50.

7. Dennis Lindsey, "Of Sound Mind? Evaluating the Workforce," *Security Management*, September 1994, p. 69.

CHAPTER 17

Security Sensitive Areas and Security-Related Sentinel Events

The terms "security sensitive area" and "sentinel event" were coined by the Joint Commission on Accreditation of the Healthcare Organizations (JCAHO) relative to their standards and intents. The security sensitive area pertains exclusively to the protection arena, while sentinel event not only relates to protection, but to a wide array of adverse patient outcomes. While non-JCAHO-accredited facilities are not bound by commission requirements, the commission requirements provide all organizations with a logical and practical method of identifying and approaching certain basic protection issues.

There is a clear distinction between the security sensitive area and the area that may have special security concerns. All healthcare organizations will identify certain risks in their respective environments that require enhanced or special security safeguards. It is the responsibility of the organization to make the decision, through the security risk analysis process, as to which areas have exceptional risk, rendering them security sensitive areas or lower risk areas of special concern. Common areas of special security concern are discussed in Chapter 18.

SECURITY SENSITIVE AREAS

For our purposes, it is helpful to view security sensitive areas in two categories. The first category involves the vulnerability to persons, such as in the birthing unit, the mental health unit, parking areas, the emergency clinical care area, and perhaps even the intensive care unit. The second category involves property. Areas that may be included in the property category are the pharmacy, medical records, information services, research labs, and cashier areas. In those cases, it is the product or function that sets up the potential for a dangerous situation. For example, the drugs in the pharmacy create a high risk of armed robbery, yet the dollar loss potential to the organization is quite low. The operation of an animal research lab, on the other hand, sets up the potential for high dollar loss in relation to information and property damage as opposed to high exposure for staff injury.

The JCAHO has not issued a clear and precise definition for their term security sensitive area. In this discussion, the term will be defined as a location whose function or activity presents an environment in which there is a significant potential for injury, abduction, or security loss that would most likely severely impact the ability of the organization rendering a high quality of patient care.

There are three major areas of healthcare that would normally involve the designation of security sensitive area: the emergency department, infant birthing, and the pharmacy. Other areas in specific healthcare delivery systems may require the organization to designate additional security sensitive areas. These include pediatric units, clinics, research labs, mental health units, and centralized information departments.

Each JCAHO-accredited hospital organization must designate their security sensitive areas in their security management plan. There are three basic security components that must be developed and implemented relative to the security sensitive area. These components are a specific security access control plan for the area; security orientation and education specific to area risks, which minimizes the danger to staff, patients, and visitors; and a critical incident response plan.

Area Access Control Plan

The security sensitive area must have an access control plan that is specific to the area and that builds on the overall facility access control plan. As discussed in previous chapters, access control is not limited to locks and keys; it consists of staff-assigned responsibilities, identification systems, as well as the various physical safeguards that may be appropriate.

Staff Security Orientation and Education

Every staff member who works in the security sensitive area must undergo specific security training. This training includes understanding the processes and staff contributions for the security of the area, how to spot potential security compromises, how to minimize security risks for all persons within the area, and how to react to specific breaches of security.

Critical Incident Response Plan

Each security sensitive area must have a specific critical incident response plan. The plan must be activated immediately when the preventive steps of access control and staff actions have failed to prevent a major security incident. This plan will generally be formulated for staff reaction to the primary security threat of the area, while more general and generic response plans will be generated by security. An example of this concept can be viewed in the infant birthing unit. The plan for this unit would be prepared by the unit manager and focus on the abduction of the newborn. Input and collaboration with the security department would of course be part of the methodology in developing the plan. There is also the possibility of other major incidents occurring in the birthing unit, such as hostage taking, bomb threats, or serious assaults. The formulation of the critical incident response plan for these so-called general, or generic, events would be the responsibility of the security department in collaboration with various facility staff and/or departments.

The responsibility for the preparation of the security sensitive area critical incident response plan rests with the unit manager. The plan will almost always involve actions of various facility departments and staff and thus is not limited to just the actions of the unit staff. In the case of an infant abduction, the response is that of a whole-house effort.

In this chapter, the three primary security sensitive areas—the infant birthing area, the emergency department, and the pharmacy—will be discussed; however, this should not infer that these are the only three areas for facility consideration. Each facility will have specific functions or areas that present major security threats.

INFANT ABDUCTIONS FROM U.S. HEALTHCARE FACILITIES

The abduction of an infant from a healthcare facility is an event that generates a considerable amount of media attention. Newspapers, magazines, and TV talk shows have addressed the various aspects of infant abduction so that the risk is now widely recognized. However, in recent years, the number of non-family infant (birth to six months) abductions from hospitals have been drastically reduced. This reduction is due, in large part, to the efforts of the National Center for Missing and Exploited Children (NCMEC). It was not until 1987, when the NCMEC studied the problem of U.S. infant abductions, that the extent of these incidents was known. Their study data dates back to 1983 and their research and tracking continues as an ongoing NCMEC program. In particular, the work of John Rabun, Vice President and Chief Operating Officer; Cathy Nahirny, Senior Analyst/Supervisor; and the staff of the NCMEC have made a difference.

The NCMEC does not just study the problem; it also provides ongoing training and education and is an instant resource to facilities and law enforcement agencies when an abduction occurs. The work of the NCMEC goes far beyond hospital infant abductions; however, this discussion focuses on non-family abductions within the healthcare delivery system.

The delivery system involves some 4 million births each year in approximately 3,500 U.S. birthing facilities and continues to a limited degree after discharge. Hospital-operated or independent home healthcare agencies frequently provide aftercare to mother and baby in the home. The healthcare security administrator must also be aware that there can be a certain degree of organizational responsibility for infant safety in the home after discharge from the hospital. In the event that information, action, or inaction on the part of the healthcare organization caused or contributed to a criminal act in the home, there could be certain legal ramifications.

In 1989, the NCMEC issued its first set of guidelines relative to the abduction of the newborn, entitled *For Hospital Professionals: Guidelines on Preventing Abduction of Infants from the Hospital*. The most current NCMEC guideline (6th edition) was published in March 2000 and is titled *For Healthcare Professionals: Guidelines on Prevention of and Response to Infant Abductions*. This publication goes beyond safety in the maternal-childcare unit to safety in special care nurseries, pediatric facilities, outpatient areas, and the home.[2]

The number of infants abducted from hospitals (from 1983 to September 2000), including the location of the abduction and degree of violence, is shown in Table 17-1. The number of infant abductions from

Table 17-1 Infants (under six months) Abducted by Non-Family Members from U.S. Healthcare Facilities: 1983 to September 2000 (Courtesy National Center for Missing and Exploited Children, Alexandria, Virginia)

Abducted from	Number	Percent
Mother's Room	59	55
Nursery	16	15
Pediatrics	17	15
On Premises	16	15
TOTAL	**108**	**100**
Outcome		
Recovered	102	94
Still Missing	6	6
TOTAL	**107**	**100**
Violence to Mother	5	5

hospitals and Homes by state (includes Puerto Rico and the District of Columbia) for the same period of time is shown in Table 17-2.

In addition to the NCMEC guidelines for preventing infant abductions, several states have enacted legislation mandating hospitals to implement certain infant security measures.

The number of infant or pediatric abductions from hospitals by family members is not known. These cases, which are generally based on custody issues, are not tracked by any central tracking organization. Likewise, the number of attempted infant abductions from hospitals is not known. Circumstances surrounding possible abductions that do not occur would be speculative at best.

Hospital Infant Environment

Since the early 1980s, there has been a relaxed environment in the delivery and care of infants in hospitals. Family members are now allowed to view the delivery process and are freely admitted to nurseries. Visitor restrictions have also been relaxed to permit greater family involvement; the crowds in some birthing rooms resemble a small family reunion.

Table 17-2 The Number of Infant Abductions from U.S. Hospitals and Homes by State: 1983–September 2000 (Courtesy National Center for Missing and Exploited Children, Alexandria, Virginia)

Alabama	3	Arkansas	2	Arizona	3
California	30	Colorado	5	Connecticut	2
District of Columbia	5	Delaware	1	Florida	13
Georgia	7	Illinois	11	Indiana	2
Iowa	1	Kansas	3	Kentucky	1
Maine	1	Maryland	8	Massachusetts	2
Michigan	3	Mississippi	3	Missouri	4
New Hampshire	1	New Jersey	3	New Mexico	4
New York	10	North Carolina	4	Ohio	4
Oklahoma	3	Oregon	2	Pennsylvania	5
Puerto Rico	3	Rhode Island	1	South Carolina	4
South Dakota	1	Tennessee	4	Texas	26
Virginia	3	Washington	3	West Virginia	1
Wisconsin	2				

Note: States that are not listed in this table have not experienced an abduction by a non-family member from a hospital or the home.

Baby viewing areas are considered quasi-public areas, and hospitals are in some sense inviting people in to view the infants. It is one place in a hospital that is upbeat, friendly, and warm. Hospital inpatients and family members often visit this area, and it can be good therapy for many.

The new relaxed environment does not mean that security safeguards should be relaxed, however. With the greater number of people involved, security must be strengthened.

Abductor Profile

The NCMEC has produced a general profile of those who have abducted infants from hospitals. These are the general characteristics of the abductor:

- Females of childbearing age (range 12–50 years old)

- Often overweight

- Low self-esteem, emotionally immature, compulsive, and manipulative

- Often married or co-habitating

- Usually resides in the community where the abduction takes place

- Usually no previous criminal record

In many cases, the abductor has convinced others that she is pregnant. The abduction occurs during the alleged ninth month when the woman must produce a baby at all costs.

Abductor Modus Operandi

The abductor will often use common methods during the abduction, including:

- Indicating to others that she has "lost" a baby or may be incapable of childbirth

- Planning the abduction, but not targeting a specific infant (except possibly race)

- Visiting multiple birthing facilities in the community, seeking an opportunity to carry out the abduction

- Impersonating a clinical provider or other healthcare person

- Spending time becoming familiar with healthcare personnel and befriending the infant's parents

- Demonstrating the desire and capability for providing "good" or appropriate care to the infant after the abduction

The Basics of the Infant Security Plan

The basics of providing infant security are identification (mom, baby, significant other, and the caregiver staff), education (mom and staff), and physical security safeguards. These three elements of infant security intertwine to provide the desired level of access control and infant safety.

Identification

The most commonly utilized method of visual identification of the infant is the four-band (bracelet) system. These four identical bands link mom, baby, and significant other. The infant is banded on the wrist and ankle, while the mom and significant other wear similar bands on their wrists. However, infant identification goes far beyond bracelets. It is a combination of elements that should be viewed as a package, each complimenting and supporting the other. Each element of the infant identification package must be completed prior to the removal of the baby from the birthing room and in all cases, within two hours of birth. The elements of identification are:

- **Footprints.** The footprint is an excellent form of identification if an infant is abducted and recovered even months later. Table 17-3 lists an NCMEC summary of methods used to identify recovered infants abducted from hospitals from 1983 to 2000. In 88 cases studied, there was a single element of identification, and in 37 cases, a combination of elements was utilized.

- **Color photograph.** The Polaroid camera is a popular method of achieving this element of identification as it can instantly become part of the infant's medical record. Other types of cameras can be utilized, although the requirement is that the photograph must be taken within two hours of birth but the film dies need to be developed in this time frame.

- **Full physical assessment.** The physical assessment of the infant must record any marks or abnormalities.

- **Cord blood.** A sample of cord blood for future identification typing should be taken and retained until 24 hours after the infant is discharged from the facility.

An additional method of identification is antibody profiling. Mother and baby share the same antibody profile for the first year. Unlike

Table 17-3 Methods (Elements) of Infant Identification Used in Recovering Infants Abducted from U.S. Hospitals through 1999 (Courtesy of National Center for Missing and Exploited Children, Alexandria, Virginia)

Identification Methods	
Single Method Utilized	Number of Cases
Visual Identification	16
Footprints	15
Blood Work	7
Abductor Confession	4
Hospital Wristband I.D.	4
DNA Testing	2
Abductor I.D. by Witness	1
Birthmark	1
Photographs	1
Total Cases	**51**
Multiple Methods Utilized	Number of Cases
Visual I.D., Hospital I.D. Bracelet	9
Visual I.D., Confession of Abductor	7
Footprints, Visual I.D.	4
Footprints, Blood Tests	3
Footprints, Blood Tests, Visual I.D.	1
Footprints, Photo	1
Footprints, Medical Charts	1
Footprints, Birthmark	1
Cord clamp, description	1
Blood tests, Cord Clamp	1
Blood Tests, Birthmark	1
Antibody Profiling, Criminal Investigation, Confession from Suspect	1
Photos, Way in Which Umbilical Cord Was Tied, Confession of Suspect	1
Description of Suspect, Witness Testimony	1
Visual I.D., Hospital I.D., Bracelet, Clothes from Hospital	1
Visual I.D., Photos, Birthmark	1
Visual I.D., Birthmark, Hospital I.D. Bracelet Found at Site Recovery	1
Visual I.D., Photos	1
Total Cases	**37**

DNA testing, which can take up to two weeks to get results, the antibody profile can be performed within hours. Such antibody profiling is most useful in resolving any question as to the mix up of babies and mothers.

A number of hospitals have prepared an attractive baby record "kit" that is provided to the parents at the birth of their infant. This kit is a duplicate of the footprint, photograph, and physical assessment that was completed for the infant's medical record.

The identification of hospital staff is a key element of the infant security plan. Each staff member who is authorized to be transporting or maintaining control of the infant must wear a unique form of identification. This identification must differ, in a noticeable way, from regular hospital identification. This identification, most often a photo identification badge, must be worn above the waist and in a manner that is visible to mother and other staff at all times. A common method in developing the unique badge is to utilize a different color background for either the staff person's photograph or for the background of the badge itself.

This special badge is generally issued permanently to regular staff; however, there must be a system for the issuing of a temporary badge on a shift-to-shift basis. The temporary badge is utilized when temporary staff or students are participating in infant care and when a regular staff member does not have their regularly issued badge for a variety of reasons. These temporary badges must be tightly controlled with a method of strict accountability. On termination of the regular mother/infant caregiver, there must be a diligent effort to retrieve and destroy the identification badge. In addition, a new regular baby staff identification badge should be developed at least every five years and whenever there is a significant security compromise involving the badge system.

Education

The proper education of mothers is crucial to the infant security system. This education often begins in prenatal classes and continues to some degree until discharge, and includes after discharge care at home. The hospital must be very clear as to whether there will be any home care provided. If such care is to be provided, the guidelines of identification and other security precautions must be thoroughly communicated.

The NCMEC has developed a checklist, entitled "What Parents Need to Know," which contains sound parenting techniques that bear directly on the safety and security of the new infant. This checklist in contained in the "guidelines" document previously referred to.

Upon admission to the hospital, the mother must be fully briefed concerning the security procedures. It is strongly recommended that there be a briefing form signed by the soon-to-be mom. This form should become a component of the mother's medical record. See Figure 17-1 for an example of a briefing form.

In addition to pre-admission and admission education, it is important to remind moms and others of the importance of security during the entire (even though it may be a very short) stay. Message stickers on the room mirrors and bedside/dresser table tents are frequently used. Iowa Methodist Medical Center in Des Moines has developed a security education poster that is placed on the back of the bathroom door, as shown in Figure 17-2.

In addition to mother education, there must be continuous education and training of the caregiver staff. In the majority of infant abductions, there have been one or more observations by staff that, properly followed up, would have prevented the abduction. When a situation does not quite look right, or there are unidentified persons on the unit, staff must act to investigate and clarify the situation or legitimacy of the unknown person. Staff must be trained concerning the profile of infant abductors and their methods of operation. In addition, a semi-annual review of the infant security plan should be completed on a formal basis with all staff members. All training should be documented.

The Mead Johnson Nutritionals Company, in cooperation with the NCMEC and the Association of Women's Health, Obstetric and Neonatal Nurses (AWHONN), has developed a comprehensive and professional infant security education program directed to healthcare organizations. This program, revised in 1999 and entitled "Safeguard Their Tomorrows," has provided education and training on infant security to thousands of healthcare providers over the past 10 years.

Physical Security

The third basic element of infant security involves the installation of certain physical security safeguards, including:

baby safety

The maternity center staff has some important hints for you to keep your new baby safe:

1. **Never leave your baby alone.**
   If you wish to shower or sleep undisturbed, return your baby to the nursery where the infant will be constantly observed by a staff member.

2. **Place your baby's crib in constant view.**
   This will alow you to observe any visitors or hospital staff as they approach the baby.

3. **Feel free to question <u>anyone</u> entering your room.**
   All staff who are allowed to handle your baby wear their photo ID badges. Your nurse will explain these badges in more detail. If you are uncomfortable with anyone entering your room to take your baby, ask to see the photo ID or use the nurse call light to have your nurse assist in the identification. A staff member working with your baby will know the identification band number that is exclusive to you and your baby. **Never** give your baby to anyone that cannot show these **two forms of identification**.

4. **Always transport your baby in the crib.**
   When going from the nursery to your room, or your room to the nursery, always put the baby in the crib and push the crib. You will find the crib pushes easier and more safely if you guide it end to end, not sideways.

5. **Remember, there are many people who work in the hospital, but only the maternity center staff have special photo ID badges.**
   If you have any questions or are unsure about any of these people, please press your nurse call light.

6. **When you leave the hospital, continue safeguarding your baby.**
   At home never open the door for people you do not know. Never leave your baby alone in the car, even with the doors locked. Be sure you know how to identify a visiting nurse/helper **before** they arrive, if one is coming to your home.

I understand these safely precautions and I will do all I can to keep my baby safe.

IOWA HEALTH SYSTEM

Parent Signature

Nurs 2957 9/95 NS

Figure 17-1 Mother Security Briefing Form (Courtesy of Central Iowa Health System)

Keep Me Safe

Keep Me Safe

Please don't give me to people that cannot identify themselves. the proper name badges and photo I.D's have this logo. (The Perinatal Center)

Please don't leave me alone in your room, even with the door closed.

Please only give me to staff that know my identiband numbers.

Love,
your baby

Figure 17-2 Infant Security Poster (Courtesy of Central Iowa Health System)

- **Nursery.** All nursery doors should be locked. The door utilized for entry and exit of staff/visitors should be equipped with self-closing hardware. An exception to all locked nursery doors would be when there is an access control person (security officer, receptionist, clerk) stationed at the door for the specific purpose of controlling and authorizing access.

- **Maternity unit (includes nursery).** All stairwell and exit doors on the perimeter of the maternity unit must have alarms that will alert unit personnel of their use. These doors can be equipped with devices that allow authorized staff entry/exit use without activating the alarm. All exit control devices must conform to the Authority Having Jurisdiction (AHJ). A closed circuit television camera should be placed at each exit point in such a manner that the face of the exiting person is captured. These cameras may be "live" on a continuous basis or activated upon door use.

- **Closed-circuit television (CCTV) cameras.** CCTV cameras should also be placed at the main corridor entry to the unit and at all elevators. These cameras should be placed so that the face of entering and exiting persons will be captured. All CCTV systems should be color equipment and each camera should be recorded. A seven-day videotape library must be maintained.

    There is no specific mandate that CCTV systems utilized for infant security need to be live monitored. In most systems however, there is live monitoring of all, or selected, cameras at the main nursing station. In addition, many of the larger systems will include some redundant monitoring at the facility central security station along with redundant alarm monitoring.

Electronic Infant Monitoring

There has been a good deal of interest by healthcare security organizations in the electronic monitoring of infants. These systems have been developed and refined over the past few years and now provide a wide range of products. The design of an electronic monitoring system begins with defining the space to be protected, often referred to as the protection zone, or safe area.

The basic electronic infant monitoring system is one that simply sounds an alarm when the device on the infant is detected by a receiving unit at a specific point. From the basic system, one can design systems that are computer-driven and that can provide a supervised system, the identification of a specific infant, the specific location of an infant within the protected zone, the ability to lock doors/elevators, anti-piggybank protection, and timed alarm activation after a set period.

These systems will cost anywhere from several thousand dollars for a single door alarm to several hundred thousand dollars for a very sophisticated system. However, the decision to install any electronic monitoring system should not be based on funding alone. There must be a complete buy-in by staff, as all systems require humans to make them work. There is considerable staff task and administrative time in operating such systems.

General Security Precautions and Guidelines

The NCMEC document previously referred to covers a number of fundamental elements of infant security. It should thus be reviewed by all persons having responsibility for protecting infants. The following is a general summary of some very important aspects of infant protection while in the hospital, at discharge, and at home:

- Infants should be transported one at a time and never left alone in a corridor

- Infants should be transported in a bassinet, never arm-carried, except in an extreme emergency

- Infants should always be in direct line of sight supervision by staff or mother/family

- Infant bassinets in the mother's room should be placed on the side of the bed farthest from the room entry door

- Birth announcements published in the newspapers or online should use surnames and should not include the family's home address or telephone number

- Staff should provide internal transportation to the discharge point and remain with the mother/infant until their departure

- Avoid the use of outdoor decorations announcing the infant's arrival at home

- Allow only well-known and properly identified persons into the home. Authorized caregivers will provide advance information of the intended visit and will produce proper identification that has been previously explained to the infant's mother/family

Critical Incident Response Plan

The response to an infant abduction should be considered a whole-house plan, as all organizational staff should be actively involved. There should be a code name for this response that is communicated to as many staff as possible, usually via an overhead paging system and group alert communication device, if available. A common code utilized by healthcare facilities to activate the infant abduction plan is "Code Pink." In the event of an abduction, the immediate involvement of law enforcement and the media is paramount in terms of enhancing a successful outcome. Most often, infants are recovered as a direct result of information generated by media coverage.

It is extremely important for both the healthcare organization and law enforcement authority to contact the NCMEC for technical assistance in handling an infant or pediatric abduction. The NCMEC's 24-hour telephone number is 1-800-843-5678.

Infant Discharged to Wrong Family

The discharge of an infant to the wrong family is a significant event, but not actually a breach of security. The security department may become involved with such a situation as a resource to investigate the occurrence and contribute to a successful outcome. However, the proper discharge of a patient is a clinical management function.

EMERGENCY DEPARTMENT SECURITY

A gunman entered a San Diego hospital emergency room and started shooting indiscriminately, killing two and wounding two. A social worker was killed in a hospital emergency room in Pittsburgh by an assailant who also took three people hostage. A man dressed in a security uniform walked into an Atlanta hospital emergency room, where he shot four people and then committed suicide. These types of incidents are weekly occurrences in emergency departments in the U.S. In fact, the emergency room chief at San Francisco General reports that threats from angry patients and or visitors occur daily, and violence breaks out at least once a week.

The physicians and nurses who staff emergency departments are demanding greater protection by hospitals. The American Medical Association passed a resolution calling for hospitals to increase security in emergency departments. Meanwhile, the American College of Emergency Physicians has been active in conducting studies and providing educational materials concerning emergency room violence. The Emergency Nurses Association, representing over 21,000 nurses, enacted a resolution calling for legislation to increase the safety and security of emergency department healthcare workers. The resolution also called for collaboration and liaison with other organizations to develop security and safety protocols, to develop educational programs, and to develop position statements, including minimal safety standards for personnel and for the physical plant.

How Much ED Security Is Needed?

Every hospital that has an emergency department must assess its own specific vulnerabilities and apply the degree of security necessary to maintain a reasonably safe and secure department. The number of patient visits, the types of patients and visitors, the area's crime rate, and the ER layout and design are among the chief assessment considerations. A variety of safeguards can be applied to any emergency department: it is the degree of application of a specific safeguard to establish proper security that must be determined. For example, one emergency department may require only periodic security patrols, another may require the presence of an officer at night, and another may require 24-hour security coverage by one or more officers.

Designing Security for Emergency Departments

The security layout and design of an emergency department can be viewed as compartments and control points.

Access Control

A major consideration in providing for safety in the emergency department is to control the access of patients, visitors, and staff. These controls may vary to some degree, according to the day and the time. In other words, it is very common to tighten access control during the night hours. In some large, inner-city departments, the control may be the same 24 hours per day.

The ambulatory and the ambulance entrances are usually separate. In small departments, these two entrances are often combined during off-peak periods. The ambulance entrance should open directly to a nursing station. The ambulance entrance is commonly locked, especially at night. Ambulance drivers and staff can use a card key, a push-button lock, or other means to gain access. An electric lock release and audio communications at the nursing station can be used to accommodate entry for others. A clearly marked communications station on the exterior side of the entrance is required, and either direct visual observation or a CCTV system is required to properly manage the control system.

The ambulatory entry point is usually not locked, but it could be, depending on the vulnerability. It is recommended that this entry point be equipped with a lock even if the entry is always open. The purpose of this lock is to have the means to lock down in the case of an unanticipated emergency condition. In most cases, the first person the patients and visitors encounter is a receptionist or triage nurse. It is imperative that this point be staffed at all times to greet those who enter. It is recommended that the receptionist or nurse sit inside an enclosed booth with a service window. The enclosure should make it difficult for someone to grab the receptionist or to jump over the counter. The degree of enclosure depends on the assessed vulnerability.

The use of protected or controlled areas is a key concept of emergency department security. The following areas should be separated:

- Walk-in areas (waiting and admissions)
- Triage area
- Treatment area
- Quiet (seclusion) rooms

Figure 17-3 shows a model layout for access control in a small emergency department.

Walk-in Area/Waiting and Admissions

Many security incidents involve visitors and occur in the walk-in area. Visitors may include family members, friends, or even enemies of the patient. The waiting area should contain washrooms, vending equipment, and telephones. Long waits and tense visitors can spell trouble, if not properly managed. An important part of this management is to keep visitors informed; the lack of information often stimulates incidents. Emergency medical care units must be staffed and organized to effectively communicate with those persons waiting for a sick or injured patient being treated or in need of treatment.

Triage Area

The triage area should be separated from the walk-in area, which is necessary for security and patient confidentiality. There must of course be a window for communications with the arriving patient to begin the triage process. In the locked triage area, the triage nurse would simply admit the patient to the assessment area, locking the door after entry. It is recommended that all triage areas, locked or unlocked, have an entry door directly into the treatment area. Upon completion of the triage process, the triage nurse would simply send the patient back to the waiting area to await treatment or take them directly into the treatment area.

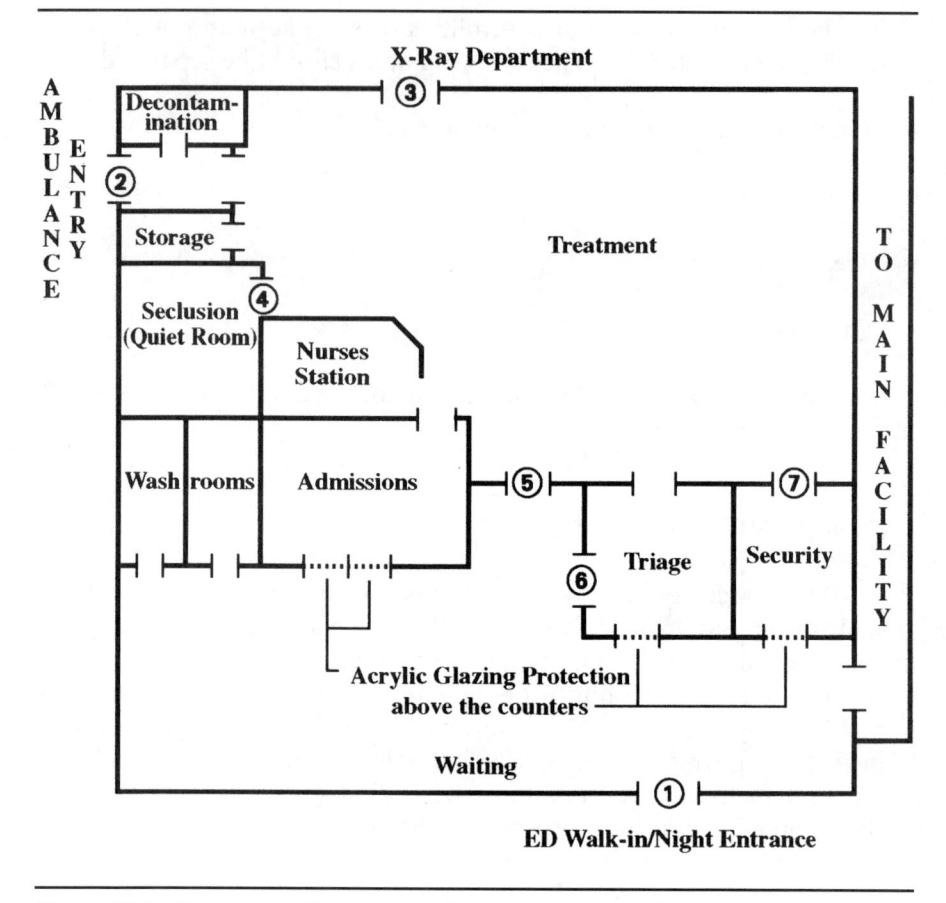

Figure 17-3 Emergency Department Security Layout and Design

Treatment Area

The treatment area is another controlled section of the emergency department. A common mistake in this regard is to lock off the treatment area from the walk-in area and then leave the entry-exit door (back door) open, which provides access to other hospital areas and departments. All entry/exit points to the treatment area must be controlled.

Quiet Room

The quiet room is a room within the treatment area used to administer care to the combative patient. In smaller facilities, it may simply be a treatment room that is very sparsely equipped or completely striped of objects. In large, higher volume facilities, this room may actually be locked and padded with tamper-proof hardware items. This type of room generally has an observation window and/or a television monitoring system.

Safe Room

The concept of a safe room, primarily in emergency departments, has recently emerged as another safeguard in managing workplace violence. A safe room merely means a designated room that can be locked from the inside, as a place for staff, patients, and even visitors to "hide" due to an immediate threat of danger. The typical safe room is a room usually utilized for day-to-day activity and equipped with telephone and/or radio communications equipment. It should be easily accessible and somewhat centrally located within the department. It is most often a regular treatment room, which may be a distinct advantage if patients are present when the safe room is actually being utilized as such.

There are many different scenarios in which the safe room would provide a secure place, such as when trouble erupts or is anticipated. An example of anticipated trouble might be when visitors, or adversarial persons, in a waiting area insist upon going back to the treatment area to see the patient who is being treated. The fear of an altercation or the medical procedure itself may preclude staff allowing such a visit. In this case, it may be a prudent security strategy to provide the patient treatment in the safe room, which could be secured if necessary. Another scenario would include the safety of a staff member relative to a domestic situation.

Physical Security Safeguards

A variety of physical security safeguards can be used when securing the emergency department. These safeguards include card access equipment, bullet-resistant glazing, duress (panic) alarms, CCTV, signage, secure storage containers including gun lockers, and metal detectors. The application of these safeguards has been discussed in previous chapters with the exception of metal detectors.

The metal detector is available as an inexpensive handheld unit or as a more elaborate walk-through type. There is very limited use of the walk-through systems in healthcare facilities due to the low cost-benefit achieved. In order to handle any significant volume of traffic, each monitoring station requires two security officers plus relief officers for meal and work breaks. Considering that one officer could operate the system during very low traffic times, perhaps 10 hours per day, the system would require a minimum of seven full-time employees at a cost exceeding $150,000 per year in direct labor alone. In addition, proper screening may not be possible with only one monitoring point. Thus, two or more stations would be required in many facilities.

In contrast to the high cost of the walk-through metal detector, a handheld unit is a very effective security device at a very low cost. It is recommended that the handheld unit be stored in the department to be operated by a security officer. The use of the handheld unit would be initiated whenever a situation develops that suggests the possibility that a person may have a weapon concealed on their body. Thus, the use of the handheld unit would be situational and used as a reactionary response as opposed to continuous screening.

Security Staffing in Emergency Departments

There is a need to provide security staff for emergency service departments in a great many healthcare facilities. In small facilities, a patrol and response capability may suffice, but very large emergency departments may require several fixed security posts on a 24-hour basis. It is quite common to staff emergency rooms with a security officer only at night. This practice can be cost effective, especially when the officer also controls nighttime visitors for the entire facility. The emergency room is also a logical location for a security operations control center, which provides a certain presence in itself.

Security personnel assigned to emergency treatment areas should generally be uniformed to achieve maximum effectiveness. Individual hospitals must decide whether to arm officers, weighing all the pros and cons regarding this important decision.

As has been discussed in previous chapters, it is generally not desirable to employ off-duty law enforcement personnel as security officers in emergency rooms. The training required is very different; police training is of little value for the function of the emergency room security officer. Police work as a whole is often measured in terms of arrests, and the security effort is measured in terms of conflict resolution and prevention. This is not to say that police service should not be called when police response is required for a specific incident.

In numerous hospital security programs, security officers are promoted to the emergency department, where they have their own specific job description and generally receive higher pay. Funding for the emergency department security coverage is sometimes provided by the emergency department. These officers should be considered as much a part of the emergency department staff as they are members of the security staff.

Security Officer Training

Security personnel stationed in emergency rooms need extensive training. Their training must include recognizing the early symptoms of disruptive behavior, verbal and nonverbal intervention skills, working knowledge of the process of trauma care, the psychology of stress, the role of supporting medical care (not giving advice or administering care), the application of physical restraints as part of a restraint team, and proper take-down procedures. Although these subjects are appropriate for all security personnel, the full-time officers assigned to busy emergency rooms must develop and hone these skills to a greater extent than generalists do.

Training should not be limited to the security staff on an individual basis. There should be joint training exercises of the emergency department staff and the security staff. This collaborative training is important to establish working protocols. Role-playing is a common method used in this training.

Interaction Protocols

Whenever security personnel support the emergency department, formally established protocols, or guidelines, must govern the actions of the officers and the ER staff. Without these guidelines, there is bound to be conflict and dissension between security and ER personnel on how specific situations are to be handled. The objective is to eliminate individual expectations and guesswork. Firmly established roles for different situations eliminate dissatisfaction and provide a high level of service. Generally, nurses or physicians take charge in dealing with patient incidents, and security officers take charge in dealing with visitor problems outside the treatment area. Visitors within the treatment area occupy a middle ground, but generally are in the purview of the medical caregiver.

Security officers must be careful to not accept the responsibilities of orderlies. There is a fine line between providing security service and assistance in the emergency department and becoming too much a part of the medical team by performing orderly duties.

The term "patient watch" is sometimes used to describe the activity of standing by to watch a particular patient. Officers are generally asked to perform a patient watch when a patient causes staff to feel fear, anger, uneasiness, potential danger, or when there is an indication that the patient may attempt to leave prior to proper medical evaluation or treatment. Staff members must recognize the considerable range of these feelings and assess the gravity of the risk they perceive. Many incidents of emergency department violence could have been avoided if personnel had erred on the side of being overly cautious. However, the risk of disruptive or harmful behavior could be escalated if inappropriate steps are taken. The overall goal is to maintain safety for everyone involved, including the patient.

The American College of Emergency Physicians has developed a dangerous subject protocol, which involves the following three levels of security alert:[3]

- **Level I.** Patients who are potentially violent but cooperative and responsive and who require close and continuous observation while being evaluated or treated

- **Level II.** Patients who are obviously dangerous, uncooperative, unresponsive, or expressing violent behavior

- **Level III.** Armed patients with the same characteristics as Level II; they generally require police or security intervention

Although this discussion focuses on patients, the same evaluations, preparations, and actions are required for visitors in treatment areas, waiting areas, or patient rooms outside the emergency department.

Emergency Signals

The emergency department should have a system of alerting other staff members of an emergency situation that requires immediate help. These systems are used primarily to summon additional medical assistance, but they may also serve as an element of the security system. Wall buttons, pull chains, and foot or other activation devices should be strategically located within the department, with particular attention given to isolated areas. The device must be placed so that staff members can easily access it, but it does not invite improper activation by patients, visitors, or even staff. There are also available devices that the caregiver can carry (as a pendant or clip on device) to summon assistance. These devices are more costly than fixed location devices as the equipment must be able to track the movement of the person to fix their location when the device is activated. As with all electronic devices, the system should be periodically tested.

Security/Police Room

In large emergency departments and hospitals that maintain a fixed security post in the ER, separate rooms or offices are provided for the police and security. In other programs, a single room can be shared. This room should be placed outside the major emergency care activity area. The security/police room provides a place to separate people for taking statements, for detention, and as a place to complete routine reports or to make telephone calls. This room should not be confused with a security post.

Conclusion

The emergency department will always have the characteristics that portend disruptive behavior. Extreme mental and physical factors, acute psychiatric manifestations, drug and alcohol abuse by patients and visitors, the mix of patients and providers outside the medical staff (that is, police, fire, ambulance, coroner, and so on), and often chaotic circumstances combine to produce a unique environment. Disruptive behavior is predictable, and it can be managed to minimize the risk in providing safety for all concerned.

THE HOSPITAL PHARMACY

The security of the hospital pharmacy begins with proper handling, supervision, and training of the pharmacy staff. Not all pharmacy employees are honest, and many pharmacy helpers, cashiers, order clerks, and pharmacists have been involved in major drug thefts. Personnel hired to work in the pharmacy should be screened thoroughly to establish their integrity. The security department should assist the chief pharmacist and the personnel department in determining the suitability of applicants for these sensitive positions. The Code of Federal Regulations Number 21 (1301.90) covers employee-screening procedures for positions involving controlled substances. Individual states may prescribe additional requirements.

Pharmacy employees are not the only ones who have access to the pharmacy and drug supplies. The cleaning and maintenance personnel are often allowed to move about without supervision and may even be scheduled to clean or to provide maintenance to the pharmacy when it is closed, which is a poor practice.

In addition to cleaning personnel, other employees such as delivery and even security personnel should have restricted access to areas where drugs are stored. Some states, such as Ohio, require that no individual be alone in a pharmacy unless it is a licensed pharmacist during business hours. Where pharmacies are not open 24 hours a day, specific procedures must be developed to detect and document any individual, other than the pharmacist, who enters the pharmacy for emergency purposes.

Pharmacy Burglary and Robbery

When street drug traffic becomes scarce, pharmacies often become the target of burglary and armed robbery. As retail outlets have become increasingly hardened against attack, and as local pharmacies have become reluctant to include dangerous drugs in their inventories, hospital pharmacies have become a tempting and vulnerable target.

Burglary protection can best be provided by installing proper physical safeguards, such as protection for windows and counter openings, locks, and alarms. Armed robbery presents a somewhat more difficult problem in part because employees often fail to utilize safeguards in place, and in part because many hospital pharmacies fail to install even minimal safeguards.

The major consideration in planning for pharmacy safeguards is to reduce the possibility of personal injury, which is, of course, directly related to avoiding a confrontation. However, confrontations cannot always be avoided, and pharmacy personnel should be trained to respond properly should a holdup occur. Pharmacy robbers are often addicts, excitable, and desperate. Pharmacy employees should obey instructions and avoid any heroics while under observation, including giving an alarm or calling for help. They should also note the physical characteristics of the perpetrator and, if possible, the direction of escape. The alarm can be given as soon as it is safe to do so. Employees who remain calm help to avoid triggering violence, and they will be more helpful to security and police investigators in providing a description of the robber and an accurate account of the event.

Holdup Alarms

The use of holdup, or panic, alarms for hospital pharmacies is discouraged. Employees confronted by an armed robber should not do anything that would jeopardize their safety. Organizations should avoid having security or the police respond to the pharmacy during an armed robbery. The telephone should be used to report the robbery when it is safe to do so. If the telephone system is damaged by the perpetrator, the delay in getting to another telephone is generally insignificant.

Those who promote the holdup alarm explain that the security force or the police will not rush to the scene to become part of the problem. Their response should be to take up strategic positions to observe and confront the robbers when they are outside of the building. This is fine in theory; however, with high turnover and varied security personnel, the safest approach for the staff during a robbery in progress is inaction.

Pharmacies that choose to install holdup alarms should make every effort to install them properly to avoid triggering false alarms. The most common mistake in the installation of the panic alarm is to not use a specifically designed activation button, which is recessed to protect against accidental activation. The high rate of false alarms has resulted in the elimination of many systems. Duress codes may prove a valuable supplement to holdup or intrusion alarms. When an alarm is activated and monitored in another location, a telephone call to the pharmacy may be in order. No answer would indicate a possible problem and call for special response procedures. When the telephone is answered, a duress code can be valuable in determining whether a crime is, in fact, being committed and whether employees are in danger.

Access Controls

The pharmacy work area should be secured so that unauthorized personnel cannot gain free access. All entrances should be fitted with good locks, and they should be kept locked at all times. Non-pharmacy personnel, including sales representatives, should not be permitted to freely enter the work areas. Insofar as possible, pharmacies should be windowless. Where windows exist, they should be secured and protected by an alarm.

Openings such as service counters are necessary for the transaction of business. They should be as small as possible, and counters should be constructed so as to preclude anyone jumping over them to gain access. Counters should also be located so that they are out of the line of sight to access doors. This prevents someone with a gun from ordering an employee to open a door without giving the employee an opportunity to gain protection before reaching the door.

In many cases, hospital pharmacies have counseling booths, or other such areas, where pharmacists and patients can interact privately. These arrangements are often not as secure as they should be and may benefit from closed-circuit television monitoring.

The staff door leading from the pharmacy to the corridor can also present a security vulnerability for exiting pharmacy employees. A robber or thief can wait outside the door for someone to exit. This vulnerability can be reduced with a closed-circuit television system. The camera is placed in the corridor, and the monitor is placed just inside the door. Exiting employees can check the monitor before opening the door.

Closed Pharmacies

Although many hospital pharmacies are open 24 hours a day, others are closed during the night hours, and nursing supervisors often require frequent access. This access presents a special vulnerability that demands a high degree of personal diligence on the part of the nursing supervisor. In most cases, depending on the frequency of required access and the assessed degree of risk, a security escort should be provided.

An emergency after-hours drug room or large cabinet can also be effective. This container can be stocked with a par value amount of drugs the facility is expected to need that night. This system eliminates many unnecessary trips to the pharmacy. In either case, procedures must be developed to carefully document who enters the pharmacy and what drugs are removed. These records should be available to the pharmacist for review when the pharmacy re-opens.

Lights should remain on in the closed pharmacy. The nurse who goes in and out of the pharmacy, turning lights on and off, informs the intruder that there is only one person to contend with. One pharmacy has entirely eliminated the on-off switch for the overhead lights, so that they remain on all the time and cannot inadvertently be turned off.

Intrusion alarms are highly recommended for all closed pharmacies, regardless of size. Not only are electronic motion detectors and other anti-intrusion devices effective in detecting illegal entry, but they also serve as a strong deterrent to break-ins. Relatively inexpensive holdup cameras can provide additional levels of protection, as well as utilizing CCTV security systems.

THE SECURITY-RELATED SENTINEL EVENT

The term "sentinel event" is a very broad term utilized by JCAHO in relation to their accreditation process, which was effective January 1999. A sentinel event is an unexpected occurrence involving death or serious physical or psychological injury, or the risk thereof. Such events are called "sentinel" because they signal the need for immediate investigation and response.[4]

There are four primary goals for the JCAHO sentinel event policy:

- To have a positive impact in the improvement of patient care

- To focus organization attention on the event to provide an understanding of the underlying cause, and to make changes in systems and procedures to reduce the probability of such an event in the future

- To increase the general knowledge about sentinel events, their causes, and preventive strategies

- To maintain the confidence of the public in the commission accreditation process

There are two basic categories of the sentinel event relative to the investigation and reporting of such incidents. The first is the event which is referred to as "reviewable" by the JCAHO. The second is an event that is handled internally within the organization. In the latter event, the organization is required to have a policy regarding a review process which meets JCAHO criteria but the event does not need to be reported to the JCAHO.

The subset of sentinel events that are subject to JCAHO review at the time of occurrence and that are security-related are: (1) an event resulting in an unanticipated death or major permanent loss of function, not related to the natural course of the patients' illness or underlying condition, or (2) the event is one specified by the JCAHO and the outcome is *not* death or major permanent loss of function. This second category specifically includes security incidents of infant abduction or discharge to the wrong family, or rape.

The JCAHO is not very clear regarding its definition of an infant nor the distinction of an abduction (stranger to stranger versus domestic custody). There is a vast difference in these two categories of infant abduction incidents.

The rape of a patient is a JCAHO-reviewable sentinel event. The determination of rape is to be based on the organization's definition, consistent with applicable law and regulation. An allegation of rape is not reviewable under the JCAHO's policy. Applicability of the policy is established when a determination is made that a rape has actually occurred.

The JCAHO encourages accredited organizations to report all reviewable sentinel events. The JCAHO may also become aware of a reviewable sentinel event through patient contact, family, media, or a staff member. Regardless of how the JCAHO is made aware of the event, the organization is expected to prepare a root cause analysis report and action plan within 45 calendar days of the event or of becoming aware of the event. The analysis and action plans are to then be forwarded to the JCAHO. Upon receipt of the information, the JCAHO will determine the acceptability of the analysis and action plan.

An organization that does not submit an acceptable analysis or action plan within the 45-day period may be put on Accreditation Watch. This designation is considered to be public information. The Accreditation Watch is not an accreditation status; rather, it is an attribute of the organization's official accreditation.

The removal of an Accreditation Watch is a determination of the JCAHO's Accreditation Committee. The decision to remove this accreditation attribute generates an Official Accreditation Decision Report. This report will assign an appropriate follow-up activity for the facility, typically a written progress report or follow-up visit to be conducted within a specified period of time.

Until a sufficient period of time passes, there will be various questions and concerns on what is a reviewable sentinel event. As situations occur and questions get answered, the picture will be much clearer than it is today. The best course of action is to have a strong in-house program to process all sentinel events, and when in doubt as to a mandated reviewable event, error on the side of reporting it to the JCAHO.

REFERENCES

1. *Comprehensive Accreditation Manual for Hospitals (CAMH)*, Joint Commission on Accreditation of Healthcare Organizations, Oakbrook Terrace, Illinois, 1999.

2. "For Healthcare Professionals: Guidelines on Prevention of and Response to Infant Abductions," National Center for Missing and Exploited Children, Arlington, Virginia, March, 2000.

3. "Emergency Department Violence—Prevention and Management," American College of Emergency Physicians, Dallas, Texas, 1988, pp. 38–40.

4. "Special Report on Sentinel Events, Perspectives, Joint Commission on Accreditation of Healthcare Organizations," Oakbrook Terrace, Illinois, November/December 1998, pp. 19–42.

CHAPTER 18

Special Security Concerns, Offsite Facilities, and Community Healthcare Provider Services

All healthcare facilities present environments that have special security vulnerabilities. Evaluating the degree of these risks is an essential element of the security assessment process. The tragedies that have recently occurred in many abortion facilities are glaring examples of such risks. As healthcare reaches further into new areas, such as community and home services, expanded security planning and the implementation of appropriate safeguards will be needed.

NARCOTICS AND DANGEROUS DRUGS

Drug abuse continues to be a major problem in our society. The majority of crimes committed in the U.S. are associated directly or indirectly with illegal drugs. One security problem thus associated with healthcare facilities is controlling narcotics and dangerous drugs. Although it is difficult to pinpoint the extent of drug thefts, there is no question that healthcare facilities are a major source of illegally obtained drugs.

The enforcement of federal laws on dangerous drugs has undergone constant reorganization. Under the Harrison Narcotics Act, the Internal Revenue Service was initially responsible for regulation and enforcement. This responsibility shifted to the Federal Bureau of Narcotics and then to the Bureau of Abuse Control. These two agencies merged in 1968 to become the Bureau of Narcotics and Dangerous Drugs (BNDD), located within the Department of Justice. In 1973, the Drug Enforcement Administration (DEA), under the Justice Department, become the nation's sole federal law enforcement agency for drug control. The Controlled Substance Act of 1970 is the federal law that now regulates the handling and safeguarding of certain drugs. This act replaced the Harrison Narcotics Act and Dangerous Drug Act.

All states regulate pharmacies. Under most laws, the pharmacy must be licensed and must be supervised by someone who is licensed to practice pharmacy. The most common state agency for regulating pharmacists is the State Board of Pharmacy, which may also be responsible for enforcing federal or state drug laws. In addition to federal laws and state regulations, standards for pharmacies have been established by organizations such as the American Pharmaceutical Association, the American Hospital Association, the Catholic Hospital Association, the American Medical Association, the American Society of Hospital Pharmacists, and the Joint Commission on Accreditation of Healthcare Organizations (JCAHO).

The illegal use of drugs is not restricted to a specific group of people. Substance abuse is a disturbing problem among healthcare workers. The incidence of dependence on alcohol and other drugs is estimated to be as high as 14 percent among physicians. The highest incidence is found among anesthesiologists, obstetricians, gynecologists, and psychiatrists. Drug abuse among physicians is difficult to curb because doctors as a whole are fairly autonomous, accounting for their performance only to their patients and their conscience.

Anesthesiologists and Certified Registered Nurse Anesthetists (CRNAs) are at particular risk because of their easy access to drugs, job stress, problems with self-esteem, and an often casual attitude toward the drug they routinely prescribe or administer. As a group, their work is not closely supervised, and many of these individuals exhibit the attitude that their established protocols take precedence over the security of narcotics. The theft of fentanyl, sufenta, and alfenta from surgery areas is a major problem.[1]

Although the number of nurses addicted to drugs is difficult to calculate, evidence suggests that the problem is real. Every state board of nursing accumulates statistics on the number of nurses receiving drug-related disciplinary action. The statistics are sent to the National Council of State Boards of Nursing. Nurses do not have the privilege of writing prescriptions for themselves, but they can use a number of diversionary methods to obtain drugs. These tactics make it difficult to prevent the illegitimate use of controlled substances.

Diverted drugs are not always for use by the person responsible for the diversion; they may be intended for use by another (friend, relative, spouse) or for resale. According to Donald E. Bogardus, a leading authority on drug diversion, the increased diversion among nurses and physicians is related to increased pressure and stress in the medical profession. In the nursing industry, long hours, six- and seven-day weeks, vacation deferment bonuses, low staffing levels, and increased responsibility contribute to elevated levels of stress. Until these stress-creating conditions are reduced, more healthcare professionals will turn to drugs and alcohol.

Pharmacists, because of their direct access to drugs, are also at great risk for abuse. It is estimated that the rate of impairment of this group is equal to that of physicians and nurses. State pharmacy boards are experiencing an increase in disciplinary hearings related to drug abuse.

Controlled Substances

Security officers must be familiar with the classes of drugs, their reaction within the body, and their slang names. Officers need this information to recognize the behavior associated with drug abuse, and they may find it important to a variety of control and investigative activities.

Controlled substances can be broken down into five major classes: depressants, stimulants, narcotics, marijuana, and anabolic steroids. In addition, hallucinogens such as LSD, glue, and hydrocarbons may require security scrutiny.

- **Depressants.** Depressants (barbiturates) will produce behavior like that of alcohol intoxication; stumbling and staggering as in a drunken state; falling asleep; difficulty concentrating; and dilated pupils.

- **Stimulants.** Stimulants (amphetamines) will produce excessive activity; irritable, argumentative, or nervous behavior; excitable talkativeness; increased blood pressure/pulse; and long periods without food or sleep.

- **Narcotics.** Narcotics (opiates and their derivatives) will produce constricted and fixed pupils; itchiness; flushed skin; muscular twitching; sniffles; watering eyes; loss of appetite; and lethargy or drowsiness.

- **Marijuana.** Marijuana will produce dilated and generally bloodshot pupils; distortions and hallucinations; rapid, loud speech with frequent laughter; and distorted depth and time perception.

- **Anabolic steroids.** Anabolic steroids will produce increase in muscle mass and an increase in secondary male sex characteristics in both males and females (deepened voice, increased hair growth, and acne).

Schedules

There are five schedules for controlled substances. Substances are placed in a specific schedule according to the following Drug Enforcement Administration (DEA) criteria:

Schedule I

- The drug or other substance has a high potential for abuse

- The drug or other substance has no currently accepted medical use in treatment in the United States

- The drug or other substance cannot be safely used, even under medical supervision

- These drugs are not usually available to physicians, pharmacies, or patients unless they are part of a research project; thus, they are not routinely seen in hospitals

Schedule II

- The drug or other substance has a high potential for abuse

- The drug or other substance has a currently accepted medical use in treatment in the U.S. or a currently acceptable medical use with severe restrictions

- Abuse of the drug or other substance may lead to severe psychological or physical dependence. Federal legislation enacted in February 1991 placed anabolic steroids in the Schedule III category

Schedule III

- The drug or other substance has some potential for abuse but less than the drugs or other substances in Schedules I and II

- The drug or other substance has a currently accepted medical use in treatment in the U.S.

- Abuse of the drug or other substances may lead to moderate or low physical dependence or high psychological dependence

Schedule IV

- The drug or other substance has a low potential for abuse relative to drugs or other substances in Schedule III

- The drug or other substance has a currently accepted medical use in treatment in the U.S.

- Abuse of the drug or other substance may lead to limited physical dependence or psychological dependence relative to the drugs or other substances in Schedule III

Schedule V

- The drug or other substance has a low potential for abuse relative to drugs or other substances in Schedule IV

- The drug or other substance has a currently accepted medical use in treatment in the U.S.

- Abuse of the drug or other substance may lead to limited physical dependence or psychological dependence relative to the drugs or other substances in Schedule IV

General Security Requirements

This discussion focuses on the practitioner's responsibility for the security of controlled substances. Practitioners include physicians, dentists, veterinarians, researchers, hospitals, pharmacies, and people who have been registered or otherwise permitted to research, distribute, dispense, or use in teaching or chemical analysis a controlled substance in the course of professional practice or research.

All practitioners are required to provide effective controls and procedures to guard against the theft and diversion of controlled substances. The overall security system provided must be approved by the Drug Enforcement Administration. The type of activity conducted determines the type of security controls that will be necessary. Considerations include the number of people who will have access, the size of the storage containers, whether the controlled substances is in useable form, the length of time the substances will be stored, the location of the registrant, the use of the effective alarm system, and the prior history of theft or diversion.

Any controlled substance listed in Schedule I must be stored in a securely locked cabinet of substantial construction. Schedule II to V substances can be stored on open shelves if they are concealed through some system of stock dispersal. If they are stored together, they must be stored in a securely locked cabinet of substantial construction. Cabinet control is recommended because container labels readily identify the controlled substances. An inventory of all controlled substances must be conducted every two years, and the results must be maintained for two years. Records of Schedule II drugs must be maintained separately from the records of other controlled substances.

When methadone is used in an approved methadone maintenance program (where large numbers of addicts may be in proximity to the substance), it must be stored and handled under secure conditions. Methadone must be stored in locked cabinets of substantial construction. Large quantities require additional security controls. Unless used as part of an approved methadone maintenance program, methadone is considered a Schedule II controlled substance and is subject to the same requirements as all other Schedule II drugs.

Prescriptions

Phony prescriptions filled by pharmacies are a major source of illegal drugs. Physicians and medical care facilities as a whole have been grossly negligent in controlling blank prescription forms. Pharmacies are also often guilty of not properly examining the controlled substance prescriptions.

An effective deterrent used to control forged prescriptions is the camera system, which photographs the customer and the blank prescription together. In addition to it being a good deterrent, this system also provides tangible evidence for an investigation.

A large Connecticut hospital has a successful system for limiting the possibility that blank prescriptions will be illegally used for controlled substances. The hospital pharmacy only honors prescriptions for controlled substances when written on a serial-numbered prescription blank that has the words "VALID FOR CONTROLLED SUBSTANCES" overprinted (screened) on the face of the blank. These blanks are bound in books of 50 and are controlled by the security department. Physicians, clinics, and division charge nurses may requisition these blanks 24 hours a day from the security office. The requisition must be accompanied by an audit record and the used book of previously issued blanks. The same facility also has a prescription blank marked for non-controlled substances only. These blanks also carry serial numbers and are issued through the general storeroom.

INTERNAL HOSPITAL DRUG CONTROLS

The loss of controlled substances is only part of the total drug loss problem. Because the volume of drugs in a medical care facility is large, and the breach of minimal controls is fairly simple, many drugs are diverted by employees for personal use or for resale. Even some non-abusable drugs can be sold to unscrupulous drug vendors for illegal resale.

Audit Committee

Several hospitals report that an active drug audit committee has significantly increased the security of hospital drugs. The audit committee should be composed of a pharmacist, a nursing supervisor, and a member of the general administrative team or a physician. The committee concerns itself primarily with controlled substances; however, other drugs are not outside its providence. The committee should meet at least weekly, and its activity should include reviewing incident reports involving medication accountability problems, reviewing control systems, and most importantly, spot-auditing the various elements of the system. Committee members might proceed directly to a nursing unit where they review physical security, take a count, or check the doctor's orders against the control sheet. These practices are administratively sound and also create a positive perception of the importance the hospital puts on good drug control.

Automated Dispensing

The unit dose system was a good step toward drug control; however, the utilization of automated dispensing machines has greatly enhanced drug accountability. These machines function just like automated teller machines for drugs and other supplies. This form of control reliably handles distribution with record keeping and audit trails. The advantage of automated dispensing is that it keeps track of missed doses and accurately captures drug charges to be billed to the patient.

Drug Losses

All missing drugs should be reported to the security department and the appropriate law enforcement agency. Losses should also be reported to the director of the pharmacy or the chief pharmacist, particularly when the losses are reported from areas outside the pharmacy, such as the nursing units or operating rooms. Many states hold the chief pharmacist or his or her designee responsible for reporting any losses. Every instance of missing drugs should be investigated.

MEDICAL RECORDS

In addition to their role in medical care, medical records are a source of information for settling insurance claims, resolving litigation, conducting research, and are used in various law enforcement actions. The task of balancing the patient's privacy rights and the facility's need for information is a difficult one. The problem is magnified by the number of medical records maintained and the electronic transfer information systems.

The Privacy Act of 1974 was enacted to stop the widespread abuse of government information systems. Under the act, hospitals are prohibited from disclosing information contained in a medical record, except under the following conditions:

1. The hospital has the patient's consent to release the medical record.

2. The hospital is legally required by a subpoena or a court order to disclose the information.

3. Public health supersedes the patient's rights, such as in cases involving infectious disease.

4. The hospital is required by law to report the information to a public agency.

The custodian of medical records determines disclosure, and the security department is rarely involved. Security's responsibility is to support the custodian in fulfilling the hospital's responsibility. The security effort focuses on protecting medical records from those who try to surreptitiously obtain information, including those who steal records or copies of records. A complication arises because in most states the theft of information is not a criminal act.

Security precautions for medical records should include the following:

- A written affidavit signed by medical records employees that they understand disclosure procedures and intend to abide by those procedures

- Restricted access to medical records during operational and non-operational periods

- Physical separation of the doctors' dictating area from the medical records storage and work area

- A floor-to-ceiling wall partition or an intrusion alarm system in the records area

- Separation of medical records concerning cases in litigation or possible future litigation; these records should be maintained by the person in charge of medical records in a secure cabinet

- Established procedures for after-hours access, including a record of all access granted

- Tight controls over photocopier use by department employees

- Built-in safeguards for computerized medical records systems to reduce the possibility that a nursing unit monitor and printer will be used to circumvent normal disclosure procedures

If security officers are involved in providing after-hours access to the medical records department, a procedure must be established for identifying individuals who seek access. The access record must be available to the head of the records department for review on the next regular workday.

COMPUTER OPERATIONS (INFORMATION SERVICES)

The computer is a common piece of equipment utilized in all healthcare organizations. This discussion focuses on the main computer area. Healthcare security administrators are generally not very knowledgeable in software security, which includes software access control, encrypted password protection, and firewalls. Their security concerns, then, are in physically protecting the hardware installation and controlling access to the main computer equipment area. Adequate physical protection can reduce the computer's exposure to fraud and sabotage. It should be remembered, however, that security violations by authorized insiders far outnumber those that occur at the hands of outsiders.

Prosecution for computer-related crimes must be vigorously pursued by healthcare organizations. Most states have, in addition to federal laws, some form of computer crime laws. These laws range from the simple to the complex.

The computer room should be located in an isolated section of the facility or in an offsite location that is not in a traffic flow area. There should be only a minimum number of access points, and fire-rated walls should surround the entire computer center. Ideally, one entry and exit point is best; however, regulations may require additional exits, depending on the size of the center. These exits should be equipped with alarm devices, as should the main entry door if the center is not staffed 24 hours a day. This alarm system should be monitored at a central monitoring point.

Once the computer center has been sealed as much as possible and has the proper fire protection systems, the main concern is access control. Limiting the number of personnel within the center and within various sections of the center is the primary principle of security control. Card access is especially appropriate for the computer operation.

Computer operations depend on power and controlled-climate conditions. Security administrators should not forget to secure the power and air-conditioning systems that supply the center.

Electronic data processing security is a multi-disciplinary problem. Knowledgeable people from operation management, application programmers, systems personnel, and internal auditors as well as the security administrator must address this specialized security situation, working as a team.

MATERIALS MANAGEMENT

The materials management responsibility is defined somewhat differently in each hospital. For the purposes of security, the general areas of concern are purchasing and receiving, storage, equipment accountability and marking, distribution, and disposing of property. All of these areas are subject to security review and support.

Purchasing and Receiving

Because hospitals purchase large amounts of goods, products, and equipment, a proactive loss-prevention program is necessary. A materials management program requires checks and balances and a separation of the people responsible for purchasing and the people responsible for receiving. Many opportunities for kickbacks exist in purchasing activities, somewhat in relation to the size of the function. The larger the program, the greater the opportunity for this type of fraud. Not only is the separation of purchasing and receiving necessary, but the rotation of job assignments is a sound management practice to deter criminal activity.

The receiving dock and the process of receiving supplies and equipment present numerous security vulnerabilities. A frequent problem that hospitals encounter is that received goods are left unattended on the dock, and thus accessible to delivery drivers or others passing by. After being checked in and signed for, all goods should immediately be removed to a controlled storage location. A small fenced holding area on the dock may provide temporary protection, pending distribution or transportation to a more permanent storage area.

All deliveries to the facility should be directed to a receiving area, and the internal distribution of light deliveries, including flowers, should be performed by organizational personnel. Many problems have occurred because delivery personnel were allowed to make their own deliveries to various departments within the organization. These problems include unnecessary traffic, extra housekeeping due to careless handling, interruption of direct or indirect patient care, and the misplacement of material delivered to the wrong location.

Storage

Although general storerooms contain many pilferable items, the losses from these areas are generally minimal compared to the losses that occur after the goods have been distributed to the units. One reason the loss is minimal is because most materials management personnel have recognized the potential for large-volume losses and have implemented at least basic security precautions.

All general storerooms should be alarmed after hours, and the sensing devices should transmit a signal to a central alarm panel. Whenever possible, storerooms should be windowless, and the number of access openings should be reduced as much as possible.

The system of perimeters is a valid concept for general storeroom operations. Certain areas within the general storeroom should be sectioned off to provide greater protection for particularly vulnerable items, including syringes, blank checks, invoices, and linens. Regular storeroom employees can thus be restricted from areas or storage containers to which they do not need access to perform their jobs.

Storerooms should be off-limits to all but department personnel. This rule is common, but so is non-enforcement. In one case, employees leaving the workplace were permitted to cut through the storeroom and leave by a side door.

After-hours access to storerooms can present a problem. If the materials management function is properly carried out, there should be little, if any, need for after-hours access. A 600-bed hospital with a firm policy restricting after-hours access required only two after-hours entries during a one-year period. On those two occasions, the storeroom manager had to come from home to provide the access.

If entry to the storeroom is necessary, a security officer should accompany the individual to the storeroom. To provide proper accountability, a requisition should be prepared by the security officer for any items removed. The security officer should also be responsible for securing the area when the business is concluded.

Equipment Accountability and Marking

A common practice in healthcare organizations is to receive a piece of equipment, assign an asset control number to it, affix the number to the equipment, assign a depreciation schedule, and deliver the equipment to the requesting department—never to see it again. For example, a computer acquired to the public relations department may end up in the nursing office, and the new location will not be recorded. After these transfers have been made several times, the computer's location cannot be readily established.

Equipment should be assigned to a specific department, and a periodic inventory is essential. When property is transferred, the record should be annotated to relieve one department and assign accountability to the other.

Related to the assigning of asset numbers—and of equal importance—is marking property with hospital identification. "Marking" refers to conspicuous identification that cannot be easily altered or removed. Many items must be marked with more than the asset control number. When marking equipment to deter theft, basic economics must be considered. A balance must be found between the cost of marking and the actual theft deterrent value achieved. Not all markings need to be readily seen. For example, desks, file cabinets, tables, and chairs should be marked on the underside, permitting ready identification but not defacing the property. Furniture is normally stenciled with the hospital's initials or logo. Etching tools are used for instruments and other metal equipment.

Distribution

The distribution of goods and equipment from storage areas to end users is accomplished by walk-up distribution counters or transported to the user by materials management personnel. The latter method is being utilized more frequently as off site storage areas are becoming common.

Regardless of the distribution method, all supplies and equipment should be signed for by an authorized staff person at the point of delivery. The person signing for the property must take time to determine that the property being signed for is actually delivered. When staff simply sign a receipt without checking it is an open invitation to receive a "short" delivery with property being fraudulently diverted. At this point the delivered property should immediately be properly stored and not exposed to passing staff or visitors.

Disposing of Property

All healthcare organizations accumulate and need to dispose of obsolete, excess, or damaged property. Hospital personnel, including the supervisory staff, should not have the authority to give away or otherwise dispose of hospital property, regardless of its value. A firm policy should be established that outlines the authorized disposition of unneeded property through the material management department.

All unneeded material should be transported to a central storage area so that is can be used by another department. Thus, property may be reassigned and properly managed. Healthcare facilities are notorious for needlessly purchasing an item because no one knew the same item was no longer needed by another department.

A committee—composed of the plant engineer, the materials manager, and administrators—should periodically survey the material in storage to determine what should be discarded. A sale accessible to employees only is a good employee relations mechanism that can eliminate the practice of favoritism, which produces negative employee relations.

LAUNDRY AND LINEN CONTROL

The loss of linens in medical facilities of all sizes has generally gone unchecked, and it continues to needlessly increase the cost of patient care. Too many administrators and laundry managers believe that satisfying unit needs is more important than trying to halt linen thefts and misuse. The theft of surgical scrub suits has attracted press coverage, which has prompted some administrators to alter methods of control. However, the majority have done nothing, thinking that the problem is not too bad or will go away with time.

Security practitioners must understand why it is so difficult to focus the attention of laundry personnel and hospital administrators on laundry theft and misuse. First, "more linen" has erroneously been translated into "better patient care." Second, many administrators falsely believe that increased linen use reduces the cost per pound of processed linen. Laundry managers in general take great pride in reducing cost per pound, rather than in reducing use. The cost of linen service should be measured in cost per patient day to be meaningful.

A hospital that succeeds in reducing the pounds of linen service per patient day will find that the linen replacement figure will increase because of the smaller weight base. For example, a loss figure of $0.75 per patient day on a volume of 20 pounds of linen per patient day will be $0.0375 per pound. If linen use per patient day is reduced to 12 pounds, the loss figure per patient day is $0.0625 per pound, which is approximately double. Yet the cost of $0.75 per day for loss did not change. As this example shows, expressing the cost of linen loss per pound is invalid.

The term "linen control" should also be examined. Most hospitals operate supply systems rather than control systems. The basis of a supply system is often to establish a quota for each item for each unit. Supplying the units is only part of a control system; the soiled linen returned from the unit must be accounted for also. If a theft problem exists, the supply system simply keeps replacing the stolen items.

Establishing Losses

Linen loss figures are difficult to establish unless strong procedural controls and adequate recording methods are instituted and maintained. One method of determining a loss in the supply system is to review the amount of linen put into the system after adjusting for the amount of linen discarded. These numbers must be viewed over a period of time because input varies over the year. Excessive amounts of linen added to the system is often rationalized by suggesting that inventories were increased due to extremely hot or extremely cold weather, a higher census, exceptional medical cases that required more frequent changes, hoarding by units, and the like. These explanations may have limited merit; however, a review over a longer period of time generally indicates whether losses are occurring.

A complete review of movement of linen, from ordering to the end user, and the hospital's reprocessing system is the first step in establishing a linen security program. Security practitioners must examine each step of this process to note the controls that are in place and to identify areas of possible compromise.

Controlling Losses

Most institutions find it difficult to pinpoint the specific areas in which linen loss occurs. In a shared laundry, the hospital causing the problem can also be difficult to identify. This leads to such generalized security efforts that the linen thieves are not usually threatened.

When losses occur, the basic problem is that the linen processing system is not a closed loop. The amount of soiled linen returned by each department, or hospital, is not determined. The problems that result would be similar to those of a car rental agency that never checked whether cars were returned. The only way to continue to rent out cars would be to purchase a new one for every one that was not returned. Unfortunately, this is the way hospitals operate in terms of linen replacement.

To combat these problems, a number of shared laundries and a few large in-hospital laundries have commenced soiled-linen counting systems. These systems return clean linen to the units based on the amount of soiled linen that was returned. The laundry replaces the linen that wears out normally, and when a unit requires new linen, it is charged directly to the unit.

Healthcare facilities personnel are not disposed to inventory routines. In view of the serious problem of linen theft, however, healthcare facilities should conduct at least one complete inventory each year; several inventories per year are highly recommended when a linen disappearance problem is suspected or there is an actual occurrence of a substantial loss.

Not all linen losses are attributed to theft. Some losses occur through waste and misuse. Employees who wipe up a spill with a washcloth and throw it into the trash or who tear up linen for rags can produce a significant loss problem. The discarding of linen should be a controlled practice, and the transformation of discarded linen into rags should be a centralized operation. Rags should be appropriately dyed and supplied to users to prevent abuse of the reusable linen supply.

Linen that has not yet been put into the system should not be stored in the laundry area. New linen should be maintained in the general storeroom and dispersed to the laundry operation through a regular requisition system.

Scrub Suits

More has been written on the loss of hospital scrub suits than on the rest of the linen theft problem. Scrub suits seem to appeal to all segments of the population, from teenagers to college professors. Some predict the scrub suit trend will continue indefinitely, but others feel it is probably just a passing fad. Whatever the future holds, the public's love of scrub suits has cost hospital patients millions of dollars.

The solution to this type of loss is quite simple. First, scrub suits should be issued to individuals. A soiled suit can be exchanged for a clean suit either through an issue window during set hours or through an automatic uniform dispenser. The dispenser works much like automated bank tellers; it credits the individual for returned suits and issues clean ones. This is another use for access control, plastic-coated ID cards.

The second step for simple scrub suit control is an administrative directive with real support. Hospital property should never leave the premises, and violators should be firmly dealt with rather than ignored.

Access Controls for the Laundry

The laundry itself must be provided with good after-hours physical controls. These safeguards include strict access control, which may include an intrusion alarm system. Personnel should not be permitted to enter the laundry to supplement inadequate unit inventories. Once the laundry is closed for the day, it should remain closed, just like the pharmacy and the general storeroom. To meet unexpected emergencies that require extra linen, one method is to provide a small emergency supply in another area. For example, a fully stocked linen cart can be placed in a locked closet that is accessible to a nursing supervisor. This emergency cart can also be stored in central supply if this area is operational 24 hours a day.

Marking Linens

Materials management personnel should be responsible for marking linen with the facility's name before releasing it to the laundry. Linen can be ordered from vendors with the hospital's markings; however, many hospitals buy unmarked linen and perform this task at the hospital. All linen, with the possible exception of washcloths, should be marked. Sheets and other large items should be marked in at least three places, on opposite ends and in the middle of the item. Despite some claims to the contrary, marking linen does not deter theft. Marking is an important step in the total control system, and it is essential for pursuing arrests and prosecution when thefts occur.

THE RESEARCH LABORATORY (ANIMAL)

The activities of animal rights groups and anti-vivisectionists have made laboratory security a high priority for facilities conducting animal research projects. These groups are well financed and sophisticated, and they enjoy the attention of a sympathetic media. Among the well known groups are: the Animal Liberation Front, Animal Liberation Provisional Front, Alliance for Animals, World Animal Net, Animal Rights Team, Students Oppression Against Animal Research, and Citizens for Animal Resources. Activists fall into two groups: the non-violent and the violent. It is the latter group that creates the security vulnerability.

Research facilities in hospitals, universities, and independent firms have been the target of demonstrations, break-ins, vandalism, and fires. In one case more than 1,200 laboratory animals were released just before two university laboratory buildings were set on fire. The Animal Liberation Front (ALF) claimed responsibility for these acts.

In addition to physical damage, graffiti, and disruption of normal work, pressure by animal rights activists can result in the suppression of important research. A leading pharmacology researcher at Cornell University Medical College, New York, was the target of demonstrations, picketing, petitions, and letters. As a result, he gave up a $600,000 grant and abandoned his 14-year project.

The defense against these disturbances requires planning for both perimeter security and the protection of the contents of the laboratory: animals, equipment, and records. When the security of sensitive materials is involved, it is of prime importance to know laboratory employees well. Information provided by an employee who is sympathetic to the animal rights movement can allow activists to gain access through even the most efficient security system.

The animal rights activist movement goes back several hundred years in Europe and expanded to the United States well over a hundred years ago. In the last five years, the activist groups have become more active, and somewhat more radical. The new leaders are young, confrontational, and dissatisfied with the lack of progress. As a result, they advocate more direct action that leads to violence and destruction of property.[2]

According to Debra Higgins Cavalier, president of the Massachusetts Society for Medical Research (MSMR), there are well over seventy animal activists groups in the United States. The MSMR is one of the leading non profit groups in the U.S. that support the biosciences in the proper use of animals in research. Massachusetts was the first of several states to enact legislation making it a felony to trespass upon, remove, damage, or interfere with any property used in animal research. There is also the Federal Animal Enterprise Protection Act of 1992 that makes it a felony to break into a laboratory and cause damage in excess of 10 thousand dollars.[3]

The ALF distributes handouts to supply operatives with tactical information. One such handout recommends eight methods of gathering information on targeted institutions.[4] These methods are:

- **Personal entry.** In this method, the operative simply walks into the facility. If challenged, the operative simply states he is looking for a friend.

- **Employment.** In this method, the operative gains employment at the targeted facility.

- **Use of disguise.** In this method, the operative impersonates a government employee, inspector, et cetera.

- **Surveillance.** In this method, the operative conducts a fixed surveillance (stakeout) of the facility.

- **Use of inside help.** In this method, the operative develops friendships with facility staff.

- **Bribery.** In this method, the operative bribes facility staff.

- **Garbage inspection.** In this method, the operative inspects the target's garbage.

- **Surreptitious entry.** In this method, the operative gains access to the facility surreptitiously.

Lab coats, required safety equipment, and badges help to identify authorized employees during normal working hours, but identification can be difficult after hours. Animal activists have preferred holidays and early morning hours for break-ins, so security personnel should make sure doors, windows, and all other possible entries are locked at the beginning and end of each workday and immediately after the last employees have left.

In addition, visitors should be restricted from sensitive areas, repair people should be carefully identified, and reliable alarm systems should be used. Because intruders often disable power substations—thus cutting off electricity to the research facility—an emergency power system is advisable for lighting, preserving specimens and agents, and maintaining animal life-support systems.

DAYCARE CENTERS

In order to attract and retain staff, many healthcare organizations operate daycare centers. These centers present unique security concerns. The first and primary security concern is the development of appropriate staff. Intense background checks of applicants must be conducted; certain checks are even legally mandated by regulatory and licensing agencies. The sexual molestation, or other physical abuse, of a child by a staff member is a situation to be prevented at all costs. Limiting access to the facility is also a primary safeguard. It is a common practice to have all ingress/egress points locked except for the normal drop-off and pick-up times. Some facilities maintain a locked facility at all times, issuing electronic access cards to authorized family members only.

An outside play area is generally a design implement in daycare centers. These play areas should be completely fenced with at least six-foot-high barriers. The access to the area should be from the daycare center itself. If there is a gate arrangement, it should be locked from the egress side and the release side should be such that small children cannot operate the release. Staff personnel should be especially watchful for persons loitering in the area around the center.

Release of a child at the end of the designated time period is an area of special concern. First, there is generally a lot of activity going on during the pick-up time, resulting in difficulty of keeping track of who is coming and going. Second, there must be strict criteria established regarding who can pick up a child. There must be a system to permit the release of a child to anyone other than a normal family member due to emergency or other extenuating circumstances. Regardless of the policy and resultant procedure, there should be strict adherence to this critical element of security.

Closed-circuit television (CCTV) has several appropriate applications to help secure a childcare center. In addition to surveillance of general areas, a camera should be placed at the main access door to record the dropping off and picking up of the children. In some cases, this will require two cameras to adequately record this activity. As with all other CCTV applications, the recorded video should be kept for a minimum of seven days. The CCTV system may also be used to allow the remote electrical release of the main entry door.

The general security plan for a daycare center should include procedures for relocation of children and staff in the event of an emergency requiring evacuation. This information should be given to parents at the time of enrollment and can be included in an overall security briefing card that is a standard handout to parents.

OFFSITE FACILITIES

The utilization of offsite freestanding facilities and lease space in larger buildings is becoming the norm for most hospitals and healthcare systems. These offsite facilities are a result of mergers, acquisitions, the need for serving a given geographical area with certain medical services, the need for privacy, and a space shortage within existing facilities. This trend will likely continue in the future as organizations seek to gain market share by delivering medical services to outlying neighborhoods and communities.

The assessment of security needs and concerns for these offsite facilities, whether down the block or many miles away from the main facility, begins with a site inspection. The same approach and utilization of information sources should be utilized as when conducting the main facility security risk assessment. An additional element of review for lease space functions is to determine the security safeguards provided by the property owner.

All too often, these offsite facilities are left on their own relative to security issues until a problem develops. The main facility security resources are then called upon to provide security. These facilities should be a part of the main facility security program in all respects, with the exception of critical incident response. In an emergency, a public agency would likely be the first responder. In terms of communications, all incident reporting and physical security (including key and access control) should be handled as if the facility were a functional unit within the main facility.

HOME HEALTHCARE (COMMUNITY PROVIDER SERVICES)

The delivery of home healthcare services had its beginning in the early 1990s and grew quickly through the mid-1990s. Today, many hospitals and private agencies (both profit and non-profit) are examining the future of their existence. There is clear distinction between home healthcare and home care. Even in home healthcare, the definitions of service and the caregiver are not consistent or clear. In terms of state regulation, there are states that regulate home healthcare but not home care. States vary to a great degree on how they regulate the whole issue of home care, with Florida being one of the more progressive states in this regard.

The home environment sets up a new and different relationship between the caregiver and the patient. The patient is now in his or her familiar surroundings, while the caregiver is providing services outside the familiar organizational setting. This change of relationship and environment creates a whole different set of security issues and concerns for the patient, the caregiver, and the organization the caregiver represents.

Patient at Risk

The caregiver is relatively independent of organizational supervision while in the home. Oftentimes, the patient cannot walk and therefore cannot provide a normal degree of surveillance of this "stranger in their home." This degree of caregiver independence can lead to a variety of security issues, including:

- Theft of patient property

- Diversion of drugs

- Verbal and physical abuse

In one case, a home health aide was hired through After-Care Professional Nurses Registry of California to care for a 96-year-old person. Little did the family know that the caregiver was on probation after serving eight months for stealing more than $500,000 from two other people who had been in her care. In fact, the family only learned of the past conviction after filing a police report regarding their own theft of property by the aide. The firm was not a licensed home care agency because it called itself a registry instead of an agency. This firm was listed in the telephone directory as "Home Health Services" and was recommended by local hospitals.[5]

A study of 150 cases from 32 states in which home care providers were found to have abused, neglected, or stolen from patients was conducted by *USA Today*.[6] Results of the study revealed that 73 percent of these cases involved theft, 19 percent involved violence (including murder and sexual abuse), and 15 percent involved behavior that put the patient at risk of physical injury. Nurses were involved in 6 percent of these cases with the remaining 94 percent involving aides.

Caregiver at Risk

The caregiver providing home healthcare is subject to a variety of risks in performing services, including:

- Automobile accidents

- Automobile theft and vandalism

- Attack by vicious animals

- Attack by the patient, family, or others present in the home

- Attack by neighbors or persons in the neighborhood

- False accusations including patient abuse and theft of property

In August of 1996, a nurse on a home healthcare visit was shot and killed by a patient who then shot himself. The patient's sister had warned the nurse she should leave due to the "mood" of the patient following a change of dressings the previous evening. The nurse followed this advice, but forgot her nurse's bag. The nurse was waiting outside while the sister retrieved the bag. The patient came out of another door and confronted the nurse, killing her and himself.[7]

In still another case that occurred in February, 2000, a home healthcare nurse in rural Kansas was shot and killed while dialing 911 to report finding two bodies on the floor of a client's home. The nurse was apparently killed by the client's 23 year old grandson, arrested at the scene, for killing his father, another woman at the home, and the nurse. The client (patient) was unharmed.[8]

There have been many cases in which family members or friends have stolen property from a patient and then accused the caregiver of being responsible for the loss. This type of false accusation is particularly true when it involves cash, jewelry, and antiques. The motive for interfamily theft is quite prevalent when a patient is near death and family members are concerned about getting their "fair share" of the estate.

Security Practices and Guidelines

There are a number of security practices and guidelines that should be taken into consideration with regards to home healthcare.

- **Initial assessment of the home environment.** Prior to the first home health visit, the agency should complete an environment assessment either by direct verbal conversation or telephone contact with the patient or close family member. This assessment should include inquiring about animals, other persons living in the home, medications, neighborhood crime/gang activity, and complete directions for finding the address and accessing the living unit.

- **First visit.** If the initial assessment of the home environment presents significant danger signals, there should possibly be two caregivers making the first visit. This practice is difficult due to funding issues; however, the safety of the caregiver must take precedence over cost. During the first visit, the caregiver should make an assessment relative to safety or other potential problems presented by the environment. This information should be noted in agency files for further references or for immediate follow-up. For example, should the patient or family openly display or talk about firearms, a safety awareness response is necessary.

- **Scheduling visits.** It is always best to schedule home visits during daylight hours. This is not always possible, but should always be a goal. Physicians can sometimes regulate specified times of treatment when they are aware of caregiver safety issues. It is always a good idea to telephone the patient just before the visit as a courtesy and to find out whether there is some legitimate reason to reschedule the visit.

- **Preparing for the visit.** Always wear name-badges and uniforms that clearly identify the healthcare agency. A cell-phone or two-way radio should always be part of the standard equipment carried into the patient's home. Caregivers should always leave supplies, equipment, and personal property not needed for the specific visit in the trunk of their vehicle. Vehicles should always be locked.

- **During the visit.** Caregivers should always spend only the time necessary in a patient's home. Instincts are to be trusted and care should be terminated when danger signals are perceived. Suspending treatment is somewhat different than abandonment of care. Immediate termination of care is justified if there is violence or threats of violence during the visit. If there is to be a termination of care, there must be a reasonable notice depending on the needs of the patient and other resources available. Notice of termination of care should be in writing and hand-delivered to the patient.

- **Caregiver security escort.** There are times when a caregiver must be provided a security escort for a home visit. There are two basic forms such a security escort can take. One is a uniformed, generally armed security officer in a work security vehicle. The escort may involve transporting the caregiver in the security vehicle or meeting the caregiver at the patient's address. In the case of the conspicuous security escort, the security officer generally remains outside but ready to respond if summoned by the caregiver. The second approach is to provide a security escort in street clothes or care agency uniform. In this case, the escort usually accompanies the caregiver into the living unit and is introduced as a team member. This type of escort normally involves an unarmed security officer.

- **Security education for the caregiver.** It is absolutely essential that all home healthcare staff receive security training and education. This training must reinforce security awareness and practice without frightening the staff. The training should also teach caregivers how to avoid or defuse dangerous situations. Professional caregivers are very focused on delivering a quality service and do not always assess the environment or perceive danger signs. In addition to formal training presentations, it is recommended that each home healthcare agency develop safety and security policies to be distributed to each caregiver to guide their everyday activities.

Information in this regard should include:

- Taking planned routes that are well traveled streets—not taking shortcuts through unknown areas.

- Utilize a reliable, well-maintained vehicle with ample gas supply.

- Drive by the client's address for a short distance while assessing the neighborhood (i.e., suspicious vehicles or persons loitering).

- Park in the direction of travel you intend to use when departing from the visit.

- Park so that your vehicle can be seen from the client's home whenever possible.

- Always lock your vehicle and do not leave property exposed in open view.

- When leaving, have keys ready, lock doors immediately upon entering the vehicle and do not sit in the vehicle checking maps or preparing documentation. Depart the neighborhood immediately heading directly to the well-traveled street. Note any vehicle that pulls out directly behind your vehicle when you depart.

There will be additional safety practices depending on the agency, such as reporting arrival and departure times, pre-planned routes, emergency notifications, route deviation procedures, etc. And it will not be long before the emergence of Global Positioning Systems (GPS) to track the movement and location of the caregiver's vehicle.

Information in this regard should include:

REFERENCES

1. Donald E. Bogardus, MPA, CHPA, CPP, "Missing Drugs III," *Medical Management System*, Gilbert, Arizona, 1997, p. 86.

2. Michael J. Geier, "Securing Research Facilities Against Activist Attacks," *Security Management*, June 1994, pp. 30–36.

3. "Renewed Violence by Animal Rights Activists Who Target Research Labs," *Hospital Security and Safety Management*, Vol. 20, #4, August, 1999, p. 13.

4. Ibid., p. 14.

5. "Home Healthcare Opens Door to Abuses," *USA Today*, November 11, 1996, p. 11B.

6. Ibid., p. 13B.

7. "Tribute to a Home Care Nurse," *Colorado Nurse*, December 1996, p. 10.

8. "Three Fatally Shot in Girard," *Topeka Capitol-Journal*, February 8, 2000.

CHAPTER 19

Parking Control and Security

The demand for medical center parking has increased drastically in recent years. Even though parking needs and parking issues have always been a major concern for healthcare organizations, they always seem to take a backseat to planning. The demand for more parking space has been driven to a large extent by the trend to expand outpatient services. Patient-to-bed census parking demand ratios are thus completely obsolete for planning purposes. In addition, many benchmarks and tools previously utilized to project medical center parking needs have been tossed out the window. Each facility has its own identity in terms of product mix (types of services), market share, patient/visitor/staff composition, and degree of public transportation, which are all basic factors in parking space needs.

The control of parking is a major activity for medical care facilities. This responsibility is sometimes considered to be within the purview of the security function, and other times is assigned elsewhere in the organization. The context of control does not always include protection. Some argue that parking control is not a true function of security and that it is a separate area of facility services.

All "parkers" want to park as close as possible to their intended destination. As facilities grow and change, the demands for parking change. It is not necessarily numbers but convenience that makes control difficult. Many healthcare organizations have undergone major relocations of entrances and services. Such renovations often create a new "front door," and parking needs change without receiving much advance planning.[1]

In designing parking accommodations, the following is a basic list of priorities:

- Handicap parking (required by law)

- Emergency services, patients

- Ambulatory patients with impaired mobility
- Outpatients
- Clinic patients
- Delivery drivers (15 minutes or less)
- Visitors
- Staff (including physicians, volunteers, and physician office staff)
- Vendors and educational program attendants

Despite the rather low parking priority for medical center staff, they account for 60 to 70 percent of the parking needs.[2]

The protection of people and property on medical center property, including parking areas, is a responsibility of the security function. This protection responsibility includes preventive patrols, escorts, response to calls for services, investigation of security-related incidents, and physical security monitoring.

The parking accommodations of different healthcare facilities present unique control and protection problems. One constant factor is that there is never enough parking space. Studies continually indicate that the shortage of spaces is most acute between 11:00 AM and 3:30 PM on weekdays.[3] The most acute shortage is when dayshift employees are still at work and the arriving second shift must find parking spaces. Once the day shift leaves, there is generally an abundance of parking spaces. Because the security department is generally responsible for enforcing parking regulations, it receives the brunt of employee, visitor, and patient dissatisfaction with the real or perceived lack of parking facilities. Unfortunately, this dissatisfaction with parking has a direct negative effect on the image of security and the entire organization.

In addition to enforcing parking regulations to effect orderly use, the security effort is concerned with the growing number of assaults, thefts, and incidents of vandalism that occurs in parking areas. Numerous major lawsuits against medical centers allege inadequate parking area security. Litigation can result in punitive as well as general damage awards.

In Pittsburgh, Pennsylvania, the security in parking structures became such an issue that the city enacted an ordinance mandating certain security provisions. The law covers any structure that charges guests, employees, or the public to use a parking space. The law has been enforced since 1985 by the Bureau of Building Inspection. It requires the following:

- A uniformed security guard must patrol all levels of the structure once every 30 minutes, unless detained for security reasons

- Patrols must be verified by having employees punch a clock or other recording device on each level

- Emergency buzzers must be installed on each level

- Lighting must project a minimum of five-foot candles in all areas

- Emergency phones must be installed in elevators

- Directional arrows must be painted on walls to indicate exits and elevators

Since the implementation of this parking structure ordinance, the complaints from parking garage operators have been few, and the wave of assaults on parkers has been virtually eliminated.

Perhaps one of the strictest parking garage security laws in the country is in effect in Minneapolis, Minnesota. The law's 29 requirements for security became effective in 1990 and have proven to be very effective in terms of public safety.

TYPES OF PARKING AREAS

Parking areas can generally be categorized as street parking, surface (or grade) lots, freestanding structures, and structures that are physically connected to healthcare facilities. Although the application of security safeguards will vary depending on the type of parking area, the objectives are the same: establish a user-friendly feeling and high level of safety in both perception and reality.

Street Parking

Parking on side streets around the medical care facilities presents a security challenge. This parking is on public property and is generally outside the realm of the organization's protection responsibility. In a practical sense, however, persons who are assaulted and vehicles that are broken into on these side streets do affect the healthcare organization. It is not uncommon for security to escort employees or visitors off facility property. Security escorts should be restricted to a maximum of one block, and this restriction should be strongly upheld by the organization. When security officers are more than one block from the property, they are not providing facility visibility, surveillance, or maximum response capability. This extended escort service may help one person to the detriment of others.

Street parking can cause community relations problems in addition to protection problems. Neighboring homeowners generally resent cars parked along their streets all day because they restrict homeowner use and bring a certain amount of congestion and litter.

Surface Parking Lots

Surface parking lots are slowly disappearing from large and urban medical centers. The cost of land and the fact that many facilities are landlocked generally results in the construction of parking structures when parking areas must be expanded or replaced. Security for surface lots generally consists of access control, emergency communication devices, fencing, lighting, security patrols, and observation posts. Enclosed observation posts, somewhat elevated, in the parking area, offer several advantages. Not only do they provide shelter for security officers, but they are also another visible safeguard. Closed-circuit television is not widely used for surface lots because of its low cost/benefit ratio. Of specific importance in surface lots is that landscaping be placed, and properly maintained, to eliminate hiding areas, reduced visibility, and reduced lighting levels.

Parking Structures

As land values increase and the available land around hospitals decreases, parking structures become a cost-effective alternative to surface lots. Modern structures can be designed to be user friendly and produce a feeling of safety. Among the new design features are raised ceilings, extensive use of glazing materials, increased lighting, bright colors, and legible signs.

Basic Parking Structure Security

Parking structures provide concentrated parking, but at the same time they create new security problems. Many potential problems can be eliminated or minimized through proper security design, which should begin with the first architectural drawing. Architectural firms without security design experience should advise their clients and take steps to obtain security advice. The basic security considerations for parking structures include the following:

• The structure should provide the maximum span of vision on the parking levels and should eliminate interior support columns and dark corners.

• Lighting must comply with the standards of the Illuminating Engineering Society of North America (IESNA). This standard includes a 3- to 5-foot candle lighting minimum throughout the structure. The installation of lighting should take into consideration the failure rate of the system. At any given time, approximately 18 to 22 percent of the lighting system may be inoperative. Thus, the lighting standards should be exceeded by approximately 25 percent so minimum lighting levels are maintained. A common method to counteract the effect of burned-out lamps is to use several lamps in one fixture. The interior of the structure should contain some light-colored surfaces (for example, supporting columns and walkway areas). Light-colored paint increases the effectiveness of lighting and conveys a feeling of security.

An important aspect of parking structure lighting is that of uniformity. Drivers should not experience passing from light to dark areas. There should be lighting in the parking stall and not just in the driving aisles. Another important lighting consideration is to reduce glare. Glare is a potential hazard for all drivers, but is particularly dangerous for senior citizens and others with impaired vision.[4]

- Parking areas should be well-maintained and clean.

- Stairwells and elevators should be enclosed with appropriate glazing materials.

- Stairwells, walkouts, and traffic ingress/egress points should whenever possible open onto the facility's property, not the street.

- Emergency exit doors should be alarmed as part of the access control system.

- Emergency telephones, or call stations, should be connected directly to the central security station or the facility's telephone operator. Call stations must be conspicuously marked in two different ways. First, they should be marked to be identifiable from great distances. Large signage may be needed within the structure to announce and point to emergency call stations. Second, the station should be prominently marked, so callers can accurately describe their location. Even though some communications equipment shows the caller's location at the answering point, it is still desirable to indicate the user's location at the calling point. There are some systems that activate a strobe light when the communications device is activated. This activation is intended to scare away potential troublesome persons and to render a clear destination to responding security personnel.

- Openings on the ground floor large enough to allow people to climb through or to pass large objects through should be eliminated. Decorative wire mesh or other barriers can be installed that meet the security objective yet provide light and visibility.

- All entrances/exits should be capable of being closed during low traffic periods or emergencies, including gates that prohibit pedestrians and vehicles from entering the structure.

- Crash bars should be installed on stairwell emergency exit doors.

- Frequent security patrols should be scheduled. The frequency will depend on the time of day, local crime rate, number of reported incidents, location, and other security safeguards that have been applied within the structure.

- Cashier booths should be placed outside the structure so that cashiers have a better view of loiterers, stairwells, and general traffic.

- Covert parking area surveillance posts should be provided. Ideally, there will be one or two posts on each level, allowing security to view any part of the structure. One-way glazed observation posts are generally used. All enclosed areas, such as equipment spaces and storage areas, provide an opportunity for observation posts with little additional cost. By simply including a small window, an added element of security can be achieved.

Cost overruns in construction seem to be a standard. When cost overruns occur, security is generally the target of cost cutting. Even when planned security applications are eliminated, the proper design can accommodate later retrofitting at a favorable cost.

CLOSED-CIRCUIT TELEVISION MONITORING (CCTV)

Many questions arise concerning the use of CCTV for parking security. The first question is whether a CCTV system is needed. Sometimes it is decided that an area should be monitored before the need has been established. The use of CCTV is somewhat prevalent in parking structures, yet many of these structures have various elements of design that don't lend themselves to CCTV.

All CCTV systems require effective monitoring, regardless of the size of the system, and this is extremely difficult to achieve. If effective monitoring is in place, the reaction to monitored incidents is of equal importance. The response of security, police, or fire personnel must be quick and properly directed.

Opponents of CCTV point out that it does not give directions, it does not generate people-to-people public relations, and it does not respond to incidents. The live monitoring or recording of an incident does little good without a quick response capability. The argument that CCTV may help solve a crime is generally a poor justification for the system.

The cost of a CCTV system does not end with its purchase and installation. Systems require monitoring, maintenance, and ongoing replacement expenditures. Maintenance may be required 24 hours per day, and weekend and off hours are quite expensive. From a liability standpoint, equipment must be repaired immediately, or alternative security safeguards must be implemented until the problem is rectified.

SIGNAGE

Signage and graphics in parking areas serve several purposes, including control of parking, the providing of general information (directions), and security. Even information signage that orients parkers and enables them to move quickly in and out of the parking area makes them less vulnerable to a security-related situation.

Security signage indicating general surveillance of the area and the availability of emergency call stations will generally provide a greater feeling of safety. This security signage also serves as a crime deterrent.

SHUTTLE SERVICE AND VALET PARKING

Some facilities that have been unable to increase campus parking capabilities have instituted shuttle services to offsite parking facilities. This type of parking arrangement is generally directed to the employee so that additional parking can be available to patients and visitors. Suitable parking areas are sometimes available near the facility but too far for staff to walk or the exposure to street crime an unexceptional factor. Shuttle buses have proved effective.

In the typical shuttle system, security department employees drive a passenger van or bus between the parking lot and the facility during the early morning and late afternoon hours. When an employee needs to leave during the middle of a shift or is held over past the closing time of the lot, security is contacted and a special trip is made for that employee. This special shuttle trip is then utilized to provide a random security patrol of the parking area. Likewise, there must be arrangements made to accommodate random arriving staff.

Organizations have tried many incentives to entice employees to use offsite parking areas, including:

- Comfortable waiting areas (heated and air-conditioned)
- Complimentary coffee, rolls, and morning papers
- Coupons for free food in the facility cafeteria
- Weekly prize drawings
- Car washes while the vehicle is parked for the day for a fee
- Attended parking lots

The main complaint of shuttle users is transportation waiting time. Thus, organizations must ensure that they have sufficient resources before embarking on a shuttle program.

One Midwest hospital asked employees to park in a church lot six blocks from the hospital and to walk to and from work. Instead of putting money into resources and incentives, they paid employees to park in the offsite area. The program was oversubscribed by employees, and there was a waiting list for vacancies.

The use of valet parking for healthcare patrons is not new, but it is growing. The shortage of convenient parking is the greatest stimulus to the valet parking system, but proponents also cite the marketing advantage of this program. Some organizations charge for valet parking; others offer the service free.

Organizations that undertake a valet parking program should provide adequate supervision, and they should review their insurance coverage regarding this type of operation. The hours of operation should be clearly stated, and the procedure for retrieving vehicles after hours should be established. Security often becomes involved in the after-hours retrieval of vehicles.

TYPES OF PARKERS

Those who use facility-provided parking can be divided into several distinct categories, including dayshift employees, afternoon shift employees, nightshift employees, outpatients, inpatients, physicians, visitors, and vendors or outside service representatives. Despite flexible scheduling and the use of 10- and 12-hour shifts, there is still a discernable day-, afternoon-, and night-shift demand for parking. The most common approach is to assign each category of parker to a specific parking area.

During the day, the nearest parking is generally assigned to outpatients, physicians, service representatives, and visitors, due to their short-term use of parking space. Whether appropriate or not, physicians usually demand and receive special attention when it comes to parking.

Afternoon-Shift Employees

The afternoon-shift employees are the ones who most often feel the inadequacy of parking space because the day shift is still on duty when they arrive. A common solution is to designate a special "3 to 11" lot (named for the hours of the afternoon shift), which is opened approximately an hour before the afternoon shift reports for work. Entry to this lot is generally controlled by a security officer unless automatic controls are installed. This lot, which is vacant during the morning hours, can also be used to accommodate people attending morning meetings, but must be tightly controlled to assure that these temporary parkers have cleared the lot by the required time.

If the 3 to 11 lot is not adequate to accommodate all afternoon personnel, the organization should consider placing some of these employees in the physician's parking lot. In most facilities, the peak time for physicians is in the morning, before they go to their offices. Of course, not all open spaces should be used by second-shift employees, because some physicians stop by the facility after their office hours.

The fact that afternoon-shift personnel may return to their cars late at night presents special security vulnerabilities. For safety reasons, it is desirable that shift employees park together. Maximum security officer coverage in the parking lots is advisable during late night and early-morning shift changes.

Late-Night–Shift Employees

Late-night–shift employees have many places to park and, left to their own options, may create a fragmented parking configuration. There should be a designated area for these employees, which is typically as close as possible to the designated night entrance(s). By concentrating these employees and their vehicles into a specific area, a maximum amount of protection for both employees and vehicles can be provided.

AUTOMATED CONTROLS

An electronic, card-activated gate is considered to be cost-effective for parking areas with as few as 20 spaces. Automatic gates with a minicomputer offer many control features, including the ability to set time parameters for card use, to invalidate a card at the output unit, and to provide data on the attempted use of invalidated cards. In addition, some systems render cards invalid once they have been used to enter the parking area until they are used to exit. This feature, known as "anti-pass back," prevents one card from being used by several people. Card-activated gates are predominantly used at the entry and exit points of parking areas. This device can also be used within the parking area itself to reserve an area for valet parking, afternoon staff, or physicians, for example. In addition, the parking card can be used to provide entry to locked physician and staff facility entrances.

TRAFFIC FLOW AND SPACE ALLOCATION

In determining traffic flow and space allocation, the trend toward small vehicles is both an advantage and a disadvantage. When most vehicles were the same size, parking spaces could also be uniform. This limited the number of available spaces, but it made space allocation a rather simple matter. Today the size of the space needed for small vehicles and the width of the traffic aisles can be reduced. The problem is to determine how many spaces of each size are required at a given time for a particular parking lot or whether certain areas should be designated for all large cars and trucks or all small cars.

Not only are one-way traffic lanes with angled parking expedient, but they are also safer than straight, or 90-degree, parking. The difficulty of parking in a space angled at 90 degrees and the excessive size of the traffic lanes required generally make this type of design unsatisfactory.

During periods of low demand, it is recommended that certain parking lots, sections of lots, or parking structure floors be closed off. This improves the safety of people walking to or from their vehicles. Naturally, the closed areas should be those that are the greatest distance from the facility. The more concentrated the parking, the greater the number of people going to and from vehicles, which to some extent deters assaults, vandalism, and break-ins. In addition, by closing lots, the security patrol area is reduced, allowing a more concentrated preventive patrol.

PAY PARKING

Recent trends have favored pay parking at medical care facilities. Facilities that have charged visitors for some time have recently decided to charge everyone who parks in their lots. Visitors are generally the first to be charged parking fees, and physicians are generally the last.

When pay parking is the responsibility of the security department, security can be transformed from an overhead cost to an income-producing department. Some organizations completely fund their security operation from parking revenues. The outpatient and visitor parking areas produce the most revenue because of their high turnover.

The method of collecting parking fees should be closely examined. For employee parking, a monthly fee can be deducted from the payroll checks at relatively little cost. The visitor lots can be controlled by automatic equipment, which has a high initial cost but proves economical over a short period of time. The decision to use personnel to collect parking fees should be carefully evaluated because theft appears to be the rule rather than the exception. In addition, providing for accounting controls and backup personnel in case of absences proves much more costly than automatic equipment. When automatic equipment is used, stringent controls should be established regarding the collection of money from the machines, and these controls should be audited frequently.

PARKING SYSTEM VIOLATORS

Parking violators present a control problem. Fire lanes must be designated and patrolled to ensure that vehicles do not block the lanes, and lots must be checked to ensure compliance with the parking plan. Most security departments issue parking violation notices to help control non-conforming parking. Figures 19-1 and 19-2 are examples of parking

Parking Control and Security 483

✚ MISSION HOSPITAL
REGIONAL MEDICAL CENTER

PARKING/TRAFFIC VIOLATION

✓	VIOLATION	✓	LOCATION
	1. Decal Not Displayed		Emergency Room Patients Only
	2. Vehicle Leaking Fluids		Physician Parking Only
	3. Tailgating Observed		Patient Unloading Only
	4. Failure to Park In Marked Stall		Lot # 1 Surface Lot
	5. Subject to Towing		Lot # 2 Surface Lot
	6. Subject to Fire/Police Citation		Lot # 3 Surface Lot
	7. Parking Prohibited:		Lot # 4 Surface Lot
	a. Patient/Visitor Parking		Lot # 5 MOBs – Rear
	b. Emergency Parking		Lot # 6 Short Term Lot
	c. Handicapped Parking		Lot # 7 Emergency Room Area
	d. Clergy Parking		Lot # 8 Pavilian – North
	e. Physician Parking		Lot # 9 Crown Valley Lot
	f. MHRMC Vehicles Only		Lot # 10 Medical Tower – West
	g. Fire Zone/Hydrant		Lot # 11 Medical Tower
	h. Driveway		Lot # 12 Surgi Center Area
	i. Rideshare/Carpool		Parking Structure – Level # ____
	j. Over 6 Ft. High Vehicles		Other:
	k. Other:		
	8. Speeding – 5 MPH Limit		
	9. Careless Driving		
	10. Driving Wrong Way		– ALWAYS USE SEAT BELTS –
	11. Other:		– PLEASE DRIVE CAREFULLY –

MAKE OF VEHICLE / MODEL	COLOR	LICENSE NUMBER	STATE
PARKING DECAL NUMBER	DATE	TIME	ISSUED BY
VIOLATOR'S NAME	EXTENSION	DEPARTMENT	CAR MOVED? YES NO

THE ABOVE VIOLATION HAS BEEN RECORDED AND DISCIPLINARY ACTION MAY RESULT IF FURTHER VIOLATIONS ARE NOTED.

SAFETY & SECURITY SERVICES: (714) 364-4288

FORM #SS-01   WHITE–VIOLATOR   CANARY–SECURITY   PINK–DIRECTOR/VP

Figure 19-1 An Example of a Parking Violation Notice (Courtesy of Mission Hospital Regional Medical Center, Mission Viejo, CA)

PARKING VIOLATION

WELLSTAR HEALTH SYSTEM
Security Services
(770) 793-7777

№ 8751

Notice: This vehicle is improperly parked for the following reason(s):

- ☐ Vehicle has NO VALID PARKING PERMIT
- ☐ Parked in DISABLED PERSONS' space/area
- ☐ Parked in NO PARKING space/area
- ☐ Parked in RESERVED or DESIGNATED space/area
- ☐ Parked in 2 SPACES
- ☐ Blocking driveway or access
- ☐ _____

_____

Location: _____

This vehicle's description has been PERMANENTLY RECORDED. Failure to conform to our regulations may result in towing and storage at DRIVER'S EXPENSE and REVOCATION OF PARKING PRIVILEGES.

PARKING PERMIT NO.	Other I.D.	
VEHICLE MAKE/MODEL		Apprx. Year
Vehicle Color(s)	Lic. Tag No.	State
Driver's Name (if known)		

Date Issued   Time   By

Form PV-224   •   PEACHTREE   1-800-241-4623

Figure 19-2 An Example of a Parking/Traffic Violation Notice (Courtesy of Wellstar Health System, Marietta, GA)

violation notices. Various other methods of increasing severity may be necessary to correct abuses. These methods include city parking tickets, immobilization devices, and towing. The immobilization device, sometimes known as the "boot," has proved effective in many programs. It forces the violator to report as directed, and thus the organization can exert a high degree of control. Towing is always the last resort but is an effective mechanism to gain compliance.

Warning letters and follow-up by department supervisors are common procedures for dealing with employee violators. In one system, the first violation earns the employee a warning notice, and subsequent violations result in successively higher fines, which are collected through automatic payroll deductions. This system works; however, strong administrative support is required to implement this type of program or any other control program that successfully meets its objectives.

COMPUTERS AND PARKING CONTROL

The use of computers is becoming commonplace in the administration of parking control systems. Software programs are readily available that permit tracking of parking violations and efficient issuing and control of parking permits. Once the database of information is established, the various programs allow a multitude of search capabilities. In addition to helping manage the day-to-day program, the computer allows the periodic production of activity and planning reports.

REFERENCES

1. Tryst M. Anderson, "Park Place: Facility Parking Can Be as Tricky as a Board Game," *Health Facilities Management*, April 1998, p. 32.

2. Catherine Quayle, "Space Odyssey," *Health Facilities Management*, June 1996, p. 30.

3. Richard A. Rich and David W. Burr, "A Plan for Parking," *Health Facilities Management*, April 1997, p. 28.

4. Jeremy Travis, "Crime Prevention Through Environmental Design in Parking Facilities," National Institute of Justice, Research in Brief, April 1996.

CHAPTER 20

Emergency Planning and Operations

Protecting the healthcare environment from a variety of emergency conditions takes a good deal of foresight and extensive planning. While some of these situations are intentionally created by people, others result from unintentional accidents and still others are weather related. Each and every day a facility somewhere is reacting to an emergency.

Emergencies can be divided into internal and external situations. Regardless of the nature of the emergency, the organizational response will be quite different when the emergency condition exists within the facility from when it occurs at some distant location.

The actual emergency response programs of healthcare facilities indicate that much more effort has gone into a prepared response to external emergencies than to internal ones. Exceptions can be found in the areas of fire safety and bomb threat programs, in which various regulatory and accrediting agencies have considerable involvement.

A complete list of situations that require emergency planning is difficult to compile; however, the situations listed in Table 20-1 should receive consideration, depending on the geographical location and type of facility.

The media and healthcare management journals have reported case histories for all of these situations. In reviewing the list of potential emergencies, security practitioners should divide these situations into two categories: those that are most likely to occur and those in which the protection system will be involved most extensively.

Security activity at the facility will be fairly standard if the emergency occurs away from the facility; that is, involvement will be in the general areas of traffic control (people and vehicles), information dissemination, and the procurement of supplies and equipment. The security response will primarily be a support role. A different involvement is indicated when the emergency occurs within or in the immediate area of the hospital.

Table 20-1 Situations Requiring Emergency Planning

Man Made	Accidental	Weather
Bombs	Fires	Earthquakes
Strikes/Pickets	Hazardous Materials	Hurricanes
Arson	Construction	Snowstorms
Civil Disturbances	Utilities Failures	Tornadoes

As a general rule, the plan for security response to any emergency should be based on everyday security routines and organizational resources. In other words, handling emergency protection needs should be viewed as an extension or expansion of regular security activity. When facilities develop complex emergency plans that differ from the routine handling of patients, confusion and inefficiency might result when the plan is activated.

A case in point is the casualty receiving area. If this activity is moved from its normal location to another, supplies and equipment must be moved, and police officers, firefighters, ambulance drivers, and facility personnel must be reoriented to respond to a new and perhaps unfamiliar location. The protection management problems also become more complex and unnecessarily burdensome.

Emergency planning in most medical care organizations is accomplished by committees. Because all departments and sections will be involved in emergency situations to varying degrees, the committee must be composed of representatives of all operating departments of the organization.

Regardless of how the committee is organized, the task is to assemble the organization's resources into a workable emergency response plan. The key to a successfully implemented plan is simplicity. This point cannot be overemphasized. The complexity and detail of some plans have proved inefficient and unworkable in actual disaster situations.

Security administrators must analyze every emergency that could possibly affect their healthcare facilities and formulate security plans within the broader organizational plan. No step-by-step answers can be given; every facility must consider its own situation. General guidelines and considerations are offered only to stimulate organizations in developing their emergency protection programming in compliance with the

Joint Commission on Accreditation of Healthcare Organizations (JCAHO) standards, if applicable.

The various plans for each type of emergency should not be independent. Great care must be taken to develop standard procedures that can apply to each emergency situation. Consider, for example, the evacuation of patients. As nearly as possible, the same evacuation method and routes should be used in response to a fire as in response to a bomb threat.

COMMON EMERGENCY CODES

Standardized code words for various emergencies are needed. Healthcare organizations use color codes, number codes, word codes, and a combination of these to announce emergency situations to staff. Most codes consist of a primary word and a secondary word, such as Doctor Red or Code Blue.

If all facilities used common codes, misunderstandings and training time would be reduced, and emergency response would be more efficient. James Hanna, an emergency response consultant in Ontario, Canada, spent years studying the use of emergency codes in hospitals.[1] He concluded that color codes were more desirable than number codes because numbers require strict memorization, and they have no real relationship to the crisis. On the other hand, colors can be related to the type of emergency.

The Ontario Hospital Association has adopted a standardized color code system developed by Hanna for disaster and emergency planning, as shown in Table 20-2.

MUTUAL AID

Planning for any type of emergency, whether internal or external, requires close liaison with other medical care facilities in the community. The security administrators of nearby facilities hospitals should meet regularly for planning purposes. An important consideration in mutual aid planning is to join with organizations that are not likely to be involved in the same emergency at the same time.

Table 20-2 Common Color Codes for Designated Healthcare Emergency Situations (Courtesy of Ontario Hospital Association, Canada)

Incident Type	Code	Color Rationale
Fire	RED	Color of fire
Cardiac Arrest	BLUE	Patient in arrest will be cyanotic (blue-tinged skin)
Disaster (patient influx)	ORANGE	International ambulance color
Evacuation (precaution)	GREEN	Green (light) has always been color for "go ahead"
Evacuation (crisis)	GREEN-STAT	Green (light) has always been color for "go ahead"
Missing Patient	YELLOW	Used in some hospitals/not commonly used for other purposes
Bomb Threat/Search	BLACK	Color of charred material from an explosion
Violent Patient	WHITE	Color of some restraints

Resources of one facility should be readily available for use in another facility. The planned exchange of resources—whether security officers, vehicles, cameras, et cetera—should be organized, and each organization should sign a formal statement of commitment.

FIRE PREVENTION AND CONTROL

Fires in medical care facilities make up many of the fires in the U.S. Some 10 percent of healthcare facilities have suffered a fire loss at some time in their history. Although this is a much lower rate than that of industry, hospital fires can mean the loss of human life as well as financial loss.

The term "fire prevention" refers to the everyday activities that eliminate hazards and prepare people to react properly should a fire actually occur. In this discussion, the term "fire control" pertains to the basic organizational reaction to an actual fire.

The fire protection problems experienced by medical care facilities essentially relate to fuel loading and occupant loading. "Fuel loading" refers to the degree of combustibility of the contents of a building. "Occupant loading" refers to the number and the ambulatory ability of people within the facility. Patients often range from those who can move freely without help to those who cannot be moved without life-support equipment. Also, infants, children, psychiatric patients, and the elderly present unique requirements that must be considered in the fire plan.

The elderly, especially those in nursing homes, are a particular concern. More than eight fires a day occur in nursing homes across the U.S., and each threatens the lives of the residents. More deaths occur each year in facilities that care for the aged than in all other healthcare facilities combined. Not only are these facilities minimally staffed, but also most of the elderly must be assisted during evacuation. The aged are generally slower to react to emergencies, and they often react unpredictably. An additional complication is that the products of combustion, even in small quantities, are often more fatal to older people.

Fire Safety Programming

A fire safety program can be viewed as five basic elements: (1) prevention, (2) detection, (3) containment, (4) evacuation, and (5) extinguishment. These elements chronologically define organizational response to a fire threat. The National Fire Protection Association document NFPA 101 refers to a fire protection program as the "Total Concept Approach." Such a program consists of construction, detection/suppression, and staff presence.

Fire Prevention

Prevention encompasses the activities of the fire safety program that occur before an actual fire, including the identification and correction of fire hazards, fire control planning, employee and occupant education, design and specifications, equipment tests, drills, and fire department liaison. Absolute fire safety is unattainable because it is impossible to exclude from the facility everything that burns and all sources of ignition. The level of safety is a balance between the ideal and that which is reasonable within economic and operating limitations.

Facility inspections are conducted by all kinds of inspectors, including representatives of insurance companies, Medicare/Medicaid, JCAHO, city building departments, state and city health departments, and fire department personnel. Some of the best inspections, however, are those conducted by organizational personnel. If they are conducted properly, a continuous, everyday fire inspection program is accomplished.

Security officers on their rounds should note and correct hazards to the extent feasible every day. Security officers on rounds should be particularly alert for people smoking in prohibited areas. Officers should correct and report doors left open that should be closed, obstructions to egress paths, careless use of oxygen cylinders, and other fire safety violations. If a hazard cannot be corrected on the spot, officers can, through proper reporting, initiate administrative action.

According to Robert Solomon, PE, Chief Building Fire Protection Engineer, National Fire Protection Association, the leading cause of fire in healthcare facilities is smoking and smoking materials. A case in point was the Petersburg VA Hospital fire in late 1994. This fire broke out in a patient's room and intensified briefly when fed by oxygen released from the hospital's piped oxygen distribution system. Smoke spread into the corridor and other patient rooms due to an open door in the room of fire origin and because the walls between patient rooms were not continuous from the floor to the underside of the floor above. This fire, resulting in the death of five patients, was caused by the improper use of smoking materials.[2]

Detection

Automatic early-warning smoke detection systems are typical in many facilities since regional and national codes often require this equipment for hospitals. In many healthcare facilities, detection equipment transmits a signal directly to the fire department, while at the same time alerting hospital personnel. In some cases, however, the alarm is only sounded in the hospital because some municipal services are not capable of providing a direct connection to the fire department or emergency dispatch center.

Smoke detectors use sensing units that respond to the presence of products of combustion that result from a fire. Other types of detectors may respond to heat or flame. When the threshold is exceeded, the sensor is activated. Most hospital fire detection systems use a combination of devices due to the varied situations the medical care environment presents. When the detector senses an abnormal condition, it transmits a signal to an annunciator. This signal may also control various items of equipment;

it may activate fire extinguishing equipment and air-handling machinery, send elevators to predetermined locations, and release magnetic hold-open devices on doors. These functions are also used to initiate human response and subsequent staff action.

Containment

The third element of the fire safety program is containing smoke and fire. The objective is to contain the fire in the room of origin. When this is not possible, the goal is to provide successive levels of defense or areas of refuge from the fire. The five basic areas of fire containment are often referred to as the "unit concept." The units are the room, the compartment, the floor, the building, and the exits, all of which have a distinct function in the fire protection features of the building.

- **Unit 1.** The room—the smallest unit—is the first line of defense. The function of Unit 1 is to provide the first barrier against the passage of smoke. The more effectively a room can be sealed, the better job it will do in containing fires.

- **Unit 2.** The compartment is the second level of defense. The intention is to provide at least two areas of refuge on every horizontal plane of the hospital. When an area must be evacuated, the initial movement is horizontal rather than vertical. The Unit 2 compartment is created by smoke and barrier walls.

- **Unit 3.** The floor, or floor assembly, is the next level of containment. The function of the floor assembly is to prevent the spread of fire and smoke from one floor to another.

- **Unit 4.** The building is the fourth level of protection. For the building to remain structurally intact for a period of time, it should maintain structural components that offer minimum contribution to any fuel load and that can withstand the effects of a fire within the facility.

- **Unit 5.** The exit path is the final unit in this concept of fire protection. At least two remote exits must be provided on each floor or fire section of the building. Two separate means of exit should be visible from any location in the corridor. Exits need not necessarily lead directly to the outside. They can include egress to interior stairs, exterior stairs, horizontal exits, ramps, and exit passageways.

Fire containment can also limit the air needed to sustain combustion. The heat and smoke from a fire generally rises as a result of the buoyancy created by the heated gases. The smoke and heat will also seek out a path to the outside air. If it cannot continue to rise, the smoke and heat will descend back to the floor level. If there is any air in the room that is breathable, it will be found closest to the floor. When a fire is contained, extreme caution must be taken when entering the area because opening the door may provide the combustion air or a ventilation path the fire is seeking.

Evacuation (Relocation)

The fourth component of the hospital fire safety plan is relocation of patients, visitors, and staff. The Life Safety Code—through its standards for exit capacities, types of exits, travel distance, door specifications, and similar details—ensures the necessary means of egress from a medical care facility during an emergency. It is the healthcare staff, however, who are responsible for moving any patients who are in imminent danger to a safe location. In hospitals, many occupants are incapable of self-preservation. This fact is recognized by the Life Safety Code, which places the main responsibility for patient safety on the healthcare facility staff.
Total building evacuation, as a measure of last resort, can and does occur in rare instances. Patient relocation between smoke-protected compartments on the same floor is usually an adequate first step. The typical scenario involves the horizontal relocation of some patients. Following the unit concept principle, the evacuation plan's first objective is to move patients to a safe compartment on the same floor. At this point, it must be determined whether to continue horizontal evacuation or whether vertical movement (to another floor) is necessary for relocating patients.
Wheelchairs and carts are useful and often necessary for relocating patients, but they may not always be available at the time and place of need. Blankets are always available, and security professionals generally agree that they can be the most important pieces of equipment on

hand for evacuation. If necessary, blankets can be used by one person to drag a patient. When two carriers are available, the blanket can be used as an improvised stretcher.

Elevators should receive special consideration in the fire evacuation plan. Generally, plans prohibit the use of elevators for egress or relocation purposes because of their recall features, which are normally activated in a fire condition. An elevator may stop at the wrong floor, exposing its occupants to the fire. On the other hand, high-rise hospitals present unique problems that may require the use of elevators for vertical relocation under controlled conditions. In addition, the fire department may need to utilize the elevator to bring hoses, fans, and other equipment to the fire.

For the purpose of this discussion, any hospital of more than seven stories is considered a high-rise. Seven stories is generally the limit of most fire department ladders, and even this height is not always reachable by ladder. A vertical evacuation plan is mandatory for high-rise buildings. One or more elevators in a wing removed from the fire area may be used to transport patients to another floor much more quickly and with fewer possible medical complications than when patients are carried down a stairwell. Although the use of elevators should not be written into the fire plan, the person in charge of the fire situation should consider their utilization.

Extinguishment

The last element of the hospital fire safety program is extinguishing the fire. The suppression of fire is achieved either manually or by automatic suppression systems required for all new construction. The automatic sprinkler system is the most common of the automatic suppression devices. The automatic sprinkler system also acts as an alarm device because all systems are installed with water-flow sensors that activate an alarm when water is flowing in the pipes. The sprinkler is activated by a thermally sensitive element (solder type or glass bulb) that automatically releases at a pre-determined temperature. Sprinkler systems used in hospitals are typically wet-pipe systems rather than dry-pipe systems. Other piped extinguishing systems include water spray, foam, carbon dioxide, dry chemical, Halon agents, and newer, environmentally sensitive, clean agents.

The standpipe and hose system, found in most U.S. medical care facilities, is used to provide quick and convenient water streams. This system is most generally used by fire department or trained fire brigade personnel. It is not uncommon to eliminate the hose at the valve locations. The rationale for this is that most fire departments supply their own hose. Further, there have been reports of vandalism by opening the valve a little, allowing the hose in the cabinet to fill slowly with water.

The hand-held extinguishers used in medical care facilities are primarily two-and-one-half gallon, stored-pressure water extinguishers, carbon dioxide extinguishers, multipurpose (ABC) extinguishers, and Halon extinguishers. The type at any given location is predicated on the primary type of hazard involved.

Employee Reaction

Proper employee reaction to a fire is one of the fundamental factors in saving lives and property. Fire safety is a race against time, and the action taken within the first few minutes can make the difference between a minor fire threat and a tragic disaster.

Because employees must act almost instinctively when fire breaks out, detailed instructions are seldom remembered. The following simple steps, expressed through an easily remembered acronym, are widely used in healthcare facilities:

R *Rescue* those in danger.
A *Activate* the alarm.
C *Contain* the smoke and fire.
E *Evacuate* and *extinguish*.

To execute these steps properly, personnel must receive continuous in-service training. The more training personnel receive, the better the chances that they will react correctly under extreme stress.

Fire Safety Training

Planning for a fire emergency requires the cooperation and understanding of every employee in the facility. Any employee could be the one who discovers a fire or who is the first to arrive at the scene of an alarm.

The high rate of personnel turnover in medical care facilities and the difficulty of retaining procedures that are not used routinely require continuous in-service and new employee training classes.

The methods of training personnel are limited only by the trainer's imagination. Typical and essential methods include training sessions where employees handle patients and discharge a fire extinguisher. Supplementing this training are posters, contests, in-service training, and fire drills.

One of the obstacles faced in fire safety training is that little uniformity exists among facility fire plans. Because of the transient characteristic of medical care personnel, an individual could work at many different facilities within a very short period of time. Hence, fire safety training may require relearning as well as learning. Organizations and facilities all have unique characteristics that require special fire planning; however, especially within a given locality, common fire plan components among facilities would reduce training time.

Basic Security Considerations

Security's role in a fire situation is part of the overall facility fire plan.

- Ensuring that responding fire department personnel gain access to the facility complex, buildings, and internal areas. This may require unlocking gates or doors, holding elevators, turning on lights, and even escorting fire personnel to the fire area.

- Controlling traffic, including vehicular traffic and people on the perimeter of the fire scene as well as the emergency operations areas.

- Assisting with the evacuation process if necessary.

- Assisting emergency personnel throughout the emergency.

- Securing the area after the conclusion of the incident. A fire watch may be required for some time after the fire has been put out. There have been many cases of re-ignition even days later.

- Preparing good documentation of the fire incident.

An important consideration of proactive security involvement concerning fire planning is fire department liaison. Security must be actively involved with the fire department; the more firefighters know about the facility, the better they can respond. Likewise, the more security personnel know about the fire department's response, the better they can assist.

Another consideration is security officer training. This training goes far beyond the general employee fire training discussed earlier. Security officers are not only the first to respond in many cases; they are the only ones to respond in small facilities. The action they take or do not take in the first minutes bears directly on the outcome. Their initial concerns involve sizing up the situation for personal safety, sounding an alarm, containment, and controlling the fire.

Beyond these basics, there may be evidence that should be protected or conversations that should be noted and retained, which may later answer some questions. Arson does happen in medical care facilities. Security officers must notice if someone has an unnatural or unusual interest in the fire. In short, security officers may be exposed to much information in the initial moments of a fire—information that must not go unnoticed or it will be lost forever.

NATURAL DISASTERS

Natural disasters, such as snowstorms, tornadoes, floods, hurricanes, and earthquakes, frequently activate facility emergency plans. All of these severe natural phenomena will affect healthcare operations to varying degrees. The concomitant problems generally involve failure of the electrical system, interruption of deliveries, lack of communications, increased demand for medical treatment, and the isolation of the facility. Fortunately, facilities are not always hit directly by these disastrous occurrences, and they can continue to serve the community's needs with minimal interruption of normal services if proper planning has been completed.

Many disaster events occurred in the 1990s that put healthcare delivery systems to the test. The more major events included:[3]

- **The 1993 World Trade Center bombing in New York.** The total number of injured is not known; however, over 450 patients were transported to hospitals by more than 150 ambulances that responded.

- **The 1994 Los Angeles earthquake.** As a result of this 6.8 magnitude earthquake, 30 people were killed and some 11,500 patients were treated for quake-related injuries.

- **Hurricane Andrew in August 1992.** Striking the coast of Florida with winds over 215 miles per hour, this hurricane had a devastating effect on over 330 square miles of land. The total destruction of property and the actual number of displaced, injured, and dead persons may never be known. The storm also damaged over 100 healthcare facilities.

- **The 1995 Hanshin earthquake in Kobe, Japan.** This earthquake lasted only 20 seconds, but killed 5,300 people and injured some 27,000 more.

- **The 1989 Loma Prieta earthquake in San Francisco.** This earthquake measured 7.1 on the Richter scale, killed 67 people, injured 4,100 others, and caused more than $7 billion in damage. Hospital operations suffered during the turmoil, facilities sustained physical damage, and some patient evacuation was necessary. Miraculously, there were no significant injuries to hospital patients.

Robert Ross, an independent consultant, is an expert on earthquake preparedness. He reviewed the experiences of several San Francisco area hospitals during the 1989 quake and found various problems:

- As many as 15 percent of hospital employees abandoned their jobs to go home to check on their families

- There were various communications deficiencies

- Hospitals experienced difficulty in calling in off-duty employees

- There was trouble transferring trucked water into hospital water systems

Ross notes that West Coast hospitals have prepared for earthquake; hospitals in other parts of the country that are also subject to earthquakes have not. For example, in the Midwest, the New Madrid fault poses a serious threat.

In many cases of severe weather conditions, handling of mass casualties is not required. The focus is on other problems, such as providing housing for employees who cannot leave; finding temporary shelter for people who have been stranded; maintaining supplies, including food; and transporting essential personnel from their homes to the hospital. When a facility operates under emergency conditions as a result of a community disaster, a unique phenomenon is readily apparent. Everyone pitches in to do practically anything required. The petty jealousies and animosities of the everyday routine quickly disappear. Even student nurses who are normally restricted in day-to-day activities are given more latitude to do the things that need to be done. The distinct feeling of camaraderie and singleness of purpose generally result in excellent patient care.

This phenomenon is not unique to the personnel employed by the facility; it extends to the community as well. Experience has indicated that medical care organizations can expect many calls from people in the community offering their assistance. During a severe snowstorm that shut down all vehicular traffic in a large city for two days, a judge was observed feeding a hospital patient while an airline pilot helped mop the floor. Both were nearby residents who were able to walk to the hospital.

Disaster Drills (Emergency Preparedness)

The disaster drill is required by the JCAHO. Every accredited facility must conduct drills and prepare a written report evaluating each drill. People who have been assigned to observe specific aspects of the plan must meet after the drill to determine the plan's effectiveness. It is generally agreed that observers should be people from outside the organization when possible.

They traditionally come from state agencies, offices of emergency preparedness, medical societies, or other medical care facilities.

Drills serve a very important purpose, and they must be conducted with all the realism possible. It is extremely difficult, however, to rehearse certain parts of a disaster plan when the facility is open and conducting routine everyday business. One of the most difficult elements to practice is traffic control. It is not practical to restrict visiting or to turn away patients who have an appointment. Physicians and the community will not accept the curtailment of normal activities for a drill.

Handling Mass Casualties

"Disaster planning" and "control," as these terms are used in most medical care facilities, generally refer to the handling of the mass casualties that result from a community disaster. The disaster plan of a medical facility should contain the following:

- An efficient system of notifying and assigning personnel.

- A unified medical command.

- An availability of adequate basic utilities and supplies, as well as essential medical and supportive materials. Hospitals should be essentially self-sustaining in these areas for a minimum of one week.

- A method of identifying patients who are immediately dischargeable or transferable and providing for their expeditious transportation.

- The conversion of all usable space to provide adequate triage, observation, and treatment areas.

- The prompt transfer of patients, when necessary, to the facility most appropriate for rendering definitive care, in accordance with any regional plan in operation.

- The use of a special disaster medical record or medical tag that accompanies the patient at all times and contains specific required information.

- The establishment of a centralized public information center with a designated spokesperson.

- Security, to minimize the presence of unauthorized individuals and vehicles in or near the triage, observation, and immediate care areas.

- A pre-established radio communication system for use when telephone communications are out or overtaxed. Cellular phones, once thought to be an answer, have simply not worked well due to systems overload.

- Instructions on the use of elevators.

The Incident Command System (ICS) has been utilized by public safety agencies for many years. Only recently, has this term "caught on" in the healthcare environment relative to managing emergency situations. In short, the concept of ICS is for a timely, structured, and focused direction of effort/activity relative to the reaction to an emergency condition. A predictable chain of management and defined authority is a key element of this concept. Other elements include common nomenclature between hospital staff and public safety responders, clear reporting channels, and defined responsibility. The ICS concept is referenced by the National Fire Protection Association and the JCAHO.

The major responsibility of the security system is to maintain order and control traffic. As simple and straightforward as this responsibility appears to be, it is a monumental task. The decision to restrict visiting and to deny certain people access to given areas is a decision to be made at the highest management level.

The most common method of traffic control is to lock perimeter doors to channel people in and out of a limited number of controlled points. The seriousness of the situation dictates the degree of control required. Signs should be prepared that indicate the emergency situation and direct those seeking entry to a specific control point.

People seeking information about the injured should be directed to an external door that leads into an easily controlled area. In some cases it is possible to use another building for this purpose. In any event, people seeking information should be completely segregated from the patient treatment areas. This procedure obviously requires a timely flow of information from the treatment area to the information center. Not only will family and friends seek information, but also the news media will insist on information. Although beyond the realm of protection services, the security operation should use all of its influence to see that information to the news media is planned in detail. This planning can help eliminate needless confrontation between security and media personnel, which often generates bad feelings on both sides.

Planning for disasters and other emergencies is an ongoing exercise. Learning from others through case histories or direct interaction with those responsible will help an organization refine its plan.

BOMBS AND BOMB THREATS

Bomb threats are a reality for medical care organizations. Although the number of threats has decreased over previous years, a significant number still occur. One of the unique features of the bomb threat is the guessing game it forces the threatened organization to play. Is it real or is it a hoax? Where do we search? Is evacuation necessary? These basic questions become the framework of the organizational plan. The plan must be flexible to the degree that the information received can be applied to these questions at the time of the crisis.

A bomb can be described as any explosive, incendiary, or gas-filled container. Many chemicals can be used to make a bomb, and most chemicals are easily obtainable. Dynamite can be purchased or stolen from construction sites. Ammonium nitrate is sold in stores that handle fertilizers. Potassium nitrate and black powder can be bought at shops that supply chemists or hunters. The most commonly used explosive is commercial dynamite. It is normally exploded using another exploding charge, most commonly called blasting caps.

Pipe bombs are commonly used by amateur bombers. These bombs are made from an ordinary pipe capped on both ends and filled generally with black powder. They are set off using a device similar to that used to detonate dynamite. When a fuse is used, the explosive cap is not needed. Open dynamite bombs are quite common due to their simple construction.

The Bomb Threat Plan

All healthcare facilities should have a written bomb threat plan. Each plan is unique to the specific facility; however, the basic steps of bomb threat programming can be categorized as follows: (1) prevention, (2) establishing authority, (3) receiving the threat, (4) searching for the bomb, (5) evacuating the building, (6) terminating the emergency, and (7) documenting the threat.

Prevention

The first area of concern is the preventive steps that can be taken against the bomb situation. These steps are the same security safeguards that should be in everyday use to protect the organization against its other security vulnerabilities. In other words, the proper functioning of the day-to-day protection system is the first line of defense against a threat. To be more specific, locking equipment rooms, switchboard rooms, utility closets, storage areas, and the like can help reduce the problem. Limited access, access controls, noting suspicious people and vehicles, and providing emergency equipment are all part of the everyday protection system.

Establishing Authority

One of the most important aspects of properly managing a bomb threat is to specifically establish organizational authority. As basic as this point seems, it is a fundamental deficiency of many healthcare institutions. Authority and responsibility for handling the crisis must be designated to a position that is readily available 24 hours a day. Logical choices would be the nursing supervisor, the house officer, or the security shift supervisor. The various field resources brought into play during this type of emergency must know to whom to report information. Authoritative answers to questions must be immediately rendered. This does not mean that a person of higher authority will not be called in later to take charge.

Receiving the Threat

The bomb threat can be received in numerous ways. The most common method is by telephone, and the most common recipient of such information is the telephone operator. When a threatening call is received, security's major objective is to obtain all of the information possible from the caller. Telephone operators and others who are likely to receive these calls should be trained to keep the caller talking as long as possible and to ask key questions, such as where the bomb is, when it will go off, why it was placed, what kind of bomb it is, and other questions that may keep the caller on the line. The person who receives the call should make notes or activate a recording device.

Some organizations receive bomb threat calls so frequently that the operator automatically reaches for a prepared bomb threat information form. Most organizations have such a form, which can be a valuable tool for obtaining and recording the necessary information.

Searching for the Bomb

The bomb threat information received must be communicated to the designated authority within the organization, who in turn initiates the notification system. The first step in the notification procedure must always be to notify the appropriate law enforcement authority. In most cases, the law enforcement authority and facility management will decide jointly the type of search required, based on the known facts. It is not practical or possible to conduct an all-out search in every case. An all-out search includes everything from checking every patient's belongings to removing all suspended ceiling tiles and all ventilation grille work. It could take at least a day or two to completely search a facility, considering all the places a bomb could be placed. It is presumed that people who carry bombs are well aware of the danger of premature detonation, and therefore in most cases they will want to get into the facility quickly and to get out even more quickly—precluding an elaborate hiding process.

If sufficient organizational personnel are available, the search should be conducted by employees rather than by the police or fire department. The proper role of the outside support agencies is to assume control if a bomb or suspected bomb is located.

Employees are used to conduct the search for two basic reasons. First, employees are in the best position to know what belongs and what does not belong in a given area. Employees are more knowledgeable of the layout of the facility and either have the capability to enter locked or controlled areas or know how to obtain access. This familiarity makes it possible for employees to conduct a better and faster search than outside personnel.

Second, using in-house personnel to search avoids unnecessary confusion and minimizes disruption. Patients do not need a police officer, or a security officer, searching their room at 2:00 A.M. The search can be emotionally upsetting, and the reaction could very easily be panic. Many experts believe that bomb threat callers are frequently interested in stirring up as much activity and causing as much disruption as possible. Thus, one objective of a bomb search is to carry out the search in a smooth, routine manner, while taking every threat seriously.

In bomb threat situations, the administrative person handling the threat decides to advise only selected employees and patients. In general, patients should not be told of the problem unless absolutely necessary. Experience has shown that patients often set off a chain reaction that is detrimental to the entire process. Many patients respond by calling their families. In turn, the family may decide to come to the facility or call the facility for detailed information. This reaction can tie up needed communications lines and hinder response capabilities.

Whether the search is full or partial, areas of responsibility must be assigned. In some plans, the search personnel are assembled as a group so that the search coordinator can relate to them the information received and assign specific areas to specific personnel. In other plans, this information is communicated by telephone or through a public address system with a code term such as "Mr. Search" or "Code Black."

A problem that must be taken into consideration is the staffing pattern of the facility. When all departments are fully operational, the facility can be more easily and quickly searched than when departments are closed and locked. During the non-operational period, security, maintenance, and environmental services personnel may be assigned an expanded role in the search effort.

Floor plans that have been divided into specific search areas are used in some facilities. Personnel are given a map of the area for which they are responsible. In other organizations, these assignments are made from an administrative checklist that defines the areas. However the parameters of the search are defined, the person responsible for searching a given area must always report back to the control center when the search has been completed.

A complete search of the entire facility may be impractical or even impossible at certain times. The main concern is for personal safety rather than property. Thus, a threat at 11:30 P.M., when a minimal staff is on duty, may preclude searching all areas. It is suggested that closed areas such as food service, business and accounting areas, administrative offices, maintenance shops, medical record areas, and the like receive only cursory examination. The occupied areas of the facility should be searched more thoroughly.

Some controversy exists over the use of two-way radios during a bomb search. It has been suggested that radios should not be used because a bomb might be constructed to detonate in response to the transmission of radio signals. However, most experts believe that this possibility is extremely remote. In almost all situations, the radio system is active before the bomb threat was received and would have already detonated the device. The benefits of two-way radios during emergency operations support their use unless specific information is received to the contrary.

Evacuating the Building

If the search produces a bomb or a suspected bomb, the cooperative efforts of security and law enforcement agencies come into play. There are all kinds of guidelines for handling a suspected bomb. Because facility employees should never touch a suspected bomb, these considerations are not applicable to this discussion. The investigation and removal of any suspect object is the responsibility of the public safety agency.

Security's basic function is to seal off the area and to commence evacuation if necessary. The decision to evacuate rests with the administrative authority working in cooperation with the law enforcement agency involved.

The evacuation of employees from a given work area presents no serious problems. Any plan for evacuating patients, however, must take into consideration the magnitude of the problems involved in moving the helpless and the seriously ill and the medical complications that may result.

The extent of the evacuation is another decision that must be made on the spot and based on the specific situation. A safe distance for evacuation is generally considered to be a 200-foot radius from the suspected object, including the floors immediately above and below. Windows and doors in the vicinity should be opened, if possible, to allow some of the force of the explosion to escape should the device detonate.

Terminating the Emergency

An important part of the organizational reaction to the bomb threat is the decision that the threat has ended. All people who were notified of the receipt of the threat should also be officially informed that the organization is resuming normal operations. In other words, the activity generated by the threat should not simply be allowed to trail off. The ending should be officially declared.

After the threat is over, environmental services, maintenance, and security departments should brief the next shift of employees in their respective departments. In the normal course of their activities, these employees may observe something of importance that was overlooked during the earlier "official search."

Documenting the Threat

The last step in bomb threat procedure is to document the incident for future reference. This task is usually assumed by the security department. Regardless of who prepares the report, it is the responsibility of the person in charge of the threat incident to make certain that this important task is completed.

The security report generally focuses on recording the facts of the situation. An additional administrative report that critiques the bomb threat response may be appropriate. The analysis may reveal deficiencies that require plan modification or further employee education.

Not all bomb threats concern a bomb that has already been planted. Some facilities report threats indicating that a bomb "would be" placed in the facility. When this occurs, access controls must be tightened, and the organization must decide whether to examine property being brought into the facility.

STRIKES AND PICKETING

A real test of a facility's protection plan comes when the facility faces a strike or picketing situation. A *strike* occurs when some of the organization's employees, represented by one or more unions, refuse to work as a protest against a serious grievance or a failure to negotiate a mutually acceptable contract. *Picketing* refers to the placement of people around the exterior of the facility for the dual purposes of informing the public of alleged problems and curtailing deliveries of supplies and equipment. This discussion is restricted to strikes and picketing related to organized labor.

The primary purpose of a strike is to create hardships for the organizations, weaken its bargaining position, and resolve the dispute in favor of the union. The hardships may include disruption of patient care, intimidation of non-striking staff, loss of revenue, damaged or stolen property, negative community reaction toward the facility, and injury to persons.

An organization need not be unionized to become the focus of a picket line. Picketing may be set up as a result of a strike or for the purpose of attempting to force the organization to recognize a collective bargaining unit. The immediate effect of a picket line is that union drivers will refuse to cross the line to make deliveries. In the initial stages, nonunion drivers will often cross the picket line until threats are made or physical violence is directed against the company, the vehicle, or the driver.

National Labor Relations Act

Before August 1974, not-for-profit hospitals were excluded from the National Labor Relations Act (Taft-Hartley Law). This act covers the broad area of collective bargaining and subjects organizations to huge and complex volumes of law. Organizations in certain states had already been subject to state laws that governed collective bargaining. Investor-owned hospitals and nursing homes were previously covered under law, and the 1974 amendments to the act had little, if any, effect on them. Federal, state, county, and municipal hospitals are excluded from coverage under the act.

The National Labor Relations Act is administered and enforced by the National Labor Relations Board (NLRB). The board has two major functions under the act: (1) to remedy unfair labor practices of either labor organizations or employers, and (2) to order secret ballot elections in which employees decide whether a labor organization or group of employees will represent them in collective bargaining. The NLRB can only act when it is formally requested to do so by individuals, employers, or unions. Board actions are set in motion when a representative petition or an unfair labor practice charge is filed. Anyone aggrieved by a final order of the board may have the order reviewed in the appropriate court of appeals.

The NLRB has issued a set of rules that recognizes eight separate bargaining units for acute care hospitals: (1) registered nurses, (2) physicians, (3) other professionals, (4) technical employees, (5) skilled maintenance employees, (6) business office clerical employees, (7) guards, and (8) other nonprofessional employees. These rules were scheduled to take effect in mid-1989; however, a U.S. District Court judge struck down the rules, and then a federal appellate court reversed the decision. The American Hospital Association appealed the case to the U.S. Supreme Court. Under the Supreme Court decision, the eight categories of workers went into effect in May 1991.[4]

Strike Control Team and Strike Action Committee

During a strike, an organization must have a unified command structure. Only one person should be in charge. The chain of command dictates the person who will substitute in the absence of the person who has been assigned the overall responsibility for strike control operations. The strike control team should operate out of a strike control center so that all employees and outside support groups know where to deliver information or seek direction.

A strike action committee should be formed by the head of strike operations to represent the various operating units of the facility and to function primarily in the pre-strike preparation phases to ensure coordinated planning. Once a strike is underway, the committee will rarely be needed; however, it may meet periodically as a communication tool to keep operating units advised of the situation.

Non-Striking Employees

The non-striking employees are the basic resource for continuing patient care and ensuring a successful conclusion to the labor action. It is extremely important that the administration support non-striking employees in every way possible.

On the day the strike begins, all non-striking employees should attend a briefing meeting designed to update employees on logistical matters, exhibit the administration's appreciation, and reassure employees. The employees should be told to expect harassing telephone calls.

These calls generally threaten not only the employees, but also their families if the employees return to work. It may be difficult for the administration to talk about this situation because administration generally wants to avoid negative issues. However, forewarning employees takes the initial shock away from these types of threats.

Non-striking employees are also vitally concerned about the protection of their vehicles while they are at work. Because experience has shown that vehicles are a major target of strikers, this concern is certainly valid. High priority must be given to this protection responsibility.

Initial Stages of the Strike

The first day or two of the typical healthcare-related strike are generally peaceful and uneventful. The strikers are in a fairly good mood and enjoy talking with one another. The greatest number of picketers are on hand in the early stages of a strike, except for major rally events when the union tries to show a high degree of support. Inside the hospital, the staff's initial reaction is enthusiastic support for the hospital and cooperation.

As the strike wears on, both picketers and staff will exhibit frustration, disappointment, and exhaustion. After a few days, when the facility seems to be functioning well, the strikers begin to wonder whether their picket line is meeting its objective. Their reaction may be to step up harassment. Incidents of intimidation, property damage, and other problems sometimes begin to appear.

Another tactic that may occur and will affect the facility is a secondary boycott by suppliers and vendors. This illegal activity usually occurs much later in the strike, but it should be anticipated during early planning.

Picket Lines

A major purpose of the picket line is to discourage employees from crossing the line to report to work. When the picketers see that employees are not being sufficiently discouraged and do cross the line to work, confrontations sometimes begin to take place. It is at this point that threats and acts of violence often occur.

Administrators and supervisory personnel should be outside during shift changes to support arriving personnel and to observe any incidents that might occur. Employees arriving to work are encouraged when they see the upper echelon there to support them rather than sitting safely behind their desks.

Most healthcare facilities have a built-in security vulnerability that can become an asset during picket activities: a multitude of entrances and exits. For the duration of the strike or picketing, as many of these access points as possible should be open for employee use. The more entrances that are available, the more difficult it becomes for the picketers to cover them all.

The law states that picket lines shall not restrict the right of people to enter and leave the facility. Despite this provision, thousands of incidents on record involve injury to people and destruction of property during picketing.

In coping with this situation, it is a common mistake to assume that law enforcement agencies will maintain law and order. Unfortunately, for a variety of reasons, police protection is not always at its best at such times. The healthcare organization has a responsibility to provide for personal safety and to protect its assets. The security department will necessarily play a strong role in achieving this objective.

Several days before the strike, there should be a thorough inspection of the exterior of the facility to remove signs and other items that could be easily vandalized. One item often overlooked is sprinkler heads—a favorite target for picketers.

Security personnel are generally deployed at the site of the picket line to show non-striking employees and others who cross the line a high degree of protective support. Security's additional responsibility is to ensure that picketers stay off facility property, to prevent accidents, and to document evidence of wrongdoing.

It is recommended that security personnel assigned to the strike detail be unarmed. Their objective is to be present but to project a fairly low profile to indicate that no trouble is expected. The type of trouble that might occur will not be deterred or corrected with the threat or use of a firearm.

Security officers should be briefed by the administration and legal counsel just before they are deployed to the picket line. The basic message this briefing should convey is that officers must be professional: They must keep their eyes and ears open and their mouths closed. The officers should be reminded that they are representatives of the hospital, regardless of their personal feelings about the situation.

A goal of the labor action is to disrupt services to pressure the administration to yield. Disruption does not always occur outside the facility, and thus internal mechanical and electrical equipment rooms, communications areas, and other vulnerable units should be protected.

Record Keeping

A step that must be initiated immediately when a strike or picket situation develops is to establish a strike control center. A major administrative mistake is to assume that the confrontation will not last long. This assumption makes it easy to ignore the central reporting and its record-keeping role until the organization is well into a prolonged strike.

All information concerning activities and incidents related to the labor action should be reported at once to the recording person. All supervisory employees should be given the responsibility of reporting all incidents brought to their attention. A chronological record of incidents, including complete details, serves a variety of purposes, not the least of which is collecting the data necessary for legal actions. A consolidated central reporting concept will also serve as a clearinghouse to verify or reject rumors and to readily assess the situation.

Depending on the problems encountered, it may be desirable to assign an investigator to the function of record keeping. The investigator would have the responsibility of following up on reported incidents to obtain statements from those involved and to make certain that all the necessary facts are properly documented.

An important tool in dealing with and documenting strikes and picketing—and one that relates very closely to the incident recording function—is the use of photography. The task of photographing the labor action should be an assigned responsibility. Because camera equipment is often antagonizing to picketers, it should be used in such a manner that a minimum of confrontation occurs.

The organization's response to the labor action may require the unexpected expenditure of funds. Special arrangements may have to be made to procure supplies, obtain drivers and vehicles, authorize meals, use taxi services, authorize overtime, and the like. During times of strife, the customary management controls tend to be loosened. Specific guidelines must be drawn up for these unexpected expenditures, and the individuals who authorize the use of funds must keep adequate records. After the turmoil is over, the administration will inevitably seek an explanation for various expenditures.

Maintaining Supply Lines

If it is to continue to carry out its mission, one of the first and most important steps a healthcare facility must take during a labor action situation is to maintain a supply line. In most instances, a supply line requires the procurement of additional labor and vehicles.

If vehicles are obtained from rental or leasing companies, it is usually only a matter of time before the rental agency demands the return of their vehicles. This tactic can be countered to some extent by having individuals rent vehicles from various agencies for onetime use. This procedure also proves valuable in avoiding harassment because the newly rented vehicle can be used to pick up supplies without being followed and subjected to threats, damage, or driver injury.

Before picketing begins, the organization should contact all suppliers who make deliveries to the facility. The facility needs to know if nonunion or supervisory personnel will be available to make deliveries. It is better to pick up the supplies directly from the vendor or to have the order shipped to a temporary receiving site than to have confrontations between picketers and truck drivers. When truck drivers refuse to cross the line, their action supports and encourages the picketers.

Because it is impossible for the facility to pick up the thousands of items it requires, particularly during a prolonged strike, offsite receiving areas are generally necessary. Offsite receiving points should be well secured and generally require security officer coverage. Depending on the severity of the strike, the location of the offsite receiving point should be changed periodically. Organizations should consider using a truck parked in a vacant lot or other out-of-the-way place and simply off-loading from one truck to the other. If the loaded trucks are not brought to the facility the same day, security precautions are important. One facility involved in a severe labor action had parked three trucks overnight in an abandoned section of a railroad yard, and all three trucks were fire-bombed.

The picket line not only inhibits the free flow of deliveries but also affects the removal of items, particularly trash. An institution of any size will find that a tremendous volume of refuse can build up in a very short time. It is essential that facilities move quickly to dispose of this material or they may find themselves in violation of health and fire standards. Inspectors from various regulatory agencies seem to proliferate during labor actions.

TERRORISM

To many, terrorism is something that takes place elsewhere—generally overseas. The fact of the matter is, however, that it is a very real problem for healthcare security professionals. Acts of terrorism, both internationally and domestically, are increasing. Fire bombings, injuries, and homicides related to the abortion issue; product tampering; and the introduction of widespread computer viruses are real security threats to be anticipated and planned for.

A topic receiving increased attention is that of weapons of mass destruction (WMD). Within the realm of WMD, there are five generally accepted categories of terrorist actions: biological, nuclear, incendiary, chemical, and explosive (B-NICE). (This acronym was coined in a federal study on terrorism that can be downloaded from a Federal Emergency Management web site.[5]) While weapons of mass destruction have not been well studied or discussed, they have serious security implications for all healthcare delivery systems.

There have been two major WMD study groups: a National Guard Bureau Work Group and the Department of Justice Stakeholders Forum. This preliminary work raised more questions than answers, with summary conclusions that hospitals are unprepared to handle a serious WMD incident. Hospital emergency departments will generally be early, if not the first, responders. While military medical services may be a resource, in all probability, they may not be mobilized in a timely manner to meet initial needs.

A biological incident is considered to be the most likely event. Anthrax or smallpox agents would be likely sources for mass contamination, which would require tremendous, instant medical care resources.[6] However, U.S. hospital emergency departments are currently often hard-pressed to deliver services for even normally occurring events. A case in point occurred in March 1999 in Denver, Colorado. On that particular day, which was normal in most respects, 13 of the 14 Denver emergency rooms and intensive care units were "on divert," meaning community emergency service responders were advised to take acute-care patients elsewhere. It is further reported that on any given day, at least one or two Denver hospitals are on a divert status.[7]

Two major problems face hospitals and other medical care facilities in such instances: maintaining an adequate staff and assuring that facilities are not overrun by hordes of patients, families, and other victims. The latter problem obviously falls under the realm of security. A likely scenario is akin to the mass exuberance of football fans intent on tearing down goal posts after a win. The sheer mass and determination involved can simply overwhelm the protective effort. The "physical hardening" of healthcare facilities is a logical step, but the question becomes the degree to which physical safeguards can be applied while still carrying out the mission of providing healthcare services to those in need.

WMD will continue to be a high priority for healthcare security planning. It is not a question of whether a WMD incident will occur in the U.S., but rather when, where, and to what extent.

The security safeguards applied against terrorist threats coincide with safeguards used against civil disturbances; that is, an expansion of the elements of the day-to-day security system in place.

MOB AND GANG ACTIVITIES

Mob and gang activities are different from riots and civil disturbances in that mobs and gangs generally focus on the hospital as the primary target of their actions.

Medical care facilities have been the object of demonstrations, ranging from peaceful picketing to sit-ins, the occupation of administrative offices, and the takeover of communications systems. The purpose of these demonstrations has been varied and has included demands for free medical care and the reinstatement of terminated employees. These disruptive activities characteristically show a complete disregard for the rights of the medical care facility and for the negative effects on patient care.

In general, hospitals prohibit the exhibition of gang colors or flashing signs. Most security professionals agree that a strong security presence and dealing firmly but fairly with gang members is the best approach. Too passive an approach usually escalates disruptive behavior.

Planning for Mob and Gang Activity

One of the most important points to consider when planning an organization's response to mob and gang activity is the policy on arrests. Specifically, will arrests be made, and who will make this decision? Once the police have been called, the facility must be prepared to sign complaints and to follow through in prosecuting demonstrators if the police are unable to persuade them to leave.

Arthur Gennan, a security consultant and former hospital security director, suggests that the following points be included in the facility plan:

1. Notify administrators, security director, police department, and employees.

2. Discontinue visiting, except for critical patients, and then only upon identification.

3. Make special arrangements for patient admission and discharge.

4. Reassign personnel to critical areas.

5. Close and lock office doors in all public areas of the hospital to avoid sit-ins.

6. Station a fire brigade to fight possible fires.

7. Place operators on all elevators.

8. Keep employees and patients away from main floors or other areas of disturbance.

9. Consider the possible use of video cameras for obtaining evidence.

10. Resume services and ease restrictions as circumstances permit.

11. Designate codes to announce the start and end of the emergency situation.

A demonstration in a healthcare facility can have a lasting effect on patients and staff alike. The prompt handling of these incidents is necessary to guarantee personal safety, to ensure the proper functioning of the facility, and to minimize adverse stress upon patients and staff.

Legal Considerations

Of the many mob activities directed against healthcare facilities, a demonstration against the Beth Israel Medical Center in New York many years ago is of particular interest to security practitioners. A group of people demonstrating under the banner of the Health Revolutionary Unity Movement disrupted services, and the hospital sought and obtained a court injunction prohibiting demonstrations within the hospital.

The decision handed down by Justice Mitchell of the New York Supreme Court clearly stated that a medical facility is not a public place, and its sole purpose is to render medical care and treatment, for which a tranquil atmosphere is required. The opinion also stated that the demonstrators were in error when they justified their conduct on the basis of their constitutional right to freedom of speech and assembly. Although the case is more than 25 years old, other case law has supported these principles. Although the law supports medical care facilities in their defense against intrusion, injunctions take time, and facility protection still requires a certain amount of planning.

CIVIL DISTURBANCES

The outbreak of rioting in the late 1960s presented a relatively new protection vulnerability for healthcare institutions. Hospitals had previously handled mass casualties, but the influx of casualties from rioting created new complications for protection services, including the following:

• Confrontations between police and rioters that often continued into treatment rooms

• Hostile visitors who demanded attention, disrupted activity, and destroyed property to obtain their objective

- Direct attacks on the facility, including fire-bombs and in one case a siege of gunfire

In short, healthcare facilities ceased to be the neutral ground they had been in the past.

During the 1970s, few if any civil disturbances involved hospital operations. In mid-1980, heavy rioting hit Miami, Florida. One hospital, Jackson Memorial Medical Center, was under siege for a few days as rioters burned and looted just outside the hospital's perimeter.

Security professionals learned three things from these riots. First, police and fire protection services may not be available as assumed or even as promised. Many facilities suffered extensive damage and disruption because the municipal protection services were stretched so thin that adequate protection could not be furnished. Every protection plan should therefore be predicated on the assumption that no external help will be available.

Second, employees may be sympathetic to the rioters and their cause. This will, of course, be governed somewhat by the purported cause for the civil disturbance. Employee sympathy may be manifested in the theft of drugs and supplies for use at first-aid stations set up by the rioters, or employees may create disturbances within the facility. For example, a wastebasket fire was set in a stairwell in one reported case. Although no real damage resulted, the smoke created confusion and panic among patients and employees.

Third, separate treatment areas for rioters and the public may be needed to minimize continuing confrontation. Strict visitor access control is paramount.

External Protection Planning

Preparations for minimizing damage to the facility and safely moving employees cannot be made at the last minute. Thus, the first step in riot protection planning is to survey the perimeter of the property. For example, this might be the time to recommend fencing the north property line to divert foot traffic from crossing through parking areas. Security administrators should also consider whether exterior lighting is adequately protected to minimize destruction, whether landscaping decorations or other external items should be removed, and how employee vehicles could be protected.

The next step is to carefully survey the exterior of the buildings that will require protection. Access doors and windows are of primary concern. Even though normal access points cannot be eliminated during normal operations, administrators must be prepared to quickly authorize locking up when a riot hits. The time to make certain that doors are equipped with the proper hardware is before a riot occurs.

Security administrators should select the access point that could be controlled best if only one entrance were to be operative. The best entrance is not necessarily the most accessible one. If the facility has an emergency department, two access points are generally required: one for the injured and another for everyone else.

Windows and other glass areas are primary targets for destruction. Unbreakable glazing material is commonly used for protection. Another method is to precut plywood and install brackets on the window frames to permit easy and quick installation. If no glass protection has been installed or if the protection is minimal, interior blinds or curtains should be closed. If beds are near a window, they should be moved as far from the window as possible.

Exterior lighting must be reviewed to determine whether the illumination is adequate. More light is needed during rioting than is needed under normal conditions. Security administrators should also check to determine whether light fixtures can be modified to prevent damage. Generally, little can be done in this regard, but making certain that lights are not within easy reach is at least one step that can be taken.

Internal Protection Planning

The interior of the facility should be reviewed to identify critical areas that need additional protection. This additional security may be in the form of hardware, or it may require establishing a security post. Areas of obvious concern are electrical distribution vaults, emergency power areas, equipment rooms (including elevator penthouses), emergency exits, traffic control, and surveillance areas. Organizations should seriously consider placing operators on all elevators. By manually controlling elevators, traffic can be controlled more readily, and in a sense the elevator operators provide an element of security.

If emergency security posts are necessary, every possible post location should be given an activation priority so that as emergency conditions develop, the posts can be activated in a logical manner. The protection level will expand and contract during a crisis according to the threat at hand.

Fire extinguishers and communications equipment are essential for every post; access lists and special equipment may be needed at particular posts. Planning may indicate that a reasonable approach to providing communications at every post is to install telephone jacks at each location or the use of cellular telephones. Most facilities do not have enough two-way radio equipment available for a significant protection posture.

A command post is required for all types of emergencies. In larger facilities the central security post is readily adaptable to this function, and as a general rule the command post should not be moved to another location. In smaller facilities, a command post location should be planned. It is suggested that two or three security employees be assigned to a task force that will be immediately available to deploy upon receiving notification from the command center that an emergency response is needed at a specific location.

Small Facilities or Clinics

Small clinics and medical office buildings must take many of the same precautions and plan in the same manner as hospitals do. One advantage of outpatient treatment facilities is that they can be locked up and need not continue to operate. However, past accounts of riot damage have shown that unoccupied buildings receive considerably more damage than occupied buildings.

Auxiliary Labor Needs

To cope with a riot, a great amount of security personnel labor is required. Having security personnel work on extended shifts will not produce sufficient coverage if the facility is one of the primary casualty treatment facilities. An auxiliary security force should be considered to supplement the regular security force. The administration may be reluctant to plan for an auxiliary security force due to the extra cost, but this reluctance will disappear when the facility is in a state of emergency.

An auxiliary security force is generally composed of volunteers from other departments within the organization. One eastern hospital created an auxiliary unit of 20 volunteers, including a computer programmer, an accounting clerk, a mail clerk, a personnel interviewer, maintenance workers, and environmental service workers. Also, security personnel can be borrowed from other facilities.

The auxiliary force should be identified as security personnel. This can be accomplished by issuing jackets or armbands, badges, and small pieces of equipment. The facility should hold periodic orientation briefings to familiarize auxiliary officers with basic protection concepts and organizational procedure. Extensive training is not generally required because auxiliary officers are usually assigned to a fixed post or as the second officer of a two-person security response team.

Auxiliary officers should receive additional pay beyond their normal salary. One plan that reportedly has worked well is to pay auxiliary officers at their normal rate plus an additional half-time rate.

Security Uniforms and Marked Vehicles

In some assignments or functions, the identification of security personnel is a detriment. Planning should take into account that uniformed authority figures may sometimes create problems. Street clothes should be worn by security personnel assigned to the emergency room and by drivers who will pass through disturbance areas. Drivers should carry a letter indicating that they are employees on official business. Marked vehicles and especially marked security vehicles may also become targets. The objective in using both street clothes and unmarked vehicles is to avoid calling attention to security activities.

Employee Travel and Housing

Another problem that requires considerable planning is that employees may not be able to travel freely to and from work because of a curfew, police lines, or fear of harm. Experience reveals that even though employees may be willing to travel to work under adverse conditions, anxious friends or relatives often persuade them to remain at home.

Curfew terms vary widely according to local conditions and objectives. A common restriction is to prohibit people under a certain age from being on the streets after a certain hour. When this condition was imposed in a major city, it created a problem for the hospital because many employees were affected. The solution was simple. Employees carried a letter addressed to the law enforcement agency that was signed by the hospital administrator, and contained the employee's name and address, the time dismissed from work, and a statement that the letter was intended for use only for the date indicated. This approach worked well and was reported to be widely accepted by law enforcement personnel.

When police lines are established, altered travel routes are an obvious course of action. When police lines surround the facility, some procedure must be devised for staff access. Identification cards or badges are one solution. Another approach may be for a facility representative to be stationed at a central point along the police line to verify employee status. Individuals who attempt to cross the police line can be identified with simple questions about their department, employee number, birth date, or other data. The facility representative will be able to verify many employees by sight.

During a civil disturbance, organizations may encourage employees to stay on the premises for their own safety and for the purpose of maintaining an adequate staff. Employees sometimes insist on staying regardless of the official stance, and thus some planning for employee housing is mandated.

An inventory of beds that can be used in an emergency should be maintained. A thorough review of a facility often uncovers more beds than expected. Beds can sometimes be found in classrooms, blood banks, on-call rooms, and electrocardiogram and electroencephalogram areas. In addition, cots can be set up in many areas for temporary accommodations.

To ensure the utilization of all beds and to keep a record of where employees are housed, assignments must be made by a designated facility representative. Employees should not be allowed to assume their own accommodations even in their own departments. When more employees request accommodations than are needed to work, a system of housing authorization by department heads may be necessary to maintain adequate control.

REFERENCES

1. James A. Hanna, "Uniform Hospital Disaster Codes," presentation, Ontario Hospital Association Annual Convention, Toronto, October 31, 1989.

2. Edward R. Comeau and Michael S. Isner, "Fire Investigation Report, Hospital Fire, Petersburg, VA," National Fire Protection Association, December 31, 1994.

3. Linda Young Landesman, "Emergency Preparedness in Health Care Organizations," Joint Commission on Accreditation of Healthcare Organizations, Oakbrook Terrace, Illinois, 1996, pp. 123–176.

4. David Burda, "Union Elections, Victories Increase Sharply," *Modern Healthcare*, July 5, 1991, p. 3.

5. "Types of Terrorist Incidents," *HHMM Newsletter*, April 2000, p. 9.

6. Susan B. McLaughling, "Briefing to JCAHO Healthcare Safety Committee," Oakbrook Terrace, Illinois, April 19, 1999.

7. Claire Martin, "Sent Elsewhere," *Denver Post*, April 19, 1999, p. 1F.

INDEX

Abductions, infants, 413–26
Abductor, modus operandi, 417
Abductor profiles, 416–17
Abuse/lose, drug, 21
Access
  to employee lockers, 88
  to locked areas, 87–88
Access control, 87–88
Access control plan, area, 412
Access controls for laundry, 460
Accident reporting, 61
  and investigation, 84
Accidents, 35–36
  employee, 61–62
  patient, 61
  visitor, 62
Acreage facilities, large, 309
Activities, and duties, 104–12
Administrative records need, 249–50
Administrators, healthcare security, 7
Admissions, waiting and, 429
After-hours badging, 308–9
Against medical advice (AMA), 280
AHJ (Authority Having Jurisdiction), 424
Aid, mutual, 489–90
AIDS, 282, 284
Alarm applications, basic, 371–72
Alarm systems
  components, 370–71
  proprietary, 372
Alarms, 369–73
  false, 373
  holdup, 437–38
ALF (Animal Liberation Front), 461–62
AMA (against medical advice), 280
American Society for Healthcare Engineering (ASHE), 147
American Society for Industrial Security (ASIS), 147, 323

Anabolic steroids, 446
Applicant background investigation, 85
Area access control plan, 412
Areas
  security sensitive, 411–13
  treatment, 430
  triage, 429–30
  types of parking, 473–77
Arming officers, considerations in, 181–84
ASHE (American Society for Healthcare Engineering), 147
ASIS (American Society for Industrial Security), 147, 323
Assaults, 14–16
Association of Women's Health, Obstetric and Neonatal Nurses (AWHONN), 421
Attitudes, morale and negative, 156–57
Audits, 357
  external, 90
  internal, 89
Authority Having Jurisdiction (AHJ), 424
Authority, program, 100–102
AWHONN (Association of Women's Health, Obstetric and Neonatal Nurses), 421

B-NICE (biological, nuclear, incendiary, chemical, and explosive), 515
Background investigations, 85, 330–31, 357
Badge programs, administering, 332–33
Badges
  identification, 333–34
  and visitor log books, 68
Badging, after-hours, 308–9
Batons, 190–91
Battery jumping service, 229–30
Belts, duty, 191–92
Biological, nuclear, incendiary, chemical, and explosive (B-NICE), 515

525

BNDD (Bureau of Narcotics and Dangerous Drugs), 443
Bodies, removal of, 91–92
Bomb threats, 17
Bombings, 17
Bombs
  and bomb threats, 503–8
  searching for, 505–7
Breaking and entering, 17
Buildings
  configuration and design of, 120
  evacuating, 507
Bulletins
  daily security, 271
  weekly security, 271
Bureau of Narcotics and Dangerous Drugs (BNDD), 443
Burglary, 17
Burglary and robbery, pharmacy, 436–38

Cameras
  CCTV (closed-circuit television), 424
  dummy, 377–78
Canine patrols, 232–33
Care, patient, 226–27
Cash registers, 92–93
Casualties, handling mass, 501–3
CBT (Computer-Based Training), 210–11
CCDs (charge-coupled devices), 377
CCTV (closed-circuit television), 42, 365, 373–80, 428, 439, 463–64
  accessories, 378–79
  applications, 374–77
  cameras, 424
  dummy cameras, 377–78
  equipment, 377
  monitoring, 379–80, 477–78
  videotape recording, 379
Centers, daycare, 463–64
Central security stations, 366–69
  advantages, 366–67
  cost, 368–69
  design, 367–68
Certified Healthcare Protection Administrator (CHPA), 146–47
Certified nurse assistants (CNAs), 24
Certified Protection Professional (CPP), 146–47
Certified Registered Nurse Anesthetists (CRNAs), 444
Charge-coupled devices (CCDs), 377
Charts, functional organization, 123–26

Check-off forms, 251
Checks, package, 93–94
Chemical gas, 190
CHPA (Certified Healthcare Protection Administrator), 146–47
Civil disturbances, 17–19, 518–23
  auxiliary labor needs, 521–22
  employee travel, 522–23
  external protection planning, 519–20
  housing, 522–23
  internal protection planning, 520–21
  marked vehicles, 522
  security uniforms, 522
  small facilities or clinics, 521
Clinics, medical/dental, 288
Closed-circuit television (CCTV), 42, 365, 373–80, 428, 439, 463–64
  accessories, 378–79
  applications, 374–77
  cameras, 424
  dummy cameras, 377–78
  equipment, 377
  monitoring, 379–80, 477–78
  videotape recording, 379
Closed pharmacies, 439
CNAs (certified nurse assistants), 24
Code of Ethics, 55
Codes
  common emergency, 489
  duress, 372–73
Combative patients, 284
Combination forms, 251–52
Commission, special police, 160–61
Commissioned police officers, 134
Communication, 155–56
  devices, 187–88
  privileged, 319
Community healthcare provider services, 443
Community provider services, 465–69
Community relations, 96–97
Compensation, wage, 171–72
Complaints, handling subordinate, 157
Computer-Based Training (CBT), 210–11
Computer operations, 452–53
Computers and parking control, 485
Conservation, 91
Contraband, 343
Contract security officers, 132–33
Contract staff, 130–32
Control
  computers and parking, 485

fire prevention and, 490–98
 parking, 471–85
Control plan, area access, 412
Controlled substances, 445–48
 anabolic steroids, 446
 depressants, 445
 marijuana, 446
 narcotics, 445
 schedules, 446–48
 stimulants, 445
Corporate approach, 135–38
Covert investigations, 359–60
CPP (Certified Protection Professional), 146–47
Crime prevention activities, security, 116–17
Criminal investigations, 319–20
Criminal justice interface, 117–18
CRNAs (Certified Registered Nurse Anesthetists), 444

Daily activity reports, 263–65
Daily security bulletins, 271
Damaged property, 343
Daycare centers, 463–64
DEA (Drug Enforcement Administration), 443, 446
Deception, detection of, 362
Decision-making process, security safeguards relating to individual, 67–72
Dental clinics, medical, 288
Department policies and procedures, 104–8
Departmental records, keeping current, 271–72
Departments, emergency, 284–86
Depressants, 445
Detectors, lie, 362
Deterrents, psychological, 64–65
Diagnostic and Statistical Manual of Mental Disorders (DSM), 169
Diligence, selecting employees through due, 329
Disasters, 36
Disasters, natural, 498–503
 disaster drills, 500–501
 emergency preparedness, 500–501
 handling mass casualties, 501–3
Discipline, security force, 172–74
Disputes, labor, 25–26
Disturbances, 20
 civil, 17–19, 518–23
Division of Occupational Safety and Health (DOSH), 397
Documentation policy, 250

DOSH (Division of Occupational Safety and Health), 397
Drug abuse/loss, 21
Drug controls, internal hospital, 449–50
Drug Enforcement Administration (DEA), 443, 446
Drugs
 narcotics and dangerous, 443–49
 testing of, 343–44
DSM (Diagnostic and Statistical Manual of Mental Disorders), 169
Due diligence, selecting employees through, 329
Dummy cameras, 377–78
Duress codes, 372–73
Duties and activities, 104–12
Duty belts, 191–92

EAPs (Employee Assistance Programs), 344
Education
 security, 85, 108
 and staff security orientation, 412–13
Elective training, 207
Electronic infant monitoring, 424–25
Electronic physical security safeguards; *See* Non-electronic physical security safeguards
Elopement, patient, 26–27
Emergencies
 internal and external, 36
 reaction to internal and external, 86
 terminating, 507–8
Emergency codes, common, 489
Emergency department security, 427–36
 designing, 428–31
 emergency signals, 435
 how much is needed?, 427–28
 physical security safeguards, 431–32
 security/police room, 435
 security staffing in emergency departments, 432–35
Emergency departments, 284–86
Emergency departments, designing security for, 428–31
 access control, 428–29
 admissions, 429
 quiet room, 431
 safe room, 431
 treatment area, 430
 triage area, 429–30
 waiting and admissions, 429
 walk-in area/waiting and admissions, 429

Emergency messages, 92
Emergency planning and operations, 487–524
  bombs and bomb threats, 503–8
  civil disturbances, 518–23
  common emergency codes, 489
  fire prevention and control, 490–98
  mob and gang activities, 516–18
  mutual aid, 489–90
  natural disasters, 498–503
  strikes and picketing, 508–15
  terrorism, 515–16
Emergency preparedness, 500–501
Emergency room activity, 314–16
Emergency shipments, 93
Emergency signals, 435
Employee
  accidents, 61–62
  identification, 331–34
  informants, 363–64
  lockers, 88, 340–41
  photographs, 331
  property losses, 33–34, 344–45
  time recording, 342
  weapons, 336
Employee Assistance Programs (EAPs), 344
Employee health records, 318
Employee orientation, new, 68
Employee security
  attitudes, 345–47
  education and motivation, 347–50
  responsibility, 335
Employee/staff involvement in protection programs, 119–20
Employee theft, 29–32
  effects of controls on, 31–32
  factors in, 30–31
Employees, 401–2
  handling problem, 157–58
  hiring and managing, 327–31
  non-striking, 510–11
  off-duty, 335–36
  police interaction with patients and, 313–14
  public, 96–97
  selecting through due diligence, 329
Employment
  application forms, 329
  conditions of, 67–68, 330
Entrances and exits, 227
Equipment
  distribution of reports and, 94–95
  fastening down, 393
  for vehicle patrols, 231–32
Equipment considerations, firearms, 180–81
Ethics, Code of, 55
Events, security-related sentinel, 411–42, 439–41
Exits and entrances, 227
Explosion, 21
External audits, 90
External emergencies, reaction to internal and, 86
External motivation, 67
External patrols, 228–33

Facilitators, 209–10
Facilities
  large acreage, 309
  maintaining orderly, 80
  offsite, 443, 464
Facility security staffing, incremental, 142–44
Facility security survey, 36–43
False alarms, 373
Family
  gifts from, 342
  infant discharged to wrong, 426
Fencing, 381–83
Field supervision, 152–55
Fire, 21, 36
Fire prevention and control, 490–98
  basic security considerations, 497–98
  employee reaction, 496
  fire safety programming, 491–96
  fire safety training, 496–97
Fire safety programming, 491–96
  containment, 493–94
  detection, 492–93
  evacuation, 494–95
  extinguishment, 495–96
  fire prevention, 491–92
  relocation, 494–95
Fire safety training, 496–97
Firearms, 180–81
Firearms programs, managing, 184–93
  miscellaneous equipment considerations, 186–92
    batons, 190–91
    bullet-resistant vest, 191
    chemical gas, 190
    communication devices, 187–88
    duty belts, 191–92
    flashlights, 189
    gloves, 189–90

handcuffs, 188–89
nightsticks, 190–91
radios, 187–88
security operations manual, 192–93
training, 192
Flag etiquette, 95
Flashlights, 189
Forensic patients, 289–93
Formats, report, 250–52
Forms
    AMA (against medical advice), 280
    check-off, 251
    combination, 251–52
    employment application, 329
    narrative, 251
Fraud, 21–22
FTEs (full-time equivalents), 171, 215, 245

Gambling, 23
Gang activities, mob and, 516–18
Gas, chemical, 190
GDP (gross domestic product), 2
General services, supportive, 90–96
    cash registers, 92–93
    conservation, 91
    distribution of reports and equipment, 94–95
    emergency messages, 92
    emergency shipments, 93
    flag etiquette, 95
    lost and found, 91
    miscellaneous services, 95–96
    package checks, 93–94
    removal of bodies, 91–92
Gifts from patients or family, 342
Glass areas, windows and, 392–93
Gloves, 189–90
Government agencies, liaison with miscellaneous, 88–89
GPS (global positioning system), 469
Grand jury subpoenas, 321–22
Gross domestic product (GDP), 2
Groups, patient risk, 280–301
Growth, professional, 53–56
Guards, prisoner, 292–98

Handcuffs, 188–89
Hazard reporting, 62
HDTV (high-definition television), 377
HEAL (Hospital Employees Assisting Law Enforcement), 323–24
Health, mental, 286–88

Health records, employee, 318
Healthcare
    categories of, 4–5
    home, 465–69
Healthcare facilities
    infant abductions from U.S., 413–26
    property losses, 32
Healthcare organizations, protecting, 45–75
Healthcare provider services, community, 443
Healthcare Safety Committee, JCAHO, 11
Healthcare security
    administrators, 7
    defining, 46–47
    evolution of, 50
    expansion of, 57
    foundation of, 13–44
    personnel, 53–56
    rationale for, 48–50
    risk/vulnerabilities, 14
Healthcare security services environment, hospitals and, 1–11
Healthcare Security Services (HSS), 292
Healthcare settings, investigative activity in, 351–64
Healthcare violence, management of, 404–7
    preventive and management steps, 404–5
    response to threats, 406–7
    threat policy, 405
High-definition television (HDTV), 377
HIV (human immunodeficiency virus), 282
Holdup alarms, 437–38
Home healthcare, 465–69
    caregiver at risk, 466–67
    patient at risk, 465–66
    security practices and guidelines, 467–69
Homicides and suicides, 23
Hospital drug controls, internal, 449–50
    audit committee, 450
    automated dispensing, 450
    drug loses, 450
Hospital Employees Assisting Law Enforcement (HEAL), 323–24
Hospital infant environment, 415–16
Hospital pharmacy, 436–39
Hospital security, progression in United States, 50–53
    1900–1950, 51
    1950–1960, 51
    1960–1975, 51–52
    1975–1990, 52
    1990 into next century, 52–53

Hospital watch, 350
Hospitals
  and healthcare security services environment, 1–11
  types of, 5–6
  unique aspects of, 47–48
Hostage-taking, 23–24
Hours
  non-operational, 307–8
  operational, non-visiting, 306–7
HR (human resources), 329
  office, 327–28
  to secure environment, 327–50
HSS (Healthcare Security Services), 292
Human immunodeficiency virus (HIV), 282
Hypnosis, 363

IACP (International Association of Chiefs of Police), 323
IAHSS (International Association of Healthcare Security and Safety), 14, 54, 146–47, 172, 197, 200, 331
  advanced security officer training, 202–4
  basic security officer training, 201–2
  safety training, 204–5
  supervisory training, 204
ICS (Incident Command System), 502
Identification badge design considerations, 333–34
Identification, employee, 331–34
Identification, infant, 418–20
IESNA (Illuminating Engineering Society of North America), 475
IHDN (Integrated Health Delivery Network), 3–4
IHSSF (International Healthcare Security and Safety Foundation), 146
Illuminating Engineering Society of North America (IESNA), 475
Imposters, 24
Incident Command System (ICS), 502
Incident investigations, 353–57
Incident reporting and investigation, 83–84
Incident response plan, critical, 413, 426
Indexes, master name, 267
Infant
  abductions from U.S. healthcare facilities, 413–26
  abductor modus operandi, 417
  abductor profiles, 416–17
  basics of infant security plan, 417–20
  critical incident response plan, 426
  education, 420–21
  electronic infant monitoring, 424–25
  general security precautions and guidelines, 425–26
  hospital infant environment, 415–16
  infant discharged to wrong family, 426
  physical security, 421–24
  discharged to wrong family, 426
  identification, 418–20
  patients, 299–301
  security plan, 417–20
Infant environment, hospital, 415–16
Infant monitoring, electronic, 424–25
Infectious patients, 282–84
Informants, employee, 363–64
Information
  centralization of, 59
  exchange of, 248–49
  loss of, 26
  releasing of, 318–22
    criminal investigations, 319–20
    employee health records, 318
    key considerations for information release, 322
    patient medical records, 318, 320–21
    personnel records, 319, 319–20
    from personnel records to criminal investigations, 319–20
    privileged communication, 319
    search warrants, 319
    searching grand jury subpoenas, 321–22
    searching warrants, 321–22
    subpoenas, 319
  requests for, 317–22
  services, 452–53
Inpatients, 276–78
Inspections, 90
  line, 153–55
  package, 336–39
  safety, 62–63
  services, 80–83
  staff, 155
Installations, lock, 388–89
Instructors, 209–10
Integrated Health Delivery Network (IHDN), 3–4
Internal and external emergencies, reaction to, 86
Internal audits, 89
Internal patrols, 234–35
International Association of Chiefs of Police (IACP), 323

International Association of Healthcare
  Security and Safety (IAHSS), 14, 54,
  146–47, 172, 197, 200, 331
 advanced security officer training, 202–4
 basic security officer training, 201–2
 safety training, 204–5
 supervisory training, 204
International Healthcare Security and Safety
  Foundation (IHSSF), 146
Interrelationships, security, 275–310
Investigations, 71
 and accident reporting, 84
 applicant background, 85
 background, 330–31, 357
 covert, 359–60
 criminal, 319–20
 incident, 353–57
 and incident reporting, 83–84
 preliminary, 353
 types of, 353–60
  audits, 357
  background investigations, 357
  covert investigations, 359–60
  incident investigations, 353–57
  spot-checks and surveillance, 357–58
  undercover investigations, 359–60
  unemployment investigations, 358
  worker's compensation investigations, 358
 undercover, 359–60
 unemployment, 358
 worker's compensation, 358
Investigative activity in healthcare settings,
  351–64
 types of investigations, 353–60
Investigators
 cooperating with, 339–40
 and their tools, 361–64
  detection of deception, 362
  employee informants, 363–64
  hypnosis, 363

JCAH (Joint Commission on Accreditation of
  Hospitals), 8
JCAHO (Joint Commission on Accreditation
  of Healthcare Organizations), 7–11, 14,
  49, 59, 99, 124, 147, 268, 331, 411, 500
 design and implementation, 9–10
 Healthcare Safety Committee, 11
 organization surveys, 10
 scoring of standards, 10
 security management plans, 110–12
Justice, criminal, 117–18

Key ring, patrol officer's, 239–41
Key systems, master, 387–88
Keys
 and locks, 90, 384–92
 making of, 390–91
Kickbacks, 21–22
Kidnappings, 24–25

Labor disputes, 25–26
Laboratory, research, 460–63
Laundry, access controls for, 460
Laundry and linen control, 457–60
 access controls for laundry, 460
 controlling losses, 458–59
 establishing losses, 458
 marking linens, 460
 scrub suits, 459–60
Law enforcement liaison, security and, 323–24
Law enforcement personnel, off-duty, 133–34
Law enforcement service, requests for, 311–13
Law, Taft-Hartley, 509–10
Liaison
 with miscellaneous government agencies,
  88–89
 with public safety, 88–89
 security and law enforcement, 323–24
 security and non-police, 324–25
Licensed practical nurses (LPNs), 24
Licensing for security personnel, 161–63
Lie detectors, 362
Lighting, 383–84
Line inspection, 153–55
Linen control, laundry and, 457–60
Linens, marking, 460
Locked areas, access to, 87–88
Lockers
 access to employee, 88
 employee, 340–41
Locks
 changes of, 389
 installations of, 388–89
 and keys, 90, 384–92
  administering system, 386–87
  key making, 390–91
  lock changes, 389
  lock installations, 388–89
  master key systems, 387–88
  padlocks, 390
  periodic inventory, 391–92
  push-button locks, 389
  seals, 392
 push-button, 389

532 Index

Log books, badges and visitor, 68
Losses
  employee property, 33–34, 344–45
  patient property, 32–33
  reporting healthcare facility property, 32
Lost and found, 91
LPNs (licensed practical nurses), 24

Malefactors, 72
Management, 145–49
  components of risk, 58
  materials, 453–57
  proprietary, 132–33
  risk, 57–59
Management cycle, security, 112–13
Management planning, security, 99–120
Management plans
  annual security, 269
  JCAHO security, 110–12
Manual, security operations, 192–93
Marijuana, 446
Marked vehicles, 522
Mass casualties, handling, 501–3
Massachusetts Society for Medical Research (MSMR), 461
Master name indexes, 267
Materials management, 453–57
  disposing of property, 456–57
  distribution, 456
  equipment accountability and marking, 455–56
  purchasing and receiving, 454
  storage, 454–55
Medical care facilities, staffing, 6–7
Medical/dental clinics, 288
Medical records, 451–52
Medical records, patient, 318, 320–21
Mental health units, 286–88
Messages, emergency, 92
Missing patients, 278–80
Mission statements, security, 100
Mob and gang activities, 516–18
  legal considerations, 518
  planning for, 517–18
Monitoring
  CCTV (closed-circuit television), 477–78
  electronic infant, 424–25
Monthly security reports, 267–69
Morale and negative attitudes, 156–57
Motivation, 156
  conscious versus unconscious, 66–67

external, 67
factors in, 65–67
  age, 65
  society and motives, 65–66
Motives, social, 65
MSBP (Munchausen Syndrome by Proxy), 300–301
MSMR (Massachusetts Society for Medical Research), 461
Mutual aid, 489–90

Name indexes, master, 267
Narcotics, 445
Narcotics and dangerous drugs, 443–49
  controlled substances, 445–48
  general security requirements, 448–49
  prescriptions, 449
Narrative forms, 251
National Center for Missing and Exploited Children (NCMEC), 414–16, 418, 421, 425–26
National Crime Information Center (NCIC), 323
National Institute for Occupational Safety (NIOSH), 59–63
National Labor Relations Act, 509–10
National Labor Relations Board (NLRB), 509–10
National Rifle Association (NRA), 186
Natural disasters, 498–503
NCIC (National Crime Information Center), 323
NCMEC (National Center for Missing and Exploited Children), 414–16, 418, 421, 425–26
NCR (no-carbon-required) paper, 252
Negative attitudes and morale, 156–57
Neighborhood stability, 116–17
New employee orientation, 68
Nightsticks, 190–91
NIOSH (National Institute for Occupational Safety) and OSHA, 59–63
NLRB (National Labor Relations Board), 509–10
Non-electronic physical security safeguards, 380–84
  fencing, 381–83
  lighting, 383–84
  trees and shrubs, 384
Non-operational hours, 307–8
Non-operational time period, 308–9

Non-police liaison, security and, 324–25
Non-striking employees, 510–11
Non-visiting hours, 306–7
Notebooks, officer's, 241–42
NRA (National Rifle Association), 186
Nursing units, general, 288

Occupational Safety and Health Act of 1970 (OSHA), 59
Occupational Safety and Health Administration (OSHA), 189, 398–99
Off-duty employees, 335–36
Off-duty law enforcement personnel, 133–34
Offenses, punishable, 175–78
Officer, security, 433
Officers
  commissioned police, 134
  considerations in arming, 181–84
    deterrent value, 183
    environmental profile, 183
    liability, 182–83
    personal safety, 181
    quality of personnel, 184
    type of weapon, holster, and ammunition, 184
    vulnerability, 181–82
  contract security, 132–33
  full-time versus part-time security, 169–71
  notebooks of, 241–42
  security, 159–63
Offsite facilities, 443, 464
OJT (on-the-job training), 207–8
Organization and staffing, security department, 121–44
Organization charts, functional, 123–26
Organization-wide security coordination, 114–16
Organizational protection programs, 72–74
Organizations, protecting healthcare, 45–75
Orientation
  new employee, 68
  staff security, 412–13
OSHA and NIOSH, 59–63
OSHA (Occupational Safety and Health Act of 1970), 59
OSHA (Occupational Safety and Health Administration), 189, 398–99
Outsourcing, 130–32

Package checks, 93–94
Package inspections, 336–39

Padlocks, 390
Paper, NCR (no-carbon-required), 252
Parkers, types of, 479–81
  afternoon-shift employees, 480
  late-night-shift employees, 480–81
Parking
  pay, 482
  street, 474
  structures, 474–77
  system violators, 482–85
  and traffic control, 85–86
  valet, 478–79
  violation notices, 266
Parking areas, types of, 473–77
  parking structures, 474–77
  street parking, 474
  surface parking lots, 474
Parking control
  and computers, 485
  and security, 471–85
    automated controls, 481
    computers and parking control, 485
    parking system violators, 482–85
    pay parking, 482
    traffic flow and space allocation, 481–82
Parking lots, surface, 474
Pass-on records, 266–67
Patients, 276–303, 401
  accidents of, 61
  assisting with, 278–80
  care units/areas, 226–27
  combative, 284
  detaining, 316
  elopement of, 26–27
  forensic, 289–93
  gifts from, 342
  infant, 299–301
  infectious, 282–84
  medical records of, 318, 320–21
  missing, 278–80
  pediatric, 299–301
  property losses of, 32–33
  property of, 301–3
  risk groups, 280–301
  VIP, 281–82
  visiting hours, 305–6
  wandering, 298–99
Patients and employees, police interaction with, 313–14
Patients and visitors, interrelationships of security with, 275–310

534 Index

Patients; *See also* Inpatients
Patrol concepts, basic, 227–42
  external patrols, 228–33
  importance of first patrol round, 235–37
  internal patrols, 234–35
  officer's notebooks, 241–42
  patrol officer's key ring, 239–41
  patrol verification, 238–39
  shift rotation, 237–38
Patrol deployment plans, basic, 222–26
  double coverage, 224
  operational versus non-operational times, 224–26
Patrol officer's key ring, 239–41
Patrol problems, 244–45
Patrol round, importance of first, 235–37
Patrol verification, 238–39
Patrols
  canine, 232–33
  external, 228–33
    battery jumping service, 229–30
    canine patrols, 232–33
    damage to vehicles, 232
    equipment for vehicle patrols, 231–32
    operating vehicles, 232
    transporting people in security vehicles, 230–31
    vehicle patrols, 228–29
  internal, 234–35
  preventive, 80–83
  security, 69–70
  vehicle, 228–29
Pay parking, 482
Pediatric patients, 299–301
People, transporting in security vehicles, 230–31
Performance improvement
  measures, 108–10
  records, 269–71
Performance standards, 108–10
Periodic security reports, 267–69
Permanent records, 247–48
Perpetrators/visitors, 399–402
Personal Identification Numbers (PINs), 241
Personal safety, 181
Personnel
  equipping security, 178–84
  healthcare security, 53–56
  off-duty law enforcement, 133–34
  quality of, 184
  records, 319, 319–20
  selecting security, 163–69

Personnel policies, security-oriented, 334–44
Pharmacies
  burglary and robbery of, 436–38
  closed, 439
  hospital, 436–39
    access control, 438–39
    closed pharmacies, 439
    holdup alarms, 437–38
Photographs, employee, 331
Physical safeguards, security, 104
Physical security, 365–95
  alarms, 369–73
  central security stations, 366–69
  electronic security systems, 365–66
  fastening down equipment, 393
  locks and keys, 384–92
  marking property, 393–94
  safes, 394–95
  windows and glass areas, 392–93
Physical security safeguards
  non-electronic, 380–84
    fencing, 381–83
    lighting, 383–84
    trees and shrubs, 384
  utilization of, 118–19
Physician role impacted, 7
Picket lines, 511–13
Picketing, and strikes, 508–15
PINs (Personal Identification Numbers), 241
Planning
  emergency, 487–524
  for mob and gang activities, 517–18
  security management, 99–120
Plans
  bomb threat
    documenting threats, 508
    establishing authority, 504
    evacuating buildings, 507
    prevention, 504
    receiving threats, 504–5
    searching for bombs, 505–7
    terminating emergencies, 507–8
  critical incident response, 413, 426
  patrol deployment, 222–26
  strategic, 99
  unique strategic, 120
Police commission, special, 160–61
Police holds, and prisoners, 316–17
Police interaction with patients and employees, 313–14
Police officers, commissioned, 134

Police room, 435
Police; *See also* Non-police liaison
Policies
  documentation, 250
  security-oriented personnel, 334–44
  solicitation and distribution of products, 341
  threat, 405
Policies and procedures, department, 104–8
Polygraphs, 362
Position descriptions/activities, 102–3
Preliminary investigations, 353
Preparedness, emergency, 500–501
Prevention, crime, 116–17
Preventive patrols, 80–83
Prisoner guard instructions, 292–98
  admission to facilities, 294
  communications, 294
  confidentiality, 292–93
  general, 292
  initial room searches, 294–95
  media contacts, 297
  medical visits, 296
  movement outside rooms, 297–98
  non-medical visitors, 296–97
  ongoing room control, 295–96
  phone calls, 297
  prisoner property, 293–94
  responsibility, 292
  security officer breaks, 296
  service paperwork, 293
  subsequent room searches, 298
Prisoners and police holds, 316–17
Private Sector Liaison Committee (PSLC), 323
Privileged communication, 319
Problem employees, handling, 157–58
Products policy, solicitation and distribution of, 341
Professional growth, 53–56
Professionals, need for safety, 63
Profiles, abductor, 416–17
Program
  authority, 100–102
  security, 104–12
Program services, managing security and basic, 77–97
Property
  damaged, 343
  destruction of, 19
  losses
    employee, 33–34, 344–45
    patient, 32–33

  reporting healthcare facility, 32
  marking, 393–94
  patient, 301–3
  surplus, 343
Proprietary alarm systems, 372
Proprietary management, 132–33
Proprietary staff, 128–30
Protection programs, employee/staff involvement in, 119–20
Protection programs, organizational, 72–74
  blending safeguards into systems, 73–74
  determining correct application of safeguards, 73
Provider services
  community, 465–69
  community healthcare, 443
PSE (psychological stress evaluator), 362–63
PSLC (Private Sector Liaison Committee), 323
Psychological deterrents, 64–65
Psychological stress evaluator (PSE), 362–63
Public employees, 96–97
Public safety
  coordination, 117
  liaison with, 88–89
Public safety agencies, security and, 311–25
  detaining patients, 316
  emergency room activity, 314–16
  police interaction with patients and employees, 313–14
  prisoners and police holds, 316–17
  requests for information, 317–22
  requests for law enforcement service, 311–13
Punishable offenses, 175–78
Push-button locks, 389

QI (Quality Improvement) reports, 269
Quiet room, 431

Radios, 187–88
Recording
  employee time, 342
  videotape, 379
Records, 211
  basic, 252–71
    annual security management plans, 269
    daily activity reports, 263–65
    daily security bulletins, 271
    master name indexes, 267
    monthly security reports, 267–69
    parking violation notices, 266
    pass-on records, 266–67

536 Index

performance improvement records, 269–71
periodic security reports, 267–69
security condition reports, 261–63
security incident reports (SIRs), 253–59
security supplemental reports, 259–61
weekly security bulletins, 271
employee health, 318
medical, 451–52
pass-on, 266–67
patient medical, 318, 320–21
performance improvement, 269–71
permanent, 247–48
personnel, 319, 319–20
purposes of, 247–50
  administrative records need, 249–50
  exchange of information, 248–49
  memory system, 247–48
  permanent records, 247–48
and reports, 247–74
  documentation policy, 250
  keeping departmental records current, 271–72
  records retention, 273
  report formats, 250–52
  security, 108
  retention, 273
Records need, administrative, 249–50
Recruitment, 164–65
Registered nurses (RNs), 24
Regulations, and enforcement of rules, 86–87
Report formats, 250–52
  check-off forms, 251
  combination forms, 251–52
  miscellaneous format considerations, 252
  narrative forms, 251
Reporting
  accident, 61, 84
  hazard, 62
  incident, 83–84
Reports
  daily activity, 263–65
  filing security incident, 259–61
  monthly security, 267–69
  periodic security, 267–69
  QI (Quality Improvement), 269
  and records, 247–74
  security condition, 261–63
  and security records, 108
  security supplemental, 259–61
Reports and equipment, distribution of, 94–95
Research laboratory (animal), 460–63

Restraining orders, 408
Retention, 169
Ring, patrol officer's key, 239–41
Risk
  assessing, 38–40
  matching safeguards to, 41–42
Risk groups, patient, 280–301
Risk management
  components of, 58
  and security, 57–59
Risk/vulnerabilities, healthcare security, 14
Risks and vulnerabilities, 13–44
RNs (registered nurses), 24
Robbery, 27
  pharmacy burglary and, 436–38
Rooms
  quiet, 431
  safe, 431
  security/police, 435
Rotation, shift, 237–38
Rules and regulations, enforcement of, 86–87

Safe room, 431
Safeguards
  blending into systems, 73–74
  determining correct application of, 73
  matching to risk, 41–42
  security physical, 104
  utilization of physical security, 118–19
Safes, 394–95
Safety
  inspections, 62–63
  liaison with public, 88–89
  personal, 181
  programming, 59
Safety agencies, public, 311–25
Safety professionals, need for, 63
Safety programs, foundation of, 60–63
Safety-related vulnerabilities, 35–36
Safety training, IAHSS, 204–5
Scrub suits, 459–60
Seals, 392
Search warrants, 319
Security
  awareness, 108
  defining healthcare, 46–47
  designing for emergency department, 428–31
  education, 108
  emergency department, 427–36
    emergency signals, 435
    how much is needed?, 427–28

Index   537

physical security safeguards, 431–32
security/police room, 435
security staffing in emergency departments, 432–35
employee, 335, 345–47, 347–50
evolution of healthcare, 50
expansion of healthcare, 57
false expectations, 70–71
foundation of healthcare, 13–44
and law enforcement liaison, 323–24
and non-police liaison, 324–25
one program approach to, 74–75
physical, 365–95
physical safeguards, 104
program overview, 104–12
and public safety agencies, 311–25
rationale for healthcare, 48–50
records and reports, 108
and risk management, 57–59
Security administrators, healthcare, 7
Security and basic program services, managing, 77–97
Security bulletins
daily, 271
weekly, 271
Security concerns, special, 443
Security condition reports, 261–63
Security coordination, organization-wide, 114–16
Security/crime prevention activities, 116–17
Security department
organization and staffing, 121–44
reporting level and support, 121–23
Security education and training, 85
Security force
administration, 145–95
communication, 155–56
equipping security personnel, 178–84
handling problem employees, 157–58
handling subordinate complaints, 157
management, 145–49
morale and negative attitudes, 156–57
motivation, 156
punishable offenses, 175–78
retention, 169
rules and regulations, 174–75
security force discipline, 172–74
security officers, 159–63
selecting security personnel, 163–69
staffing security supervisors, 158–59
supervision, 149–55

wage compensation, 171–72
discipline, 172–74
training, 197–213
Security in United States, progression of hospital, 50–53
Security incident reports, filing, 259–61
Security Incident Reports (SIRs), 253–59, 293
Security management cycle, 112–13
Security management planning, 99–120
Security management plans
annual, 269
JCAHO, 110–12
Security mission statements, 100
Security officer responses, 242–43
Security officer training, 433
IAHSS advanced, 202–4
IAHSS basic, 201–2
Security officers, 159–63
authority of, 159–60
contract, 132–33
full-time versus part-time, 169–71
licensing, 161–63
special police commission, 160–61
Security operations manual, 192–93
Security-oriented personnel policies, 334–44
Security, parking control and, 471–85
Security patrols, 69–70
Security personnel
equipping, 178–84
considerations in arming officers, 181–84
firearms, 180–81
uniforms, 178–80
healthcare, 53–56
selecting, 163–69
recruitment, 164–65
selection criteria, 165–67
selection process, 167–68
Security plan, infant, 417–20
Security/police room, 435
Security-related sentinel events, 411–42
Security-related vulnerabilities, 34–35
Security reports
monthly, 267–69
periodic, 267–69
Security safeguards
relating to individual decision-making process, 67–72
utilization of physical, 118–19
Security sensitive areas, 411–13
area access control plan, 412
critical incident response plan, 413

staff security orientation and education, 412–13
Security services environment, hospitals and healthcare, 1–11
Security staff
  deployment of, 215–46
    basic patrol concepts, 227–42
    basic patrol deployment plans, 222–26
    deployment objectives, 216–17
    deployment patterns and concepts, 219–20
    entrances and exits, 227
    patient care units/areas, 226–27
    patrol problems, 244–45
    post assignments, 220–21
    scheduling security staff, 218–19
    security officer responses, 242–43
  scheduling, 218–19
  training, 104
  types of, 126–38
Security staffing
  in emergency departments, 432–35
  incremental facility, 142–44
Security stations, central, 366–69
Security strategic plan, 113–18
Security supervisors, number needed, 158–59
Security supplemental reports, 259–61
Security survey, facility, 36–43
Security systems
  developing, 63–67
  electronic, 365–66
Security uniforms, 69, 522
Security vehicles, transporting people in, 230–31
Security vulnerabilities, primary, 14–34
Security with patients and visitors, interrelationship of, 275–310
Sensitive areas, security, 411–13
Sentinel events, security-related, 411–42
Services
  information, 452–53
  inspection, 80–83
  miscellaneous, 95–96
  response to requests for, 84
  supportive general, 90–96
Shared services approach, 134–35
Shift rotation, 237–38
Shipments, emergency, 93
Shrubs, trees and, 384
Shuttle service and valet parking, 478–79
SICDS (Sudden In Custody Death Syndrome), 189
Signage, 478

Signals, emergency, 435
Signs, 69–70
SIRs (Security Incident Reports), 253–59, 293
Social motives, 65
Spot-checks and surveillance, 357–58
Staff
  contract, 130–32
  contributions to secure environment, 327–50
  deployment of security, 215–46
  inspection, 155
  involvement in protection programs, 119–20
  proprietary, 128–30
  scheduling security, 218–19
  security orientation and education, 412–13
  size of, 139–42
  types of security, 126–38
Staff training, security, 104
Staffing
  incremental facility security, 142–44
  medical care facilities, 6–7
  security department organization and, 121–44
Staffing in emergency departments, security, 432–35
  interaction protocols, 433–35
  security officer training, 433
Stalking, 27–28
Steroids, anabolic, 446
Stimulants, 445
Strategic plan, security, 113–18
Strategic plans, 99, 120
Street parking, 474
Strikes
  initial stages of, 511
  and picketing, 508–15
    initial stages of strikes, 511
    maintaining supply lines, 514–15
    National Labor Relations Act, 509–10
    non-striking employees, 510–11
    picket lines, 511–13
    record keeping, 513–14
    strike action committee, 510
    strike control team, 510
Structures, parking, 474–77
Subordinate complaints, handling, 157
Subpoenas, 319
  grand jury, 321–22
Substances, controlled, 445–48
Sudden In Custody Death Syndrome (SICDS), 189
Suicides and homicides, 23
Suits, scrub, 459–60

Supervision, field, 152–55
Supervisors
　security, 158–59
　selecting, 150–52
Supervisory training, IAHSS, 204
Surface parking lots, 474
Surplus property, 343
Surveillance and spot-checks, 357–58
Surveys
　facility security, 36–43
　　assessing risk, 38–40
　　continuos process, 42–43
　　details of surveys, 37–38
　　matching safeguards to risk, 41–42
　　material included in surveys, 38
　　those conducting surveys, 37
　material included in, 38
Suspects, patterns of wrongdoing and, 356–57
Systems approach, 135–38

Taft-Hartley Law, 509–10
Terrorism, 28
Testing, drug, 343–44
Theft, 28–34
　effects of controls on employee, 31–32
　employee, 29–32
　factors in employee, 30–31
　items taken, 29
Threat policy, 405
Threat response team, 406–7
Threats
　documenting, 508
　receiving, 504–5
　response to, 406–7
Time periods, non-operational, 308–9
Time recording, employee, 342
Traffic control and parking, 85–86
Traffic flow and space allocation, 481–82
Training
　concepts, 199–201
　elective, 207
　fire safety, 496–97
　IAHSS advanced security officer, 202–4
　IAHSS basic security officer, 201–2
　IAHSS safety, 204–5
　IAHSS supervisory, 204
　managing firearms programs, 192
　materials, 210–11
　on-the-job, 207–8
　resources and records requirements, 209–11
　and security education, 85

security force, 197–213
security officer, 433
security staff, 104
specialized or supplemental, 205–6
types of, 200–201
Treatment areas, 430
Trees and shrubs, 384
Triage areas, 429–30

UAP (unlicensed assistant personnel), 7
UGH (United General Hospital), 102
UIRs (unusual incident reports), 253
UL (Underwriters Laboratory), 371, 395
Undercover investigations, 359–60
Unemployment investigations, 358
Uniforms, 178–80
　security, 69, 522

Valet parking, and shuttle service, 478–79
Vandalism, 19
Vehicle patrols, 228–29
　equipment for, 231–32
Vehicles
　damage to, 232
　marked, 522
　operating, 232
Verification, patrol, 238–39
Vests, bullet-resistant, 191
Videotape recorders (VTRs), 379
Videotape recording, 379
Violators, parking system, 482–85
Violence
　management of healthcare, 404–7
　　preventive and management steps, 404–5
　　response to threats, 406–7
　　threat policy, 405
　managing workplace, 397–409
　　what and why, 402–3
　　when and where, 403–4
　　the who (perpetrators/visitors), 399–402
　preventing in workplace, 407–8
　threat of, 398
VIP patients, 281–82
Visiting hours, patient, 305–6
Visitor log books and badges, 68
Visitors, 303–9, 400–401
　accidents of, 62
　after-hours badging, 308–9
　interrelationships of security with patients and, 275–310
　large acreage facilities, 309
　non-operational hours, 307–8

non-operational time period, 308–9
operational, non-visiting hours, 306–7
patient visiting hours, 305–6
time periods, 304–9
VTRs (videotape recorders), 379
Vulnerabilities
healthcare security risk and, 14
loss of information, 26
primary security, 14–34
risks and, 13–44
safety-related, 35–36
security-related, 34–35

Wage compensation, 171–72
Waiting and admissions, 429
Walk-in area/waiting and admissions, 429
Wandering patients, 298–99
Warrants, 321–22
search, 319
Watch, hospital, 350
Weapons, employee, 336
Weekly security bulletins, 271
Windows and glass areas, 392–93
WMD (weapons of mass destruction), 515–16
Worker's compensation investigations, 358
Workplace, preventing violence in, 407–8
Workplace violence, managing, 397–409
what and why, 402–3
when and where, 403–4
the who (perpetrators/visitors), 399–402
Wrongdoing and suspects, patterns of, 356–57